Refactoring with C#

Safely improve .NET applications and pay down technical debt
with Visual Studio, .NET 8, and C# 12

Matt Eland

BIRMINGHAM—MUMBAI

Refactoring with C#

Copyright © 2023 Packt Publishing

Group Product Manager: Kunal Swant
Associate Publishing Product Manager: Debadrita Chatterjee
Senior Editor: Esha Banerjee
Technical Editor: Jubit Pincy
Copy Editor: Safis Editing
Project Coordinator: Manisha Singh
Proofreader: Safis Editing
Indexer: Rekha Nair
Production Designer: Ponraj Dhandapani
Marketing Co-ordinator: Sonia Chauhan

First published: November 2023

Production reference: 1271023

Published by Packt Publishing Ltd.
Grosvenor House
11 St Paul's Square
Birmingham
B3 1RB, UK

ISBN 978-1-83508-998-9

www.packtpub.com

To my dear wife, Heather, who encouraged me to dream big and supported me while I did so.

To our dads, who we wish could be here to see this.

To all those I have had the privilege to teach, mentor, manage, and inspire – and to those I've yet to impact: may your learning journeys be amazing.

Matt

Foreword

Matt Eland, aka Integerman, has, like me, been writing software for over three decades. Upon delving this book, it became clear to me that *he has seen some things*. It's hard to have a lengthy career in software development and not encounter the grim effects of legacy code and technical debt. What separates Matt from many other developers, though, is that rather than shying away from the challenges these things pose, he's developed a rich set of techniques to combat them. It is these techniques and skills that he shares with you in *Refactoring with C#*.

Technical debt is a ubiquitous presence in virtually every codebase. It's a metaphor for the small (and sometimes not so small) shortcuts, messes, and design mismatches left behind as the software evolves, often due to the software's failure to adapt to changing external factors. Left unchecked, these problems can slow productivity to a crawl, and refactoring is the main tool developers have to deal with this problem. It's a vital skill every developer should have.

This book has a great conversational style. Reading it is like having Matt sitting next to you, walking you through the examples. Many of them start out with a fair bit of complexity, but Matt does a great job of breaking this complexity down into understandable chunks, which he then demonstrates how to break down further through refactoring techniques.

Another technique Matt employs with great effectiveness is his use of tools and screenshots to demonstrate the effective usage of tools. Most of the book leverages Visual Studio, but there's coverage for VS Code and other tools as well. Wherever a tool can be used to assist with a refactoring technique, Matt shows how to do so in a clear, concise manner, with effective use of screenshots. As they say, a picture is worth a thousand words!

The breadth of the book you're holding is also impressive. In addition to demonstrating refactoring techniques that involve rearranging a few lines of code, Matt provides invaluable tips for effectively communicating the concepts of technical debt and the importance of refactoring to your managers and business stakeholders. There's content dedicated to keeping your code up-to-date with the latest software changes. He doesn't just mention that refactoring benefits from having automated tests, he even dedicates a couple of chapters to testing techniques and tools!

Whether you're a novice developer or have been coding for decades, I'm confident you'll find some useful tips and techniques in *Refactoring with C#*. I know I did, despite having taught refactoring to .NET developers for many years.

Steve "ardalis" Smith
Principal Architect, NimblePros. Pluralsight author. 20x Microsoft MVP.

Contributors

About the author

Matt Eland is a Microsoft MVP in Artificial Intelligence (AI) who has been working with .NET since 2001. Matt has served as a senior engineer, software engineering manager, and .NET programming instructor. He is currently an AI specialist and senior consultant at Leading EDJE near Columbus, Ohio, where he helps companies with their software engineering and data science needs using C# and related technologies. Matt speaks and writes in his community and co-organizes the Central Ohio .NET Developers Group while pursuing a master's degree in data analytics. You can find more of Matt's work at `MattEland.dev`.

Matthew, Brad, Calvin, Sam, Steve, and Esha: thank you for your hard work in refactoring this book. Debadrita, thank you for pitching this idea to me. To Heather, our families, Wren, Sadukie, Matt, Angelia, my fellow EDJErs, the Dads, and countless others: thank you for your encouragement and support. Microsoft, thank you for 20+ years of C# and giving us the tools we need to build great things. Finally, I am grateful to God for granting me the skills, knowledge, time, and health to write this.

About the reviewers

Brad Knowles is a Cloud Application Architect (CAA) with AWS Professional Services, specializing in migrating and optimizing .NET workloads running in the cloud. With over two decades of experience in the software industry, Brad has written applications for several industries, including supply chain and healthcare. During that time, he has deployed from single on-premises web servers all the way up to multiple containerized microservices. As an architect, his primary goal is to build resilient systems, minimize complexity, and balance the trade-offs between the two. He shares his knowledge at local meetups and conferences and blogs about .NET and architecture-related topics at `https://bradknowles.com`.

Calvin A. Allen is highly involved in the tech community. He is a recognized Microsoft MVP for his contributions to the developer community, which include mentoring, writing technical articles/blog posts, and organizing tech events. Calvin is also a contributor to various open-source projects and is passionate about sharing his knowledge and expertise with others through his blog, Coding with Calvin, which can be found at `https://www.codingwithcalvin.net`.

Matthew D. Groves is a guy who loves to code. It doesn't matter whether it's C#, jQuery, or PHP: he'll submit pull requests for anything. He has been coding professionally ever since he wrote a QuickBASIC point-of-sale app for his parent's pizza shop back in the 90s. He currently works for Couchbase, helping developers in any way he can. His free time is spent with his family, watching the Reds, and getting involved in the developer community. He is the author of *AOP in .NET*, co-author of *Pro Microservices in .NET*, a Pluralsight author, and a Microsoft MVP.

Samuel Gomez has worked in software development for 15+ years (mostly Microsoft technologies) and he thoroughly enjoys the problem-solving aspect of the work. In recent years, he has become passionate about AI and machine learning technologies and how they can be applied to different aspects of our lives. When not coding, he enjoys spending time with his family, soccer (watching, playing, and coaching), video games, and watching movies.

Table of Contents

Part 1: Refactoring with C# in Visual Studio

1

Technical Debt, Code Smells, and Refactoring   3

2

Introduction to Refactoring   11

3

4

5

Object-Oriented Refactoring   99

Part 2: Refactoring Safely

6

Unit Testing   143

7

Test-Driven Development   171

8

Avoiding Code Anti-Patterns with SOLID   185

9

Advanced Unit Testing   201

10

Defensive Coding Techniques   227

Part 3: Advanced Refactoring with AI and Code Analysis

11

AI-Assisted Refactoring with GitHub Copilot   255

12

Code Analysis in Visual Studio   281

13

Creating a Roslyn Analyzer   303

14

Refactoring Code with Roslyn Analyzers   323

Part 4: Refactoring in the Enterprise

15

Communicating Technical Debt   343

Preface

Software projects quickly go from greenfield paradises to brownfield wastelands filled with legacy code and technical debt. Every engineer will encounter projects that are more difficult than they should be due to existing technical debt. This book covers the process of refactoring existing code into more maintainable forms.

In Refactoring with C#, we focus on using modern C# and Visual Studio features to safely pay down technical debt in a sustainable way – while continuing to deliver value to the business.

Who this book is for

This book is for two distinct types of readers.

The first is junior and mid-level C# developers in the first few years of their careers. This book will teach you the programming techniques and mentalities needed to advance in your career. You'll learn how to safely refactor your code and find new ways of improving the overall structure of your code.

The second type of reader is the software engineer or engineering manager dealing with a particularly troublesome codebase or a project or organization resistant to refactoring. This book will help you make the case for refactoring, ensure you can do it safely, and give you alternatives to all-or-nothing approaches of complete rewrites.

This book also features a number of libraries and language features you may not have encountered or thought about recently. I hope that this book gives you new perspectives, tools, and techniques that will aid you as you refactor your code and build a better codebase.

What this book covers

Chapter 1, Technical Debt, Code Smells, and Refactoring, introduces the reader to the concept of technical debt and the things that cause it. The chapter covers legacy code and its impact on the development process and code smells that help you find it. The chapter closes with the idea of refactoring, which is the focus of the rest of the book.

Chapter 2, Introduction to Refactoring, illustrates the process of refactoring C# code in Visual Studio by taking a sample piece of code and progressively refining it with built-in refactorings and custom actions.

Chapter 3, Refactoring Code Flow and Iteration, focuses on refactoring individual lines and blocks of code. We focus on program flow control, object instantiation, handling collections, and using LINQ appropriately.

Chapter 4, Refactoring at the Method Level, expands the scope of the previous chapter by refactoring methods and constructors to more maintainable forms. Maintaining consistency within the class and building small, maintainable methods is a core focus.

Chapter 5, Object-Oriented Refactoring, takes the ideas of the previous refactoring chapters and applies them at the entire class level. This shows how introducing interfaces, inheritance, polymorphism, and other classes in general can lead to better patterns of code and more maintainable software systems.

Chapter 6, Unit Testing, serves as an introduction to unit testing in C#, moving quickly from the idea of a unit test to a tour of how to write one in xUnit, NUnit, and MSTest. We also cover parameterized tests and unit testing best practices.

Chapter 7, Test-Driven Development, introduces the reader to test-driven development and red/green/ refactor by following the TDD process to improve code and enact refactorings. Code generation quick actions are also discussed here.

Chapter 8, Avoiding Code Anti-Patterns with SOLID, focuses on what makes code good or bad and how common patterns such as SOLID, DRY, and KISS can help make your code more resistant to technical debt.

Chapter 9, Advanced Unit Testing, covers a variety of testing libraries for data generation, mocking, pinning existing behavior, and safely making changes with A/B tests. We cover Bogus, Fluent Assertions, Moq, NSubstitute, Scientist .NET, Shouldly, and Snapper.

Chapter 10, Defensive Coding Techniques, shows off a wide range of C# language features that can make your code more reliable and resistant to defects. This chapter covers nullability, validation, immutability, record classes, pattern matching, and more.

Chapter 11, AI-Assisted Refactoring with GitHub Copilot, introduces the reader to the latest AI tooling in Visual Studio with GitHub Copilot Chat. This chapter shows the reader how to use GitHub Copilot Chat to generate code, give refactoring suggestions, write draft documentation, and even help test your code. We also stress on data privacy concerns and ways of guarding your company's intellectual property.

Chapter 12, Code Analysis in Visual Studio, highlights the code analyzers built into modern .NET by showing how code analysis profiles can help detect issues in your code. We also explore code metrics and prioritize technical debt areas using those metrics. The chapter closes by looking at the SonarCloud and NDepend tools, which can help track technical debt over time.

Chapter 13, Creating a Roslyn Analyzer, introduces the idea of custom Roslyn Analyzers that can detect issues in your code. The chapter guides the reader through writing their first analyzer, unit testing it with RoslynTestKit, and deploying it using a Visual Studio extension.

Chapter 14, Refactoring Code with Roslyn Analyzers, shows how Roslyn Analyzers can also fix the issues they detect. The chapter picks up where the previous one left off by expanding the analyzer to provide a code fix. We then discuss packaging analyzers in NuGet packages and publishing them on NuGet.org or other NuGet feeds.

Chapter 15, Communicating Technical Debt, covers the systematic process of tracking and reporting technical debt in a way that business leaders can understand. We cover many common obstacles to refactoring and building a culture of trust and transparency where business management can understand the risks that technical debt represents.

Chapter 16, Adopting Code Standards, talks about the process of determining code standards that are appropriate for your development team and getting developer buy-in. The chapter covers code styling in Visual Studio, code cleanup profiles, and sharing EditorConfig files to promote consistent style choices across your team.

Chapter 17, Agile Refactoring, closes the book with a discussion of refactoring in agile environments and the unique challenges agile can pose to refactoring. We talk about ways of prioritizing and paying down technical debt inside of agile sprints. The chapter also covers larger projects, such as upgrades and rewrites, and ways to help those larger projects succeed.

To get the most out of this book

The ideal reader should be familiar with the C# programming language and the Visual Studio IDE. Knowledge of object-oriented programming, classes, and LINQ will be particularly helpful.

Software/hardware covered in the book	Operating system requirements
Visual Studio 2022 v17.8 or higher	Windows
.NET 8 SDK	

This book works with any edition of Visual Studio from 2022 v17.8 onward, including Visual Studio Community. You can download Visual Studio from `https://visualstudio.microsoft.com/downloads/`.

The latest version of the .NET 8 SDK can be downloaded from `https://dotnet.microsoft.com/en-us/download/dotnet/8.0`.

If you are using the digital version of this book, we advise you to type the code yourself or access the code from the book's GitHub repository (a link is available in the next section). Doing so will help you avoid any potential errors related to the copying and pasting of code.

Many chapters feature step-by-step instructions that you can follow along with by using the beginning code for a chapter to produce the code featured in the chapter's final code folder. You can also keep an eye on other code you work with as you read the book and think about how the topics apply to that code. However, you may want to refrain from applying your refactoring techniques to real-world codebases until you've read the chapters covering safely testing your code.

Download the example code files

You can download the example code files for this book from GitHub at `https://github.com/PacktPublishing/Refactoring-with-CSharp`. If there's an update to the code, it will be updated in the GitHub repository.

We also have other code bundles from our rich catalog of books and videos available at `https://github.com/PacktPublishing/`. Check them out!

Conventions used

There are a number of text conventions used throughout this book.

`Code in text`: Indicates code words in text, database table names, folder names, filenames, file extensions, pathnames, dummy URLs, user input, and Twitter handles. Here is an example: "Let's look again at the `IFlightUpdater` interface from earlier."

A block of code is set as follows:

```
public interface IFlightRepository {
   FlightInfo AddFlight(FlightInfo flight);
   FlightInfo UpdateFlight(FlightInfo flight);
   void CancelFlight(FlightInfo flight);
   FlightInfo? FindFlight(string id);
   IEnumerable<FlightInfo> GetActiveFlights();
   IEnumerable<FlightInfo> GetPendingFlights();
   IEnumerable<FlightInfo> GetCompletedFlights();
}
```

When we wish to draw your attention to a particular part of a code block, the relevant lines or items are set in bold:

```
public interface IFlightUpdater {
   FlightInfo AddFlight(FlightInfo flight);
   FlightInfo UpdateFlight(FlightInfo flight);
   void CancelFlight(FlightInfo flight);
}
```

Any command-line input or output is written as follows:

```
Assert.Equal() Failure
Expected: 60
Actual: 50
```

Bold: Indicates a new term, an important word, or words that you see onscreen. For instance, words in menus or dialog boxes appear in **bold**. Here is an example: "Click **Next**, then give your test project a meaningful name and click **Next** again."

> **Tips or important notes**
> Appear like this.

Get in touch

Feedback from our readers is always welcome.

General feedback: If you have questions about any aspect of this book, email us at `customercare@packtpub.com` and mention the book title in the subject of your message.

Errata: Although we have taken every care to ensure the accuracy of our content, mistakes do happen. If you have found a mistake in this book, we would be grateful if you would report this to us. Please visit `www.packtpub.com/support/errata` and fill in the form.

Piracy: If you come across any illegal copies of our works in any form on the internet, we would be grateful if you would provide us with the location address or website name. Please contact us at `copyright@packt.com` with a link to the material.

If you are interested in becoming an author: If there is a topic that you have expertise in and you are interested in either writing or contributing to a book, please visit `authors.packtpub.com`.

Share Your Thoughts

Once you've read *Refactoring with C#*, we'd love to hear your thoughts! Scan the QR code below to go straight to the Amazon review page for this book and share your feedback.

`https://packt.link/r/1835089984`

Your review is important to us and the tech community and will help us make sure we're delivering excellent quality content.

Download a free PDF copy of this book

Thanks for purchasing this book!

Do you like to read on the go but are unable to carry your print books everywhere?

Is your eBook purchase not compatible with the device of your choice?

Don't worry, now with every Packt book you get a DRM-free PDF version of that book at no cost.

Read anywhere, any place, on any device. Search, copy, and paste code from your favorite technical books directly into your application.

The perks don't stop there, you can get exclusive access to discounts, newsletters, and great free content in your inbox daily

Follow these simple steps to get the benefits:

1. Scan the QR code or visit the link below

https://packt.link/free-ebook/9781835089989

2. Submit your proof of purchase
3. That's it! We'll send your free PDF and other benefits to your email directly

Part 1:
Refactoring with C# in
Visual Studio

In the first part of the book, we'll discuss the nature of technical debt, code smells, and refactoring. We'll focus on the mechanical process of refactoring C# code in Visual Studio.

Throughout this part, you'll learn how to safely alter the form of your code without changing its functionality. We'll cover high-level concepts and then walk through refactoring individual lines of code. After this, we'll zoom out to refactor entire methods and see how they interact with each other. Finally, we'll look at some object-oriented approaches to refactoring that can help truly reshape your code by altering how classes interact with each other.

This part of the book can either be read as a traditional book or used as a step-by-step tutorial for refactoring the starting code found in each chapter.

This part contains the following chapters:

- *Chapter 1, Technical Debt, Code Smells, and Refactoring*
- *Chapter 2, Introduction to Refactoring*
- *Chapter 3, Refactoring Code Flow and Iteration*
- *Chapter 4, Refactoring at the Method Level*
- *Chapter 5, Object-Oriented Refactoring*

1

Technical Debt, Code Smells, and Refactoring

New software projects start out clean and optimistic, but quickly grow in complexity and difficulty to maintain until the code is difficult to understand, brittle to change, and impossible to test.

If you've worked with code for any length of time, chances are you've come across code like this. In fact, if you've been in development for even a little bit of time, it's likely you've *written* code you now regret.

It could be that the code is hard to read or understand. Maybe the code is inefficient or prone to errors. Perhaps the code was built under a certain set of business assumptions that later changed. Maybe the code simply no longer conforms to the standards you and your team have agreed to. Whatever the reason, bad code feels like it is practically everywhere in codebases of any significant size or age.

This code litters our software projects and reduces our development speed, causes us to introduce bugs, and generally makes us less happy and productive as software engineers.

In this book, we'll talk about how technical debt arises and what we can do about it through the process of refactoring, guided by tests and code analysis.

In this chapter, we're going to cover the following main topics:

- Understanding technical debt and legacy code
- Identifying code smells
- Introducing refactoring

Understanding technical debt and legacy code

While computer science education, books, tutorials, and online courses all focus on creating new projects from scratch, the reality is that almost all development jobs you'll have will center around understanding, maintaining, and expanding pre-existing code that may not meet your current standards.

This pre-existing code is referred to as **legacy code**. You almost always inherit some amount of legacy code when joining a new project. This can be a large amount of code for pre-existing projects or a smaller set of libraries your code must work with.

There are many different definitions of the term *legacy code*. One that stands out to me from my readings is Michael C. Feather's definition, in *Working Effectively with Legacy Code*, that legacy code is *code without tests*.

While I like Michael's definition and believe testing is critically important, as we'll see in *Part 2* of this book, I personally define legacy code as follows:

Legacy code refers to any pre-existing code that would be implemented significantly differently were it rewritten today.

One key factor in legacy code is that it is *code you don't currently fully understand* and as a result, its presence causes some degree of anxiety and apprehension.

This anxiety you feel when maintaining old systems is a prime symptom of something called **technical debt**.

Simply put, technical debt is *the negative effect of legacy code on future development efforts*.

In other words, legacy code has a certain amount of inherent *risk* that bad things will happen when the code is modified. These bad things could be bugs that are introduced due to the brittleness of the pre-existing code (or our lack of understanding of it), slower development speed, or even catastrophic issues such as critical bugs or security breaches from out-of-date security practices or deprecated dependencies.

What's worse is that technical debt will only grow over time – particularly if left unchecked.

Where technical debt comes from

Before we move on, I want to address a common point of confusion I see in organizations: technical debt is not the same thing as bad code.

Certainly, some of the technical debt we have in our systems may be simply poor-quality code. It could be that an inexperienced developer wrote it and didn't properly benefit from code review by other developers. Sometimes, projects are in a rush and the team didn't have time to write the code properly to begin with, and never got to go back and clean it up.

Sometimes, "quick and dirty" code written for prototypes makes it into production applications when "throwaway prototypes" get hastily promoted to actual production applications, as we'll explore in *Chapter 15: Communicating Technical Debt*.

Of course, there are other causes of technical debt as well.

Sometimes, the development team is under the impression that they are building software to accomplish a specific task and then that task changes as business needs evolve and new information is discovered. In these cases, teams often don't start over with the code they were writing. They simply evolve the old code to suit the new task at hand. The result is code that works but isn't ideally suited for the new task.

This change in requirements is normal and even expected in software development environments. Modern software development occurs in an agile manner where requirements and plans naturally evolve over time and understanding them up-front is virtually impossible.

Even if development teams understood requirements perfectly and wrote perfect code, this code will eventually become a form of technical debt due to the changing nature of software engineering.

In software development, tools and libraries change over time. At the time of writing, **.NET 8** and **C# 12** are the latest ways to run C# code, but these technologies will go out of support at some point in the future only to be replaced by newer versions.

Even entire ways of thinking about software can change. Over the last twenty years, organizations have shifted from having their own on-premises servers to using cloud hosting on **Azure**, **AWS**, or **Google Cloud**. Even the very nature of what a server is has changed with technologies, including containerization technologies such as **Docker**, **platform as a service** (**PaaS**) offerings such as **Azure App Services**, and serverless computing offerings such as **Azure Functions** and **AWS Lambda**.

Nowadays, newer AI technologies such as **ChatGPT** and **GitHub Copilot Chat** are poised to change what it even means to be a software developer, and this only underscores how much constant change is at the heart of the software engineering industry.

> **Change in software projects**
>
> In software development, change is a constant and can be unpredictable and sudden. All this change leads to code that was once considered perfect to later be considered a significant risk to the ongoing success of the business.

In other words, technical debt is to some degree or another an unavoidable part of software development. Thankfully, you can take some steps to reduce the rate at which it accumulates (as we'll discuss in *Part 2* of this book). Fortunately, we can detect technical debt through its symptoms, or "smells."

Identifying code smells

So, how do you know whether your code has issues?

How do you know whether food has spoiled, clothing needs to be washed, or a diaper needs changing? It turns out that it just smells bad.

There are some metrics about what constitutes "good" and "bad" code, and we'll explore them in *Chapter 12: Code Analysis in Visual Studio* and *Chapter 16: Adopting Code Standards*. Smelly code can be subjective to some degree or another. A developer who wrote a section of code or frequently modifies that portion of code may find the code to be more tolerable than a developer encountering the code for the first time.

While not all pieces of technical debt are identical, it turns out that many pieces of legacy code share a set of common symptoms.

These symptoms are commonly referred to as "code smells" and can include the following:

- It's difficult to understand what it does or *why* it does it
- You or people on your team avoid working with it
- It's slower to modify than other areas or tends to break when modified
- It's hard to test or debug

New code starts out good and pristine, but real code that lives in a business setting evolves over time as more capabilities are required and additional features and fixes are introduced. As that happens, code that was once nice and neat starts to accumulate code smells.

Not all code is created equal, and not all code lasts as long as other pieces of code. Certainly, there are things we can do to make our code more resilient (as we'll see in *Chapter 8: Avoiding Code Anti-Patterns with SOLID*). However, at some point in time, your nice and shiny new code will start to get smelly and will need to be cleaned up through a process called refactoring.

Introducing refactoring

Refactoring is one of those words that doesn't make a lot of sense to newer programmers, but here's a simple definition:

Refactoring is the act of changing the shape or form of code without changing its functionality or behavior.

There are two key concepts here:

- The first concept is that refactoring is an effort to improve the maintainability of existing code. Sometimes, restructuring means introducing a new variable, method, or class. Other times, refactoring simply changes how individual lines of code are arranged or which language features are used. Even something as simple as renaming a variable could be considered a small act of refactoring.
- The second concept in this definition is that refactoring does not alter the *behavior* of the code in question. Refactoring is a structural change done to bring some piece of technical merit without altering the existing behavior of your code. If a method typically returned a certain value before you refactored it and now it returns a different value, that is a *change* and not a refactoring.

Refactoring also should provide some benefit to the engineering team. The code resulting from refactoring should be easier to understand, less likely to break when changed, and have less technical debt and fewer code smells than the starting code did.

Every line of code the development team produces should have a business value. Refactoring is no different, except the business value it produces should be more maintainable code with fewer issues and delays arising from its presence.

Sometimes, we try to improve our code through refactoring and we accidentally introduce new behavior – typically in the form of new bugs. This makes our refactoring become an unintentional change in the software that can result in emergency fixes to restore code to a working state.

Breaking code while refactoring can be a critical problem and a significant barrier to being allowed to perform refactored code in the future, which in turn can allow technical debt to thrive.

In *Part 2* of this book, we'll explore ways of safely refactoring your code so that you don't accidentally introduce bugs, while in *Part 4*, we'll discuss getting organizational buy-in to refactor your code, and what to do when a defect does arise out of your refactoring efforts.

Refactoring tools in Visual Studio

Thankfully, all editions of **Visual Studio** now include refactoring tools built into the editor that allow you to quickly perform a set of common refactorings in a reliable and repeatable manner.

In *Chapter 2: Introduction to Refactoring* and the remaining chapters in *Part 1*, we'll see a number of refactorings in action. Here's a preview of some of the refactoring options Visual Studio provides the user:

Figure 1.1 – Visual Studio Quick Actions context menu showing a set of refactoring operations

Tool-assisted refactorings such as these are fantastic for a few reasons:

- They are fast and efficient

- They are reliable and repeatable

- They *rarely* introduce defects

> **Caution**
>
> Note that I use the word *rarely* when talking about bugs introduced by refactoring tools. There are a few rare scenarios where using the built-in refactoring tools without thinking about their actions may introduce bugs into your application. We'll talk specifically about those areas as we encounter them in the following chapters.

Over the rest of *Part 1*, we'll explore using these tools to quickly and effectively refactor your C# applications and talk about the types of scenarios in which you might use each one of these.

With all that our tools can do, it is important to remember that these tools are just one way of refactoring code. Often, the most effective ways of removing code smells involve a combination of writing code yourself and using the built-in refactoring tools.

Refactoring's key value is the long-term health of an organization, but many obstacles to refactoring can come from the organization itself. To help illustrate the practical aspects of refactoring in a real organization, each chapter will involve a case study from a fictitious organization. Some chapters will focus entirely on code from the case study while others, such as this chapter, will conclude with a dedicated case study section. These case study sections illustrate the concepts of the chapter applied to a fictitious organization.

Let's meet our first case study section and see how technical debt and legacy code affect a typical company.

Case study – Cloudy Skies Airlines

The rest of this book will follow code examples from an airline called **Cloudy Skies Airlines**, or **Cloudy Skies** for short. Through these examples, we should be able to see how technical debt and refactoring can apply to a "real" organization and its software.

> **Note**
>
> Cloudy Skies is a fictitious airline company created for this book for teaching purposes only. Any resemblance to any real company is purely coincidental. Additionally, I have never worked in aviation, so the code examples presented in the book are likely significantly different from actual software systems used in the industry.

Cloudy Skies is an airline that's been around for the past 50 years and currently operates a little over 500 jets in its fleet, serving around 70 cities in its region.

Twenty years ago, the airline made a major move and started replacing its aging software systems with custom in-house applications built by its development team. Cloudy Skies chose to use .NET and C#. The initial systems performed well and resulted in increased developer productivity and high-performance software applications, so Cloudy Skies continued to migrate its applications to .NET.

As time went by, the airline and its systems grew. The engineering team at Cloudy Skies was once held in high esteem as the pride and joy of the organization and a key to its future.

However, management has been somewhat frustrated by its engineering team over the past few years. Some of its key complaints include the following:

- Product managers are frustrated by large estimates for seemingly simple changes to existing systems, and a growing amount of time between software releases due to long implementation times and numerous bugs.

- The Quality Assurance department has been overwhelmed by a growing number of bugs present in the software, a tendency for the same things to break repeatedly, and bugs appearing in seemingly unrelated areas when changes occur in other parts of the application.

For its part, the engineering team feels overwhelmed by the code it's working with. Strategic initiatives have been pushed aside for years while the organization has the team focus on urgent changes or tight deadlines for new releases. As a result, nobody has had time to address the growing amount of technical debt the team is facing.

The Cloudy Skies codebase is constantly growing in complexity to account for each new feature or "special case" added to the system. This complexity in turn makes the application harder to test, understand, and modify, which has led to difficulties in onboarding new developers and some experienced developers leaving the organization.

Out of frustration after several severe delays and high-profile bugs, Cloudy Skies brings in a new engineering manager and empowers the team to make changes to ensure the airline can stay efficient and effective in the years to come.

This engineering manager determines that the primary cause of these problems is technical debt and that targeted refactoring of the most critical areas throughout the suite of applications could significantly reduce risk and improve the team's effectiveness going forward.

To its credit, management agrees and allows the team to allocate resources to pay down technical debt and improve the maintainability of the code through refactoring.

Throughout the rest of this book, we'll follow aspects of this fictitious team's journey in paying down technical debt and paving the way to a better future through refactoring.

Summary

Legacy code is an unavoidable byproduct of the forces of time and constant change that are present in software development projects. This legacy code becomes a breeding ground for technical debt, which threatens our productivity as developers and the quality of our software.

While technical debt can arise due to a number of reasons, refactoring is the cure. Refactoring reworks existing code into a more maintainable and less risky form, reducing our technical debt and helping us control our legacy code.

The more you understand the causes and effects of technical debt in your code, the better you'll find yourself equipped to explain technical debt to others in your organization, advocate for refactoring, and avoid things that cause your code to decline in effectiveness over time.

In the next chapter, we'll explore refactoring in more depth by walking through a set of targeted changes to improve a piece of sample code from the Cloudy Skies Airlines codebase.

Questions

1. What is the difference between technical debt and legacy code?
2. What are some causes of technical debt?
3. What are some of the effects of technical debt?
4. Is it possible to avoid technical debt?
5. Is it possible to get to a point where your code cannot be refactored further?

Further reading

You can find more information about technical debt, legacy code, and refactoring at the following URLs:

*   *Defining Technical Debt*: `https://killalldefects.com/2019/12/23/defining-technical-debt/`
*   *Identify Technical Debt*: `https://learn.microsoft.com/en-us/training/modules/identify-technical-debt/`
*   *The True Cost of Technical Debt*: `https://killalldefects.com/2019/11/09/the-true-cost-of-technical-debt/`
*   *Code refactoring*: `https://en.wikipedia.org/wiki/Code_refactoring`

2
Introduction to Refactoring

The best way to learn refactoring is to look at an example. In this chapter, we'll explore a sample refactoring scenario using C# and Visual Studio and see firsthand how refactoring can transform the maintainability of code without altering its functionality.

In this chapter, we're going to cover the following main areas:

- Refactoring a baggage price calculator
- Refactoring in other editors

Along the way, we'll cover refactorings around introducing locals, constants, and parameters, extracting methods, and removing unreachable/unused code, as well as touching upon the importance of testing in any refactoring endeavor.

Technical requirements

If you want to follow along with this chapter, you can clone this book's code from GitHub at `https://github.com/PacktPublishing/Refactoring-with-CSharp`.

The starting code for this chapter can be found in the `Chapter02/Ch2BeginningCode` folder after cloning the repository.

Refactoring a baggage price calculator

We'll start by examining a baggage price calculator used by the staff of Cloudy Skies Airline during baggage checks to determine the amount an individual customer must pay.

The rules for baggage pricing are as follows:

- All carry-on baggage costs $30 per bag
- The first checked bag a passenger checks costs $40

- Each subsequent checked bag costs $50

- If the travel occurs during the holidays, a 10% surcharge is applied

This code lives in a C# `BaggageCalculator` class that we'll review in a few blocks of code, starting with the class definition, field, and full property:

BaggageCalculator.cs:

```csharp
public class BaggageCalculator {
  private decimal holidayFeePercent = 0.1M;
  public decimal HolidayFeePercent {
    get { return holidayFeePercent; }
    set { holidayFeePercent = value; }
  }
}
```

This is a simple class with an older style of property definition setting `holidayFeePercent` to a `decimal` value (identified by the M suffix) of `0.1` or 10%.

The class also has a `CalculatePrice` method that returns a `decimal` value indicating the total cost of baggage fees:

```csharp
public decimal CalculatePrice(int bags,
  int carryOn, int passengers, DateTime travelTime) {
  decimal total = 0;
  if (carryOn > 0) {
    Console.WriteLine($"Carry-on: {carryOn * 30M}");
    total += carryOn * 30M;
  }
  if (bags > 0) {
    if (bags <= passengers) {
      Console.WriteLine($"Checked: {bags * 40M}");
      total += bags * 40M;
    } else {
      decimal checkedFee = (passengers * 40M) +
        ((bags - passengers) * 50M);
      Console.WriteLine($"Checked: {checkedFee}");
      total += checkedFee;
    }
  }
  if (travelTime.Month >= 11 || travelTime.Month <= 2) {
    Console.WriteLine("Holiday Fee: " +
      (total * HolidayFeePercent));
    total += total * HolidayFeePercent;
  }
```

```
        return total;
    }
```

That logic has some complexity to it, but it matches up with the business rules described earlier.

Finally, the class ends with a `CalculatePriceFlat` method that was introduced in an earlier version of the application and is no longer used (which we'll discuss later):

```
    private decimal CalculatePriceFlat(int numBags) {
        decimal total = 0;
        return 100M;
        return numBags * 50M;
    }
}
```

While this code isn't the worst in the world by any stretch, this is a class that is slowly growing in complexity and becoming harder to understand and maintain as new rules are added to the application.

Fortunately, this class is supported by a series of passing unit tests and is generally agreed to calculate the correct amount by all users.

Over the course of the chapter, we'll apply a series of targeted refactorings to improve this code to prevent it from being an issue in the future.

Converting properties to auto properties

The class starts with the declaration of the `HolidayFeePercent` property as shown here:

```
private decimal holidayFeePercent = 0.1M;
public decimal HolidayFeePercent {
    get { return holidayFeePercent; }
    set { holidayFeePercent = value; }
}
```

This code is fine and has no issues whatsoever. However, C# is a language that continues to evolve and developers generally prefer to write and maintain fewer lines of code when given the choice.

Because of this, Microsoft gave us the ability to write *automatically implemented properties* (commonly called **auto properties**) that automatically generate their own field with a getter and setter when the code is compiled.

While we could delete the property and its field and redeclare it, there's a possibility that we could make a spelling or capitalization mistake when doing so. Instead, let's take a look at how Visual Studio can do this for us automatically.

In Visual Studio, if you move your typing cursor onto a property name, either by using the arrow keys or by clicking on the name of the property, you'll see a light bulb appear in the margin as shown in *Figure 2.1*:

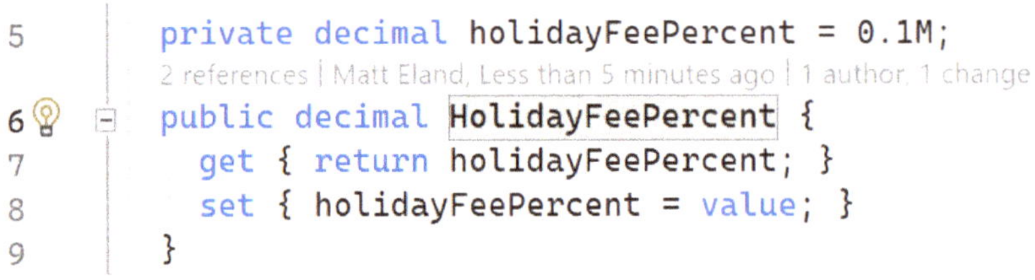

```
5        private decimal holidayFeePercent = 0.1M;
         2 references | Matt Eland, Less than 5 minutes ago | 1 author, 1 change
6 💡  ⊟   public decimal HolidayFeePercent {
7            get { return holidayFeePercent; }
8            set { holidayFeePercent = value; }
9        }
```

Figure 2.1 – The light bulb Quick Actions icon

If you click on this light bulb (or press *Ctrl* + . by default), the **Quick Actions** menu will appear and list several refactorings.

The refactoring choices are context-sensitive, so only those that Visual Studio believes are relevant to the code you have currently selected will appear.

In this case, the first option, **Use auto property**, is the refactoring action we want. See *Figure 2.2*:

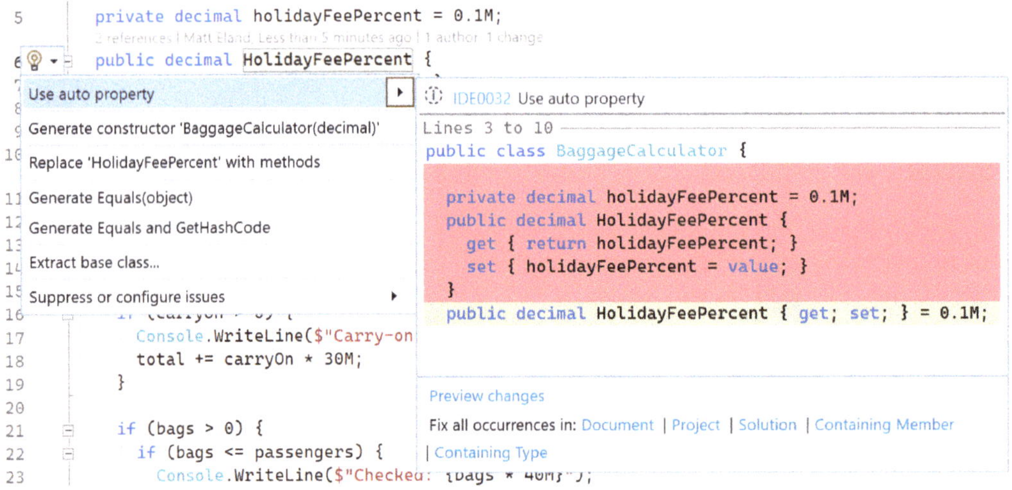

Figure 2.2 – Previewing the Use auto property refactoring

When this option is selected, the pane on the right will display a preview of the change this will make to your code. Here it lists the lines it will remove in red and the line it adds in green.

Clicking **Use auto property** or pressing *Enter* on the keyboard will accept the suggestion and replace your code with the auto property version:

```
public decimal HolidayFeePercent { get; set; } = 0.1M;
```

Admittedly this is a simple refactoring, but there are a couple of things I want to stress about the refactoring process:

- Visual Studio took care of making the change and did so in an automated way that was free of potential typos or other mistakes a human might make.

- If you didn't know that you could move a full property to an auto property, this **Quick Action** helped you discover that. These **Quick Actions** can actually *teach* you a lot about the C# programming language as it continues to evolve and change every year.

With the mechanics of refactoring in Visual Studio out of the way, let's explore some additional refactorings.

Introducing locals

One of the problems the `CalculatePrice` method has is that there are a few expressions, such as `carryOn * 30M` and `bags * 40M`, that appear multiple times throughout the method.

These are small issues but can lead to maintainability problems. If the nature of the expressions changed, we would need to modify multiple places within our code.

In general, one of the reasons you may want to refactor code is if you find yourself modifying multiple places to make a single change on a regular basis. For example, if the pricing structure changed we should modify multiple lines of code to support the new pricing model. Each one of those lines we should modify is a place we might fail to make a change. Missing changes like this typically introduce bugs.

Even if we didn't miss any code that needed to be modified, most developers would prefer to have to make a change in one place instead of multiple.

The **Introduce local** refactoring can help with this by introducing a local variable containing the result of the expression.

To use this refactoring, select the expression that is repeated as shown in *Figure 2.3*, noting that Visual Studio helpfully highlights any places it is repeated:

```
11        if (carryOn > 0) {
12            Console.WriteLine($"Carry-on: {carryOn * 30M}");
13            total += carryOn * 30M;
14        }
```

Figure 2.3 – Selecting a repeated expression in Visual Studio

Next, use the **Quick Action** button by pressing *Ctrl + .* or clicking on the screwdriver icon.

> **A note on the Quick Actions icon**
>
> The **Quick Action** button sometimes appears as a light bulb and sometimes appears as a screwdriver, depending on your code analysis rules and the exact issues a line is facing. They are effectively the same option, but the light bulb tells you a suggested refactoring is present while a screwdriver indicates a less critical refactoring option to consider.

Once the context menu is open, expand the right arrow next to **Introduce local** by using the arrow keys to navigate the menu. This will let you view more detailed options.

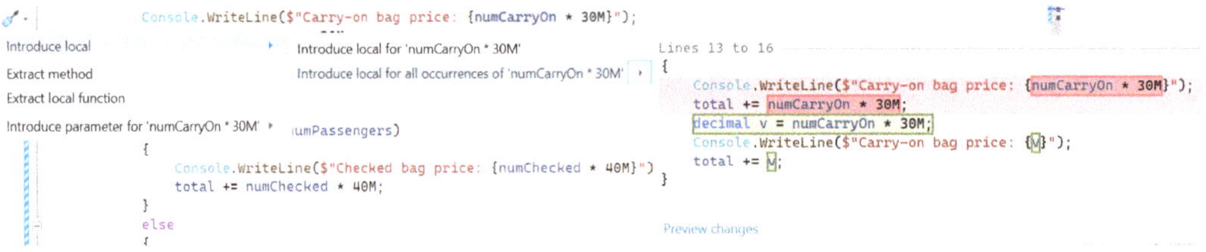

Figure 2.4 – Drilling into the specialized forms of the Introduce local refactoring

Here it gives you the ability to introduce a local variable just for the expression you selected or to do so **for all occurrences** of this expression. I generally recommend using the **for all occurrences** option, but it will depend on the context of what you're trying to improve.

Once you select the **Introduce local** option, Visual Studio will prompt you for a name for your variable (see *Figure 2.5*):

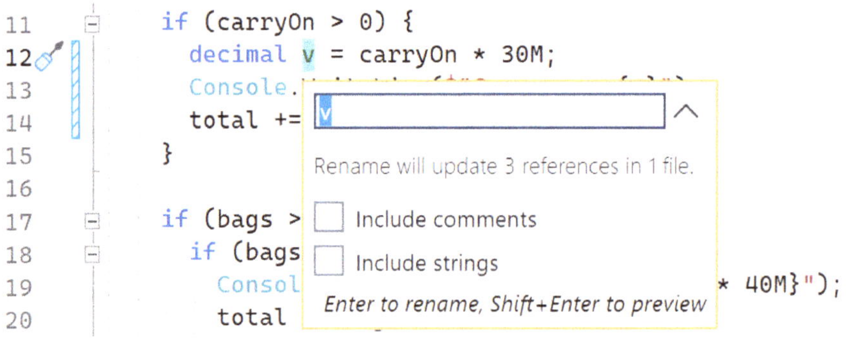

Figure 2.5 – Naming your new local variable

Type in the name you would like and then press *Enter* to make the box disappear.

In my case, I called the variable `fee` and it replaced it in both lines as shown here:

```
if (carryOn > 0) {
  decimal fee = carryOn * 30M;
  Console.WriteLine($"Carry-on: {fee}");
  total += fee;
}
```

While this is certainly cleaner for the carry-on baggage fee logic, there's still a `bags * 40M` expression repeated in the checked baggage logic and a `total * HolidayFeePercent` expression that is also repeated.

You can use the **Introduce local** refactoring to make complex lines more understandable by pulling some logic out of dense lines into their own smaller lines.

Applying the **Introduce local** refactoring throughout this method results in a longer method, but one that's easier to understand:

```
public decimal CalculatePrice(int bags,
   int carryOn, int passengers, DateTime travelTime) {
  decimal total = 0;
  if (carryOn > 0) {
    decimal fee = carryOn * 30M;
    Console.WriteLine($"Carry-on: {fee}");
    total += fee;
  }
  if (bags > 0) {
    if (bags <= passengers) {
      decimal firstBagFee = bags * 40M;
      Console.WriteLine($"Checked: {firstBagFee}");
      total += firstBagFee;
    } else {
      decimal firstBagFee = passengers * 40M;
      decimal extraBagFee = (bags - passengers) * 50M;
      decimal checkedFee = firstBagFee + extraBagFee;
      Console.WriteLine($"Checked: {checkedFee}");
      total += checkedFee;
    }
  }
  if (travelTime.Month >= 11 || travelTime.Month <= 2) {
    decimal holidayFee = total * HolidayFeePercent;
    Console.WriteLine("Holiday Fee: " + holidayFee);
    total += holidayFee;
  }
  return total;
}
```

As a programming instructor, I saw many students under the mistaken assumption that the shortest way to implement something was always the best.

Instead, the best code tends to be the code that's easier to maintain over time, less likely to break, and easier to think about as you go about development tasks.

Less code is often easier to think about, but when code gets too concise or too complex it can be hard to maintain. Find a happy medium between brevity and readability, keeping in mind that many times, programmers skim code looking for a specific section.

Introducing constants

The **Introduce constant** refactoring is very similar to **Introduce local** except it introduces a `const` value that will never change during the program's runtime.

However, **Introduce constant** is often used for a different purpose than **Introduce local**. While **Introduce local** tends to be used to reduce repetition or simplify complex lines of code, **Introduce constant** is often used to eliminate **magic numbers** or **magic strings** from code.

In programming, a magic number is a number that exists in your code without any explanation of what that number means or why it is there. This is bad because the person maintaining your code later doesn't understand why that number was chosen.

The `CalculatePrice` method has three magic numbers: `30M`, `40M`, and `50M`, representing the various baggage fee amounts.

Introducing a constant for these is the same as introducing a local. Just highlight the number and open the **Quick Actions** menu, then select **Introduce constant** and then **Introduce constant for all occurrences** in the sub-menu as shown here:

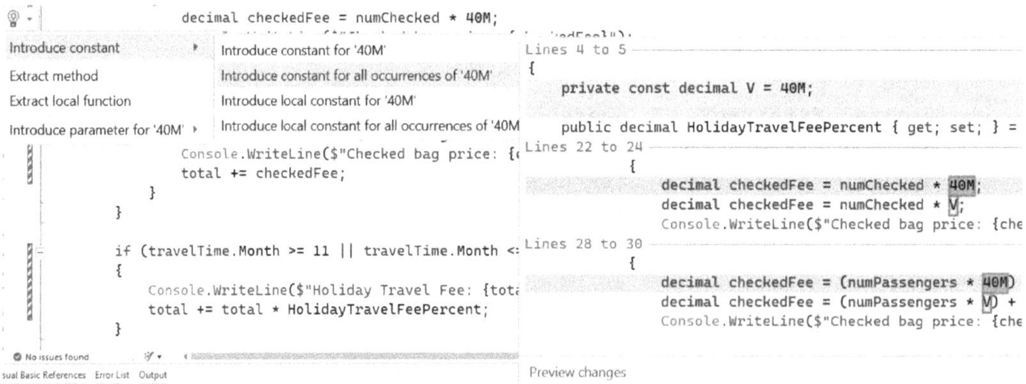

Figure 2.6 – Introducing a constant for all occurrences of the 40M decimal literal

Doing this to the various magic numbers in our application and choosing appropriate names results in the following new constants at the top of the class:

```
private const decimal CarryOnFee = 30M;
private const decimal FirstBagFee = 40M;
private const decimal ExtraBagFee = 50M;
```

Introducing these constants has the added benefit of putting our price rules in a centralized place, making them more discoverable by new developers joining the team.

This also makes our code a lot easier to read:

```
if (carryOn > 0) {
    decimal fee = carryOn * CarryOnFee;
    Console.WriteLine($"Carry-on: {fee}");
    total += fee;
}
```

Programmers spend disproportionally more time *reading* code rather than *writing* code. Optimizing your code for maintainability is a key habit that will help your application resist technical debt as time goes by.

Introducing parameters

One refactoring technique I wish I saw more people use is the **Introduce parameter** refactoring.

This refactoring takes an expression or variable in a method and removes it from the method entirely, instead adding its value as a new parameter to the method.

For example, right now the `CalculatePrice` method has logic inside of it for determining which travel dates should be considered for holiday travel:

```
if (travelTime.Month >= 11 || travelTime.Month <= 2) {
  decimal holidayFee = total * HolidayFeePercent;
  Console.WriteLine("Holiday Fee: " + holidayFee);
  total += holidayFee;
}
```

This is logic that could become more complex as more holidays are added and holidays from different countries are considered. As the code is written now, the additional complexity would need to go into this `if` statement.

Instead, introducing a parameter for `isHoliday` gives the callers of this method the responsibility of telling whether the method is holiday travel or not. This ultimately allows us to leave this method to focus on pricing the customer's baggage and to be aware of holidays but it is not responsible for determining what is and what isn't a holiday.

Introducing a parameter can be done by selecting the variable or expression you wish to move to a parameter and then triggering the **Quick Actions** menu:

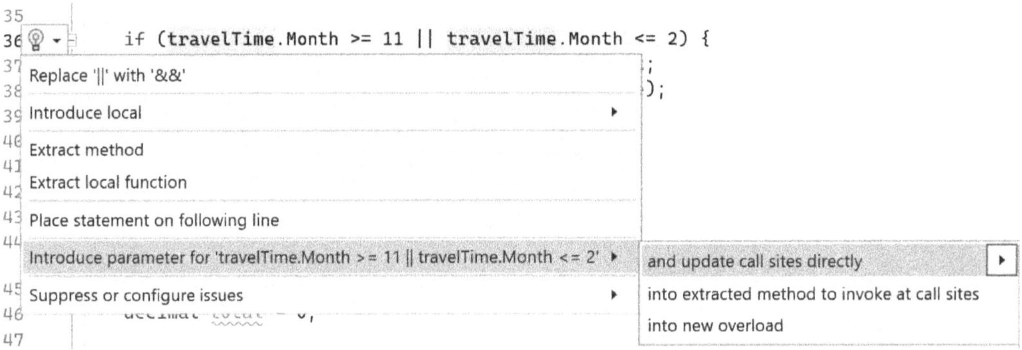

Figure 2.7 – Introducing a parameter using the Quick Actions menu

There are multiple options to choose from when introducing a parameter. Choosing **and update call sites directly** is usually a good option – provided you review the code it generates.

Once we introduce the parameter and name it appropriately, the holiday fee logic becomes much easier to read:

```
if (isHoliday) {
   decimal holidayFee = total * HolidayFeePercent;
   Console.WriteLine("Holiday Fee: " + holidayFee);
   total += holidayFee;
}
```

Introducing a parameter also changed the method signature line to add a Boolean isHoliday parameter:

```
public decimal CalculatePrice(int bags, int carryOn,
   int passengers, DateTime travelTime, bool isHoliday) {
```

As a result of this refactoring, any code that called the CalculatePrice method now calculates and passes a value for isHoliday to the method.

I find that **Introduce parameter** is particularly helpful for letting a method focus on just a few key pieces of logic.

It can also be very helpful in places where you have very similar methods of doing similar things but only differing by a few key details. It can sometimes be possible to merge many different methods into a single method that takes in a few details as parameters.

For example, the following code might perform logging for different actions:

Fee.cs

```
public void ChargeCarryOnBaggageFee(decimal fee) {
    Console.WriteLine($"Carry-on Fee: {fee}");
    Total += fee;
}
public void ChargeCheckedBaggageFee(decimal fee) {
    Console.WriteLine($"Checked Fee: {fee}");
    Total += fee;
}
```

These two methods both take in a numeric fee and write the charge name and charged fee to the console. In fact, the only way they differ is the charge name.

This code could be consolidated into a single method by introducing a parameter:

```
public void ChargeFee(decimal fee, string chargeName) {
    Console.WriteLine($"{chargeName}: {fee}");
    Total += fee;
}
```

Never underestimate the value of making a method more generalized by having outside code provide additional details.

With the charge logic largely improved, let's move on to the final method in the code that has several warnings associated with it.

Removing unreachable and unused code

If you opened the beginning code from this chapter in Visual Studio, you would likely notice that `CalculatePriceFlat` and a few variables inside it appear in gray with a number of wavy underscore suggestions as shown in *Figure 2.8*.

```
0 references | Matt Eland  6 hours ago | 1 author, 2 changes
private decimal CalculatePriceFlat(int numBags) {
    decimal total = 0;

    // Business says to use a flat 100 regardless of count
    return 100M;

    // Old logic: $50 per bag
    return numBags * ExtraBagFee;
}
```

Figure 2.8 – The CalculatePriceFlat method with gray text for many lines of code

Visual Studio can sometimes detect when variables, parameters, and even methods are not being used. If it does so, Visual Studio usually renders these identifiers in more muted tones and often includes suggestions to investigate or remove these items.

In this case, nothing is ever calling the `CalculatePriceFlat` method, and nothing is referencing the `numBags` parameter. The `total` variable is declared and given a value but is never read from after that, and the final `return` line is unreachable given the return line above it.

Each one of these issues can be addressed with a *remove unused member*, *remove unused variable*, or *remove unreachable code* refactoring.

All these refactorings do what you'd expect: they remove the offending code.

Since nothing is calling the method at all, the entire method can be removed.

Removing unused parameters

There's another piece of code from earlier that can be removed as well: the `CalculatePrice` method has a `travelTime` parameter that is no longer being used after we introduced the `isHoliday` parameter.

There is no *remove unused parameter* in Visual Studio at the time of writing, but you can remove it safely using some of the method-level refactorings we'll discuss in the next chapter.

To perform this refactoring, select the `travelTime` parameter and then select **Change signature…** as shown here:

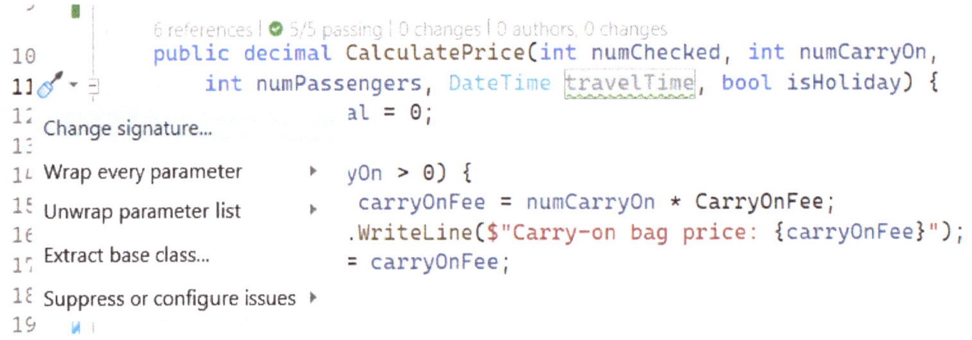

Figure 2.9 – Changing the signature of a method

Clicking **Change signature…** will show the **Change Signature** dialog.

Select the `travelTime` parameter and click **Remove**. The parameter will appear crossed out in the dialog:

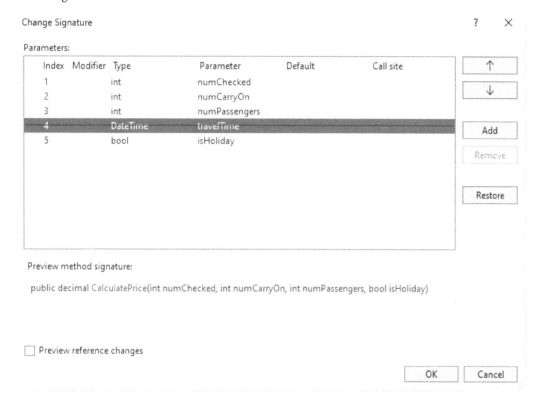

Figure 2.10 – The Change Signature dialog with travelTime removed

Click **OK** and the dialog will close and the parameter will be removed.

Any code that was referencing your method will also have their signatures updated to not pass anything for the `travelTime` parameter.

Avoiding pitfalls when removing code

One cautionary note on removing code: be particularly careful about removing `public` members from code. Sometimes Visual Studio is not aware of all the places using code. This is particularly true for serialization/deserialization logic, properties that exist for data binding, and members that are accessed using reflection.

Additionally, if your code is being deployed as a **NuGet package** or otherwise being shared in other projects, it is possible that code outside of your solution may depend on a method or parameter, and your change could cause their code to no longer compile.

> **Reminder on testing**
>
> It is *your* responsibility to test any refactorings you make and ensure they do not bring about unintended changes in program behavior.

That may sound scary, but don't let these edge cases stop you from removing dead code.

I've known a number of developers hesitant to remove code in case they need it later. Instead, these developers will either keep the code there untouched or comment the entire block of code out.

The problem with commenting out dead code is that it increases the amount of distracting and unhelpful comments in a file. This reduces the amount of importance developers place on the comments that are present and also increases the amount of scrolling the developers must do.

Delete dead code. Your code should be in source control anyway, so if you really need to find the code later, you can look at the history to recover it – assuming, of course, you checked the code into source control to begin with.

Extracting methods

Our code is now looking fairly clean, but the `CalculatePrice` method has a lot of logic in it for the checked baggage price calculation.

This logic is complex enough for us to extract a method just for this logic and call that method from our existing code.

To do this, select the lines of code that represent the method you want to extract. Be mindful of the various { } instances that you select, as your selection must make sense as a related block of code to Visual Studio. See the following screenshot.

```
21        if (bags > 0) {
22            if (bags <= passengers) {
23   Quick Actions (Ctrl+.)  al firstBagFee = bags * FirstBagFee;
24            le.WriteLine($"Checked: {firstBagFee}");
25                total += firstBagFee;
26            } else {
27                decimal firstBagFee = passengers * FirstBagFee;
28                decimal extraBagFee = (bags - passengers) * ExtraBagFee;
29                decimal checkedFee = firstBagFee + extraBagFee;
30
31                Console.WriteLine($"Checked: {checkedFee}");
32                total += checkedFee;
33            }
34        }
```

Figure 2.11 – Extracting a method from a block of code

Once your block of code is selected, open the **Quick Actions** menu, choose **Extract Method**, and then name the method in the prompt before pressing *Enter* to confirm your name.

```
21        if (bags > 0) {
22            total = ApplyCheckedBagFee(bags, passengers, total);
23        }
24            ApplyCheckedBagFee                    ∧
25        if (isHoli
26            decimal    Rename will update 2 references in 1 file.      eePercent;
27            Console.    ☐ Include comments                            olidayFee);
28
29            total +=   ☐ Include strings
30        }            Enter to rename, Shift+Enter to preview
```

Figure 2.12 – Naming the extracted method

This will result in a new method being added to your code:

```
private static decimal ApplyCheckedBagFee(int bags,
    int passengers, decimal total) {
    if (bags <= passengers) {
        decimal firstBagFee = bags * FirstBagFee;
        Console.WriteLine($"Checked: {firstBagFee}");
        total += firstBagFee;
    } else {
        decimal firstBagFee = passengers * FirstBagFee;
        decimal extraBagFee = (bags - passengers)* ExtraBagFee;
        decimal checkedFee = firstBagFee + extraBagFee;
        Console.WriteLine($"Checked: {checkedFee}");
        total += checkedFee;
    }
    return total;
}
```

Note that Visual Studio will make the method `private` by default and will mark the method as `static` if it does not access instance members on the class.

I generally prefer `private` methods, but your preferences on `static` may vary depending on what method you're working with and whether it makes sense for the method to ultimately be `static`.

The extract method refactoring also removes the code from the original method and replaces it with a call to the new method:

```
public decimal CalculatePrice(int bags, int carryOn,
    int passengers, DateTime travelTime, bool isHoliday) {
    decimal total = 0;
```

```
if (carryOn > 0) {
  decimal fee = carryOn * CarryOnFee;
  Console.WriteLine($"Carry-on: {fee}");
  total += fee;
}
if (bags > 0) {
  total = ApplyCheckedBagFee(bags, passengers, total);
}
if (isHoliday) {
  decimal holidayFee = total * HolidayFeePercent;
  Console.WriteLine("Holiday Fee: " + holidayFee);
  total += holidayFee;
}
return total;
}
```

This results in a much more concise and readable **CalculatePrice method** and makes it easier to think about everything the method is doing. This reduced complexity greatly improves the long-term quality of the method by helping developers fully understand the method and avoids costly mistakes that can occur when maintaining complex blocks of code.

Refactoring manually

Up until this point, we've performed a number of refactoring operations supported by Visual Studio. These have been fairly safe given the quality of the tools we've used, but there are some things the built-in tools just won't do.

Visual Studio is powerful, but it can't think about code like a human can (despite the exciting new AI features we'll talk about in *Chapter 11, AI-Assisted Refactoring with GitHub Copilot Chat*).

Sometimes there will be opportunities to improve the code that no built-in refactoring can perform for you. At those points, you'll have to make the changes manually.

The `ApplyCheckedBagFee` method we extracted earlier is a good method, but a few things could be improved.

First, the method takes in a total, increases it by a fee, and then returns that new total. It'd be easier for others to understand the method if the method returned the fee instead of the adjusted total.

Secondly, the method is performing the same `Console.WriteLine` operation twice. Additionally, all other `WriteLine` statements in the class are in the `CalculatePrice` method, making the user interface slightly hard to fully trace.

Let's modify the method so that it returns only the fee, doesn't require the `total` parameter, and doesn't log anything:

```
private static decimal ApplyCheckedBagFee(int bags,
   int passengers) {
   if (bags <= passengers) {
     decimal firstBagFee = bags * FirstBagFee;
     return firstBagFee;
   } else {
     decimal firstBagFee = passengers * FirstBagFee;
     decimal extraBagFee = (bags-passengers) * ExtraBagFee;
     decimal checkedFee = firstBagFee + extraBagFee;
     return checkedFee;
   }
}
```

Next, we'll need to update the code that calls this method:

```
if (bags > 0) {
   decimal bagFee = ApplyCheckedBagFee(bags, passengers);
   Console.WriteLine($"Checked: {bagFee}");
   total += bagFee;
}
```

Note that the result is stored in a bagFee variable, `total` is no longer passed to ApplyCheckedBagFee, and Console.WriteLine now appears here in this method.

Additionally, the ApplyCheckedBagFee name might not apply anymore since the method no longer actually applies the fee, but rather calculates it. In this case, applying the *rename method* refactoring would help the final code have a more appropriate name.

Testing refactored code

As I mentioned earlier, it is *your responsibility* to ensure that your refactoring efforts have not altered how the system fundamentally behaves.

In our case, this means that BaggageCalculator should still calculate the same prices it did before for any valid set of inputs.

One of the many tools we have at our disposal for determining whether code still meets our needs is running **unit tests**.

We'll talk more about unit tests in *Chapter 6, Unit Testing*, but for now, know that unit tests are code that verifies that other code is working as expected.

`BaggageCalculator` has five tests that can be run by clicking on the **Test** menu and then choosing **Run All Tests**.

The **Test Explorer** window should show all tests as passing with green check marks:

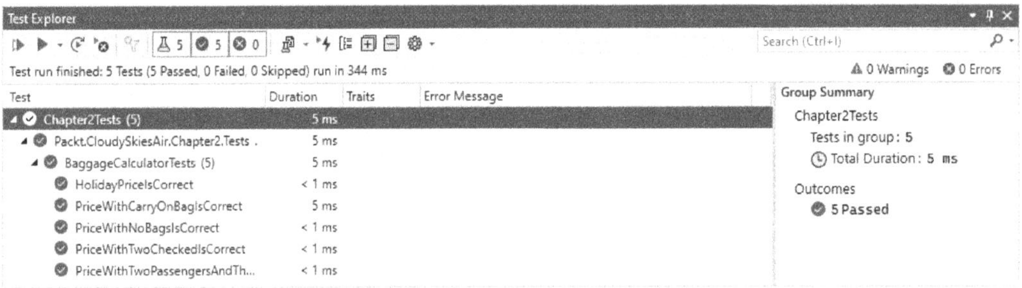

Figure 2.13 – Five passing tests in Test Explorer

If a test is now failing and didn't fail before, this is a good thing, since it means the test found an issue you caused in the code's behavior. Investigate the failing test and then resolve the issue before continuing.

We'll explore testing in much more detail in *Part 2* of this book, but as it stands, it appears that our refactorings have been successful.

> **Final code**
>
> The final refactored code from this chapter is available in the `https://github.com/PacktPublishing/Refactoring-with-CSharp` repository, inside the `Chapter02/Ch2FinalCode` folder.

The code we produced in this chapter is simple, readable, and maintainable. Certainly, there are things that could still be improved, but the code is less likely to cause issues as it grows in complexity in the future.

Refactoring in other editors

Before we end the chapter, let's talk about refactoring in editors other than Visual Studio.

This book primarily focuses on refactoring in Visual Studio because that's the current primary development environment for .NET developers. However, there are a few other editors and extensions that are frequently used for .NET development and offer refactoring support:

- **Visual Studio Code**
- **JetBrains Rider**
- **JetBrains ReSharper** (Visual Studio Extension)

These tools will not be featured in examples throughout the remainder of the book since Visual Studio is the primary editing experience. However, most of what I'll show you in the remainder of the book is also possible using these tools.

Refactoring in Visual Studio Code with the C# Dev Kit

Visual Studio Code (**VS Code**) is rapidly becoming a highly capable editing environment for .NET projects with its C# extension.

Where VS Code really comes into its own is with the newer **C# Dev Kit**, which gives an editing experience almost identical to Visual Studio, including the solution explorer. The C# Dev Kit integrates with the other C# extensions to provide code suggestions and refactoring **Quick Actions** with the same style of light bulb icons you see in Visual Studio.

Figure 2.14 – Refactoring with the C# Dev Kit in VS Code

VS Code won't give you the full set of refactoring options Visual Studio currently does, but it is cross-platform and will work on Mac and Linux.

Licensing note

VS Code is free, but the C# Dev Kit extension requires a paid Visual Studio license key.

I expect we'll see VS Code featured much more prominently in .NET development with the improvements from the C# Dev Kit and VS Code's cross-platform capabilities, along with its ability to run in-browser to some extent through **GitHub Codespaces**.

Refactoring in JetBrains Rider

JetBrains Rider is a separate editor developed on the same set of editing software used by the popular **IntelliJ** Java editor.

Rider works with most .NET projects and has a fantastic set of refactoring capabilities built in. These capabilities will often be similar to those mentioned in this book, but the exact naming and user experience will be slightly different.

```
                              Matt Eland
37          private decimal CalculatePriceFlat(int numBags) {
38              decimal total = 0;
39
40              // Business says to use a flat 100 regardless of count
41              return 100M;
42
43              // Old logic: $50 per bag
44              return numBags * 50M;
45      💡 Remove unreachable code
        💡 Comment unreachable code
46      🔧 Compiler warning: 'CS0162: Code is unreachable'      ▶
47      🔧 Inspection: 'Heuristically unreachable code'         ▶
        ⓢ Navigate To...                          Alt+`
        🔬 Inspect This...                  Ctrl+Alt+Shift+A
        →§ Generate Code...                      Alt+Insert
```

Figure 2.15 – Refactoring in JetBrains Rider

Like VS Code, one major advantage Rider has over Visual Studio is that it is fully cross-platform and can run on macOS or Linux.

Refactoring in Visual Studio with ReSharper

If you love working with Visual Studio but want the same rich set of refactorings that Rider offers, JetBrains also offers a Visual Studio extension called **ReSharper**.

ReSharper replaces many Visual Studio features with enhanced versions, including Visual Studio's code analysis and refactoring tools.

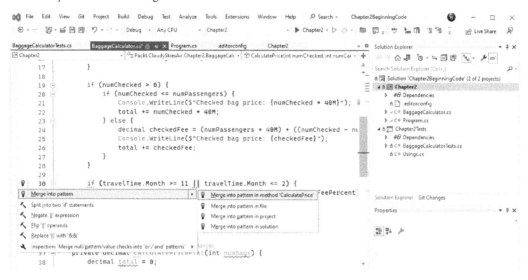

Figure 2.16 – Refactoring with ReSharper in Visual Studio

Nowadays, Visual Studio tends to have most of the refactoring capabilities ReSharper and Rider offer, but the capabilities of ReSharper and Rider can sometimes be a bit more advanced.

Summary

Throughout this chapter, we explored refactoring by taking a class with a bit of complexity and applied targeted refactorings to make it easier to read, maintain, and expand.

We went from a modestly complex class to a relatively simple one by following a set of repeatable actions that transformed the code from one form to another without changing its overall behavior or result.

Although Visual Studio supports very capable refactoring tools, it is up to you as an experienced developer to know when you might want to apply each individual refactoring, based on the current level of complexity of your code and the code smells you're observing.

Over the next three chapters, we'll explore the built-in refactorings in more depth by exploring refactorings related to methods, classes, and individual lines of code.

Questions

1. What are some ways of triggering Quick Actions for a block of code?

2. Does Visual Studio ever indicate that refactorings are possible or recommended?

3. How can you know what a Quick Action will do before performing it?

4. Are Visual Studio Quick Actions the only way to refactor code?

Further reading

You can find more information about refactoring in Visual Studio and other environments at these URLs:

- *Quick Actions Overview*: `https://learn.microsoft.com/en-us/visualstudio/ide/quick-actions`

- *JetBrains Rider vs Visual Studio (with and without ReSharper)*: `https://www.jetbrains.com/rider/compare/rider-vs-visual-studio/`

- *Announcing C# Dev Kit for Visual Studio Code*: `https://devblogs.microsoft.com/visualstudio/announcing-csharp-dev-kit-for-visual-studio-code/`

3

Refactoring Code Flow and Iteration

While other chapters in *Part 1* focus on refactorings that can be applied to entire methods or classes, this chapter focuses on improving the readability and efficiency of individual lines of code.

Developers spend the majority of their time reading over individual lines of code and only a fraction of that time modifying code. So, it is important to make our lines of code as maintainable as possible.

In this chapter, we'll explore the following topics related to improving small pieces of code:

- Controlling program flow
- Instantiating objects
- Iterating over collections
- Refactoring LINQ statements
- Reviewing and testing our refactored code

Technical requirements

The starting code for this chapter is available from GitHub at `https://github.com/PacktPublishing/Refactoring-with-CSharp` in the `Chapter03/Ch3BeginningCode` folder.

Refactoring the boarding app

This chapter's code focuses on a pair of applications for Cloudy Skies Airline:

- A *Boarding Status Display* app that tells the user if it's time for them to board their flight based on the current boarding group and the person's ticket, military status, and whether or not they need assistance getting down the jetway.

- A *Boarding Kiosk* app that allows airline employees to view the passengers scheduled to be on the flight and provides information regarding whether each passenger has boarded. *Figure 3.1* shows the application in action:

```
Boarding Group 4

Torrey Kilback          Group 1: Onboard
Cielo Connelly          Group 1: Onboard
Justine Bergstrom       Group 1: Onboard
Myrna Brekke            Group 1: Onboard
Herminia Schultz        Group 1: Board Now via Priority Lane
Hollis Kirlin           Group 1: Onboard
Chase West              Group 2: Onboard
Dave Nader              Group 2: Onboard
Perry Ritchie           Group 2: Onboard
Brant Flatley           Group 2: Board Now via Priority Lane
Mary Gutmann            Group 3: Onboard
Mitchell Ritchie        Group 3: Onboard
Ernestina Sipes         Group 4: Onboard
Alberta Medhurst        Group 5: Onboard
Audie Brown             Group 6: Please Wait
Dayana Heller           Group 6: Please Wait
Samantha O'Kon          Group 6: Please Wait
Delta Brekke            Group 7: Onboard
```

Figure 3.1 – The Boarding Kiosk app

Since we're exploring not one but two applications, we'll meet the application code in small chunks as we progress through this chapter. However, feel free to peruse it yourself on GitHub if you'd like to orient yourself first.

As we go through this chapter, we'll take its existing functioning code and see how small refactoring steps can improve the maintainability of the code using various C# language features.

We'll start by looking at how refactoring can improve the overall flow of code.

Controlling program flow

One of the most basic things new developers learn is how programs execute lines of code in sequence and how **if statements** and other language features control what statements execute next.

In this section, we'll focus on the `BoardingProcessor` class's `CanPassengerBoard` method. The method starts simple enough:

```
public string CanPassengerBoard(Passenger passenger) {
  bool isMilitary = passenger.IsMilitary;
```

```
bool needsHelp = passenger.NeedsHelp;
int group = passenger.BoardingGroup;
```

Here, `CanPassengerBoard` takes in a `Passenger` object and returns a string. The method also declares a few local variables holding pieces of data from the object passed in.

These variables aren't necessary and could be removed by performing an inline variable refactoring, which we'll talk about later in this chapter. However, as they improve the readability of the code that follows, their existence is largely helpful. This is part of the reason why we sometimes introduce local variables, as we covered in *Chapter 2*.

The logic that follows gets significantly harder to read, as seen here:

```
if (Status != BoardingStatus.PlaneDeparted) {
  if (isMilitary && Status == BoardingStatus.Boarding) {
    return "Board Now via Priority Lane";
  } else if (needsHelp&&Status==BoardingStatus.Boarding) {
    return "Board Now via Priority Lane";
  } else if (Status == BoardingStatus.Boarding) {
    if (CurrentBoardingGroup >= group) {
      if (_priorityLaneGroups.Contains(group)) {
        return "Board Now via Priority Lane";
      } else {
        return "Board Now";
      }
    } else {
      return "Please Wait";
    }
  } else {
    return "Boarding Not Started";
  }
} else {
  return "Flight Departed";
}
}
```

This method primarily uses `if`/`else` statements with a few scattered variable declarations and periodic return statements. These are fundamental structures of computer programming, and yet it takes a moment to understand what this code truly does.

For those not wanting to sort through the logic, this code follows these rules:

• If the plane has departed, return `"Flight Departed"`

• If the plane is not yet boarding, return `"Boarding Not Started"`

- If the plane is boarding and the passenger needs help or is active military, return `"Board Now via Priority Lane"`

- If the plane is boarding and the passenger's group is not boarding yet, return `"Please Wait"`

- If the passenger's group can board, tell them to board either by the normal lane or via the priority lane if their boarding group is one of the priority groups

However, the code is complex enough that puzzling out these rules can take a bit of time, and the complexity results in uncertainty, making it difficult for others to understand the rules in their entirety.

Understanding these rules is important if you're going to maintain the code. So, improving the readability of this code is important to the code's long-term success.

Inverting if statements

One of the quickest tricks to simplifying complex logic involving nested `if` statements can be to invert the `if` statement and return early.

Currently, our high-level logic looks like this:

```
if (Status != BoardingStatus.PlaneDeparted) {
  // 17 lines of additional if statements and conditions
} else {
  return "Flight Departed";
}
```

By the time we get back to the `else` statement associated with the plane departed check, the reader has forgotten what the original `if` statement was to begin with!

Here, since the `else` branch is so simple and easy to understand, it's helpful to invert the `if` statement by taking the following actions:

1. Swap the contents of the `if` block and the `else` block.

2. Invert the boolean expression in the `if` statement. When inverting ==, it becomes != and vice versa. In cases where we do a > or < check, you flip the operand and toggle whether equality is included. Under these rules, >= becomes < and >= becomes >.

In our case, we check that `Status != BoardingStatus.PlaneDeparted`. In this case, we'd change != to == and wind up with this:

```
Status == BoardingStatus.PlaneDeparted
```

These steps preserve the program's existing behavior but change the order of the statements in the code. This can increase the readability of our source code.

If this sounds complicated, don't worry, because Visual Studio has a **Quick Action** refactoring for it called **Invert if**, as shown in *Figure 3.2*:

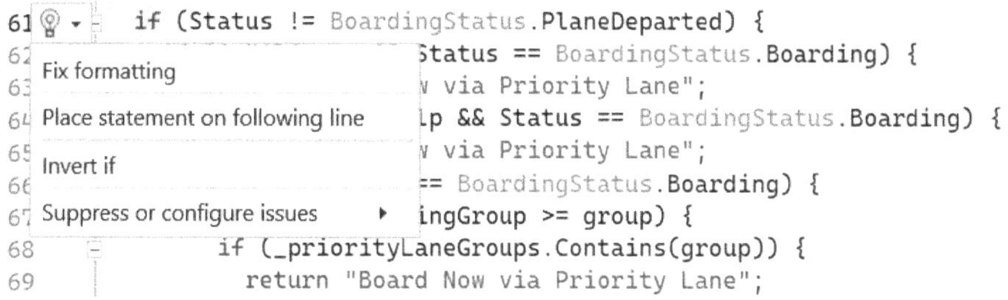

Figure 3.2 – The Invert if Quick Action refactoring

Performing the refactoring here effectively changes our logic to the following:

```
if (Status == BoardingStatus.PlaneDeparted) {
  return "Flight Departed";
} else {
  // 17 lines of additional if statements and conditions
}
```

While this is easier to read since the reader no longer must remember what the if statement even pertains to 17 lines later, the code can be improved further.

Dropping else statements after return statements

Since the return statement always leaves the method immediately, you never explicitly *need* an else statement after a return statement because you know that if you get to the return statement, logic after the if block won't execute.

This lets us remove the else keyword and its curly braces. Then, we can outdent the code that was previously in the else block.

The resulting code keeps the if statement:

```
if (Status == BoardingStatus.PlaneDeparted) {
  return "Flight Departed";
}
```

After this statement, the code that follows is now at the same indentation level as the original `if` statement and is easier to read and understand:

```
if (isMilitary && Status == BoardingStatus.Boarding) {
  return "Board Now via Priority Lane";
} else if (needsHelp&&Status == BoardingStatus.Boarding) {
  return "Board Now via Priority Lane";
} else if (Status == BoardingStatus.Boarding) {
  if (CurrentBoardingGroup >= group) {
      if (_priorityLaneGroups.Contains(group)) {
        return "Board Now via Priority Lane";
      } else {
        return "Board Now";
      }
  } else {
    return "Please Wait";
  }
} else {
  return "Boarding Not Started";
}
```

We can repeat this refactoring a few more times if we want to since the code has a few more `if`/`return`/`else` sequences.

I'll leave those for the moment since there's another refactoring I want to show you that can help with what we're seeing here.

Restructuring if statements

Looking at the previous code, some of the logic stands out as repetitive:

```
if (isMilitary && Status == BoardingStatus.Boarding) {
  return "Board Now via Priority Lane";
} else if (needsHelp&&Status == BoardingStatus.Boarding) {
  return "Board Now via Priority Lane";
} else if (Status == BoardingStatus.Boarding) {
  // Code omitted for brevity
} else {
  return "Boarding Not Started";
}
```

Here, we have an `if`/`else` chain where three different things are checking whether the flight is currently boarding. Although each of these three `if` statements is different, there's enough overlap between them that it makes me question if we could be less repetitive.

The first option we could consider might be a simple *introduce local variable* refactoring, as we saw in *Chapter 2*:

```
bool isBoarding = Status == BoardingStatus.Boarding;
if (isMilitary && isBoarding) {
  return "Board Now via Priority Lane";
} else if (needsHelp && isBoarding) {
  return "Board Now via Priority Lane";
} else if (isBoarding) {
  // Code omitted for brevity
} else {
  return "Boarding Not Started";
}
```

I find this code easier to read, even though we gained an extra line from the new local variable. However, let's take a slightly different approach.

Instead of introducing a variable, we can rearrange our if statements to have an additional layer of nesting:

```
if (Status == BoardingStatus.Boarding) {
  if (isMilitary) {
    return "Board Now via Priority Lane";
  } else if (needsHelp) {
    return "Board Now via Priority Lane";
  } else {
    // Code omitted for brevity
  }
} else {
  return "Boarding Not Started";
}
```

Here, pulling a common condition from a set of if statements into an outer if statement helped clarify those if statements, although it did so at the expense of an additional degree of nesting.

However, this simplification helps spot a few other refactoring opportunities, such as combining the isMilitary and needsHelp checks since they return the same value if either is true:

```
if (isMilitary || needsHelp) {
  return "Board Now via Priority Lane";
}
```

We can also drop the else statement after the if/return code to outdent our code a bit more, leaving just the boarding group logic:

```
if (CurrentBoardingGroup >= group) {
  if (_priorityLaneGroups.Contains(group)) {
```

```
      return "Board Now via Priority Lane";
    } else {
      return "Board Now";
    }
  } else {
    return "Please Wait";
  }
```

This looks like another place where we can invert `if` and drop the `else` statement to simplify the code even more. Remember that we must change `>=` to `<` to do this:

```
if (CurrentBoardingGroup < group) {
  return "Please Wait";
}
if (_priorityLaneGroups.Contains(group)) {
  return "Board Now via Priority Lane";
} else {
  return "Board Now";
}
```

As you can see, the code is getting significantly easier to read as we simplify it.

Let's take a step back and look at our conditional logic after these refactorings:

```
if (Status == BoardingStatus.PlaneDeparted) {
  return "Flight Departed";
}
if (Status == BoardingStatus.Boarding) {
  if (isMilitary || needsHelp) {
    return "Board Now via Priority Lane";
  }
  if (CurrentBoardingGroup < group) {
    return "Please Wait";
  }
  if (_priorityLaneGroups.Contains(group)) {
    return "Board Now via Priority Lane";
  } else {
    return "Board Now";
  }
} else {
  return "Boarding Not Started";
}
```

The code is now easier to read and harder to misinterpret. We could invert the Boarding status check to return early, but we'll do something else with here later.

Let's look at how we can reduce our line count even further through a more divisive language feature: the **ternary operator**.

Using ternary operators

If you're a fan of the ternary operator, you may have noticed an opportunity to use one in the code as we've been refactoring.

For those not familiar or not fully comfortable with the ternary conditional operator, think of it as a condensed *if my condition is true use this value, otherwise use this other value* type of an operator.

The syntax for ternary is `boolExpression ? trueValue : falseValue;`.

In other words, you could write code without a ternary like this:

```
int value;
if (someCondition) {
  value = 1;
} else {
  value = 2;
}
```

However, the same code could be written using a ternary in a single line:

```
int value = someCondition ? 1 : 2;
```

As you can see, the ternary operator lets us take six lines of code and condense it down to a single line. This conciseness is a key factor for those who like using ternaries in their code.

Those who are less fond of ternary operators often point out that ternaries are difficult to read – particularly when trying to read through code quickly. In other words, while they make code more concise, this conciseness can slow you down in the long run by making the code less easy to maintain.

Let's look at a small part of our code and see how a ternary could be applied:

```
if (CurrentBoardingGroup < group) {
    return "Please Wait";
}
if (_priorityLaneGroups.Contains(group)) {
    return "Board Now via Priority Lane";
} else {
    return "Board Now";
}
```

Here, we are checking if the current boarding group is a priority group and then telling the user to board with the priority lane or to board normally based on the result of the `Contains` call.

Since we're returning a single value based on the result of a boolean expression, we could rewrite the code with a ternary as follows:

```
if (CurrentBoardingGroup < group) {
  return "Please Wait";
}
return _priorityLaneGroups.Contains(group)
       ? "Board Now via Priority Lane"
       : "Board Now";
```

This chops five lines of code down to three lines of code or a single line of code if you want to put the ? and : segments on the same line as the boolean expression.

You might have noticed that this refactoring now puts the whole block of code into a position where you could introduce another ternary based on the boarding group, return "Please Wait", if that expression is true, and return the result of the earlier ternary expression if the expression is false:

```
return (CurrentBoardingGroup < group)
  ? "Please Wait"
  : _priorityLaneGroups.Contains(group)
    ? "Board Now via Priority Lane"
    : "Board Now";
```

While this is valid C#, I can attest that if a coworker showed this to me in code review, I would be tempted to utter some not-very-nice words!

> **Tip**
> Remember: fewer lines of code don't always equate to greater maintainability.

At a personal level, my preference is to avoid the ternary in many places and always avoid chaining ternaries together. However, I do sometimes use ternaries when I feel it is right for a piece of code.

For example, sometimes, a method is very simple and can be condensed to a single line of code if you use a ternary expression. This particular change lets you use the expression-bodied members feature, which we'll talk about in *Chapter 4*.

When I use a ternary, I format my ternary expressions on three separate lines, as shown earlier, with the first line containing the boolean expression. The second line will feature the ? operator and the value to use if the expression was true, and the third line will feature the : operator and the value to use if the expression was false:

```
var myVar = booleanExpression
            ? valueIfTrue
            : valueIfFalse;
```

I find that this approach strikes a happy medium between the benefits of more concise code from the ternary and the penalties of code becoming more difficult to read quickly and accurately when using a ternary.

Converting if statements into switch statements

The logic of this method is now a lot easier to understand, and simplifying it down to this level highlights that we're doing one of three things, depending on the current boarding status:

- Notifying the user the flight has departed if its status is `PlaneDeparted`

- Checking military status, whether help boarding is needed, and the boarding group for `Boarding` status

- Notifying the user that boarding hasn't started yet for other statuses (`NotStarted` is the only other status at the moment)

When working with enumerated values, this kind of branching logic is common.

In our case, our `enum` value only has three states:

BoardingStatus.cs

```
public enum BoardingStatus {
   NotStarted = 0,
   Boarding = 1,
   PlaneDeparted = 2,
}
```

In cases where you find yourself checking the same variable for different values, you can usually rewrite them to use a **switch statement** instead.

`switch` statements are essentially a streamlined series of `if`/`else if`/`else` types of checks that all check the same value, as our code does with `Status`. We'll see an example of a `switch` statement shortly, but if you're not familiar with them, you can think of them as just a different way of writing a series of related `if`/`else if` statements.

This can be done manually, or you can use a specific refactoring built into Visual Studio if your code is built in an `if`/`else if`/`else` type of structure, as the following code illustrates:

```
if (Status == BoardingStatus.PlaneDeparted) {
   return "Flight Departed";
} else if (Status == BoardingStatus.Boarding) {
   if (isMilitary || needsHelp) {
      return "Board Now via Priority Lane";
   }
```

```
    if (CurrentBoardingGroup < group) {
       return "Please Wait";
    }
    return _priorityLaneGroups.Contains(group)
            ? "Board Now via Priority Lane"
            : "Board Now";
  } else {
    return "Boarding Not Started";
  }
}
```

Note here that I did add the else keyword (in bold in the previous snippet) to our earlier code to get into that if/else if/else structure, which lets Visual Studio identify the refactoring we're about to use.

Once we have the code in this pattern, the **Convert to 'switch' statement** refactoring option will appear in the **Quick Actions** menu when you have the if statement selected, as shown in *Figure 3.3*:

Figure 3.3 – The Convert to "switch" statement refactoring option

This refactoring makes our status-based logic much more apparent:

```
switch (Status) {
  case BoardingStatus.PlaneDeparted:
    return "Flight Departed";
```

```
case BoardingStatus.Boarding:
    if (isMilitary || needsHelp) {
        return "Board Now via Priority Lane";
    }
    if (CurrentBoardingGroup < group) {
        return "Please Wait";
    }
    return _priorityLaneGroups.Contains(group)
            ? "Board Now via Priority Lane"
            : "Board Now";
default:
    return "Boarding Not Started";
}
```

As someone reading this code, I find this a lot easier to scan and interpret compared to an if/else if/else chain, even though the logic functions identically. With an if/else if/else statement, I *may* notice that logic is comparing the same value several different times, while a switch statement makes it explicit.

Another benefit you get with a switch statement is that it unlocks a built-in refactoring option when your switch compares an enum value (such as BoardingStatus) and you're missing a case for one or more enum values.

This option shows up in the **Quick Actions** menu for the switch statement as **Add missing cases**, as shown in *Figure 3.4*:

Figure 3.4 – The Add missing cases refactoring option in the Quick Actions menu

> **Warning**
>
> I want to point out that the **Add missing cases** refactoring option here potentially causes a change in behavior. The built-in implementation of that refactoring adds the `NotStarted` status and has it break out of the switch instead of returning a value as it previously would have through the `default` keyword.
>
> The C# compiler will flag this mistake for us in this case since the method won't return a value for this path, but adding missing cases when a `default` case is present in a `switch` statement typically does introduce a change in behavior.

In our case, we can merge the `NotStarted` status with the default case and get a more explicit list of options:

```
switch (Status) {
  case BoardingStatus.PlaneDeparted:
     return "Flight Departed";
  case BoardingStatus.Boarding:
     if (isMilitary || needsHelp) {
        return "Board Now via Priority Lane";
     }
     if (CurrentBoardingGroup < group) {
        return "Please Wait";
     }
     return _priorityLaneGroups.Contains(group)
              ? "Board Now via Priority Lane"
              : "Board Now";
  case BoardingStatus.NotStarted:
  default:
     return "Boarding Not Started";
}
```

This code is now significantly easier to read than it was before, and the flow of logic by status is now readily apparent.

In a real-world application, I might change the default case to throw an exception, explicitly telling me that a specific `Status` was not supported by this logic. This would look something like the following logic:

```
case BoardingStatus.NotStarted:
  return "Boarding Not Started";
default:
  throw new NotSupportedException($"Unsupported: {Status}");
```

I might also be tempted to perform *extract method* refactoring – as we saw in *Chapter 2* – to move the logic for handling the boarding status into its own method. However, I'll hold off on doing that to showcase switch expressions instead.

Converting to switch expressions

Switch expressions are an evolution of switch statements that rely on **pattern-matching** expressions to simplify and expand what's possible inside switch statements.

`switch` expressions are a relatively new feature in C# that was released as part of C# 8 in 2019. While that's more than a few years old at the time of writing, I still find switch expressions to be new enough that many C# developers are unfamiliar or unpracticed with them.

A simple `switch` expression looks a lot like a switch statement:

```
return Status switch {
  BoardingStatus.PlaneDeparted => "Flight Departed",
  BoardingStatus.NotStarted => "Boarding Not Started",
  BoardingStatus.Boarding => "Board Now",
  _ => "Some other status",
};
```

These `switch` expressions look very similar to switch statements except for the following aspects:

- They start with the value you want to evaluate followed by the `switch` keyword instead of starting with `switch (value)`

- We don't use the `case` or `break` keywords

- Individual cases have some condition that might be true on the left, an arrow notation (`=>`), and then the value to use on the right if the condition on the left is true.

- Instead of the `default` keyword, we have `_`, indicating any other match

One of the nice things about `switch` expressions is that they're extremely concise while still being somewhat readable. However, there's more power to `switch` expressions than what I've shown you so far.

You may have noticed the sample `switch` expression I introduced a moment ago doesn't adequately handle the logic for boarding. Specifically, we had rules for active military members, people who need assistance boarding, boarding groups, and priority lanes, and none of that is represented in the previous block of code.

Let's take a look at a `switch` expression that does handle these things:

```
return Status switch {
  BoardingStatus.PlaneDeparted => "Flight Departed",
  BoardingStatus.NotStarted => "Boarding Not Started",
```

```
    BoardingStatus.Boarding when isMilitary || needsHelp
        => "Board Now via Priority Lane",
    BoardingStatus.Boarding when CurrentBoardingGroup < group
        => "Please Wait",
    BoardingStatus.Boarding when
      _priorityLaneGroups.Contains(group)
        => "Board Now via Priority Lane",
    BoardingStatus.Boarding => "Board Now",
    _ => "Some other status",
};
```

This code is a bit different than the last `switch` expression we saw. Here, the `Boarding` status is repeated four times and sometimes accompanied by the `when` keyword.

What this code is doing is using pattern matching to check not just that `Status` is `Boarding`, but that other conditions are true as well. Effectively, we're able to check the status and optionally another boolean expression after the `when` keyword.

If both things are not true, the `switch` expression evaluates the next line in sequence. This makes `switch` expressions a set of matching rules that ensure the first rule evaluates to true.

Pattern matching

Pattern matching is a newer C# syntax that allows you to concisely check different properties and aspects of objects and variables. We'll explore pattern-matching syntax more in *Chapter 10, Defensive Coding Techniques*, but this section serves as a good introduction to some of its capabilities.

In other words, this `switch` expression checks the following rules and reacts to the first one that is true:

1. The plane has departed.
2. Boarding hasn't started yet.
3. Boarding has started and the passenger is active military or needs assistance.
4. The passenger's boarding group hasn't been called yet.
5. The passenger's group is boarding and it's a priority lane group.
6. The passenger's group is boarding but they're not in the priority boarding lane.
7. Any other status

`switch` expressions are concise and allow you to mix the structured clarity of `switch` statements with the power of pattern matching and the `when` keyword to make very readable ordered logic apparent.

As with any tool in your programming toolbelt, `switch` expressions won't be the solution to every problem and you and your team may not be as fond of reading `switch` expressions as I am. However, they remain a valuable tool in your toolbox for simplifying code while keeping it easy to read, maintain, and expand.

We'll revisit some of the pattern-matching syntax in *Chapter 10*, but let's move on to looking at what we can do to improve working with collections of objects.

Instantiating objects

Now that we've sufficiently improved our `CanPassengerBoard` method, let's look at how we can create objects and see a few simple improvements you can make that will simplify object **instantiation** in your code.

> **Terminology notes**
>
> New developers are often tripped up by a handful of phrases that are commonly used by developers. For example, in this section, we will talk about instantiating objects. This is a common way of phrasing this for developers, but all it means is the process of creating a specific *instance* of a class using the `new` keyword. When you see the term instantiating, you can think of it simply as creating a specific instance of something.
>
> This section's code could come from anywhere, but we'll focus on code found in a pair of methods in the `PassengerTests.cs` file in the test project that accompanies this chapter.

Replacing var with explicit Types

The first line of code I want to focus on comes from one of our unit tests:

PassengerTests.cs

```
var p = Build(first, last);
```

Here, I've deliberately omitted the context of the code from the surrounding lines to reinforce a point, and the point is this: take a moment and try to determine what data type the p variable is.

p stores the result of `Build`, which takes in a pair of parameters named `first` and `last`, but we can't make a confident assertion about what type of data p holds from this line alone.

This is because p was declared with the `var` keyword. The `var` keyword is a shorthand way of saying "Hey, compiler, when you're compiling this code, I want you to determine what data type this is going to be and replace the `var` keyword in the compiled code with the actual type of the data."

In other words, `var` is usually a shortcut for not typing out the full name of the data type in question. However, it comes with a small penalty in that it makes it harder to read what data type the variable contains.

This makes sense for when you have a complex data type such as `IDictionary<Guid, HashSet<string>>`, but it can get a little ridiculous for short type names such as `int`.

> **Other uses of var**
>
> The `var` keyword does have other uses beyond what I've described here. For example, it can easily store **anonymous types** and other difficult-to-represent type structures, but for this book, I'm focusing on the common applications of `var` in most codebases.

Visual Studio does let you hover over the variable declaration and see the actual Type being used. In this case, p represents a `Passenger` object, but this still slows down your reading of the code.

Instead, I recommend that you take advantage of the built-in **Use explicit type instead of 'var'** refactoring. See *Figure 3.5*:

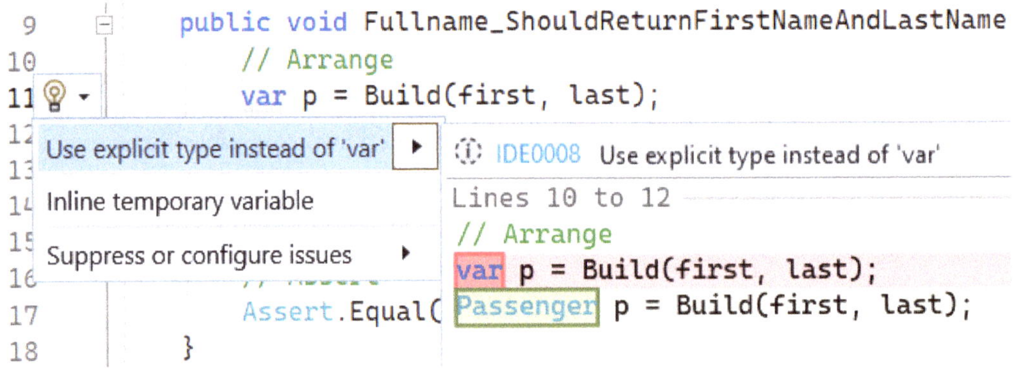

Figure 3.5 – Using explicit types

This makes your code significantly easier to read:

```
Passenger p = Build(first, last);
```

Of course, `var` exists for a reason and it was introduced to solve certain problems, including redundancy in assignment statements. We'll take a look at the **target-typed new** keyword next that offers a different solution to that problem.

Simplifying creation with target-typed new

One of the things the `var` keyword was built to help with was lines such as the following variable instantiation:

```
private Passenger Build(string firstName, string lastName){
    Passenger passenger = new Passenger();
    passenger.FirstName = firstName;
    passenger.LastName = lastName;
    return passenger;
}
```

When we instantiate a new `Passenger` object and assign it to the new passenger variable, we repeat ourselves slightly on the left and right-hand sides of the assignment operator (=) by using the name of the `Passenger` class twice.

The `var` keyword allowed us to simplify the creation of this object down to the still readable syntax of `var passenger = new Passenger();`. Here, `var` allows us to simplify the left-hand side of this assignment statement by abbreviating the type that's used for the new variable.

C# 9 introduced the **target-typed new** keyword, which lets us simplify the right-hand side of the assignment operator by effectively saying that the type of class we're instantiating is the same as the variable that acts as the target of the assignment operator.

In other words, target-typed new is a way of telling C# to create the same type as the variable we'll store the value in. This allows us to avoid `var` and not repeat ourselves:

```
Passenger passenger = new();
```

I love this syntax and tend to use it in all my code. It can cause small bits of confusion for other developers the first time they see the feature, but that's a minor one-time penalty for something that keeps your code concise and readable at the same time.

> Tip
> Visual Studio gives you a **Use 'new(…)'** option in the **Quick Action** menu that will let you change a traditional object instantiation to the target-typed new syntax.

While we're talking about creating objects, let's look at how **object initializers** can help set properties on objects as you create them.

Using object initializers

Let's take another look at that `Build` method from the previous example while focusing on configuring the created passenger object:

```
private Passenger Build(string firstName, string lastName){
    Passenger passenger = new();
    passenger.FirstName = firstName;
    passenger.LastName = lastName;
    return passenger;
}
```

This code isn't bad at all, but it does repeat itself a little.

Specifically, the code repeats the information of the object it configures each line by putting `passenger.` in front of each property before assigning a value to that property.

This is very minimal with only two properties. But imagine a larger object with 10 or more properties you want to configure. This code would get very repetitive and might even distract from the names of the properties that are being configured.

While using a constructor that takes in parameters representing property values is one solution (and one we'll explore in the next chapter), another solution is to use an **object initializer**. As you're likely guessing, Visual Studio provides a **Quick Actions** refactoring for this, though the name **Object initialization can be simplified** (shown in *Figure 3.6*) is a bit unusual:

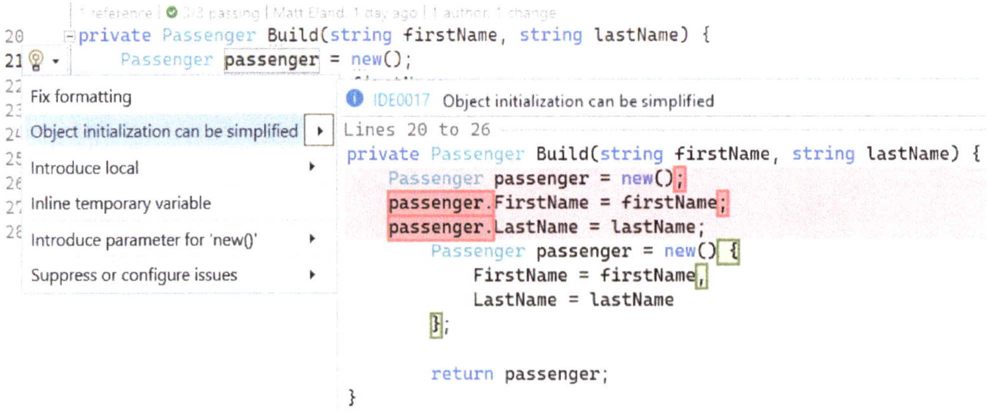

Figure 3.6 – Simplifying object initialization

Using this refactoring transforms our code into a sparser format:

```
private Passenger Build(string firstName, string lastName){
    Passenger passenger = new() {
        FirstName = firstName,
```

```
        LastName = lastName
    };
    return passenger;
}
```

I love this syntax and it plays very nicely with the `init` and `required` properties, which we'll explore in *Chapter 10, Defensive Coding Techniques*. However, there is a downside to using object initializers: stack traces.

When you have an object initializer that sets several different properties of an object and an exception occurs that calculates the value to store, the exception doesn't indicate which line of code the error occurred on or which property was about to be updated, only that it occurred somewhere in the initializer.

On the other hand, if you were using multiple lines setting individual properties, the exception details would identify the line in question. Of course, this might be an argument to avoid doing calculations in initializers that might produce exceptions.

We'll revisit initializers more in *Chapter 10* when we discuss `init`, `required`, and `with` expressions, but for now, let's move on to talking about collections.

Iterating over collections

To start exploring collections, let's go back to the `BoardingProcessor` class and look at its `DisplayPassengerBoardingStatus` method. We'll explore this method a bit at a time, starting with its method signature:

```
public void DisplayBoardingStatus(
    List<Passenger> passengers, bool? hasBoarded = null) {
```

Here, we can see that the method takes in a list of `Passenger` objects and, optionally, a nullable boolean `hasBoarded` parameter that can store `true`, `false`, or `null`. This `hasBoarded` parameter is used to optionally filter down our list of passengers based on its value:

- `true`: Only include passengers who have boarded the plane

- `false`: Only include passengers who have not yet boarded

- `null`: Do not filter by boarded status (default option)

This nullable filtering parameter is a common one I see while building search methods and we'll explore it in more depth again in *Chapter 5, Object-oriented Refactoring*.

The next portion of code in `DisplayBoardingStatus` deals with the filtering logic:

```
    List<Passenger> filteredPassengers = new();
    for (int i = 0; i < passengers.Count; i++) {
        Passenger p = passengers[i];
```

```
    if (!hasBoarded.HasValue || p.HasBoarded==hasBoarded) {
        filteredPassengers.Add(p);
    }
  }
}
```

This is the portion of code we'll be focusing on for the rest of this section. It builds a new list of passengers that matches the filtering option the user selected by iterating over the passengers in `passengers`. and conditionally adds it to our new list of passengers.

> **Terminology note**
>
> **Iterating** over something is another term that confuses new developers. It just means looping through each item in a collection.

The remainder of the method focuses on displaying passengers to the agent at the boarding kiosk:

```
DisplayBoardingHeader();
foreach (Passenger passenger in filteredPassengers) {
    string statusMessage = passenger.HasBoarded
        ? "Onboard"
        : CanPassengerBoard(passenger);
    Console.WriteLine($"{passenger.FullName,-23} Group
        {passenger.BoardingGroup}: {statusMessage}");
  }
}
```

Essentially, for every passenger that we want to display, we write out their name, boarding group, and the message they see on their boarding app or `"Onboard"` if they've already boarded the plane.

Overall, this method is simple and comes in at less than 20 lines of code long, which tends to lead to easy-to-maintain code.

That said, let's look at a few ways we could improve this code.

Introducing foreach

Take another look at the code to filter the passenger list into a new list of passengers:

```
List<Passenger> filteredPassengers = new();
for (int i = 0; i < passengers.Count; i++) {
  Passenger p = passengers[i];
  if (!hasBoarded.HasValue || p.HasBoarded == hasBoarded) {
      filteredPassengers.Add(p);
  }
}
```

While this code isn't very involved, one of the things that jumps out to me is that we're using a `for` loop to enumerate through the passengers. Inside this loop, we're not doing anything with our index variable, `i`, aside from getting a passenger out of the list by its index.

Whenever you have a `for` loop like this that isn't doing anything complex (for example, starting anywhere but the beginning of the list, looping in reverse, or skipping every other item), you can usually replace the loop with a `foreach` loop.

To convert a `for` loop into a `foreach` loop, you can select the `for` loop and then use the **Convert to 'foreach'** refactoring feature that's built into Visual Studio (*Figure 3.7*):

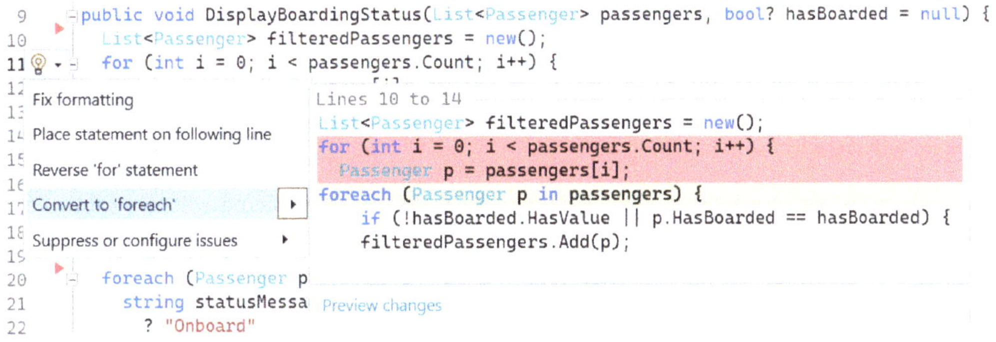

```
 9      public void DisplayBoardingStatus(List<Passenger> passengers, bool? hasBoarded = null) {
10          List<Passenger> filteredPassengers = new();
11          for (int i = 0; i < passengers.Count; i++) {

    Fix formatting                        Lines 10 to 14
                                          List<Passenger> filteredPassengers = new();
14  Place statement on following line     for (int i = 0; i < passengers.Count; i++) {
15                                             Passenger p = passengers[i];
16  Reverse 'for' statement
17  Convert to 'foreach'          ▶       foreach (Passenger p in passengers) {
18                                             if (!hasBoarded.HasValue || p.HasBoarded == hasBoarded) {
    Suppress or configure issues  ▶           filteredPassengers.Add(p);
19
20      foreach (Passenger p
21          string statusMessa  Preview changes
22              ? "Onboard"
```

Figure 3.7 – The Convert to 'foreach' refactoring option in the Quick Actions menu

This moves to a `foreach` loop and gets rid of the variable declaration entirely:

```
List<Passenger> filteredPassengers = new();
foreach (Passenger p in passengers) {
  if (!hasBoarded.HasValue || p.HasBoarded == hasBoarded) {
     filteredPassengers.Add(p);
  }
}
```

I use `foreach` wherever I can because not only does it remove a variable declaration and use of the indexer, but it makes the overall code easier to read.

Almost all `for` loops start at 0 and loop up to the end of the collection one item at a time, but not every `for` loop does this. As a result, whenever I read a `for` loop, I need to check if it is a standard `for` loop or if there's something special about it. With a `foreach` loop, I don't need to do this because the syntax doesn't support it. This increases reading comfort and speed and improves the maintainability of your code through simplicity.

Additionally, a `foreach` loop can be used with anything that implements `IEnumerable`, while `for` loops require the collection they loop over to have an indexer. This means that `foreach` loops can loop over more types of collections than `for` loops can.

> **Collection interfaces**
>
> .NET provides several collection interfaces, including `IEnumerable`, `ICollection`, `IList`, `IReadOnlyList`, and `IReadOnlyCollection`. Knowledge of these collection types is helpful but not required to read this book. See the *Further reading* section at the end of this chapter for a link to more information on these interfaces, but for now, know that an `IEnumerable` interface is just a fancy way of referring to something that can be looped over in a foreach loop.

Converting to for loops

While `foreach` loops are fantastic and my default loop in most cases, sometimes, you want to have a `for` loop for a little bit of added control. If you ever need to loop over a collection in a non-standard way or need to use the index variable for something other than reading a variable out of the collection, you usually will want to use a `for` loop.

Visual Studio gives us a **Convert to 'for'** refactoring that will transform `foreach` loops into `for` loops for you. See *Figure 3.8*:

```
9      public void DisplayBoardingStatus(List<Passenger> passengers, bool? hasBoarded = null) {
10         List<Passenger> filteredPassengers = new();
11         foreach (Passenger p in passengers) {
12
13
14                                           Lines 10 to 12
      Fix formatting
15                                           List<Passenger> filteredPassengers = new();
16    Place statement on following line      foreach (Passenger p in passengers) {
17                                              for (int i = 0; i < passengers.Count; i++) {
      Convert to LINQ                              Passenger p = passengers[i];
      Convert to LINQ (call form)                  if (!hasBoarded.HasValue || p.HasBoarded == hasBoarded) {
18    Convert to 'for'              ▶
19
20    Use implicit type                      Preview changes
21    Suppress or configure issues  ▶
22                    CanPassengerBoard(passenger);
```

Figure 3.8 – Converting a foreach loop back to a for loop

I don't find myself using this refactoring very much, but it's handy when you need it.

For now, let's leave the code in a `foreach` loop and look at how LINQ can help us make it better.

Converting to LINQ

You may have noticed that, in *Figure 3.8*, there were a pair of suggestions to convert the `foreach` loop into LINQ.

LINQ stands for **Language INtegrated Query** and provides a set of extension methods that work on any collection that implements `IEnumerable`. This allows you to perform quick aggregation, transformation, and filtering operations on that collection using arrow functions.

> **Arrow functions**
>
> Arrow functions (also called Lambda expressions) use "fat arrow" (=>) syntax to represent small methods in an abbreviated format. This book assumes a basic understanding of arrow functions. See the *Further reading* section of this chapter if you need more information or want a refresher on how arrow functions work.

Let's look at what happens to our `foreach` loop when we use the **Convert to LINQ (call form)** refactoring in the `foreach` loop's **Quick Actions** menu:

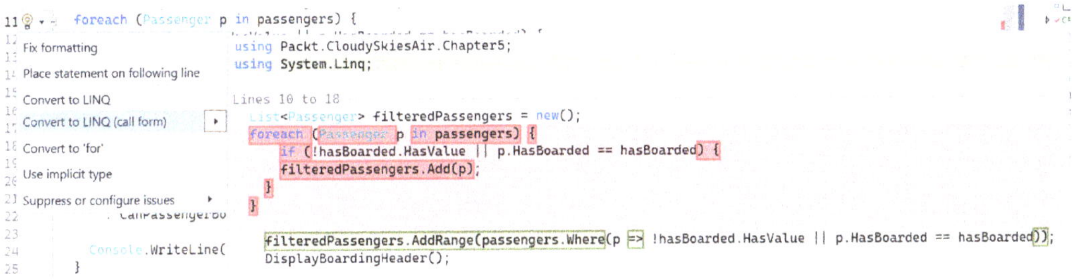

Figure 3.9 – Converting a foreach loop to use LINQ

This refactoring transforms our `foreach` loop into just a tiny portion of code:

```
List<Passenger> filteredPassengers = new();
filteredPassengers.AddRange(passengers.Where(p => !hasBoarded.HasValue
|| p.HasBoarded == hasBoarded));
```

This code takes our `passengers` collection and calls the `Where` extension method. The `Where` method will create and return a new `IEnumerable` sequence of `passengers` and only includes passengers where the arrow function, `p => !hasBoarded.HasValue || p.HasBoarded == hasBoarded`, returns a value of `true` for that passenger.

> **Extension methods**
>
> Extension methods are static methods defined in static classes that allow you to build syntax that looks like it adds new methods to existing types. LINQ relies heavily on extension methods attached to various interfaces. We'll explore creating extension methods in *Chapter 4*.

This won't modify our original collection, instead creating a new collection of `Passenger` objects that are then passed into the `filteredPassengers.AddRange` method.

While this code is already very brief, we can improve it further by taking advantage of a constructor on the generic `List` class.

The `List<T>` class has a constructor that takes in an `IEnumerable<T>` interface and allows you to efficiently create a new list around a sequence of elements. This will let us avoid needing the `AddRange` call and helps simplify our code down to a single statement:

```
List<Passenger> filteredPassengers =
  new(passengers.Where(p => !hasBoarded.HasValue ||
      p.HasBoarded == hasBoarded));
```

If we wanted to, we could also get rid of the `filteredPassengers` variable entirely by filtering passengers down and reassigning it back into itself:

```
passengers = passengers.Where(p=>!hasBoarded.HasValue ||
      p.HasBoarded==hasBoarded).ToList();
```

Here, we perform the `Where` call to generate an `IEnumerable<Passenger>` interface containing our passengers and then call the `ToList` method on that `IEnumerable` interface to convert it back into a `List` method so that it can be stored in the `passengers` parameter.

Also, note that any place that was using `filteredPassengers` before will need to be updated to use `passengers` instead:

```
foreach (Passenger passenger in passengers) {
  string statusMessage = passenger.HasBoarded
    ? "Onboard"
    : CanPassengerBoard(passenger);
  Console.WriteLine($"{passenger.FullName,-23} Group
    {passenger.BoardingGroup}: {statusMessage}");
}
```

I love LINQ and find it to be invaluable for creating simple and maintainable applications, but it does take some getting used to if you're not familiar with LINQ or not used to reading arrow function (`=>`) notation.

That said, I do see some common mistakes in LINQ code. So, let's look at a few of those before we close out this chapter.

Refactoring LINQ statements

In this final section of this chapter, we'll review a few of the more common optimizations with LINQ code by focusing on some common improvements most codebases that use LINQ will benefit from.

Choosing the correct LINQ method

LINQ has several different ways of finding a specific item in a collection.

If you had an `IEnumerable<Passenger>` interface named `people` and wanted to find someone by their name, you might write code like this:

LinqExamples.cs

```
PassengerGenerator generator = new();
List<Passenger> people = generator.GeneratePassengers(50);
Passenger me =
  people.FirstOrDefault(p => p.FullName == "Matt Eland");
Console.WriteLine($"Matt is in group {me.BoardingGroup}");
```

This code uses the LINQ `FirstOrDefault` method, which searches the collection until it finds the first value that the arrow function evaluates as true. In this example, it'd find the first person with `FullName` set to `"Matt Eland"`, return that value from the `FirstOrDefault` method, and store it in the `Passenger` variable named `matt`.

However, if no items returned `true` from the arrow function, `FirstOrDefault` will use the default value of the `Passenger` type, which would be null for a reference type such as a class.

> **Default values**
>
> In .NET, the default value of `bool` is `false`, numeric types such as `int` and `float` default to 0, and reference types including `string`, `List`, and other classes default to `null`.

In other words, this `FirstOrDefault` call will find Matt if he exists in passengers and return him or return `null` if he doesn't.

The problem with this is that the very next line attempts to read the value of `matt.BoardingGroup`. This is fine if we found the element, but if we didn't, this code will get a `NullReferenceException` error upon trying to access `BoardingGroup`, which is likely not what its author intended.

Note that how we fix this code depends on what our expectations are.

With LINQ, when you are looking for an element in a collection, you need to decide on two things:

- Am I okay with more than one item matching my arrow function or do I need to make sure that *at most* one item returns true?

- Am I okay with the item I'm looking for not being present at all?

The first decision governs whether you are making a call to `First` or `Single`. With `First`, the logic will find the first element that matches the query and return it. However, with `Single`, the logic will keep going past the first match to determine if any other element in the collection matches that expression as well. If one does match the expression, an `InvalidOperationException` error is thrown, telling you that the sequence contains more than one matching element.

Most developers don't like seeing exceptions when they're running their code. However, sometimes, you need to know if there's more than one match to your query. In general, it's better to fail early than fail later in a more confusing spot that hides where the program first got off track.

The second decision you make when finding an element in a collection involves being okay with objects not being present that match the query. If that's fine, then you will generally want to make a call to `FirstOrDefault` or `SingleOrDefault` (depending on your decision earlier on whether multiple matches are permissible). However, if it is never acceptable to not have a match, then you'll use `First` or `Single` instead of `FirstOrDefault` or `SingleOrDefault`.

`First` and `Single` will both throw an `InvalidOperationException` error if the sequence contains no matching element. If you use `First` or `Single` and nothing in the collection returns `true` from the arrow function, the exception will be thrown. This makes it impossible to deal with `null` values with the result of `First` or `Single`, which can be very helpful for simplifying your code.

> **Tip**
>
> Having an `InvalidOperationException` error thrown at the exact position your code encounters a problem can be immensely more helpful than encountering a `NullReferenceException` error 30 lines later in your code and having to figure out how a value got where it was supposed to be.

Null-state analysis is another feature that can help prevent a `NullReferenceException` error from occurring. We'll explore this in more depth in *Chapter 10*.

Let's move on and discuss ways of combining LINQ methods.

Combining LINQ methods

One of the nice things about LINQ is that it lets you "chain together" different methods by calling a LINQ method on the result of another LINQ method. This lets you do things such as filter down to a subset of items using `Where`, reorder the results with `OrderBy`, and transform them into new objects via `Select`.

However, as .NET has evolved, LINQ has grown a few more specialized overloads of its existing methods, which makes some of these chained-together methods unnecessary or even inefficient.

Look at this block of code as an example:

```
bool anyBoarded =
  people.Where(p => p.HasBoarded).Any();
int numBoarded =
  people.Where(p => p.HasBoarded).Count();
Passenger firstBoarded =
  people.Where(p => p.HasBoarded).First();
```

At first glance, this code looks fine. Each of these three variable assignments is filtering down and then looking at the results of that filtering option. Sure, there's an opportunity to introduce a local variable for `people.Where(p => p.HasBoarded)`, but otherwise, the code often looks fine at a glance.

However, LINQ offers overloaded versions of `Any`, `Count`, `First`, and a few other methods that take in a **predicate** (which is just a fancy word for an arrow function).

These overloaded versions allow you to combine `Where` methods and other methods into a more concise format:

```
bool anyBoarded = people.Any(p => p.HasBoarded);
int numBoarded = people.Count(p => p.HasBoarded);
Passenger firstBoarded = people.First(p => p.HasBoarded);
```

Not only is this way of writing things more concise, but these overloads can be more efficient in some cases.

For example, before, when we were doing `people.Where(p => p.HasBoarded).Any()`, this code evaluated left to right, filtering down a large list of items into a smaller list of items. Once the entire list had been filtered down, the `Any` method call occurred, which returned `true` if at least one item was found in that resulting list.

Contrast this to the `people.Any(p => p.HasBoarded)` version. This method loops over the items and as soon as it sees any element that returns `true` from the arrow function, it knows it can stop evaluating because its ultimate result is going to be true.

Always look for opportunities to use these specialized LINQ overloads as they can result in very concise and even more performant code.

Transforming with Select

Let's say you wanted to create a list of strings for all the passengers who hadn't boarded the plane yet. For each name, you want it formatted with the person's name and then their boarding group. So, a sample entry might be `"Priya Gupta-7"`.

You could write this code as follows:

```
List<string> names = new();
foreach (Passenger p in people) {
   if (!p.HasBoarded) {
      names.Add($"{p.FullName}-{p.BoardingGroup}");
   }
}
```

However, LINQ has a method named `Select` that allows you to transform items from one form into another, which would be perfect for this case.

> **Tip**
>
> For those of you with a JavaScript background, `Select` is similar to the `Map` function.

The `Select` version of this looks like this:

```
List<string> names =
        people.Where(p => !p.HasBoarded)
                .Select(p => $"{p.FullName}-{p.BoardingGroup}")
                .ToList();
```

Here, the `Where` call filtered the results down to non-boarded passengers and the `Select` call transformed those objects from `Passenger` objects into strings.

`Select` isn't limited to just strings. You can select whatever data type is relevant for you, including integers, other objects, lists, or even **anonymous types** or **tuples**.

Ultimately, whenever you have a collection of objects in one shape and you need those same objects but in a different form, `Select` is a great method to consider.

Reviewing and testing our refactored code

While we didn't modify a lot of code in this chapter, the code we did change shrunk in size, thus becoming easier to read, understand, and modify in the process.

This is why we refactor. Refactoring should actively improve the maintainability of our applications and pay down strategic pieces of technical debt that threaten to introduce bugs and delays in the future.

> **Refactored code**
>
> The final refactored code from this chapter is available in the `https://github.com/PacktPublishing/Refactoring-with-Csharp` repository inside the `Chapter03/Ch3RefactoredCode` folder.

Since the art of refactoring involves changing the form of code without changing its functionality, we must test the application before moving on.

We'll talk more about manual and automated tests in *Chapter 6*, but for now, run the tests by selecting the **Test** menu at the top of Visual Studio and then clicking **Run All Tests**.

This will show **Test Explorer** and a sea of green check marks, as shown in *Figure 3.10*:

Figure 3.10 – Passing tests for this chapter's code

Now, let's summarize what we've learned in this chapter.

Summary

In this chapter, we explored refactoring techniques to help better control program flow, instantiate objects, iterate over collections, and write more efficient code through LINQ.

Each refactoring technique we covered is one tool in your toolbelt that might improve the readability and maintainability of your code in the right circumstances. As you practice refactoring more, you'll learn more about when to apply which refactoring to improve the code you're working with.

In the next chapter, we'll move on from improving individual lines of code and focus on a slightly bigger picture as we work to refactor entire methods of C# code.

Questions

Answer the following questions to test your knowledge of this chapter:

1. Is it more important to have concise code or readable code?

2. Scroll through a file of code in a project you are working on. What do you notice about the if statements in your code?

3. How frequently are nested if statements used?

4. Is any logic repeated frequently in conditions of your if statements?

5.   Do you see any places where inverting the `if` statement or switching to a `switch` statement or `switch` expression could improve things?

6.   Do you think your team has been using LINQ to its fullest potential when working with collections? What opportunities for improvement do you see?

Further reading

You can find more information about the materials discussed in this chapter by reading the following resources:

- *Switch Expressions*: `https://learn.microsoft.com/en-US/dotnet/csharp/language-reference/operators/switch-expression`

- *Differences between .NET Collection Interfaces*: `https://newdevsguide.com/2022/10/09/understanding-dotnet-collection-interfaces/`

- *Query Syntax and Method Syntax in LINQ*: `https://learn.microsoft.com/en-us/dotnet/csharp/programming-guide/concepts/linq/query-syntax-and-method-syntax-in-linq`

- *Explore Ranges of Data*: `https://learn.microsoft.com/en-us/dotnet/csharp/tutorials/ranges-indexes`

- *Arrow Functions and the Lambda Operator*: `https://learn.microsoft.com/en-us/dotnet/csharp/language-reference/operators/lambda-operator`

4

Refactoring at the Method Level

In the last chapter, we covered improving individual lines of code. We'll expand on those lessons to cover refactoring entire methods and solving issues with how code comes together to form larger methods that then interact with each other.

We saw a little of this in *Chapter 2* when we covered the extract method refactoring. However, in this chapter, we'll expand our set of tools covering the basics of refactoring methods and then move into more advanced areas as we cover the following main topics:

- Refactoring the flight tracker
- Refactoring methods
- Refactoring constructors
- Refactoring parameters
- Refactoring to functions
- Introducing static methods and extension methods

Technical requirements

The starting code for this chapter is available from GitHub at `https://github.com/PacktPublishing/Refactoring-with-CSharp` in the `Chapter04/Ch4BeginningCode` folder.

Refactoring the flight tracker

This chapter's code focuses largely on a single `FlightTracker` class intended to track and display the outgoing flights from a commercial airport for passengers in the terminal, as pictured in *Figure 4.1*:

FLIGHT	DEST	DEPARTURE	GATE	STATUS
CSA2024	ORD	Sun Jul 09 23:27 PM	A01	Inbound
CSA2028	ATL	Sun Jul 09 23:41 PM	C01	Delayed
CSA2034	ORD	Mon Jul 10 00:04 AM	A01	OnTime
CSA2040	ORD	Mon Jul 10 00:13 AM	A01	OnTime
CSA2043	MCI	Mon Jul 10 00:17 AM	C04	OnTime
CSA2049	ATL	Mon Jul 10 00:31 AM	A03	OnTime
CSA2050	ORD	Mon Jul 10 00:55 AM	C01	OnTime
CSA2052	PNS	Mon Jul 10 00:57 AM	A02	OnTime
CSA2054	SAN	Mon Jul 10 01:00 AM	C03	OnTime
CSA2058	CMH	Mon Jul 10 01:17 AM	A01	OnTime
CSA2061	PNS	Mon Jul 10 01:27 AM	C04	Inbound
CSA2062	MCI	Mon Jul 10 01:47 AM	A04	Cancelled
CSA2067	CHS	Mon Jul 10 01:52 AM	A03	Delayed
CSA2073	MCI	Mon Jul 10 01:55 AM	A03	Delayed
CSA2075	MCI	Mon Jul 10 02:04 AM	A04	Cancelled

Figure 4.1 – FlightTracker displaying outbound flight statuses

The `FlightTracker` class has a number of methods related to managing and displaying flights. It is supported by the `Flight` class which represents an individual flight in the system and the `FlightStatus` enum which represents all relevant statuses of a flight, as shown in the class diagram in *Figure 4.2*:

Figure 4.2 – A class diagram showing FlightTracker and supporting classes

We'll explore these pieces of code throughout this chapter, but for now, we need to understand that the key responsibilities of `FlightTracker` include the following:

- Tracking a list of flights
- Scheduling new flights (adding them to the list)
- Marking flights as arrived, departed, or delayed
- Displaying all flights
- Finding a flight by its ID

This is a fairly simple flight tracker class, but we'll see a slightly more complicated version of one in the next chapter as we explore object-oriented refactoring.

For now, let's look at a few simple steps we can take to improve these methods.

Refactoring methods

In this section, we'll explore a number of refactorings related to methods and their interactions. We'll start by discussing the access modifier of a method.

Changing method access modifiers

During my time as a professional C# instructor, I noticed my students often tended to not think about the **access modifiers** they used in their code. Specifically, my students would usually do one of two things:

- They marked all methods as **public** by default unless someone (usually me) suggested they use a different access modifier
- They marked all methods as **private** by default (or omitted the access modifier entirely, defaulting to **private** anyway) until the compiler gave them an issue requiring them to make a method more accessible

Both approaches are insufficient for a simple reason: we want to explicitly declare the visibility level of our methods. This way, whenever you read code, you are reminded explicitly by the access modifier what other code can access the code you're working with. This is particularly useful when working with non-private methods that can be referenced outside of the class.

> **Access modifiers**
>
> C# has several access modifiers as of C# 12 that govern what other areas can refer to your code. The current access modifiers are `public`, `private`, `protected`, `internal`, `protected internal`, `private internal`, and the new `file` access modifier that restricts access to something within a single source file. While these access modifiers all have their uses, I'm going to focus primarily on `public` and `private` in this section for simplicity's sake.

If we mark a method as **public**, **protected**, or **internal**, there should be a good reason for that – typically related to the method being a primary way in which we intend for others to use our code.

Our `FlightTracker` class has a `public` method called `FindFlightById` that is used by most of the other methods in the class but nothing outside of the class. This method looks up the flight by ID and returns it if one is found:

```
public Flight? FindFlightById(string id) {
   return _flights.Find(f => f.Id == id);
}
```

Given these circumstances, you might make an explicit decision to mark the method as `private`, restricting its usage within this class, as shown in the following code:

```
private Flight? FindFlightById(string id) {
   return _flights.Find(f => f.Id == id);
}
```

By marking this method as `private`, you have greater freedom in the future to rename it, change how it works, modify its parameters, or remove it entirely.

Changing the access modifier is generally safe if nothing outside the class uses the method. Otherwise, this decision will cause compiler errors.

Renaming methods and parameters

Let's take a look at three very similar methods for managing flights in `FlightTracker`:

```
public Flight? DelayFlight(string fId, DateTime newTime) {
   // Details omitted
}
public Flight? MarkFlightArrived(DateTime time, string id){
   // Details omitted
}
public Flight? MarkFlightDeparted(string id, DateTime t) {
   // Details omitted
}
```

Each of these methods takes in a `DateTime` and a flight identifier string. However, the naming of these parameters and even these methods are not incredibly consistent.

`DelayFlight` calls its flight ID variable `fId` and its new departure time `newTime`. `MarkFlightArrived` uses `time` for the arrival time and `id` for the flight identifier. `MarkFlightDeparted` uses `id` but chose `t` to denote the departure time.

While some of these naming choices are better than others on their own, the lack of naming consistency in methods within the same class can hurt other people's ability to work effectively with your code. This can lead them to feel less confident in your abilities and can even introduce bugs from misunderstandings of what parameters or methods represent – all due to a lack of consistency.

To fix this, we can use the *rename parameter* refactoring to rename individual parameters to ensure consistency. This can be done by right-clicking on a parameter and selecting **Rename…** from the context menu, or pressing *Ctrl + R* twice with the parameter selected. See *Figure 4.3*:

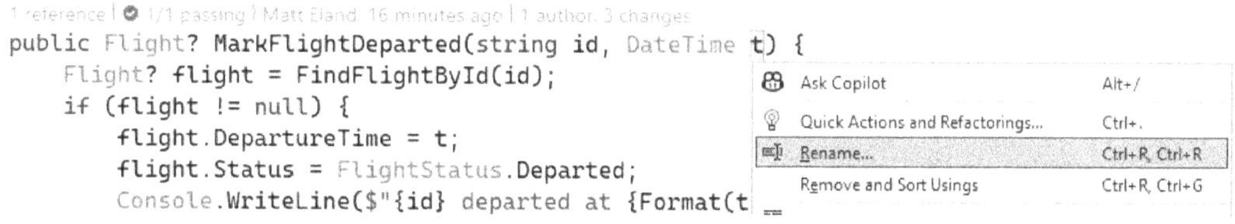

Figure 4.3 – Activating the rename parameter refactoring via the context menu

Next, type the new name you want to use for the parameter and press *Enter* to complete the change. See *Figure 4.4*:

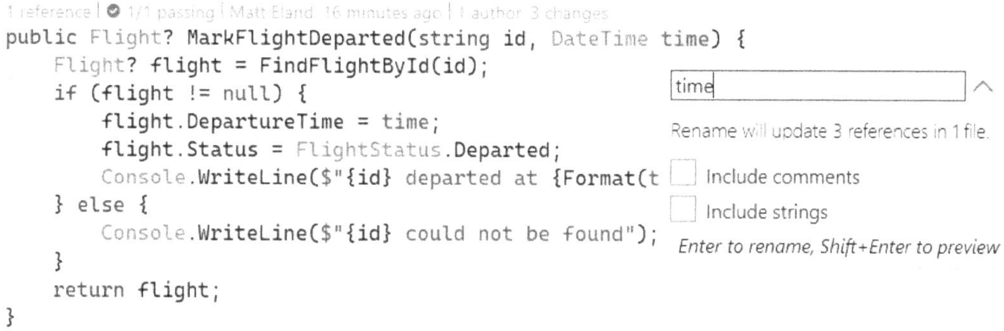

Figure 4.4 – Renaming the parameter

While choosing your names, you'll want to pick something that is clear and consistent with the terminology and names you use in your class already. Avoid very short and single-letter parameters wherever possible (excluding some cases, such as `x` and `y` for coordinates or other established usages of short parameter names).

In the case of this code, I chose to rename all the flight identifiers to `id` and chose to be more explicit about the names of the `DateTime` parameters to indicate what the parameter represented.

I also chose to use the same rename tool to rename the entire method of `DelayFlight` to `MarkFlightDelayed` to be more consistent with the other methods in this class:

```
public Flight? MarkFlightDelayed(
  string id, DateTime newDepartureTime) {
  // Details omitted
}
public Flight? MarkFlightArrived(DateTime arrivalTime,
  string id) {
  // Details omitted
}
public Flight? MarkFlightDeparted(string id,
  DateTime departureTime) {
  // Details omitted
}
```

Some of these names are perhaps a bit longer than I might like (particularly when trying to fit code onto a page in a book!), but clear parameter and method names can save a lot of confusion and even prevent certain bugs from occurring later.

> **Note**
>
> If the inconsistent ordering of parameters annoys you, don't worry. We'll fix parameter ordering later on in this chapter.

Overloading methods

Let's shift gears and talk about how methods can work together in tandem. First, we'll look at an example of **overloading** and then an example of **chaining**.

Let's start by looking at the `ScheduleNewFlight` method:

```
public Flight ScheduleNewFlight(string id, string dest,
  DateTime depart, string gate) {
  Flight flight = new() {
    Id = id,
    Destination = dest,
    DepartureTime = depart,
    Gate = gate,
```

```
        Status = FlightStatus.Inbound
    };
    _flights.Add(flight);
    return flight;
}
```

This method takes in four parameters representing flight information. It uses them to instantiate a `Flight` object, adds the flight to the private list of flights, and then returns the newly-created `Flight` object.

As the system grows, it's reasonable to expect that someone might want to provide their own `Flight` object. To accommodate that, you can overload the `ScheduleNewFlight` method.

Overloading

Overloading is where you offer a method with the same name as another method but a different set of types of parameters that can be accepted by the method. For example, you can have a method that takes in an `int` and another method that takes in two `strings`, but you can't have two methods that both take in only a single `int`, even if the parameter names are different. From the compiler's perspective, overloaded methods are entirely separate methods that just happen to have the same name.

The overloaded `ScheduleNewFlight` method that takes in a `Flight` object might look something like the following:

```
public Flight ScheduleNewFlight(Flight flight) {
  _flights.Add(flight);
  return flight;
}
```

Overloading the `ScheduleNewFlight` method is helpful because it helps people discover the different options for scheduling a flight based on Visual Studio's suggestions, as shown in *Figure 4.5*:

```
Flight flight = flightTracker.ScheduleNewFlight()

_ = rand.Next(8)    ▲ 1 of 2 ▼  Flight FlightTracker.ScheduleNewFlight(Flight flight)
```

Figure 4.5 – Visual Studio suggestions showing available overloads for ScheduleNewFlight

By providing overloads, following standard conventions, and having consistent and predictable methods and parameters, you help others discover how to use your classes safely and effectively.

Chaining methods

You may have noticed a few lines of duplication between our two `ScheduleNewFlight` overloads. Let's take a look at them side by side for reference:

```
public Flight ScheduleNewFlight(string id, string dest,
   DateTime depart, string gate) {
   Flight flight = new() {
       Id = id,
       Destination = dest,
       DepartureTime = depart,
       Gate = gate,
       Status = FlightStatus.Inbound
   };
   _flights.Add(flight);
   return flight;
}
public Flight ScheduleNewFlight(Flight flight) {
   _flights.Add(flight);
   return flight;
}
```

While this duplication is very minimal, I could see new requirements come in that would necessitate changing both places. For example, the business might require that whenever a new flight is scheduled, a log entry should be written, or perhaps a new `LastScheduleChange` property needs to be set to the current time.

When these types of changes occur, developers run the risk of introducing bugs unless they change all the affected areas. This means that code duplication, even minor code duplication such as this example, leads to additional work and additional sources of bugs if not every place with similar logic is updated.

One thing that can help with this is **method chaining**. Method chaining is when one method calls another related method and has it accomplish its work for it.

In this case, we can modify our first `ScheduleNewFlight` method to be responsible for creating a `Flight` object and then handing off that object to the other `ScheduleNewFlight` overload, as follows:

```
public Flight ScheduleNewFlight(string id, string dest,
   DateTime depart, string gate) {
   Flight flight = new() {
       Id = id,
       Destination = dest,
       DepartureTime = depart,
       Gate = gate,
```

```
      Status = FlightStatus.Inbound
   };
   return ScheduleNewFlight(flight);
}
public Flight ScheduleNewFlight(Flight flight) {
   _flights.Add(flight);
   return flight;
}
```

Not only is this less code, but if we ever need to alter what happens when a new flight is scheduled, we now only have one place to modify.

Now that we've covered some of the basics of refactoring methods, let's look briefly at some parallels with **constructors**. After all, constructors are essentially a special type of method that gets called when an object is instantiated.

Refactoring constructors

When you think about the job of a constructor, its whole reason for being is to get the object into its correct initial position. Once the constructor completes, the object is generally considered ready for use by other code.

This means that constructors can be very handy for ensuring that certain pieces of information are in place.

Right now, our Flight class is defined fairly minimally and only has the default constructor that .NET provides in the absence of any explicit constructor:

Flight.cs

```
public class Flight {
    public string Id { get; set; }
    public string Destination { get; set; }
    public DateTime DepartureTime { get; set; }
    public DateTime ArrivalTime { get; set; }
    public string Gate { get; set; }
    public FlightStatus Status { get; set; }
    public override string ToString() {
        return $"{Id} to {Destination} at {DepartureTime}";
    }
}
```

The problem with our Flight class lacking any explicit constructor is that flights don't make sense without some of these pieces of information.

While more recent versions of C# have given us things such as the `required` keyword, which we'll explore in *Chapter 10*, the classic approach to requiring some piece of information at object creation has been to make the constructor take it in as a parameter. To demonstrate this, let's add a parameterized constructor next.

Generating constructors

While we could manually write a constructor, Visual Studio gives us some great code generation tools, including a *generate constructor* refactoring.

To use this refactoring, select the class and open the **Quick Actions** menu. Then, select **Generate constructor...**, as shown in *Figure 4.6*:

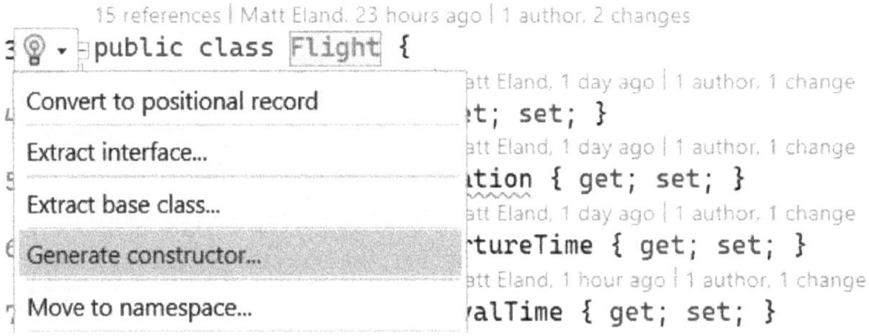

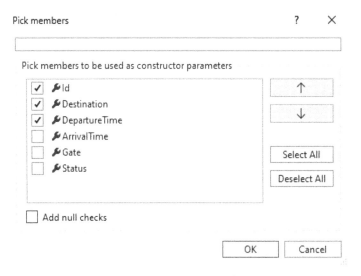

Figure 4.6 – Generating a constructor

This will open a dialog that will allow you to select what members get initialized from the constructor when creating a `Flight`, as shown in *Figure 4.7*:

Figure 4.7 – Selecting required members for the constructor

In this case, I chose to make `Id`, `Destination`, and `DepartureTime` part of the constructor and left the others unchecked. I also unchecked the **Add null checks** checkbox to prevent the generated code from being too complex for this example.

This generated the following constructor:

```
public Flight(string id, string destination,
  DateTime departureTime) {
  Id = id;
  Destination = destination;
  DepartureTime = departureTime;
}
```

The resulting code correctly sets the required properties based on its parameters.

If you wanted to, you could go back in and generate a new constructor with a different set of parameters, since classes can have any number of overloaded constructors.

In fact, we'll add another constructor in the next section to illustrate this. However, for now, we have a problem we need to resolve in the form of a build error:

```
5 references | ✓ 4/4 passing | Matt Eland  23 hours ago | 1 author, 2 changes
public Flight ScheduleNewFlight(string id, string dest, DateTime depart, string gate) {
  Flight flight = new() {
    Id = id,
    Destination = des    CS7036: There is no argument given that corresponds to the required parameter 'id' of 'Flight.Flight(string, string,
    DepartureTime = c    DateTime)'
    Gate = gate,
    Status = FlightSta      Show potential fixes (Ctrl+.)
  };
  return ScheduleNewFlight(flight);
```

Figure 4.8 – Build error trying to instantiate a Flight instance

If you tried to build your project after adding the `Flight` constructor, you'll see an error similar to that shown in *Figure 4.8*. This "no argument given that corresponds to the required parameter" error exists because the `Flight flight = new()` code in `ScheduleNewFlight` is trying to invoke the default constructor for `Flight`, but that constructor no longer exists.

When we added our constructor a moment ago, this didn't move the `Flight` class from having no constructors to one constructor. Instead, we went from having .NET's default constructor with no parameters to one constructor with the new parameters we generated, removing the default constructor entirely.

We can add the default constructor back manually by explicitly defining it:

```
public Flight() {
}
```

This constructor does nothing aside from allowing others to instantiate the class by providing no parameters to the constructor. As soon as you declare your own constructor, .NET no longer provides the default constructor for you.

To fix this compiler error, we can either add a new constructor that takes in no parameters or we can adjust the `ScheduleNewFlight` code to use our new constructor instead of the default one that no longer exists.

Since part of the intent of adding a new constructor is to require certain pieces of information at the time of object creation, it makes more sense to change `ScheduleNewFlight` to use the new constructor, as follows:

FlightTracker.cs

```
public Flight ScheduleNewFlight(string id, string dest,
    DateTime depart, string gate) {
    Flight flight = new(id, dest, depart) {
        Gate = gate,
        Status = FlightStatus.Inbound
    };
    return ScheduleNewFlight(flight);
}
```

A nice side effect of doing this is that we no longer need to set those properties in the object initializer since the constructor does that for us.

Chaining constructors

Earlier, we saw how we can chain together overloaded methods to work together to reduce code duplication. I also hinted that constructors are really just special methods. When you have multiple constructors, they act exactly like overloaded methods.

We can put all of these concepts together by **chaining constructors** together, so one constructor calls to the other.

First, let's look at an example of *not* doing this:

Flight.cs

```
public Flight(string id, string destination,
    DateTime departureTime) {
    Id = id;
    Destination = destination;
    DepartureTime = departureTime;
}
```

```
public Flight(string id, string destination,
  DateTime departureTime, FlightStatus status) {
  Id = id;
  Destination = destination;
  DepartureTime = departureTime;
  Status = status;
}
```

Here, we have two constructors for `Flight` that are nearly identical, except the second one also accepts a `status` parameter.

While this isn't an excessive amount of duplication, it can be avoided by chaining constructors together with `: this()` syntax, as follows:

```
public Flight(string id, string destination,
  DateTime departureTime) {
  Id = id;
  Destination = destination;
  DepartureTime = departureTime;
}
public Flight(string id, string destination,
  DateTime departureTime, FlightStatus status)
  : this(id, destination, departureTime) {
  Status = status;
}
```

In this case, the second `Flight` constructor starts out by calling the first constructor through its use of `: this`. Once that call completes, control will move back to the second constructor and it will execute the `Status = status;` line.

Chaining constructors together adds a little complexity to your code, but it also reduces duplicated code while making it such that you can add new initialization logic in one place and multiple constructors can take advantage of the addition.

Refactoring parameters

Now that we've explored the basics of methods and constructors, let's talk about managing parameters. This is important because it is possible that poorly thought-out parameters can quickly reduce the maintainability of your code.

Let's look at a few common refactorings you'll want to perform over the life of your methods.

Reordering parameters

Sometimes, you'll realize that the order of parameters in a method doesn't make as much sense as another arrangement might. At other times, you might notice that a few of your methods take in the same kinds of parameters, but with inconsistent ordering. In either case, you'll find yourself wanting to reorder your method parameters.

Let's look at a practical example from the various `MarkX` methods we saw earlier:

FlightTracker.cs

```
public Flight? MarkFlightDelayed(string id,
  DateTime newDepartureTime) {
  // Details omitted...
}
public Flight? MarkFlightArrived(DateTime arrivalTime,
  string id) {
  // Details omitted...
}
public Flight? MarkFlightDeparted(string id,
  DateTime departureTime) {
  // Details omitted...
}
```

Here, we have three methods that all take in `string` and `DateTime` parameters, but their ordering is inconsistent.

In this case, looking at these three methods, you decide that the most intuitive order is to put the flight ID first and then the time component as the second parameter. This means that `MarkFlightDelayed` and `MarkFlightDeparted` are correct but `MarkFlightArrived` needs to be adjusted.

You can add, remove, and reorder parameters from the same refactoring dialog in Visual Studio by selecting the method you want to refactor and then choosing **Change signature…** from the **Quick Actions** menu, as shown in *Figure 4.9*:

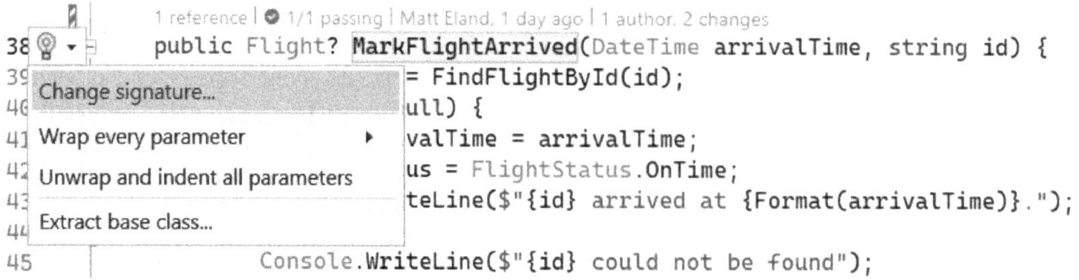

Figure 4.9 – Triggering the Change signature… refactoring

This will bring up the **Change Signature** dialog (see *Figure 4.10*) and allow you to use the up and down buttons in the upper right to reorder parameters until the order in the preview matches your expectations:

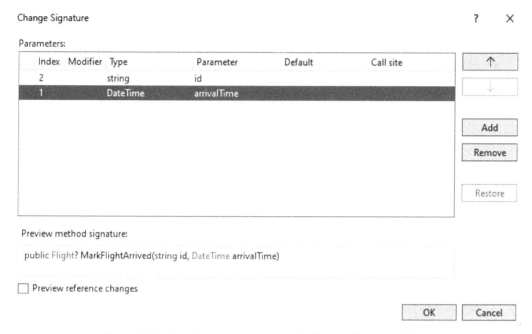

Figure 4.10 – Reordering parameters in the Change Signature dialog

Once you are done, click **OK** and Visual Studio will update your method as well as everything that was called out to that method to use the revised parameter order.

> **Tip**
>
> There are other ways of making which parameters a method requires more explicit using C#. One such way would be to use the **named arguments** feature of C# that allows you to specify method parameters by name followed by a colon, making the parameter usage explicit.
>
> An example of using this to call our `MarkFlightArrived` method would be `MarkFlightArrived(arrivalTime:DateTime.Now, id:"MyId")`. Note that when using named arguments, you can specify arguments in whatever order you prefer. See the *Further reading* section for more details.

Adding parameters

Occasionally, you'll want to add a new parameter to your method. The most natural thing to do is generally to add the parameter to the end of the list of parameters. This, however, can have two downsides:

- The new parameter might not make the most sense when added to the end of the list instead of earlier on in the sequence of parameters

- Manually adding a parameter means you must now manually adjust anything that was calling your method and provide a new value for the parameter

Let's look at a practical example and see how the **Change Signature** dialog can help.

The MarkFlightArrived method currently finds the flight by its Id and then updates its arrival time and status to match the parameters:

```
public Flight? MarkFlightArrived(string id,
  DateTime arrivalTime) {
  Flight? flight = FindFlightById(id);
  if (flight != null) {
    flight.ArrivalTime = arrivalTime;
    flight.Status = FlightStatus.OnTime;
    Console.WriteLine($"{id} arrived at {Format(arrivalTime)}.");
    } else {
      Console.WriteLine($"{id} could not be found");
    }
    return flight;
}
```

Let's say we need to update this method to take in the gate that the plane should taxi to. While we could manually add it to the end of the parameter list, this would break every method that calls out to this method.

Right now, that's not a lot of places, since only the tests are calling this method.

FlightTrackerTests.cs

```
Flight? actual =
  _target.MarkFlightArrived(flightId, arrivalTime);
```

However, the *Change Signature* refactoring tools in Visual Studio provide a safer option when you click the **Add** button:

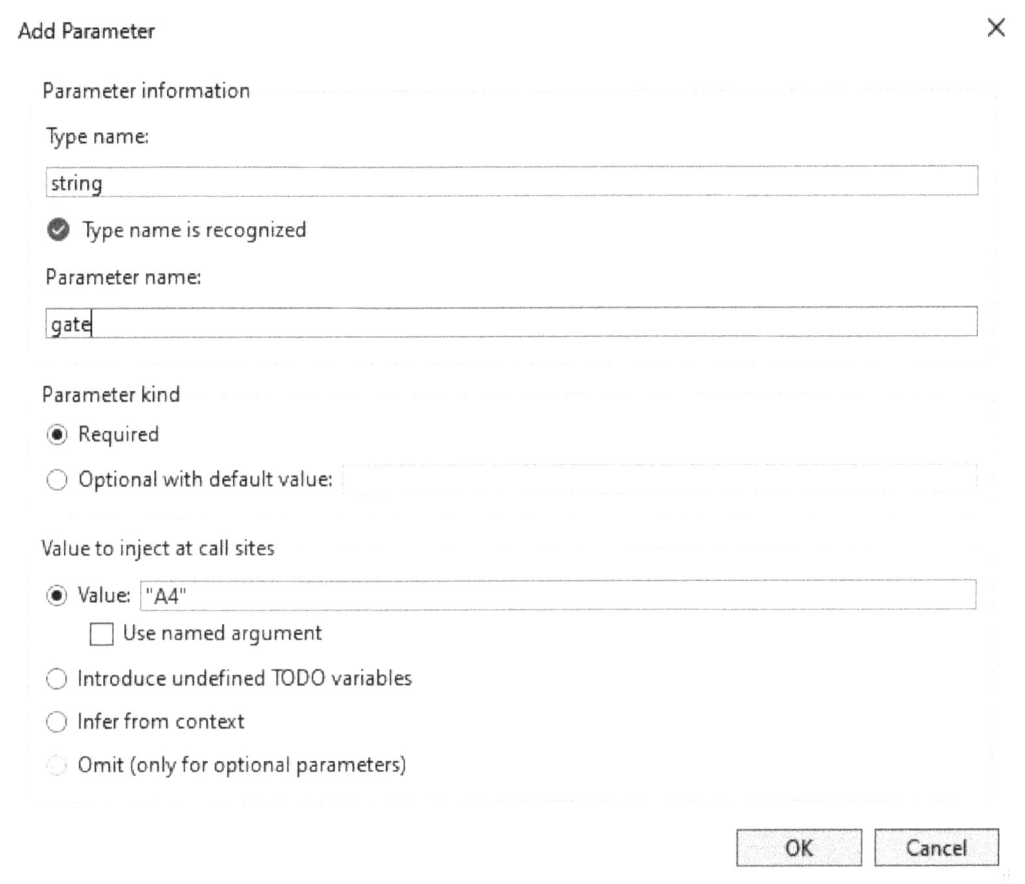

Add Parameter   ✕

Parameter information

Type name:

```
string
```

✔ Type name is recognized

Parameter name:

```
gate
```

Parameter kind

◉ Required

○ Optional with default value:

Value to inject at call sites

◉ Value: `"A4"`

☐ Use named argument

○ Introduce undefined TODO variables

○ Infer from context

○ Omit (only for optional parameters)

[OK]   [Cancel]

Figure 4.11 – Adding a new gate parameter to MarkFlightArrived

The **Add Parameter** dialog is one of the more complex ones in Visual Studio, but all it really needs is the following few things:

- The parameter name and type that is being added
- Whether this parameter is required or optional (more on this shortly)
- The value to use in places that are already calling the method

In this case, our new parameter is going to be a `string` named `gate`. Callers must provide a value and any existing callers should use the `"A4"` string for now.

This use of `"A4"` may seem like a random string because it is. The only place using this method right now is a unit test where the gate really doesn't matter for that test. If more places were using this method, I'd likely choose **Infer from context** or **Introduce undefined TODO variables**.

Clicking **OK** will display the *Change Signature* dialog again with your new parameter listed, allowing you to reorder it as needed. Clicking **OK** in this dialog will add the parameter to your method and update your code.

This updates your method signature for MarkFlightArrived and the test calling your code:

```
Flight? actual =
  _target.MarkFlightArrived(flightId, arrivalTime, "A4");
```

With the new parameter in place, you can update the MarkFlightArrived method to use it to set the flight's Gate property:

```
public Flight? MarkFlightArrived(string id,
  DateTime arrivalTime, string gate) {
  Flight? flight = FindFlightById(id);
  if (flight != null) {
    flight.ArrivalTime = arrivalTime;
    flight.Gate = gate;
    flight.Status = FlightStatus.OnTime;
    Console.WriteLine($"{id} arrived at {Format(arrivalTime)}.");
  } else {
    Console.WriteLine($"{id} could not be found");
  }
  return flight;
}
```

This workflow is a common one you'll go through as you find yourself expanding methods to take in new parameters.

Next, let's see some ways to simplify method calls using optional parameters.

Introducing optional parameters

If you're not a fan of the **Change Signature** dialog and would rather write the code yourself, you can always take advantage of optional parameters to safely add new parameters to the end of your parameter list.

With an optional parameter, you specify a default value. Places that call your method can either specify the value for this parameter or not pass any value at all. In cases where no value is passed, the default value will be used instead.

> **Note**
>
> This only works with parameters at the end of your parameter list due to how optional parameters work in C#. Additionally, the compiler doesn't allow certain types of default values such as new objects and certain literals.

If you wanted to declare gate as optional and default to "TBD" (short for "to be determined"), your method would look like the following:

```
public Flight? MarkFlightArrived(string id,
  DateTime arrivalTime, string gate = "TBD") {
  // Details omitted...
}
```

The code calling your method could then be left in its prior state:

```
Flight? actual =
  _target.MarkFlightArrived(flightId, arrivalTime);
```

Here, the code would compile, but "TBD" would be used for the gate.

Alternatively, you could specify the value for gate manually by providing a value for that parameter:

```
Flight? actual =
  _target.MarkFlightArrived(flightId, arrivalTime, "A4");
```

Optional parameters can be particularly nice not just for expanding methods, but also for providing common defaults that callers can customize if they want.

Removing parameters

Currently, the code requires you to specify the gate whenever a new flight is scheduled:

```
public Flight ScheduleNewFlight(string id, string dest, DateTime
depart, string gate) {
    Flight flight = new(id, dest, depart) {
        Gate = gate,
        Status = FlightStatus.Inbound
    };
    return ScheduleNewFlight(flight);
}
```

Let's say that you decide that since gates are now assigned at arrival, you shouldn't need to specify the gate when you schedule a new flight.

While you could go in and just remove the gate parameter from the code, this won't update any methods that are calling that method and will result in compiler errors you must resolve.

Instead, you can use the **Change Signature** dialog, select the parameter you want to remove, and click **Remove**, as shown in *Figure 4.12*:

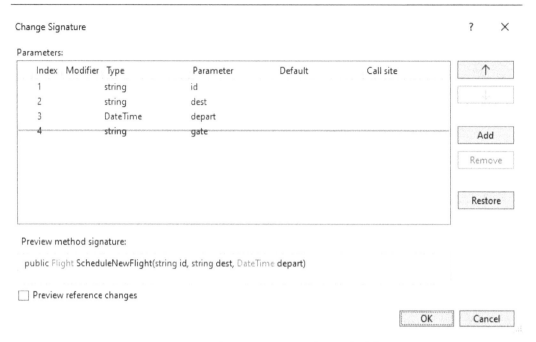

Figure 4.12 – Removing the gate parameter from ScheduleNewFlight

When you click **OK**, Visual Studio will update your method and any callers to simply not have the `gate` parameter.

Of course, this isn't magic, and it will leave behind code that relied on that gate parameter or code that was put in place to get the value ready to pass into `ScheduleNewFlight`. Still, the refactoring does a remarkable job of cleaning up the method definition and the direct calls of that method.

Applying the refactoring to remove the `gate` parameter results in a simpler method:

```
public Flight ScheduleNewFlight(string id, string dest,
    DateTime depart) {
    Flight flight = new(id, dest, depart) {
        Status = FlightStatus.Inbound
    };
    return ScheduleNewFlight(flight);
}
```

Now that we've covered the basics of methods, constructors, and parameters, let's get into the more adventuresome aspects of refactoring methods: working with functions.

Refactoring to functions

In this section, we'll explore some aspects of refactoring related to **functional programming**. Functional programming is an approach to programming that focuses on functions and their interactions instead of purely on objects and classes.

Functional programming has become more popular over the last decade and that popularity has influenced the C# language with the addition of new forms of syntax.

We'll explore a few of the syntactical improvements related to functional programming and see how they can help make concise and flexible programs. While this is not a book about functional programming, we'll still find ourselves exploring a few of these concepts in this section and *Chapter 10, Defensive Coding Techniques*.

Using expression-bodied members

To start dipping our toes into the waters of the more functional syntax, let's take a look at the FindFlightById method in FlightTracker:

```
private Flight? FindFlightById(string id) {
    return _flights.FirstOrDefault(f => f.Id == id);
}
```

Clearly, this is a very brief method with only a single statement. At the same time, this method takes up three lines of the screen. Since developers usually leave a blank line above and below each method, the existence of this simple method takes up five lines of the screen. These five lines can be a significant portion of the visible region of the screen, as shown in *Figure 4.13*:

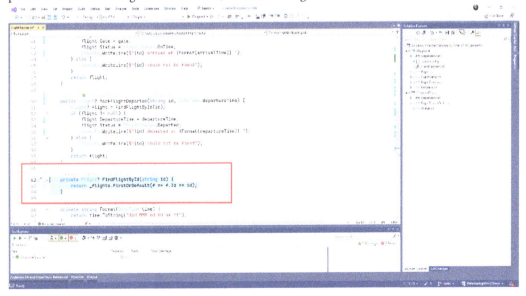

Figure 4.13 – The visual footprint of a method with a single statement

Instead, we can take advantage of expression-bodied members and convert our method to a single-line declaration using this new syntax by activating the **Use expression body for method** refactoring on the **Quick Actions** menu with the method selected, as shown in *Figure 4.14*:

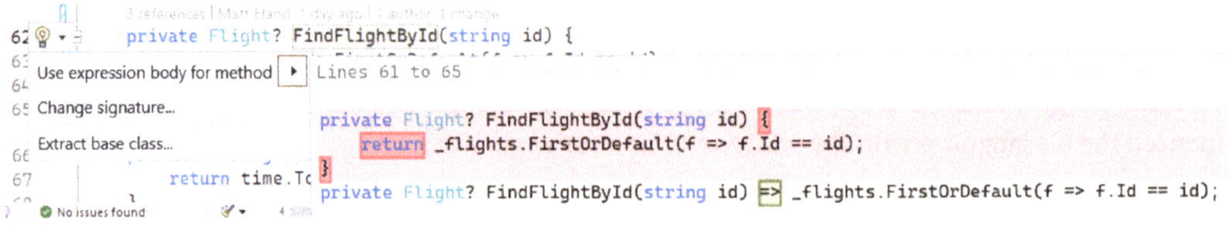

Figure 4.14 – Triggering the Use expression body for method refactoring^

This converts our code to the following, more concise format:

```
FindFlightById(string id) =>
    _flights.FirstOrDefault(f => f.Id == id);
```

This style only works for single-line implementations and it isn't for everyone. However, if you use it for simple code, it helps reduce the "scrolling penalty" you face with many small methods in a larger file.

Passing functions as parameters with actions

While expression-bodied members are less functional programming and more functional syntax, let's shift gears and get a taste of what's possible by thinking about methods as **actions** that you can store in variables and pass around to other methods.

Before we talk about *how* to do this, let's explore *why* we'd want to do this by looking at our `MarkFlightX` methods in `FlightTracker`. We'll start with the `MarkFlightDelayed` method:

```
public Flight? MarkFlightDelayed(string id,
    DateTime newDepartureTime) {
    Flight? flight = FindFlightById(id);
    if (flight != null) {
        flight.DepartureTime = newDepartureTime;
        flight.Status = FlightStatus.Delayed;
        Console.WriteLine($"{id} delayed until
            {Format(newDepartureTime)}");
    } else {
        Console.WriteLine($"{id} could not be found");
    }
    return flight;
}
```

This method does a few discrete things:

- It searches for a flight by its ID
- If it finds the flight, it updates the properties on the flight and writes out the delay
- If the flight can't be found, a warning is written to the console

On its own, this method is fine. Let's look at `MarkFlightDeparted` now:

```
public Flight? MarkFlightDeparted(string id,
  DateTime departureTime) {
  Flight? flight = FindFlightById(id);
  if (flight != null) {
    flight.DepartureTime = departureTime;
    flight.Status = FlightStatus.Departed;
    Console.WriteLine($"{id} departed at {Format(departureTime)}.");
  } else {
    Console.WriteLine($"{id} could not be found");
  }
  return flight;
}
```

Compare this method to the last one and you'll see that there are few differences between them. The method still must find a flight by its ID, check to see whether the flight was found or not, and update the flight. The only difference in this method is what updates occur to the flight and what message gets written to the console.

Let's round out our look at these methods with a look at `MarkFlightArrived`:

```
public Flight? MarkFlightArrived(string id,
  DateTime arrivalTime, string gate = "TBD") {
  Flight? flight = FindFlightById(id);
  if (flight != null) {
    flight.ArrivalTime = arrivalTime;
    flight.Gate = gate;
    flight.Status = FlightStatus.OnTime;
    Console.WriteLine($"{id} arrived at {Format(arrivalTime)}.");
  } else {
    Console.WriteLine($"{id} could not be found");
  }
  return flight;
}
```

Here, the pattern repeats itself. The only major difference between these three methods is what happens if the flight is found.

Thinking about it in that way, consider our logic with the following pseudocode:

```
Flight? flight = FindFlightById(id);
if (flight != null) {
  ApplyUpdateToFlight(flight);
} else {
  Console.WriteLine($"{id} could not be found");
}
return flight;
```

Here, `ApplyUpdateToFlight` is a placeholder for some method or function we could apply to the flight object. This is because the *action* we take turns out to be the only thing that varies here.

In fact, .NET has a class called an `Action` that can serve this very purpose:

```
private Flight? UpdateFlight(string id,
  Action<Flight> updateAction) {
  Flight? flight = FindFlightById(id);
  if (flight != null) {
    updateAction(flight);
  } else {
    Console.WriteLine($"{id} could not be found");
  }
  return flight;
}
```

Here, the `updateAction` parameter represents a specific function that can be called. What function is it? We don't know. The exact function will be provided by whoever called the `UpdateFlight` method – just like any other parameter.

However, because `updateAction` is defined as `Action<Flight>`, we know that the function takes in a single parameter of the `Flight` type, which is why we can provide that parameter to the function when we invoke it inside this method.

To help the idea of `Action` syntax sink in a little more, let's see a few other signatures:

- `Action<int>` – A function taking in a single integer parameter
- `Action<string, bool>` – A function taking in a string and then a boolean
- `Action` – A function taking in no parameters at all

Now that declaring the `Action` parameters makes a little more sense syntactically, let's see how one of our old methods might be updated to use this new method:

```
public Flight? MarkFlightDelayed(string id,
  DateTime newDepartureTime) {
```

```
  return UpdateFlight(id, (flight) => {
    flight.DepartureTime = newDepartureTime;
    flight.Status = FlightStatus.Delayed;
    Console.WriteLine($"{id} delayed to {Format(newDepartureTime)}");
  });
}
```

Here, the MarkFlightDelayed method calls directly into the UpdateFlight method and provides an Action<Flight> in the form of the (flight) => { } syntax.

When the UpdateFlight method runs, it checks to see whether the flight exists and, if it does, the method calls the arrow function we provided to actually update the flight.

If the syntax of this is difficult, here's a different way of representing the same thing, by using a local variable to hold the Action<Flight>:

```
Action<Flight> updateAction = (flight) => {
  flight.DepartureTime = newDepartureTime;
  flight.Status = FlightStatus.Delayed;
  Console.WriteLine($"{id} delayed to {Format(newDepartureTime)}");
};
return UpdateFlight(id, updateAction);
```

It's undoubtedly possible to have a happy and productive career as a developer without declaring an Action variable. However, I've found that when I'm able to think in terms of discrete Actions, it can open some very interesting and flexible solutions to problems.

Returning data from Actions with Funcs

Before we move on to talking about static and extension methods, let's take a brief look at Funcs.

A **Func** is very similar to an Action in that it represents a *function* that can be invoked and potentially passed parameters. However, while Actions do not return any results, Funcs do.

Let's examine a simple C# method that adds two numbers together and displays their result in an equation string:

```
public void AddAction(int x, int y) {
    int sum = x + y;
    Console.WriteLine($"{x} + {y} is {sum}");
}
```

This method has a `void` return type, meaning it doesn't return any value. As a result, it could be stored in an `Action` and invoked in that way:

```
Action<int, int> myAction = AddAction;
myAction(2, 2);
```

Now, let's look at a slightly different version of the `Add` method:

```
public string AddFunc(int x, int y) {
    int sum = x + y;
    return $"{x} + {y} is {sum}";
}
```

Here, `AddFunc` has a return type of `string`. Because the method no longer returns a void, it can no longer be considered an `Action` and is now considered a `Func` because it returns some value.

As a result, if we wanted to store a reference to this method, we'd need to do so in a `Func`, as shown here:

```
Func<int, int, string> myFunc = AddFunc;
string equation = myFunc(2, 2);
Console.WriteLine(equation);
```

Note that in addition to using a `Func` instead of an `Action`, we now have a third **generic type parameter** that we're providing. The last parameter to a `Func` represents the return type of the `Func`. In the case of `myFunc`, the third generic type parameter indicates that `AddFunc` returns a `string`.

`Action` and `Func` are very closely related with the only significant difference being that `Func` returns a value. In practice, I tend to use `Action` when I want to accomplish something, such as in the earlier example of updating flights. On the other hand, I tend to use `Func` to determine when to do something or how to get a specific value I need.

For example, I might declare a method that takes in a `Func<Flight, bool>` that it uses to determine whether a flight from a list of flights should be displayed:

```
public void DisplayMatchingFlights(List<Flight> flights,
  Func<Flight, bool> shouldDisplay) {
  foreach (Flight flight in flights) {
    if (shouldDisplay(flight)) {
      Console.WriteLine(flight);
    }
  }
}
```

This method calls the `shouldDisplay` Func for every flight in the list in order to determine whether it should be displayed. Flights only display if the `shouldDisplay` Func returns `true` for that flight.

This structure allows the same method to be used for different scenarios, including the following:

- Listing upcoming flights
- Listing delayed flights
- Listing flights heading to a specific airport

The only difference between these is what the `shouldDisplay` parameter holds.

Introducing static methods and extension methods

Now that we've explored some of the more functional aspects of method refactoring, let's take a look at some of the features that helped revolutionize .NET: **static methods** and **extension methods**.

Making methods static

Sometimes, your classes will have methods that don't work directly with instance members (fields, properties, or non-static methods) of that class. For example, `FlightTracker` has a `Format` method that converts a `DateTime` to a string resembling "Wed Jul 12 23:14 PM":

```
private string Format(DateTime time) {
    return time.ToString("ddd MMM dd HH:mm tt");
}
```

Here, `Format` doesn't rely on anything other than the parameters it is provided to calculate a result. Because of this, we can make `Format` a static method.

Static methods are methods associated with the class itself and not with an instance of the class. As a result, you don't need to instantiate an instance of the class to call them. The C# compiler is also able to make occasional optimizations surrounding static code that can result in faster code.

Typically, static methods can also be considered **pure methods** – that is to say, methods without direct side effects that always produce the same result when given the same input.

As shown in *Figure 4.14*, you can mark a method as static by adding the `static` keyword after the access modifier or by choosing the **Make static** option on the **Quick Actions** menu:

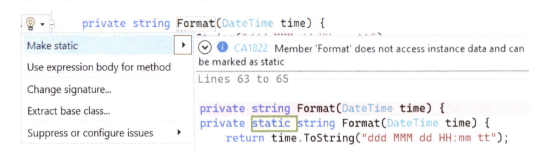

Figure 4.15 – Moving a method to a static method

The static version of **Format** looks very similar and works almost identically:

```
private static string Format(DateTime time) {
    return time.ToString("ddd MMM dd HH:mm tt");
}
```

The `Format` method can still be called simply with `Format(DateTime.Now)` as it could before, but adding static also allows you to call it from the class itself, such as `FlightTracker.Format(DateTime.Now)`.

Marking a method as static has a few advantages:

- The compiler can make optimizations resulting in faster runtime performance
- Code can call the static method without needing to instantiate the class
- The static method could be converted to an extension method, as we'll see later

The `static` keyword may seem like a great thing to use everywhere you can due to these added features. Unfortunately, `static` has some drawbacks as well. Marking a method as `static` also means it can no longer call non-`static` methods or access instance-level data.

There are certainly many uses for `static`, but it's still something that many developers find distasteful or consider an anti-pattern in excess.

Personally, I find `static` is appropriate for "helper methods" and, in some cases, to simplify unit testing complex classes that can be complex to instantiate in testing scenarios. However, I draw the line at making fields `static` whenever possible, as `static` data can lead to many problems in developing and testing applications.

Moving static members to another type

Sometimes, it doesn't make sense for a static method to remain in the class it started in.

For example, our `Format` method takes any `DateTime` and returns a customized string appropriate to Cloudy Skies Airlines' business needs. This logic is currently inside of the `FlightTracker` class, and yet is completely unrelated to tracking flights and could be useful to have in any number of places throughout their application.

In this scenario, it makes sense to pull `Format` into a different class where other developers can more readily discover these formatting capabilities.

Visual Studio provides a built-in refactoring for this. To use it, select a static method and open the **Quick Actions** menu, then click **Move static members to another type...**, as shown in *Figure 4.16*:

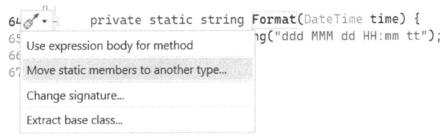

Figure 4.16 – Moving static members to another type

Next, you will be prompted to select the Type your static methods should be moved to. This can be the name of a new class if you don't currently have a class suitable for this. For Cloudy Skies, there is no existing Type that should own this, so creating one named `DateHelpers` makes sense.

Additionally, you will be asked to check or uncheck the static methods you want to move with an option to **Select Dependents** (see *Figure 4.17*) and select any methods that your selected static methods call:

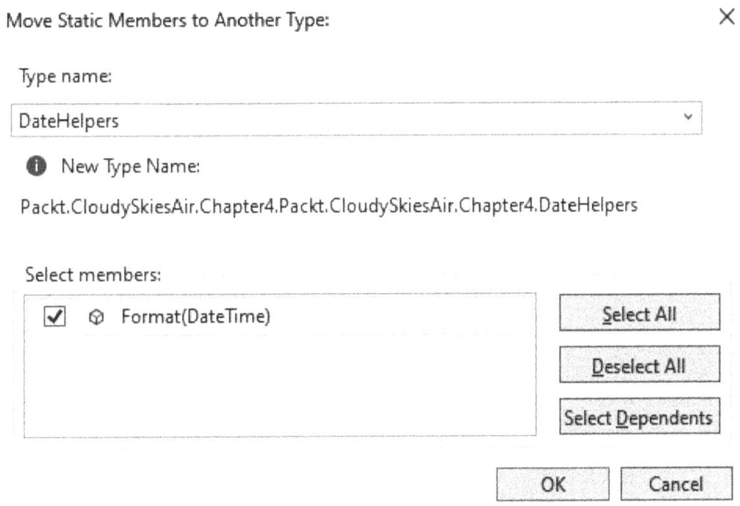

Figure 4.17 – Selecting the destination type and the members to move

Click **OK** to move your selected method and create a new class.

> **Important note**
>
> The current behavior of Visual Studio is to keep your method's current access modifier and create the new static class as `internal`. This may introduce compiler errors if your method was `private`, as code at the old location will no longer be able to access your code. I recommend changing your static class and its methods to `public` to avoid issues.

Here's the resulting **static class** after adjusting its modifiers:

```
public static class DateHelpers {
    public static string Format(DateTime time) {
        return time.ToString("ddd MMM dd HH:mm tt");
    }
}
```

Now we have a dedicated class just for "helper methods" associated with dates and times.

> **Static classes**
>
> If you're not familiar with static classes, a static class can only have static methods in it and cannot be instantiated or inherited from. Static classes are required for extension methods.

The refactoring we just performed also updated any code that was using the old `Format` method to point to `DateTimeHelpers.Format`. For example, in `FlightTracker`, the `MarkFlightArrived` method's flight logging now says `Console.WriteLine($"{id} arrived at {DateHelpers.Format(arrivalTime)}.");`.

By pulling static members into their own dedicated type, we've created a home where date-related logic can live and help a wide variety of classes, and we've made our `FlightTracker` class more focused on its core job instead of being focused on date formatting as well as flight tracking.

Unfortunately, this change has somewhat hurt the readability of our code because callers must now specify `DateHelpers.Format` instead of just `Format`. An extension method can help with this, as we'll see next.

Creating extension methods

Extension methods allow you to "extend" an existing Type by adding your own static methods that appear like they're part of that Type.

That might sound intimidating, but if you've used LINQ, you've seen extension methods in action. Let's look at the FindFlightById method in FlightTracker as an example:

```
private Flight? FindFlightById(string id) =>
    _flights.FirstOrDefault(f => f.Id == id);
```

Here, _flights is defined as a List<Flight>. Given that the code to find a flight by its ID, it's understandable to suspect that List must have a method called FirstOrDefault; however, it does not.

Instead, the FirstOrDefault method is not defined on the List<T> type in the System. Collections.Generic namespace, but rather is defined as an extension method in a static class called Enumerable in the System.Linq namespace.

In other words, it is perfectly feasible to rewrite our code from earlier to explicitly use the Enumerable class, as follows:

```
private Flight? FindFlightById(string id) =>
    Enumerable.FirstOrDefault(_flights, f => f.Id == id);
```

While this is perfectly valid code, nobody I've ever worked with writes code in this way because using FirstOrDefault as an extension method is far more intuitive and readable.

This highlights the key point of extension methods: *extension methods allow you to add new features to existing classes in a way that appears like those methods were present on the object to begin with*, resulting in more intuitive code.

To declare a method as an extension method, the following things must be true:

- The method must be static
- The method must be inside a static class
- The first parameter of the method must start with the this keyword

Our DateHelpers class and its Format method are both static, which means we can convert the method to an extension method by adding the this keyword to the method signature:

```
public static class DateHelpers {
    public static string Format(this DateTime time) {
        return time.ToString("ddd MMM dd HH:mm tt");
    }
}
```

Moving a static method to an extension method doesn't mean you have to use it as an extension method and so our previous code will still compile. However, in order to get the most value out of our extension method, we should update prior code to take advantage of its new syntax.

Let's take another look at the `MarkFlightArrived` method in `FlightTracker`. This time, if you delete the `DateFormatHelpers.Format(arrivalTime)`, instead write `arrivalTime.For`, and allow Visual Studio's **IntelliSense** to suggest values, it will list your new extension method:

```
1 reference | ● 1/1 passing | 0 changes | 0 authors, 0 changes
public Flight? MarkFlightArrived(string id, DateTime arrivalTime, string gate = "TBD") {
    return UpdateFlightIfFound(id, flight => {
        flight.ArrivalTime = arrivalTime;
        flight.Gate = gate;
        flight.Status = FlightStatus.OnTime;
        Console.WriteLine($"{id} arrived at {arrivalTime.For}.");
    });
}
                                                         Format        (extension) string DateTime.Format()
                                                         GetDateTimeFormats
```

Figure 4.18 – IntelliSense suggesting the new extension method

Because `arrivalTime` is a `DateTime` and our extension method is built to work on any `DateTime`, the new `Format` method we wrote appears here on the `DateTime` type provided in .NET through the power of extension methods.

Rewriting the call to `arrivalTime.Format()` has the correct effect of calling out to the extension method, resulting in a far more readable experience.

If you'd prefer, you can still call out to the `Format` method via `DateHelpers.Format(arrivalTime)`. Introducing an extension method just gives you another option for how your syntax is structured.

The downsides of extension methods are, primarily, as follows:

- Extension methods require the use of static, which some teams avoid because it tends to spread throughout your code
- It can be confusing that you're using an extension method
- It can be confusing where the new extension methods are defined

Thankfully, Visual Studio allows you to go to the definition of any method, member, or type simply by holding *Ctrl* and clicking on the item you want to navigate to. Alternatively, you can select the identifier and press *F12* on your keyboard or right-click on it and choose **Go To Definition** to navigate to where the extension method is declared.

Reviewing and testing our refactored code

Over the course of this chapter, we took a repetitive `FlightTracker` class and restructured it to ensure that its method signatures were more consistent and that common logic was reused wherever possible.

> **Refactored code**
>
> The final refactored code from this chapter is available in the `https://github.com/PacktPublishing/Refactoring-with-CSharp` repository inside of the `Chapter04/Ch4RefactoredCode` folder.

Before we move on, we should ensure that all tests still pass by running the unit tests from the **Test** menu and then selecting the **Run All Tests** menu item.

Summary

In this chapter, we saw how various methods, constructors, and parameter refactorings can be applied to keep your code orderly. We saw how overloading and chaining together methods and constructors gives you more options, while renaming, adding, removing, and reordering parameters helps ensure consistency.

Near the end of this chapter, we covered `Actions`, `Funcs`, static methods, and extension methods, and showed how thinking about your code in terms of small, reusable functions can help solve certain types of problems more effectively.

In the next chapter, we'll cover object-oriented refactoring techniques and revisit our parameter refactorings in this chapter by exploring how large sets of parameters can be brought under control by extracting classes.

Questions

1. Are there any areas of your code where you seem to be confused more frequently by the parameter ordering or naming?

2. Can you think of any places in your code where slightly different actions are performed based on the same or similar conditions? If so, does moving to use an `Action` or a `Func` make sense?

3. Does your code have a set of "helper methods" that might make sense to make static and put into a static class? If so, would switching to extension methods improve your code elsewhere?

Further reading

You can find more information about the materials discussed in this chapter at the following URLs:

*   *Refactor into pure functions*: `https://learn.microsoft.com/en-us/dotnet/standard/linq/refactor-pure-functions`

*   *Action-Oriented C#*: `https://killalldefects.com/2019/09/15/action-oriented-c/`

- *Refactor using an extension method*: `https://learn.microsoft.com/en-us/dotnet/standard/linq/refactor-extension-method`

- *Named and Optional Arguments*: `https://learn.microsoft.com/en-us/dotnet/csharp/programming-guide/classes-and-structs/named-and-optional-arguments`

5

Object-Oriented Refactoring

In the last chapter, we saw how refactoring can help improve classes and their methods. In this chapter, we'll explore the bigger picture with creative uses of **object-oriented programming** (**OOP**) to refactor a series of classes into more maintainable forms. These tools will help you perform larger and more impactful refactorings and make a bigger difference in improving your code.

We'll cover the following topics in this chapter:

- Organizing classes via refactoring
- Refactoring and inheritance
- Controlling inheritance with abstract
- Refactoring for better encapsulation
- Improving classes with interfaces and polymorphism

Technical requirements

The starting code for this chapter is available from GitHub at `https://github.com/PacktPublishing/Refactoring-with-CSharp` in the `Chapter05/Ch5BeginningCode` folder.

Refactoring the flight search system

This chapter's code focuses on a flight scheduling system for Cloudy Skies Airlines.

The flight scheduling system is a simple one that tracks all active flights through a `FlightScheduler` class and allows external callers to search for flights of interest. This class in turn tracks flights through a collection of `IFlightInfo` instances, which may either be a `PassengerFlightInfo` or a `FreightFlightInfo` instance, depending on whether the flight carries passenger or freight.

The high-level interactions of these classes can be seen in *Figure 5.1*:

Figure 5.1 – Classes involved in the Cloudy Skies Airline flight scheduling system

The code currently works and even uses polymorphism effectively to track a variety of different flights. That being said, there are some opportunities for improvement, as we'll see. Throughout this chapter, we'll make targeted improvements while demonstrating the breadth of refactoring possibilities present when using object-oriented programming.

Organizing classes via refactoring

It's not uncommon for solutions to have organizational challenges such as misnamed files or types existing in the wrong file or namespace.

These problems may seem small, but they can make it harder for developers to find the code they're looking for – particularly when first joining the project.

Let's look at a few refactorings that help developers navigate code more easily.

Moving classes to individual files

One common mistake I've seen teams make is putting multiple types inside of the same file. Usually, a file starts with a single class or interface and then a developer decides to add a related type. Instead of putting the new type in a file of its own, the class gets added to the existing file. Once this happens for a few small classes, it tends to snowball after that with developers continuing to add new types to the file as time goes on.

> **Types**
>
> If you're not familiar with the use of the word "type" in the .NET world, a type is a generic term that refers to anything supported by the **common type system** (**CTS**). Essentially, if you can use it to declare a variable, it's probably a type. Some examples of types include classes, interfaces, structs, enums, and the various record type variants.

The `IFlightInfo.cs` file from the Flight Scheduling System has a few different types defined in it:

```
public interface IFlightInfo {
  // Details omitted....
}
public class PassengerFlightInfo : IFlightInfo {
  // Details omitted...
}
public class FreightFlightInfo : IFlightInfo {
  // Details omitted...
}
```

While this example might not seem so bad, having multiple types in a single file does cause a few problems:

1. New developers who are looking for a specific type have trouble finding which file contains that type without using search features.

2. Version control systems, such as git, track changes to each file. This can increase confusion when teams must merge code or even determine what changed in any given software release.

The fix for this is to move each type to its own dedicated file. This can be done by going to the **Quick Actions** menu on a type whose name doesn't match the file name. Next, select the **Move type to [new file name].cs** option as shown in *Figure 5.2*:

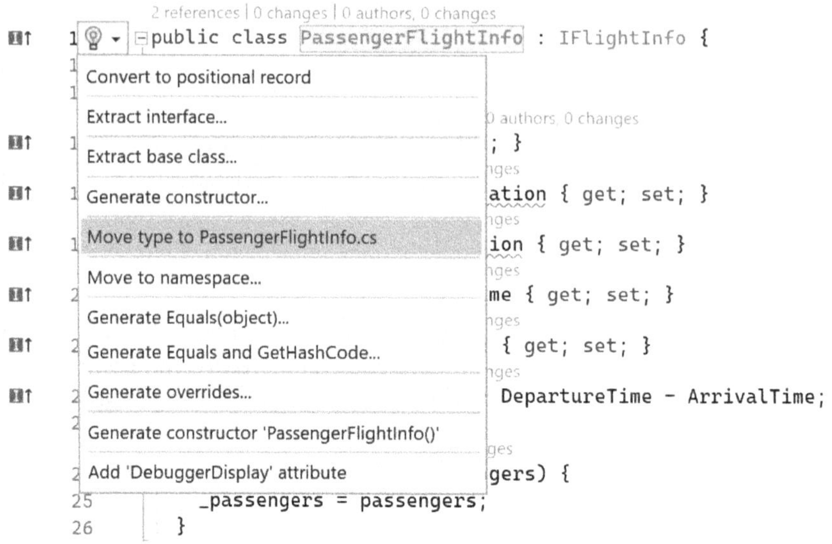

Figure 5.2 – Moving a type to its own file

Selecting this option removes the type from the original file and creates a new file containing only the type you selected.

You'll need to repeat this for every type that doesn't match the name of the file in Visual Studio. One of the extra refactoring tools that ReSharper and Rider provide allows you to perform this refactoring for every type in the file, folder, or solution. This can be particularly handy if you encounter a single file with hundreds of types in it.

Renaming files and classes

Occasionally, you'll find cases where a file and the type that it contains don't match. This often happens when developers create a new class and then decide to rename it later without using the rename refactoring built into Visual Studio.

The `AirportInfo.cs` file and its `Airport` class are an example of this:

```
namespace Packt.CloudySkiesAir.Chapter5.AirTravel;
public class Airport {
  public string Country { get; set; }
  public string Code { get; set; }
  public string Name { get; set; }
}
```

Usually, the fix for this is to rename the file to match the name of the type (though occasionally you'll determine the file was named correctly) and the class should be renamed to match the name of the file.

With either option, open the **Quick Actions** menu on the type in question and select either **Rename file** or **Rename type** to ensure the file and type name match. See the following figure:

Figure 5.3 – Options to rename the file or rename the type

I chose to rename the file to `Airport.cs`, as either option will ensure that the file and type have the same name. This naming consistency is a small improvement, but it helps developers navigate your project more easily over time.

Changing namespaces

.NET uses **namespaces** to organize types into a hierarchical structure. By convention, these namespaces should match the folders inside the project in **Solution Explorer**.

The project will start with a namespace such as `Packt.CloudySkiesAir.Chapter5`, and each folder nested inside of a project adds to this namespace. For example, a `Filters` folder in that project should use a `Packt.CloudySkiesAir.Chapter5.Filters` namespace.

When classes don't use the expected namespace, it can lead to confusion.

As a practical example, let's look at the `Airport.cs` file in the root of the `Chapter5` project as shown in *Figure 5.4*:

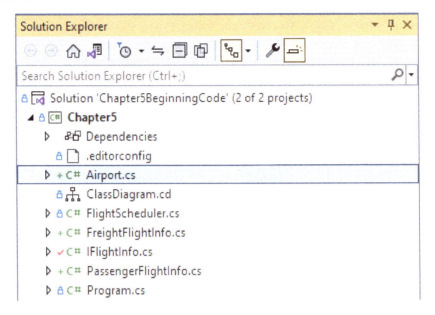

Figure 5.4 – A project with the Airport class directly nested inside of the project

In this scenario, you would expect the `Airport` class to live in the `Packt.CloudySkiesAir.Chapter5` namespace. However, the file uses a different namespace, as shown in the following code:

```
namespace Packt.CloudySkiesAir.Chapter5.AirTravel;
public class Airport {
  public string Country { get; set; }
  public string Code { get; set; }
  public string Name { get; set; }
}
```

This discrepancy can be fixed through manual editing of the namespace declaration or by using the **Change namespace to match folder structure** under **Quick Action** refactoring, as shown in *Figure 5.5*:

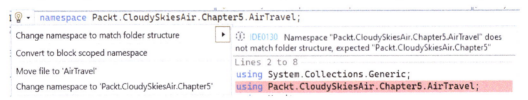

Figure 5.5 – Changing the namespace to match the folder structure

I personally recommend using the **Quick Actions** refactoring instead of typing the new namespace name manually. When you do this, you're less likely to make a typo. Additionally, the refactoring will add `using` statements to other files as needed to support the namespace change.

Avoiding partial classes and regions

Before we move on to refactoring and inheritance, I want to cover two related **anti-patterns** I've seen in C# code when dealing with large classes.

When developers have large classes with many different blocks of related code, there's a temptation to use several language features to make organizing the file easier.

Many developers use the `#region` preprocessor directive to create regions of code that can expand and collapse.

For example, you could use a statement such as `#region Stuff I don't want to look at right now` with a matching `#endregion` statement on its own line. This would create a collapsible region of code in the editor, as the collapsed region from lines 33–84 in *Figure 5.6* illustrates:

```
28
                 0 references | Matt Eland, 1 day ago | 1 author, 1 change
29           ⊟   public void RemoveFlight(IFlightInfo flight) {
30                   _flights.Remove(flight);
31               }
32
33           ⊞   Stuff I don't want to look at right now
85
                 2 references | ⊘ 1/1 passing | Matt Eland, 1 day ago | 1 author, 1 change
86           ⊟   public IEnumerable<IFlightInfo> GetAllFlights() {
87                   return _flights.AsReadOnly();
88               }
89           }
```

Figure 5.6 – A collapsed region of code

`#region` is viewed as a bad thing to rely on for code organization; it leads to extremely large classes instead of refactoring code into more maintainable patterns.

So, why does it exist at all?

The `#region` directive was introduced to help hide auto-generated code commonly built into older versions of .NET applications. This is code that developers were not expected to work with and often encouraged not to modify for fear of breaking things.

Eventually, .NET got **partial classes** to help in scenarios that regions were previously used in.

Partial classes are classes that are defined in *multiple files* within the *same project*. This will allow you to have `FlightScheduler.ItemManagement.cs` and `FlightScheduler.Search.cs` files that each contain parts of the larger class. This lets you define a large class over multiple files:

```
public partial class FlightScheduler {
  // Details omitted...
}
```

Like region directives, partial classes are intended to support automatically generated code. While I personally prefer partial classes to `#region` directives, I view both as anti-patterns when they are applied to reducing pains caused by large classes.

Usually, when your classes are big enough for you to want to consider `#region` or partial classes, you are violating the single responsibility principle and your class should be broken up into multiple smaller classes that are distinctly different from one another.

We'll discuss the single responsibility principle and other design principles in *Chapter 8, Avoiding Code Anti-patterns with SOLID*.

Refactoring and inheritance

Now that we've covered some of the ways refactoring can help organize your code, let's dive into refactorings related to inheritance. This is a collection of refactorings that involve either overriding methods, introducing inheritance, or altering in-place inheritance relationships to improve the maintainability of code.

Overriding ToString

`ToString` is one of the four methods that any .NET object is guaranteed to have due to the `virtual` definition of `ToString` on `System.Object`. This method is used whenever an object is converted to a string and can be particularly handy for logging and debugging purposes.

Sometimes overriding `ToString` can simplify your code in unexpected ways.

Let's look at the `BuildFlightIdentifier` method in `FreightFlightInfo.cs`. This method relies on the `DepartureLocation` and `ArrivalLocation` properties of type `Airport` to produce a string:

FreightFlightInfo.cs

```
public string BuildFlightIdentifier() =>
  $"{Id} {DepartureLocation.Code}-" +
  $"{ArrivalLocation.Code} carrying " +
  $"{Cargo} for {CharterCompany}";
```

It's annoying to have to drill into these location properties to reach their `Code` property.

If `Airport` overrides the `ToString` method and returns the airport code, we would be able to simplify the readability of our code:

```
public string BuildFlightIdentifier() =>
  $"{Id} {DepartureLocation}-{ArrivalLocation} " +
  $"carrying {Cargo} for {CharterCompany}";
```

To do this, you can either go to `Airport.cs` and add the override manually or use the built-in refactoring option through the **Generate overrides...** refactoring (see *Figure 5.7*):

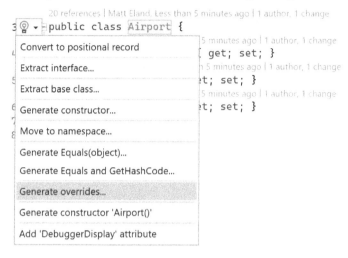

Figure 5.7 – Generating overrides on a class

From there, you'll need to specify which methods or properties you want to override. As shown in the following image, any abstract or virtual member of a class you're inheriting from will be available:

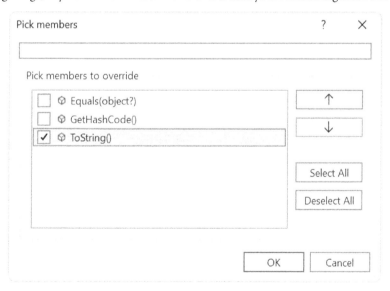

Figure 5.8 – Selecting the members to override

Selecting `ToString()` and clicking **OK** generates a stubbed-out method that can be quickly replaced with an actual implementation.

In this class, the `ToString` method should return the airport code:

```
public class Airport {
  public string Country { get; set; }
  public string Code { get; set; }
  public string Name { get; set; }
  public override string? ToString() => Code;
}
```

With this override in place, existing code can still use the `Code` property without issues. However, any code that previously tried to write an `Airport` object to the console now will see its code instead of the namespace and name of the class.

> **Note**
>
> The default implementation of `ToString` in .NET is to return a string with the namespace and the name of the type. In this case that would have been `Packt.CloudySkiesAir.Chapter5.AirTravel.Airport`.

Next, we should look at everywhere the `Code` property is currently being read from and see if it would be more readable to rely on the `ToString` override instead.

You can do this in any edition of Visual Studio 2022 by right-clicking on the `Code` property declaration and choosing **Find All References**, as shown in *Figure 5.9*:

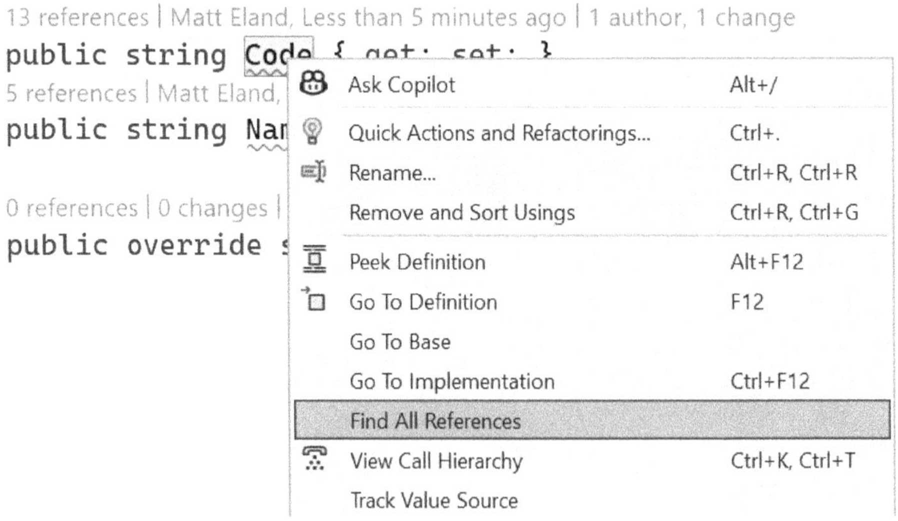

Figure 5.9 – The Find All References context menu option

This opens a new pane with all references of that property highlighted:

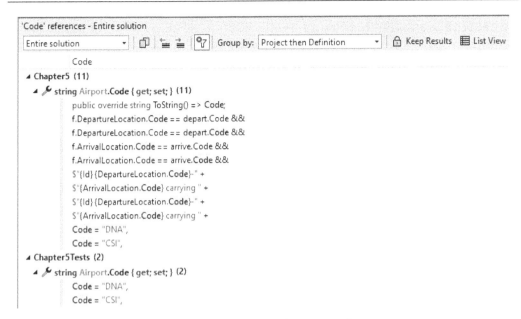

Figure 5.10 – Find All References results

You can then modify these areas to use ToString where appropriate, such as in this modification to PassengerFlightInfo:

```
public string BuildFlightIdentifier() =>
    $"{Id} {DepartureLocation}-{ArrivalLocation} " +
    $"carrying {_passengers} people";
```

One added benefit of overriding ToString in your objects is an improved display of the class when viewing the Visual Studio debugger:

```
24          PassengerFlightInfo flight = new() {
25              ArrivalLocation = arr,
26              DepartureLocation = dep,
27              DepartureTime = DateTime.Now,
28              ArrivalTime = DateTime.Now.AddHours(4),
29              Id = "CS0004",
30          };
31
32          int passengers = 308;
33          flight.Load(passengers);
34
35          Console.WriteLine(flight);
36                          ▶ ⌾ flight    (CS0004 DNA-CSI carrying 308 people)
```

Figure 5.11 – ToString override displaying in debugging tools

We'll explore debugging more in *Chapter 10: Defensive Coding Techniques.*

Generating equality methods

In C#, equality for reference types (such as classes) is done using **reference equality** –determining whether the two objects are located at the same location in the **heap**.

Sometimes it's more convenient to compare different properties on two objects to see if their values are equivalent, even if the two objects represent two separate locations on the heap.

The following code from the `FlightScheduler` class shows how its `Search` method checks to make sure the airport you're searching for has the same airport code and country. Note the repeated logic when determining if two airports are equivalent:

```
if (depart != null) {
  results = results.Where(f =>
    f.DepartureLocation.Code == depart.Code &&
    f.DepartureLocation.Country == depart.Country
  );
}
if (arrive != null) {
  results = results.Where(f =>
    f.ArrivalLocation.Code == arrive.Code &&
    f.ArrivalLocation.Country == arrive.Country
  );
}
```

This code could be simplified by overriding equality members with our own customized implementation.

> **Equality members**
>
> .NET provides two methods to determine equality: `Equals` and `GetHashCode`. The `Equals` method determines whether two objects are equivalent while `GetHashCode` is used to determine which major "bucket" an object is sorted into for **hashing** algorithms, such as those used in `Dictionary` and `HashSet`.
>
> You should never override only one of these two methods; whenever you override `Equals`, you will need to override `GetHashCode` as well. Furthermore, you want to make sure you use a good implementation of `GetHashCode` that evenly and consistently distributes objects in your class into different hash values.
>
> .NET also provides an `IEquatable<T>` interface that you can implement for strongly typed equality comparisons, which can improve performance. Implementing `IEquatable<T>` is generally recommended when overriding equality members but is not detailed in this book. See the *Further reading* section for more information.

Equality and hash codes can get complex very quickly, but thankfully we have some very good tooling for generating equality members in Visual Studio. Just select your class and then choose **Generate Equals and GetHashCode…** from the **Quick Actions** menu, as shown in *Figure 5.12*:

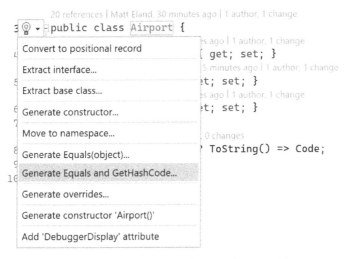

Figure 5.12 – Generating equality member overrides

Once you select this, Visual Studio will ask you what members should contribute to equality and hash code checks, as shown in *Figure 5.13*:

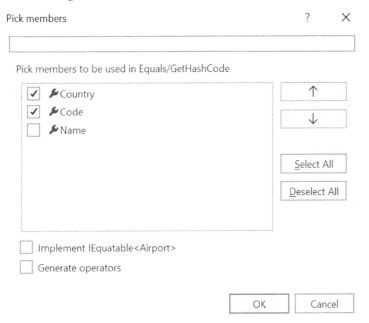

Figure 5.13 – Selecting equality members

Select the members that *must* be equal and click **OK** to generate your overrides:

Airport.cs

```
public class Airport {
  public string Country { get; set; }
  public string Code { get; set; }
  public string Name { get; set; }
  public override bool Equals(object? obj) {
    return obj is Airport airport &&
           Country == airport.Country &&
           Code == airport.Code;
  }
  public override int GetHashCode() {
    return HashCode.Combine(Country, Code);
  }
  public override string? ToString() => Code;
}
```

Here, Visual Studio generated a pattern matching the `Equals` implementation that compares the relevant properties. Additionally, the `GetHashCode` implementation uses the newer `HashCode.Combine` method to safely simplify the process of hash code generation for you.

> **Updating equality members**
>
> If you ever add new properties to your class that should factor into equality checks, be sure to update `Equals` and `GetHashCode` to include these properties.

With custom equality members in place, code that previously checked both the airport `Code` and `Country` can be simplified to use the equality operator (`==`) instead:

FlightScheduler.cs – Search

```
if (depart != null) {
  results=results.Where(f=> f.DepartureLocation == depart);
}
if (arrive != null) {
  results=results.Where(f=> f.ArrivalLocation == arrive);
}
```

Overriding equality members can be handy when you have many similar objects on the heap that contain identical values. This can happen when working with **web services** or other places where **deserialization** occurs.

Equality and records

You don't always need to override equality members to get value-based equality. In *Chapter 10: Defensive Coding Techniques*, we'll explore strategic uses of the `record` keyword for controlling equality. In fact, whenever I find myself thinking about overriding equality members, I usually decide to make my class a record instead.

Extracting a base class

Sometimes you'll encounter cases with a high degree of duplication between classes. These classes are conceptually related and share not just similar member signatures, but identical implementations of those members.

In these cases, it often makes sense to introduce a base class that defines the common shared code. **Inheritance** then allows us to remove the common code from multiple classes in the system and maintain it in a centralized place.

In our flight scheduler example (see *Figure 5.14*), the passenger and freight flight classes have several shared properties:

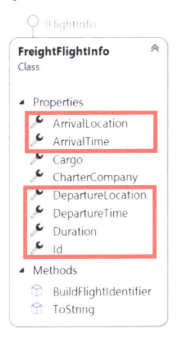

Figure 5.14 – Shared members between freight and passenger flights

To address this, go to either of the two classes and choose **Extract base class...** from the **Quick Actions** menu:

Figure 5.15 – Extracting a base class

Next, name the new class and select which members you want to move into it, as shown in *Figure 5.16*. You can also decide whether you want any of those members to be declared as abstract, but note that this will mark your class as abstract as well.

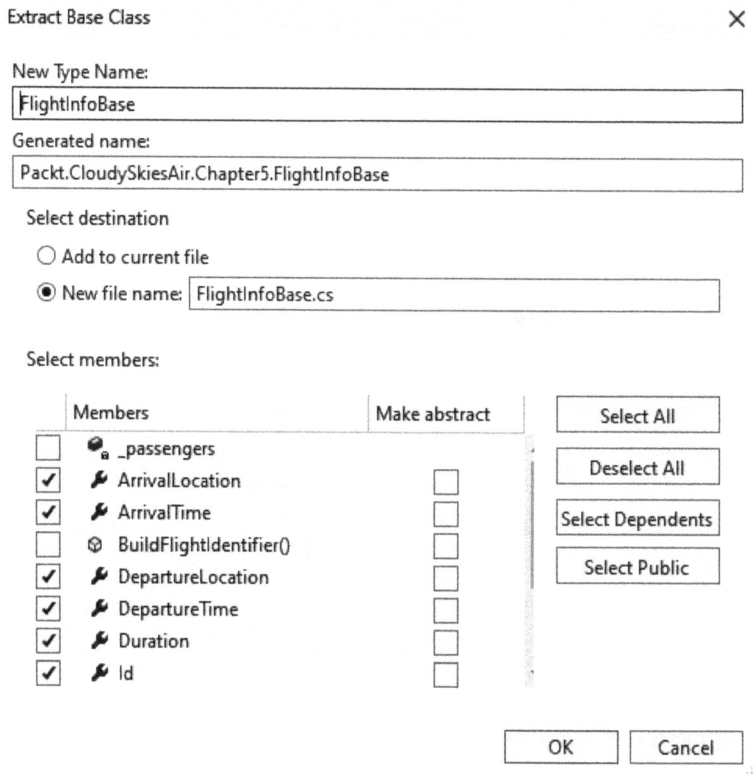

Figure 5.16 – Configuring the new base class

Once you click **OK**, the new class will be created:

FlightInfoBase.cs

```
public class FlightInfoBase {
  public Airport ArrivalLocation { get; set; }
  public DateTime ArrivalTime { get; set; }
  public Airport DepartureLocation { get; set; }
  public DateTime DepartureTime { get; set; }
  public TimeSpan Duration => DepartureTime - ArrivalTime;
  public string Id { get; set; }
}
```

The class you started with now inherits from this new class and the non-abstract members you selected have been removed from the file:

PassengerFlightInfo.cs

```
public class PassengerFlightInfo : FlightInfoBase,
                                   IFlightInfo {
  private int _passengers;
  public void Load(int passengers) =>
    _passengers = passengers;
  public void Unload() =>
    _passengers = 0;
  public string BuildFlightIdentifier() =>
    $"{Id} {DepartureLocation}-{ArrivalLocation} carrying"
    + $" {_passengers} people";
  public override string ToString() =>
    BuildFlightIdentifier();
}
```

Extracting a base class can be very helpful for promoting code reuse, but it's only half of the refactoring work; extracting a base class did not modify your other class.

If you want the related flight class to also inherit from the new class, you'll have to make that change manually by specifying the base class and removing any members that were "pulled up" to that class:

FreightFlightInfo.cs

```
public class FreightFlightInfo : FlightInfoBase,
                                 IFlightInfo {
  public string CharterCompany { get; set; }
  public string Cargo { get; set; }
```

```
public string BuildFlightIdentifier() =>
  $"{Id} {DepartureLocation}-{ArrivalLocation} " +
  $"carrying {Cargo} for {CharterCompany}";
public override string ToString() =>
  BuildFlightIdentifier();
}
```

The result of this is that our two flight classes are now focused on the things that are distinct to them. Additionally, if new logic needs to be added for every flight, it can now be added to the base class and all inheriting classes will receive it.

Moving interface implementations up the inheritance tree

One oddity you might have noticed in the last two code listings is that even though FreightFlightInfo and PassengerFlightInfo both now inherit from FlightInfoBase, they both separately implement the IFlightInfo interface, as shown in *Figure 5.17*:

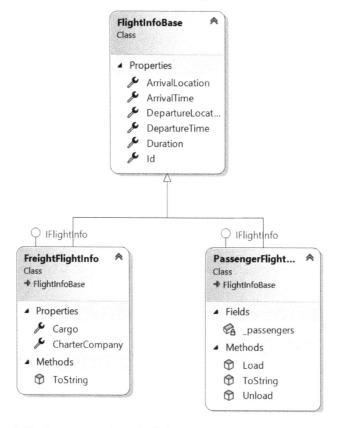

Figure 5.17 – Passenger and Freight flights separately implementing IFlightInfo

When every class inheriting from a base class implements an interface, there's usually a good chance that you can pull the interface implementation up into the base class itself.

In this case, FlightInfoBase has all required members defined by the IFlightInfo interface. So, it makes sense to implement the interface, as shown here:

FlightInfoBase.cs

```
public class FlightInfoBase : IFlightInfo {
   public Airport ArrivalLocation { get; set; }
   public DateTime ArrivalTime { get; set; }
   public Airport DepartureLocation { get; set; }
   public DateTime DepartureTime { get; set; }
   public TimeSpan Duration => DepartureTime - ArrivalTime;
   public string Id { get; set; }
}
```

With the change in place, we can remove the IFlightInfo implementation from both PassengerFlightInfo and FreightFlightInfo. This simplifies the class definitions while still inheriting the interface implementation, as pictured here:

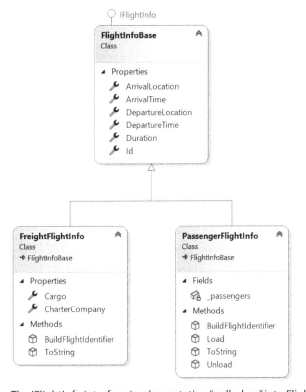

Figure 5.18 – The IFlightInfo interface implementation "pulled up" into FlightInfoBase

By pulling the interface up into the base class, we now *guarantee* that any class inheriting from this class will also implement the `IFlightInfo` interface.

Controlling inheritance with abstract

Now that we've covered some refactoring patterns around inheritance, let's look at using **abstract classes** and other C# features to restrict our classes and ensure they're used appropriately.

Communicating intent with abstract

One quirk about our current design is that it is possible to instantiate a new instance of `FlightInfoBase` simply by writing the following code:

```
FlightInfoBase flight = new FlightInfoBase();
```

While it might not make sense to you – for a new flight to exist that isn't explicitly a passenger or freight flight, because the `FlightInfoBase` class is not marked as abstract – there's nothing preventing anyone from instantiating it.

To mark a class as abstract, add the `abstract` keyword to its signature:

FlightInfoBase.cs

```
public abstract class FlightInfoBase : IFlightInfo {
  public Airport ArrivalLocation { get; set; }
  public DateTime ArrivalTime { get; set; }
  public Airport DepartureLocation { get; set; }
  public DateTime DepartureTime { get; set; }
  public TimeSpan Duration => DepartureTime - ArrivalTime;
  public string Id { get; set; }
}
```

Marking classes as abstract when you do not intend for anyone to instantiate them accomplishes a few things:

- It communicates that the class is not intended to be instantiated
- The compiler now prevents others from instantiating your class
- As we'll see next, it allows you to add abstract members to your class

Introducing abstract members

Now that `FlightInfoBase` is abstract, it opens new possibilities for refactoring.

For example, both `FreightFlightInfo` and `PassengerFlightInfo` have `BuildFlight-Identifier` methods and `ToString` overrides.

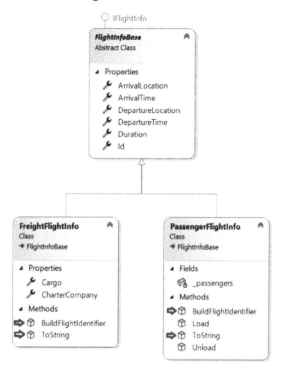

Figure 5.19 – Repeated members in flight info classes

While the implementation details of the `BuildFlightIdentifier` method differ, `ToString` overrides the return of the result of `BuildFlightIdentifier`.

We can take advantage of these commonalities by pulling both methods into the base class using **Pull [Member name] up...**, as shown in *Figure 5.20*:

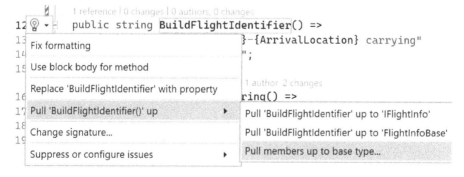

Figure 5.20 – Pulling members up to the base type

Next, select the members you want to pull up into the parent class, making sure to check the **Mark abstract** checkbox for any member you want the *definition* of to be pulled up without also having its *implementation* pulled up.

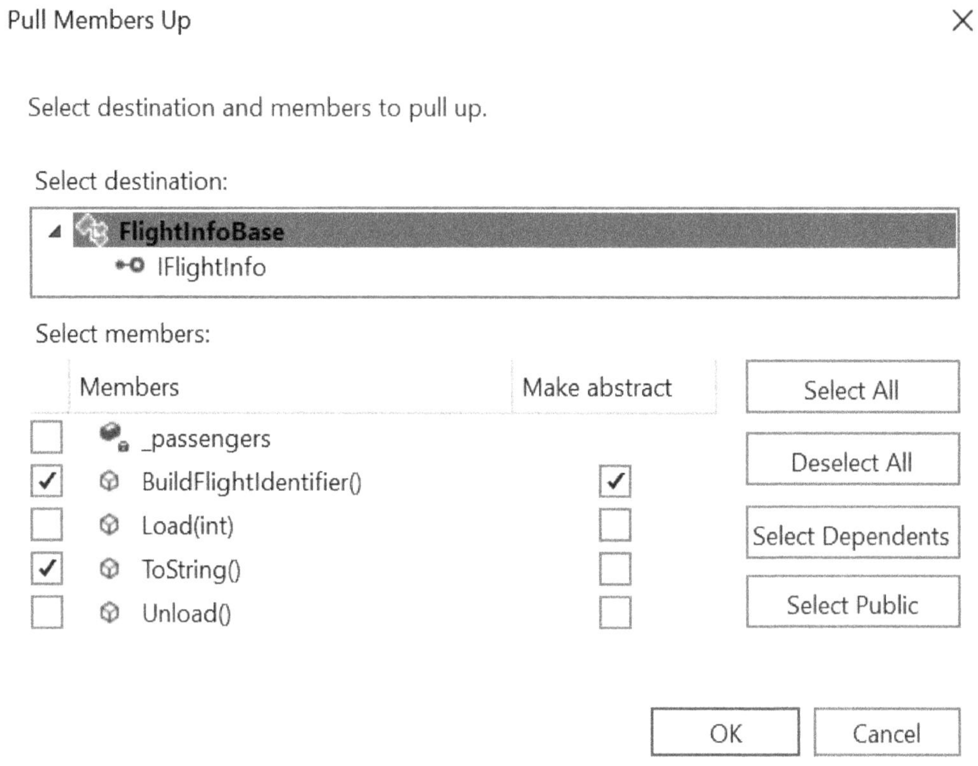

Pull Members Up   ✕

Select destination and members to pull up.

Select destination:

| ▲ 🔷 **FlightInfoBase** |
| •O IFlightInfo |

Select members:

Members	Make abstract	
☐ 🔒 _passengers		Select All
☑ 🔷 BuildFlightIdentifier()	☑	Deselect All
☐ 🔷 Load(int)	☐	Select Dependents
☑ 🔷 ToString()	☐	
☐ 🔷 Unload()	☐	Select Public

OK   Cancel

Figure 5.21 – Selecting destination and making members abstract

The result of this is that `FlightInfoBase` now has the `ToString` override as well as an abstract definition for the `BuildFlightIdentifier`:

FlightInfoBase.cs

```
public abstract class FlightInfoBase : IFlightInfo {
  // Other members omitted...
  public abstract string BuildFlightIdentifier();
  public override string ToString() =>
    BuildFlightIdentifier();
}
```

With `BuildFlightIdentifier` abstract, our original method call remains in place, but it is now marked as an override:

PassengerFlightInfo.cs

```
public class PassengerFlightInfo : FlightInfoBase {
  // Other members omitted...
  public override string BuildFlightIdentifier() =>
    $"{Id} {DepartureLocation}-{ArrivalLocation} carrying"
    + $" {_passengers} people";
}
```

Unfortunately, the **Pull Members Up** refactoring does not modify other classes that also inherit from the same base class, so you now must add the override manually in the other flight class:

```
public class FreightFlightInfo : FlightInfoBase {
  // Other members omitted...
  public override string BuildFlightIdentifier() =>
    $"{Id} {DepartureLocation}-{ArrivalLocation} " +
    $"carrying {Cargo} for {CharterCompany}";
}
```

Making this refactoring has simplified our code: the individual flight classes no longer need to override `ToString`. More importantly, if we ever add a new type of flight, the compiler will force it to provide a valid flight identifier through a `BuildFlightIdentifier` override.

Sealed methods and classes

While we're talking about abstract, virtual, and overriding methods, we should touch on `sealed`. The **sealed** keyword can be applied to a class or any overridden method in a syntax similar to abstract syntax. The `sealed` keyword has almost the opposite effect. When a class is marked with `sealed`, it cannot be inherited from. When a *method* is marked with `sealed`, that method may not be overridden further in inheriting classes. Both uses of the `sealed` keyword exist to protect what a class does from external modification. Additionally, there can be some performance benefits to marking members as sealed.

Converting abstract methods to virtual methods

Occasionally, you'll mark a method as abstract and later realize that many overrides of this method have similar implementations. When this occurs, it can make sense to move the method from `abstract` to `virtual` in order to provide a base implementation that others can *optionally* override.

Our `FlightInfoBase` class defines `BuildFlightIdentifier` as abstract:

```
public abstract string BuildFlightIdentifier();
```

This would imply that each implementation of this method *should* be different from the others. However, let's take a look at the actual implementations of this:

- PassengerFlightInfo.cs

```
public override string BuildFlightIdentifier() =>
  $"{Id} {DepartureLocation}-{ArrivalLocation}
    carrying " +
  $"{_passengers} people";
```

- FreightFlightInfo.cs

```
public override string BuildFlightIdentifier() =>
  $"{Id} {DepartureLocation}-{ArrivalLocation}
    carrying " +
  $"{Cargo} for {CharterCompany}";
```

While the strings for both methods are built, they both start with the flight identifier, the departure airport, and the arrival airport.

If we ever wanted to change the way all flights display this basic information, we'd need to change every class inheriting from `FlightInfoBase`.

Instead, we can modify `FlightInfoBase` to provide a good starting point with this shared information:

```
public virtual string BuildFlightIdentifier() =>
  $"{Id} {DepartureLocation}-{ArrivalLocation}";
```

With this change, two things have happened:

- New flight classes no longer *need* to override `BuildFlightIdentifier`
- Existing overrides can call `base.BuildFlightIdentifier()` to get the common format of the basic flight information

In our case, it makes sense to continue to override the method, but we can now change the code to take advantage of common formatting at the base level:

- PassengerFlightInfo.cs

```
public override string BuildFlightIdentifier() =>
  base.BuildFlightIdentifier() +
  $" carrying {_passengers} people";
```

- `FreightFlightInfo.cs`

```
public override string BuildFlightIdentifier() =>
  base.BuildFlightIdentifier() +
  $" carrying {Cargo} for {CharterCompany}";
```

Combining our abstract class with a virtual method lets us keep flight formatting logic in one centralized place while still giving us the freedom to extend the class and modify its behavior.

Refactoring for better encapsulation

Another core tenet of object-oriented programming is **encapsulation**. With encapsulation, you assert control of the data in your classes and ensure others work with data in ways that make sense both immediately and as the code grows over time.

The following refactorings deal with the various pieces of data composing classes along with the data passed along to methods as parameters.

Encapsulating fields

The simplest encapsulation refactoring allows you to wrap all uses of a field into a property.

In the following code example, the `PassengerFlightInfo` class has a `_passengers` field storing the count of passengers on the flight, and this field is used throughout the class when referring to the passenger count:

```
public class PassengerFlightInfo : FlightInfoBase {
  private int _passengers;
  public void Load(int passengers) =>
    _passengers = passengers;
  public void Unload() =>
    _passengers = 0;
  public override string BuildFlightIdentifier() =>
    base.BuildFlightIdentifier() +
    $" carrying {_passengers} people";
}
```

This code isn't bad, and I'd be fine with this logic in a production application. However, it does have a few potential drawbacks:

- Nothing outside of the class can read the count of passengers on the flight.

- Several places modify the `_passengers` field. If we wanted to add validation or do something every time the value changes, we'd have to modify several different methods.

Wrapping all uses of the `_passengers` field into a property can help with this by giving us a centralized place to perform validation and a property for things outside of the class to read.

You can use the **Encapsulate field** refactoring in the **Quick Action** menu to quickly wrap an existing field into a property:

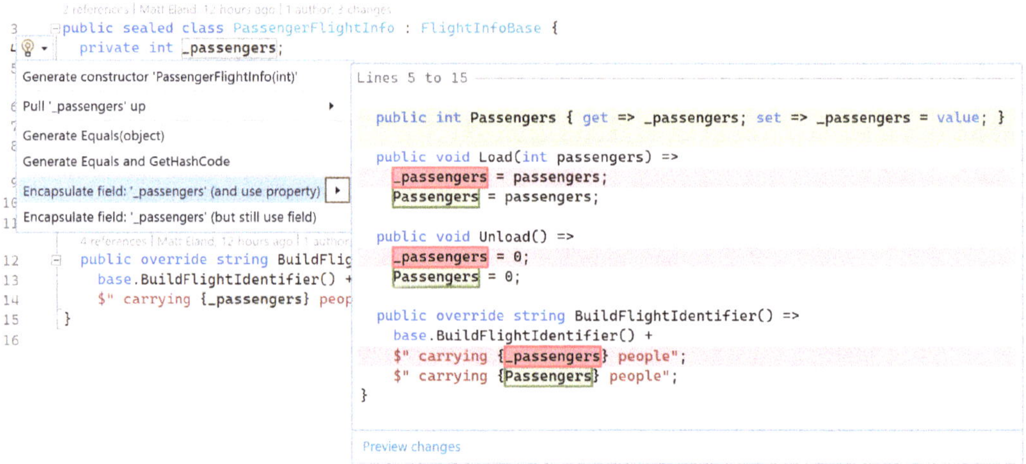

Figure 5.22 – Encapsulating the passengers field into a property

This adds a property that your class can use to read and modify the value in a centralized location:

```
public sealed class PassengerFlightInfo : FlightInfoBase {
  private int _passengers;
  public int Passengers {
    get => _passengers;
    set => _passengers = value;
  }
  public void Load(int passengers) =>
    Passengers = passengers;
  public void Unload() =>
    Passengers = 0;
  public override string BuildFlightIdentifier() =>
    base.BuildFlightIdentifier() +
    $" carrying {Passengers} people";
}
```

Keep in mind that this refactoring does make the setter public by default, which would allow code outside of the class to modify the `passengers` value. If you don't want this, you can mark the property as having a `private` or `protected` set instead.

Wrapping parameters into a class

As software systems grow, more features get added along with the code needed to support them. This can cause methods that were once simple to grow significantly in complexity and the information they require to operate.

It's not unusual for a method that took three parameters in the early days of a project to suddenly find itself needing seven or eight parameters to function after a significant amount of development occurs.

`FlightScheduler`'s search method is an example of this since there are so many things that can factor into a flight search:

FlightScheduler.cs

```
public IEnumerable<IFlightInfo> Search(
   Airport? depart, Airport? arrive,
   DateTime? minDepartTime, DateTime? maxDepartTime,
   DateTime? minArriveTime, DateTime? maxArriveTime,
   TimeSpan? minLength, TimeSpan? maxLength) {
```

This method currently takes in eight different pieces of information, which makes calls to the method extremely hard to read:

```
IEnumerable<IflightInfo> flights = scheduler.Search(cmh,
   dfw, new DateTime(2024,3,1), new DateTime(2024,3,5),
   new DateTime(2024,3,10), new DateTime(2024,3,13),
   TimeSpan.FromHours(2.5), TimeSpan.FromHours(4.5));
```

While I made that example a little hard to read on purpose, in my experience, complex method signatures exist in the real world. These complex methods can lead to subtle bugs due to confusion over which value you're passing to which parameter as you read a long list of parameters.

Looking at this code, it's easy to imagine new things that someone might want to search for with regard to flights, including low and high prices, in-flight beverage service, free Wi-Fi, and the type of aircraft being flown. Each one of these new search features would further expand both the method definition and every caller to the method.

One common solution to this problem is to encapsulate related pieces of information into a new class. In our case, we can define a new `FlightSearch` class to wrap everything related to searching for a flight:

FlightSearch.cs

```
public class FlightSearch {
   public Airport? Depart { get; set; }
   public Airport? Arrive { get; set; }
```

```
public DateTime? MinArrive { get; set; }
public DateTime? MaxArrive { get; set; }
public DateTime? MinDepart { get; set; }
public DateTime? MaxDepart { get; set; }
public TimeSpan? MinLength { get; set; }
public TimeSpan? MaxLength { get; set; }
}
```

This new class allows us to track information on searches in a centralized place and significantly improves the signature of the search method:

FlightScheduler.cs

```
public IEnumerable<IFlightInfo> Search(FlightSearch s) {
  IEnumerable<IFlightInfo> results = _flights;
  if (s.Depart != null) {
    results =
      results.Where(f => f.DepartureLocation == s.Depart);
  }
  // Other filters omitted for brevity...
  return results;
}
```

Adding the FlightSearch class shrunk the method signature from eight parameters to just one. Additionally, if new search logic needs to be added in the future, these pieces of information can be added to the FlightSearch object without needing to further modify the Search method's signature.

Unfortunately, changing the signature of the search method breaks callers to the method until they are updated to use the new search object. To fix this, you have a few options:

- Update all usages of the Search method to pass a FlightSearch object

- Create a temporary overload of the Search method that passes a FlightSearch object to the new method.

The first option is somewhat self-explanatory, so let's take a look at the second option.

Here, we'll create an overload of the Search method that takes in the eight old parameters, creates a FlightSearch object, and passes it to the new method:

```
[Obsolete("Use the overload that takes a FlightSearch")]
public IEnumerable<IFlightInfo> Search(
  Airport? depart, Airport? arrive,
  DateTime? minDepartTime, DateTime? maxDepartTime,
  DateTime? minArriveTime, DateTime? maxArriveTime,
  TimeSpan? minLength, TimeSpan? maxLength) {
```

```
FlightSearch searchParams = new() {
  Arrive = arrive,
  MinArrive = minArriveTime,
  MaxArrive = maxArriveTime,
  Depart = depart,
  MinDepart = minDepartTime,
  MaxDepart = maxDepartTime,
  MinLength = minLength,
  MaxLength = maxLength
};
return Search(searchParams);
}
```

Note that we marked this method as obsolete. This will warn programmers trying to use it and tell them what method to use instead (see *Figure 5.23*). Marking things with the `Obsolete` attribute helps guide developers towards the more recent version. Typically, a method will be marked as obsolete and then removed from the project later.

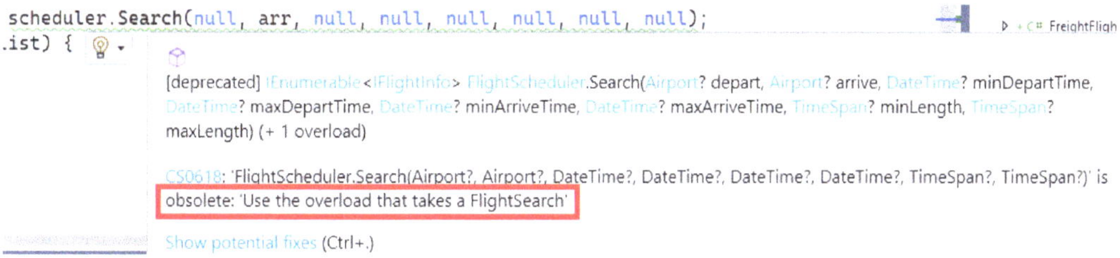

Figure 5.23 – An obsolete warning telling the developer which method to use instead

The result of this is that we were able to simplify our method and provide a safe place for the data that the method needs to grow over time by introducing a class.

Introducing classes for common sets of parameters significantly speeds up development time for teams, particularly when these same objects are passed around throughout the system.

Wrapping properties into a class

Sometimes you'll find classes with sets of properties that are related to each other. For example, the `FlightInfoBase` class needs to track both the airport a plane departs from or arrives at and the time and date of that event:

FlightInfoBase.cs

```
public abstract class FlightInfoBase : IFlightInfo {
  public Airport ArrivalLocation { get; set; }
  public DateTime ArrivalTime { get; set; }
```

```
    public Airport DepartureLocation { get; set; }
    public DateTime DepartureTime { get; set; }
    // Other members omitted ...
}
```

In this scenario, information about the arrival and departure need both their `Airport` and the associated `DateTime` to make sense. If we needed to track the terminal, gate, or runway in the future, we'd need to add in properties for both arrival and departure.

Because these sets of properties grow together, it makes sense to wrap them together in their own `AirportEvent` class:

```
public class AirportEvent {
  public Airport Location { get; set; }
  public DateTime Time { get; set; }
}
```

Now, if we need to expand the information we track on each leg of a flight, we can add it to this class and it will be available to both arrivals and departures.

Of course, for this to fully work we'll need to modify `FlightInfoBase` to use the new class instead of tracking its properties separately:

FlightInfoBase.cs

```
public abstract class FlightInfoBase : IFlightInfo {
  public AirportEvent Arrival { get; set; }
  public AirportEvent Departure { get; set; }
  public TimeSpan Duration => Departure.Time-Arrival.Time;
  public string Id { get; set; }
  public virtual string BuildFlightIdentifier() =>
    $"{Id} {Departure.Location}-{Arrival.Location}";
  public sealed override string ToString() =>
    BuildFlightIdentifier();
}
```

However, this change on its own won't be enough until we update the `IFlightInfo` interface to match our new signature:

IFlightInfo.cs

```
public interface IFlightInfo {
  string Id { get; }
  AirportEvent Arrival { get; set; }
  AirportEvent Departure { get; set; }
```

```
    TimeSpan Duration { get; }
}
```

With this change, the compiler is now satisfied with our flight classes, but there are now compiler errors in `FlightScheduler`'s `ScheduleFlight` method:

FlightScheduler.cs

```
PassengerFlightInfo flight = new() {
  Id = id,
  ArrivalLocation = arrive,
  ArrivalTime = arriveTime,
  DepartureLocation = depart,
  DepartureTime = departTime,
};
```

This method is still trying to set the old properties, so it will need to be updated to use `AirportEvent` objects instead:

```
PassengerFlightInfo flight = new() {
  Id = id,
  Arrival = new AirportEvent {
    Location = arrive,
    Time = arriveTime,
  },
  Departure = new AirportEvent {
    Location = depart,
    Time = departTime,
  },
};
```

`FlightScheduler` also has a few more compiler errors in the search method due to uses of the old properties:

```
if (s.Depart != null) {
  results =
    results.Where(f => f.DepartureLocation == s.Depart);
}
```

These pieces of code will need to reference the new properties instead:

```
if (s.Depart != null) {
  results =
    results.Where(f => f.Departure.Location == s.Depart);
}
```

You may have noticed that for this simple change of wrapping properties together into a new object we had to make a number of changes just to get the code to compile again.

This can be normal when making structural changes like this, but the compiler supports you on your refactoring journey here by ensuring your code makes structural sense as you make your changes. In fact, I wouldn't be brave enough to make some of these changes without being able to lean a little on the compiler to help me find places where I missed using the old way of doing things. I would encourage you to view the compiler as an ally on your refactoring journey.

Favoring composition over inheritance

Let's close our discussion on encapsulation by exploring the directive to *favor composition over inheritance*. This was a phrase I heard a lot in the early days of my career, though it took me a while to grasp its meaning and implications.

By favoring composition over inheritance, we make a conscious decision that classes should *have something* instead of *being something*. If a class has another object it can hand off a responsibility instead of relying on inheritance to make the class more special and able to handle a specific scenario.

Let's look at the flight scheduling system, for example.

Cloudy Skies Airlines has decided it wants to offer charter flights. These are small flights that carry both passengers and cargo paid for by various companies. In this case, a charter flight is neither a passenger flight nor a freight flight, but in fact a bit of both.

A direct implementation of this using inheritance would look something like this:

```
public class CharterFlightInfo : FlightInfoBase {
  public string CharterCompany { get; set; }
  public string Cargo { get; set; }
  public int Passengers { get; set; }
  public override string BuildFlightIdentifier() =>
    base.BuildFlightIdentifier() +
    $" carrying {Cargo} for {CharterCompany}" +
    $" and {Passengers} passengers";
}
```

Note here that a single class has both cargo and passengers.

On its own, this isn't so bad, but what if we wanted our charter flight to hold multiple pieces of cargo? We'd now need to have a collection of cargo strings with their charter companies (which might be different from one another).

Any customizations to this cargo or how it would be displayed would require either additional customization of this class or a separate but related class also inheriting from FlightInfoBase. It's not too hard to imagine this system spawning a swarm of related classes such as BulkCargoFlightInfo, ExpressFlightInfo, MedicalFlightInfo, HazardousCargoFlightInfo, and more.

While this inheritance-based approach would work, using **composition** will result in more maintainable code and fewer classes.

Composition lets us say that an individual flight is *composed of* cargo items. Cargo items can be defined using a simple `CargoItem` class:

```
public class CargoItem {
  public string ItemType { get; set; }
  public int Quantity { get; set; }
  public override string ToString() =>
    $"{Quantity} {ItemType}";
}
```

This simple approach stores the item type and its quantity and provides a string representation of the two.

We can then incorporate this into an alternative version of `CharterFlightInfo`:

```
public class CharterFlightInfo : FlightInfoBase {
  public List<CargoItem> Cargo { get; } = new();
  public override string BuildFlightIdentifier() {
    StringBuilder sb = new(base.BuildFlightIdentifier());
    if (Cargo.Count != 0) {
      sb.Append(" carrying ");
      foreach (var cargo in Cargo) {
        sb.Append($"{cargo}, ");
      }
    }
    return sb.ToString();
  }
}
```

This approach allows a charter flight to be composed of different cargo items. Each item is then displayed in the `BuildFlightIdentifier` method using its `ToString` method. See the following diagram:

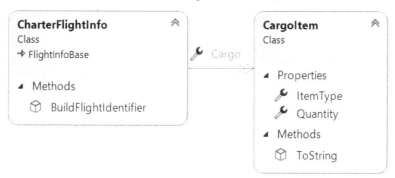

Figure 5.24 – CharterFlightInfo is composed of CargoItems

Composing our charter flight with `CargoItems` gives us additional flexibility. Not only does this arrangement pattern allow a charter flight to have multiple cargo items, but it also allows it to do so without you having to declare different classes for different cargo loads.

Improving classes with interfaces and polymorphism

We're nearly at the close of this chapter on object-oriented refactoring. However, before we close the chapter, let's discuss a few places where introducing interfaces and polymorphism can help further improve our code.

Extracting interfaces

At the moment, our `CharterFlightInfo` class stores a list of `CargoItems` representing its cargo:

```
public class CharterFlightInfo : FlightInfoBase {
  public List<CargoItem> Cargo { get; } = new();
  // Other members omitted...
}
```

Each cargo item the charter flight includes must be a `CargoItem` or something that inherits from it. For example, if we were to create the `HazardousCargoItem` we discussed in the last section and try to store it in the cargo collection, it *must* inherit from `CargoItem` to compile.

In many systems, you don't want to force people to inherit from your classes if they want to customize the system's behavior. In these places, it can be helpful to introduce an interface.

Let's do that with our `CargoItem` class by selecting the class and then choosing **Extract interface...** from the **Quick Actions** menu.

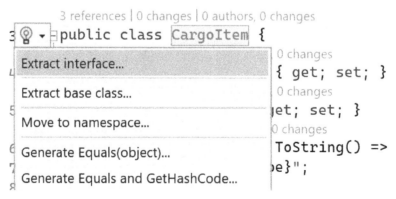

Figure 5.25 – Extracting an interface

Once you've done this, as shown in *Figure 5.25*, you now need to specify which members of the class should be included in the interface as well as what the interface should be called:

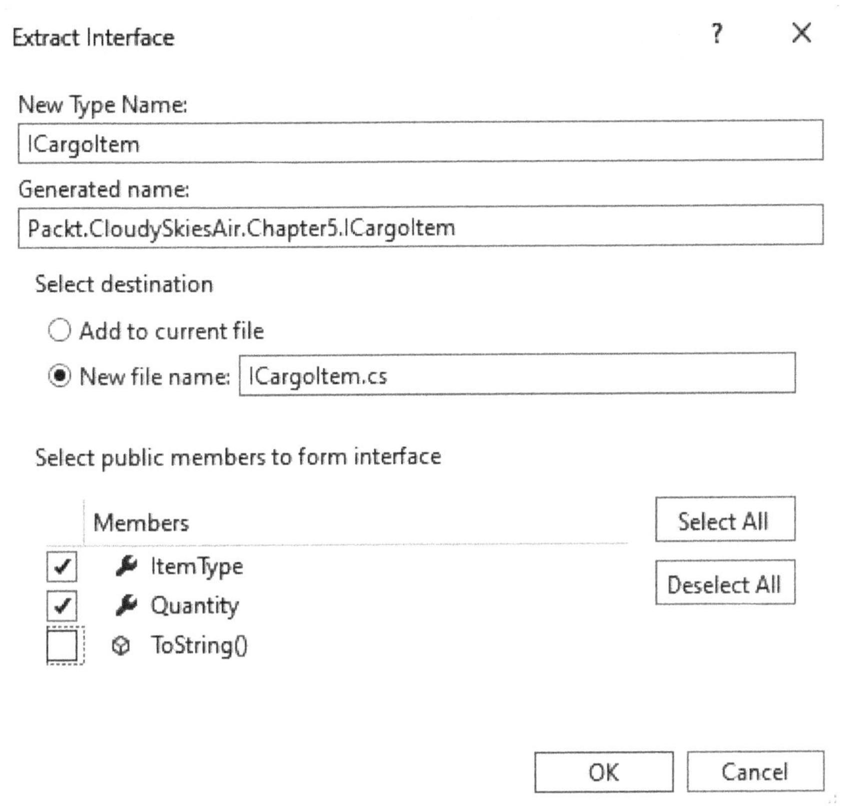

Extract Interface   ?   X

New Type Name:

ICargoItem

Generated name:

Packt.CloudySkiesAir.Chapter5.ICargoItem

Select destination

○ Add to current file

◉ New file name: ICargoItem.cs

Select public members to form interface

Members	
☑ 🔧 ItemType	
☑ 🔧 Quantity	
☐ ⊚ ToString()	

Select All

Deselect All

OK   Cancel

Figure 5.26 – Customizing the extracted interface

Name your interface `ICargoItem`, select both `ItemType` and `Quantity`, and then click **OK**. This will generate a new `ICargoItem` interface in a new file:

```
public interface ICargoItem {
  string ItemType { get; set; }
  int Quantity { get; set; }
}
```

This will also modify `CargoItem` to implement this interface:

```
public class CargoItem : ICargoItem {
  public string ItemType { get; set; }
  public int Quantity { get; set; }
  public override string ToString() =>
    $"{Quantity} {ItemType}";
}
```

Note that by default, extracting an interface will introduce both getters and setters on properties. If you do not need your interface to expose a way of modifying a property, you can remove the `set` from the property definition in the interface:

```
public interface ICargoItem {
  string ItemType { get; }
  int Quantity { get; }
}
```

Removing the set *does not prevent you* from having a setter on your property in `CargoItem`; it just means you're not *required* to have a setter on the property.

With our new interface in hand, let's go in and modify `CharterFlightInfo` to store `ICargoItems` instead of `CargoItems`:

```
public class CharterFlightInfo : FlightInfoBase {
  public List<ICargoItem> Cargo { get; } = new();
  // Other members omitted...
}
```

This change allows us to store anything that implements the interface and improves the flexibility of what `CharterFlightInfo` can store. However, this does introduce another interface to your code, which slightly increases the complexity and can slow down development time in the long run.

Be careful when introducing interfaces. Interfaces that exist for the sake of added abstraction will ultimately do more harm than good in your application. However, interfaces that are implemented by more than one class or designed to give another set of developers greater freedom or flexibility can ultimately do a lot of good in a software system.

We'll talk more about the appropriate place for interfaces in *Chapter 10* when we explore SOLID. For now, let's move on to a newer feature in C# interfaces.

Providing default interface implementations

While we're exploring interfaces, let's see how **default interface implementations** can simplify the experience of implementing an interface.

Default interface implementations allow you to provide a default implementation inside the interface. When a class chooses to implement this interface, it is not *forced to* provide implementations of methods with default implementations.

Let's see what this means by adding a `ManifestText` property with a default getter and a `LogManifest` method with a default implementation to `ICargoItem`:

```
public interface ICargoItem {
  string ItemType { get; }
```

```
    int Quantity { get; }
    string ManifestText => $"{ItemType} {Quantity}";
    void LogManifest() {
      Console.WriteLine(ManifestText);
    }
  }
```

By adding these new members to the interface, we'd normally break anything that implemented the interface, such as the `CargoItem` class, unless it had those members. However, because we provided a *default implementation* of both properties, `CargoItem` no longer *must* provide implementations. Instead, it effectively inherits these default implementations.

We can still provide a version of these new members. If we did, that version would be used instead of the default implementation:

CargoItem.cs

```
public class CargoItem : ICargoItem {
  public string ItemType { get; set; }
  public int Quantity { get; set; }
  public void LogManifest() {
    Console.WriteLine($"Customized: {ToString()}");
  }
  public override string ToString() =>
    $"{Quantity} {ItemType}";
}
```

I don't like default interface implementations very much because they confuse the concept of an interface with a contract to provide certain members.

However, I must concede that when adding a simple member to an interface, it sometimes makes sense to add a default implementation so that you don't need to change existing implementations of the interface. This can save you from having to add the same code to many different implementations of your interface throughout your solution. Additionally, default interface implementations reduce the work needed for classes trying to implement the interface by providing a default implementation.

Introducing polymorphism

Whenever you are working with an interface, you are intentionally supporting **polymorphism** in your application. This is the ability to treat different objects based on their similarities instead of on their differences.

The `ICargoItem` approach introduced earlier with charter flights is an example of polymorphism. A charter flight doesn't care about what type of cargo it has as long as the cargo implements the interface. This means that we can load a charter flight full of different types of cargo and the class works fine with them.

The chapter's code has another place that could strongly benefit from polymorphism: the `FlightScheduler` `Search` method:

```
public IEnumerable<IFlightInfo> Search(FlightSearch s) {
  IEnumerable<IFlightInfo> results = _flights;
  if (s.Depart != null) {
    results =
      results.Where(f => f.Departure.Location == s.Depart);
  }
  // Many filters omitted...
  if (s.MaxLength != null) {
    results =
      results.Where(f => f.Duration <= s.MaxLength);
  }
  return results;
}
```

This method has some very repetitive code (much of it omitted) that checks to see if the search object specifies a property. If the property was specified, the potential results are filtered down to only include those that match the filter.

The search method uses this approach to filter based on:

- Departure and arrival locations
- Minimum/maximum departure time
- Minimum/maximum arrival time
- Minimum/maximum flight length

It's not too hard to imagine new things we might filter for, such as the price of the flight, whether the flight has a beverage service or even the type of aircraft.

An alternative approach would be to take in a collection of filter objects. These filter objects would determine whether each flight should be included in the results through a common `FlightFilterBase` class and a `ShouldInclude` method:

```
public abstract class FlightFilterBase {
  public abstract bool ShouldInclude(IFlightInfo flight);
}
```

With this change, `Search` could be modified to loop over all filters and only include results that pass through all the provided filters:

```
List<IFlightInfo> Search(List<FlightFilterBase> rules) =>
   _flights.Where(f => rules.All(r => r.ShouldInclude(f)))
            .ToList();
```

This cuts our `Search` method down from over 40 lines long to only 3 lines of code through polymorphism.

> **Alternative implementation**
>
> An interface would also work fine instead of an abstract base class.

By following this design, we can create a series of classes that inherit from `FlightFilterBase` to provide specific filtering capabilities:

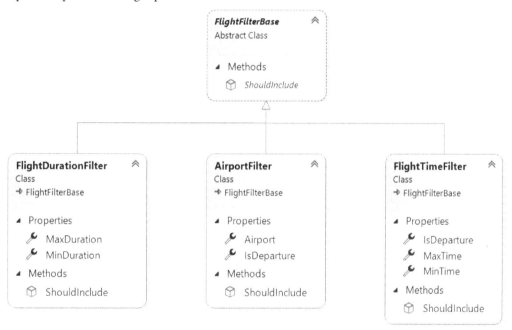

Figure 5.27 – Distinct filter classes to help simplify our search code

We now have dedicated filters that filter out flights that don't match their specific criterion. For example, the `AirportFilter` would filter out flights that don't specify an airport:

```
public class AirportFilter : FlightFilterBase {
   public bool IsDeparture { get; set; }
   public Airport Airport { get; set; }
   public override bool ShouldInclude(IFlightInfo flight) {
```

```
    if (IsDeparture) {
      return flight.Departure.Location == Airport;
    }
    return flight.Arrival.Location == Airport;
  }
}
```

Each individual filter class is small and easy to understand, maintain, and test.

Additionally, if we want to add a new way of filtering flights in the future, all we need to do is add a new class inheriting from `FlightFilterBase`. No modifications would be needed for the `Search` method to support this because all the method needs is a collection of individual filters. The `Search` method doesn't need to know which filters are involved – it just needs to call the `ShouldInclude` method and interpret the result.

I find a lot of beauty in polymorphic solutions and have found my programming style changing over the years in search of more opportunities to take advantage of polymorphism through inheritance or interfaces.

Reviewing and testing our refactored code

With these changes made, let's take a step back and look at the result.

We took a flight search system and used object-oriented programming techniques to improve its flexibility and maintainability by doing the following:

- Reorganizing the code into appropriate files and namespaces
- Introducing a base class and improving code reuse in flight information
- Controlling a large number of parameters by moving them into a new class
- Introducing another new class to manage common information about airport events including both an airport and a time component
- Adding a charter flight class with a flexible cargo tracking system
- Introducing a polymorphic way of searching flights that will be more flexible and maintainable over time

> **Refactored code**
>
> The final refactored code from this chapter is available in the `https://github.com/PacktPublishing/Refactoring-with-CSharp` repository inside of the `Chapter05/Ch5RefactoredCode` folder.

As always, refactoring should never be done without testing the code to make sure that no new defects were introduced in the refactoring process. Running the tests (see *Figure 5.28*) provided in the solution shows a full slate of passing tests, which will suffice for now until we get to *Part 2* and explore testing in more depth.

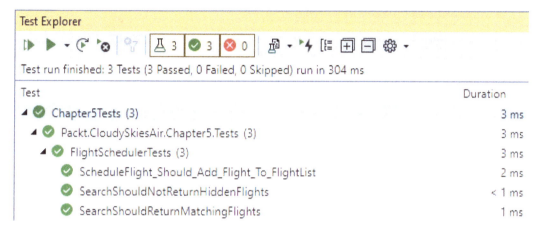

Figure 5.28 – Test Explorer showing that all tests pass

Summary

In this chapter, we explored the various ways that object-oriented programming techniques such as inheritance, encapsulation, and polymorphism can be used to refactor code toward more maintainable forms.

Refactoring can be a complex endeavor, and yet so many of the fundamental concepts of object-oriented programming can come together to build elegant, flexible, and maintainable solutions.

This concludes *Part 1* of the book. In the next part of the book, we'll look at how testing can give you the safety and freedom needed to safely refactor your code and move forward with confidence that your changes have improved the application without breaking anything.

Questions

1. Does your code follow a well-structured and consistent namespace hierarchy with not too many or too few classes in each namespace?

2. Is there any part of your code that might be improved by using inheritance to promote code reuse?

3. Can you think of any repetitive rules or other structures in your code that might benefit from polymorphism?

Further reading

You can find more information about materials discussed in this chapter at these URLs:

- *Inheritance in C#:* `https://learn.microsoft.com/en-us/dotnet/csharp/fundamentals/tutorials/inheritance`

- *Sealed Modifier:* `https://learn.microsoft.com/en-us/dotnet/csharp/language-reference/keywords/sealed`

- *IEquatable<T>:* `https://learn.microsoft.com/en-us/dotnet/api/system.iequatable-1`

Part 2: Refactoring Safely

In the second part of the book, we'll cover coding techniques such as unit tests that help ensure your refactoring efforts don't result in unintentional changes.

This chapter focuses on various testing frameworks and standard testing practices before moving on to discussions about programming best practices and writing SOLID code.

The final two chapters in this part focus on more advanced testing strategies and ways the C# language can help you detect and prevent errors from reaching your users.

This part contains the following chapters:

- *Chapter 6, Unit Testing*
- *Chapter 7, Test-Driven Development*
- *Chapter 8, Avoiding Code Anti-Patterns with SOLID*
- *Chapter 9, Advanced Unit Testing*
- *Chapter 10, Defensive Coding Techniques*

6

Unit Testing

In the first part of this book, we covered the process of refactoring and some of the more common refactoring techniques. Now, it's time for us to take a step back and remind ourselves of what refactoring is: *refactoring is the process of changing the form or shape of the code without changing how it behaves.*

In other words, we can make our code as clean and easy to maintain as we can, but if those changes introduce bugs, that's not refactoring since refactoring is about changing the form of code *without changing its behavior*. To improve our code without introducing bugs, we need a safety net: **unit testing**.

In this chapter, we'll explore unit tests and cover the following main topics:

- Understanding testing and unit tests
- Testing code with xUnit
- Refactoring unit tests
- Exploring other testing frameworks
- Adopting a testing mindset

Technical requirements

The starting code for this chapter is available from GitHub at `https://github.com/PacktPublishing/Refactoring-with-CSharp` in the `Chapter06/Ch6BeginningCode` folder.

Understanding testing and unit tests

Whenever I was managing or mentoring another developer and they wanted to make a change to a system I'd ask them a question: *"How can you be sure your change won't break things?"*

This simple question can be deceptively hard to answer, but every answer I've ever heard boils down to a single concept: testing.

I define **testing** as *the process of verifying software functionality and detecting unwanted changes to program behavior.*

This testing could be done by a human, such as a developer or a quality assurance analyst, or it could be done via software, depending on the type of test involved.

Types of tests and the testing pyramid

Testing is a broad field that encompasses many different types of activities, including the following:

- **Manual testing**, which involves a person performing some activity manually and verifying the outcome.

- **Exploratory testing**, a subset of manual testing that focuses on exploring how the system reacts to things to find new types of bugs.

- **Unit tests**, in which small parts of the software system are tested in isolation.

- **Component tests**, where larger components of the system are tested.

- **Integration tests**, which involve two components, such as an API and a database, that are tested together.

- **End-to-end tests**, in which entire paths through the system are tested. This usually involves multiple sets of components interacting in sequence.

Most of these activities are automated tests where computer code interacts with the system to verify its behavior. We'll talk more about what factors make up good tests at the end of this chapter.

Automated tests do have some drawbacks. First, automated tests take time to create. Typically, a human must write code or use some tool to script out the test. Secondly, these tests often require ongoing maintenance as the software system changes to stay relevant. Finally, these tests can offer a false sense of security. For example, let's say a developer wrote a test to navigate to the "book a flight" web page and verify that open seats display as available. This test may pass even if the web page has obvious errors and misalignments on it, simply because the test was only coded to check a small part of the web page.

On the other hand, human testers are intelligent. They have free agency and initiative and can make objective judgments about software that machines cannot. They can find issues that nobody ever thought of writing a test for, and they can provide valuable feedback about the functionality of your products. However, people are usually a lot slower than automated tests and it may take some time for a quality assurance analyst to test a feature once it is ready for testing.

There are strengths and weaknesses when it comes to both automated and manual tests. One is not better than the other; instead, they combine to make for an effective solution to quality issues in software projects.

A popular concept in software quality is the idea of a **testing pyramid**. A testing pyramid shows the various types of tests an organization might perform. Additionally, as shown in *Figure 6.1*, the width of each segment of the pyramid indicates the quantity of that type of test:

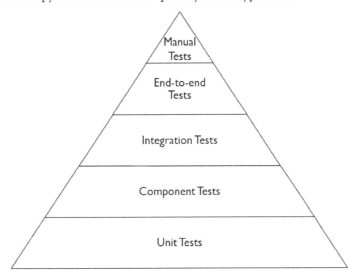

Figure 6.1 – An example of a testing pyramid

In a testing pyramid, such as this one, the items at the base should be the most numerous and the items at the top of the pyramid should be the rarest. Almost every diagram of a testing pyramid is different in the exact types of tests listed in the pyramid, but all of them agree that the most common form of testing should be the unit test and the least common should be manual testing.

Many organizations get this wrong early in their software development maturity. When that happens, they have a lot of manual tests, few unit tests, and typically no end-to-end, integration, or component tests. As a result, the pyramid would look a little like *Figure 6.2*:

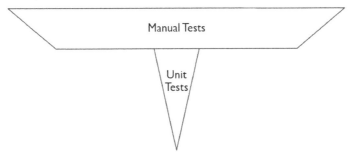

Figure 6.2 – Testing pyramid with many manual tests, few unit tests, and no other tests

This pyramid *should* look ridiculous because having very little test automation is almost always a recipe for slow processes, delayed releases, and software bugs reaching production environments!

The larger your system becomes, the less feasible manual testing will be and the longer it will take to discover bugs manually.

The solution to this is **automated testing**, particularly automated unit testing.

Unit tests

Unit tests are small methods of code that test other methods in your system to verify those methods perform correctly given a specific scenario.

More succinctly, unit tests are code that tests other code.

> **Already familiar with tests?**
> You may already be familiar with unit tests if you work with unit tests regularly. If that's true, you may want to skim the rest of this chapter and resume with the next one.

To illustrate the idea of unit testing, let's look at a simple method that generates a flight status message:

```
public class Flight {
  public string BuildMessage(string id, string status){
    return $"Flight {id} is {status}";
  }
}
```

While this method is very simple, let's think about the steps we'd need to take to verify it works correctly:

1. Instantiate the `Flight` class and store that object in a variable.

2. Declare a pair of string variables representing `id` and `status`.

3. Invoke the `BuildMessage` method on our flight object from *Step 1*.

4. Store the result of *Step 3* in a new string variable.

5. Verify the string we just stored matched what we expected.

This is essentially what a unit test would do. It would instantiate your class, *arrange* the variables it needs, *act* on the method the unit test is trying to verify, and finally *assert* that the result of the method matched what we expected. We call this pattern the **arrange/act/assert** pattern and we'll discuss it more later in this chapter.

To help illustrate this concept, here's a sample test for the `BuildMessage` method:

```
public class FlightTests {
  [Fact]
  public void GeneratedMessageShouldBeCorrect() {
    // Arrange
    Flight flight = new();
    string id = "CSA1234";
    string status = "On Time";

    // Act
    string message = flight.BuildMessage(id, status);

    // Assert
    Assert.Equal("Flight CSA1234 is On Time", message);
  }
}
```

Don't worry about the specific syntax here as we'll get into this shortly. For now, understand that the `GeneratedMessageShouldBeCorrect` method is an example of a unit test that tests a small unit of code to verify a specific piece of functionality.

Specifically, this method verifies that the `Flight` class's `BuildMessage` method calculates and returns an accurate status message given the `id` and `status` parameters it receives.

This test can be run quickly alongside all the other tests in the solution and will either pass if the `BuildMessage` method is acting as expected or will fail if the result of `BuildMessage` ever changes, as shown in *Figure 6.3*:

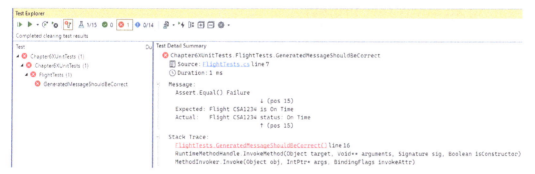

Figure 6.3 – A failing unit test

Test failures such as this are helpful because they highlight bugs that developers might otherwise release into production without the failing test flagging the potential issue.

In the next section, we'll explore unit tests more by introducing the most popular unit testing framework: **xUnit**.

Testing code with xUnit

xUnit.net, commonly referred to as xUnit, is currently the most popular unit testing library in .NET, followed by **NUnit** and **MSTest**. All three libraries provide `Attributes` that you can use to identify your test code, as we'll see shortly. Using these attributes lets a test runner, such as Visual Studio's **Test Explorer**, recognize your methods as unit tests and run them.

This chapter's code starts with most of the classes from the chapters up to this point, organized into various namespaces inside of the `Chapter6` **project** within the `Chapter6BeginningCode` **solution**.

Solutions and projects

In .NET, a project represents a distinct assembly of .NET code that accomplishes some purpose. Different projects have different types, from desktop applications to web servers to class libraries and test projects. Solutions, on the other hand, group all of these projects together into a collection of interrelated projects.

In the remainder of this chapter, we'll write tests for a number of the classes from the previous chapters. Since xUnit is currently the most popular testing library, let's start by adding a new xUnit test project to the solution.

Creating an xUnit Test Project

To add a new project to a solution, right-click on the solution's name at the top of **Solution Explorer**, just below the search bar, and then choose **Add**, followed by **New Project…**

Next, search for `xUnit` and select the **xUnit Test Project** result with the C# label attached to it, as shown in *Figure 6.4*. Note that there are also versions of this test project that use other languages, such as VB or F#:

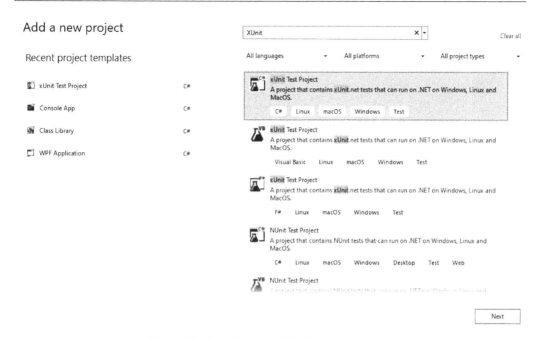

Figure 6.4 – Selecting the xUnit Test Project option

Click **Next**, then give your test project a meaningful name, such as `Chapter6XUnitTests`, and click **Next** again.

After this, you'll need to select the version of .NET to use. Since the code in this book uses **.NET 8**, you can select that option and click **Create**.

This should open a new file in your editor that contains some basic test code:

UnitTest1.cs

```
namespace Chapter6XUnitTests {
    public class UnitTest1 {
        [Fact]
        public void Test1() {
        }
    }
}
```

Additionally, a new project was added to your solution that now appears in **Solution Explorer**, as shown in *Figure 6.5*:

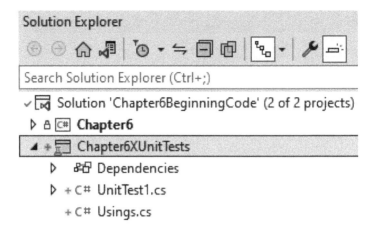

Figure 6.5 – The test project in Solution Explorer

There are still a few more steps that we'll need to do to test our code in the other project. But before we do that, it may surprise you that the code xUnit created is already a runnable unit test.

Click on the **Test** menu at the top of Visual Studio and then select **Run All Tests**. **Test Explorer** should now show your Test1 unit test, which will turn into a green check mark once the test runs, as shown in *Figure 6.6*:

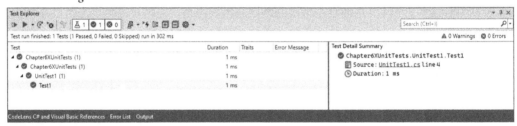

Figure 6.6 – Test Explorer with tests expanded to the point where Test1 is visible

> **Troubleshooting**
> If you do not see **Test Explorer** after running your tests, click on the **View** menu and then select **Test Explorer**. You may also need to build your solution before running tests becomes an option.

Note that our current test isn't much of a test and we still haven't covered the code or how it works. We'll get there shortly, but first, let's take the final step in setting up our tests and connect our test project to our Chapter6 project.

Connecting the xUnit Test Project to your main project

In .NET, projects can depend on code in other projects. This allows you to have a class defined in one project and another project uses that class. This is something we'll need to be able to do to test code from our unit test project. So, we'll need to set up a project dependency from the test project to the Chapter6 project.

Right-click on the **Dependencies** node inside of the test project in **Solution Explorer** and choose **Add Project Reference…**, as shown in *Figure 6.7*:

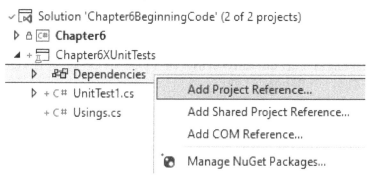

Figure 6.7 – Adding a project reference to our test project

After this, click the checkmark next to Chapter6 and click **OK**. This will add a reference from your test project to the Chapter6 project so that the test project can now reference classes defined in the other project.

With all this in place, we're ready to write our first real test.

Writing your first unit test

Our first tests will test the BaggageCalculator class we built in *Chapter 2*.

BaggageCalculator has a CalculatePrice method with the following method signature:

```
public decimal CalculatePrice(int bags, int carryOn,
   int passengers, bool isHoliday)
```

We also know the following rules for this method:

- All carry-on baggage costs $30 per bag
- The first checked bag a passenger checks in costs $40
- Each subsequent checked bag costs $50
- If the travel occurs during the holidays, a 10% surcharge is applied

We won't be able to test all this logic in a single test, and we shouldn't try. Unit tests should be small and related to one specific piece of logic. If a test fails, that failure should tell you a lot about what is wrong in your system. If unit tests try to do too much, they become harder to understand and a failure tells you less about what is wrong.

Let's start by taking our `UnitTest1` class and renaming it using the rename refactoring we covered in *Chapter 2*. Tests are generally named after the class they test. Since our class tests `BaggageCalculator`, let's rename it `BaggageCalculatorTests`.

Next, we'll rename the `Test1` method to reflect what we're trying to verify. The name of this test will show up in a test failure. So, my general rule of thumb is that if I get a notification that a test failed, its name alone should tell me what went wrong.

In our case, we're trying to verify that carry-on baggage is priced correctly. So, let's rename `Test1` to something like `CarryOnBaggageIsPricedCorrectly`.

Our code now reads as follows:

```
namespace Chapter6XUnitTests {
  public class BaggageCalculatorTests {
    [Fact]
    public void CarryOnBaggageIsPricedCorrectly() {
    }
  }
}
```

Before we move on to writing our test code, let's highlight a few key things:

- First, our method has a `Fact` attribute applied to it. This lets xUnit tell the test runner about our test and effectively registers the test for potential execution.

- Next, `CarryOnBaggageIsPricedCorrectly` returns `void` and accepts no parameters. Test methods using the `Fact` attribute cannot accept parameters and must either return `void` or `Task` for asynchronous tests. We'll discuss `Theory` and `InlineData` later in this chapter as they allow you to pass in parameters to unit tests.

- Finally, both the class and the method are `public`. Both must be `public` for the unit test to appear in the test runner.

Now that we've covered some of the basic mechanics of unit tests, let's follow the *arrange/act/assert* pattern to build our test.

Organizing tests with Arrange/Act/Assert

The **arrange/act/assert pattern** is a structural pattern that's used when writing tests. When following *arrange/act/assert*, you perform the following steps:

1. **Arrange** the things that you need for your tests by declaring variables.

2. **Act** on the specific thing you're trying to test.

3. **Assert** that the result of your action produced the desired outcome.

Let's start by arranging the code. Since we're testing the `CalculatePrice` method on the `BaggageCalculator` class, we'll need to instantiate an instance of the baggage calculator.

We also know we'll need to pass in the number of checked and carry-on bags, as well as the number of passengers and whether the travel is during a holiday season. These values should be whatever we think will make the most relevant or representative test, so they're up to our discretion.

Filling out our *arrange* section with variable declarations results in the following code:

```
[Fact]
public void CarryOnBaggageIsPricedCorrectly() {
    // Arrange
    BaggageCalculator calculator = new();
    int carryOnBags = 2;
    int checkedBags = 0;
    int passengers = 1;
    bool isHoliday = false;
```

Here, we're setting up everything we need to carry out the *act* phase. Also, note that I included an `// Arrange` comment to group related code together. This is something I and many other developers I know do in our test code to help organize tests.

Now that we have our variables in place, we can act upon the code we're testing: the `CalculatePrice` method. To do this, we must call the method and store the `decimal` value it returns:

```
// Act
decimal result = calculator.CalculatePrice(checkedBags,
    carryOnBags, passengers, isHoliday);
```

Unlike the *arrange* section, the *act* section is very brief, usually only a single line long. This is because the *act* section focuses on the thing you're trying to test. We call the method we're testing on the calculator object that was instantiated earlier and pass it the parameters it needs to do its job.

> **The system under test**
>
> In our example, the `calculator` variable stores the instance of the class we're testing. This is commonly referred to as the **system under test** (**SUT**). Some teams use the `sut` variable name for the object they're about to test.

Here's the cool thing: from our test's perspective, we don't care how it does its job. All we care about is that we give the method a set of inputs and we expect a specific output.

We verify this behavior in our *assert* section by asserting that one or more things are true. If these things turn out *not* to be true, our test will fail. If all of them turn out to be true, the test will pass.

Assertions typically use the `Assert` class to verify that values match their expected value. In our case, the scenario has 2 carry-on bags and no other bags. At $30 per carry-on bag, this should work out to $60, so our test code becomes as follows:

```
// Assert
Assert.Equal(60m, result);
```

The first parameter of the `Equal` method is the expected value. That's the value *you* expect your result to be. You should *not* be calculating this value in code; otherwise, you risk repeating the same potentially bad logic in the code you're testing to begin with!

The second parameter is the actual value, which is almost always the result of calling your method in the *act* section.

Often, developers new to testing expect the first parameter to be the actual value and the second value to be the expected value. However, this is incorrect and will lead to confusing test failures with swapped values.

For example, if the result was 50 and we verified it correctly with `Assert.Equal(60m, result);` as we did earlier, you'd see a failure like this:

```
Assert.Equal() Failure
Expected: 60
Actual:    50
```

This is helpful and tells the developer what went wrong.

If you confused the two parameters and wrote `Assert.Equal(result, 60m);` you'd get this much more confusing message:

```
Assert.Equal() Failure
Expected: 50
Actual:    60
```

This mistake has caused a lot of confusion and hair loss for me in the past. Do yourself a favor and remember that the first parameter is always the value you expect the result to be.

In *Chapter 9, Advanced Unit Testing*, we'll introduce a cleaner way of writing assertions with the **Shouldly** and **FluentAssertions** libraries. For now, remember that the expected value goes first and the actual value goes second.

> **Other Assert methods**
>
> The `Assert` class has more methods than just `Assert.Equal`. You can also use `Assert.True` and `Assert.False` to verify whether a boolean condition is true or false. `Assert.Null` and `Assert.NotNull` can help verify if something is or isn't null. `Assert.Contains` and `Assert.DoesNotContain` will verify the presence or absence of an element in a collection. These are just a few of the methods available through the `Assert` class. For each of these messages, you can also provide a custom failure message to use when an assertion causes your test to fail.

Now that we've added our first unit test, let's talk specifically about what makes a test pass and what makes a test fail.

Understanding tests and exceptions

Every unit test that runs will pass – unless it encounters something that makes it fail.

That failure could be an `Assert` statement not matching the expected value, or it could be your program or test throwing an exception without catching it.

When you investigate how `Assert` methods are implemented, you'll see that they all throw exceptions when their conditions aren't met. When these exceptions are thrown, the test runner catches them and fails the test, displaying the failure message and stack trace appropriately.

This is why an empty test will pass even without any `Assert` statements, and this is why you generally never write a `try/catch` block in your unit tests unless you are explicitly trying to verify some form of exception-handling logic.

Armed with this understanding of what makes a test fail, let's write a second test.

Adding additional test methods

Just like classes can have multiple methods inside of them, test classes can have multiple test methods inside of them. This is because unit tests are just code in every sense of the word. Unit tests live in classes that are ordinary in every regard, except they live in a special project type and individual unit test methods have `[Fact]` just before the method is declared.

Let's illustrate this by adding a test for the next scenario: *The first checked bag costs $40*. Here's what that test would look like:

```
[Fact]
public void FirstCheckedBagShouldCostExpectedAmount() {
  // Arrange
  BaggageCalculator calculator = new();
  int carryOnBags = 0;
  int checkedBags = 1;
  int passengers = 1;
  bool isHoliday = false;
  // Act
  decimal result = calculator.CalculatePrice(checkedBags,
carryOnBags, passengers, isHoliday);
  // Assert
  Assert.Equal(40m, result);
}
```

There are a lot of similarities between this test and the prior one, but the key differences are that the number of carry-on and checked bags has changed to match the new scenario we're testing, and the expected total is now $40 instead of $60.

Each test you write should be different. However, if you start to notice a lot of commonalities between tests, it's probably time to refactor your unit tests.

Refactoring unit tests

Unit tests are code, and like other types of code, they can degrade in quality over time when not given proper respect and proactive refactoring.

Hence, when you see code smells such as duplicated code that appears in most of your tests, it's a sign that your tests need to be refactored.

In this section, we'll explore several ways of refactoring your test code.

Parameterizing tests with Theory and InlineData

When we think about the similarities between our two tests, they only vary based on the values being passed into the method we're testing and the value we expect the result to be.

Thinking about our test method, this is a clear case where it'd be wonderful to have parameters that could go into one test method that could represent multiple unit tests, each testing something slightly different, but with similar code.

As you may recall from earlier, unit tests that use `Fact` cannot have any parameters to them. However, xUnit gives us another attribute called `Theory` that allows us to pass data into the unit test as parameters.

There are multiple different ways of providing data to these parameters, but the most common way is to use an `InlineData` attribute to provide the test parameter data next to the method.

Here's an example of using `Theory` and `InlineData` to test four different scenarios around baggage pricing using the same test code:

```
[Theory]
[InlineData(0, 0, 1, false, 0)]
[InlineData(2, 3, 2, false, 190)]
[InlineData(2, 1, 1, false, 100)]
[InlineData(2, 3, 2, true, 209)]
public void BaggageCalculatorCalculatesCorrectPrice(
  int carryOnBags, int checkedBags, int passengers,
  bool isHoliday, decimal expected) {
    // Arrange
    BaggageCalculator calculator = new();
    // Act
    decimal result = calculator.CalculatePrice
      (checkedBags, carryOnBags, passengers, isHoliday);
    // Assert
    Assert.Equal(expected, result);
}
```

While this is only a single method, each `InlineData` line represents a unique unit test and, as shown in *Figure 6.8*, it will show up as an individual test in the test runner:

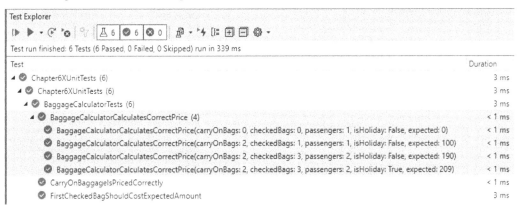

Figure 6.8 – The four theory-based tests in Test Explorer grouped under a single test

Although using `Theory` instead of `Fact` can initially be harder to read, the maintainability advantage is huge. First, parameterized tests have less code duplication. Secondly, if you need to update your tests later, you only need to update a single method instead of the many separate methods if you wrote the same tests using `Fact`.

Initializing test code with constructors and fields

`Theory` isn't the only way to improve your test code. If you find that your tests do a lot of work that is potentially sharable, you can introduce private methods to help organize your test code.

For example, let's say you wanted to test the `FlightScheduler` class from *Chapter 5* and you wanted to start with testing that adding a flight to the schedule via `ScheduleFlight` results in that flight showing up when `GetAllFlights` is called.

To do this, you've created a `FlightSchedulerTests` class and are working on a `ScheduleFlightShouldAddFlight` unit test.

As you begin to write the test, you notice the `ScheduleFlight` method requires an `IFlightInfo` instance, which, in turn, needs several `AirportEvent` objects. These `AirportEvent` objects require their own `Airport` instances.

These dependencies result in you writing a lot of *arrange* code to set up for your test:

```
[Fact]
public void ScheduleFlightShouldAddFlight() {
  // Arrange
  Airport airport1 = new() {
    Code = "DNA",
    Country = "United States",
    Name = "Dotnet Airport"
  };
  Airport airport2 = new() {
    Code = "CSI",
    Country = "United Kingdom",
    Name = "C# International Airport"
  };
  FlightScheduler scheduler = new();
  PassengerFlightInfo flight = new() {
    Id = "CS2024",
    Status = FlightStatus.OnTime,
    Departure = new AirportEvent() {
        Location = airport1,
        Time = DateTime.Now,
    },
    Arrival = new AirportEvent() {
```

```
        Location = airport2,
        Time = DateTime.Now.AddHours(2)
    }
  };
```

This large volume of code isn't necessarily *bad*, but it does distract from the rest of the test method, which performs the scheduling and verifies that the flight was added:

```
  // Act
  scheduler.ScheduleFlight(flight);
  // Assert
  IEnumerable<IFlightInfo> result =
    scheduler.GetAllFlights();
  Assert.NotNull(result);
  Assert.Contains(flight, result);
}
```

While a lengthy *arrange* section isn't the end of the world, other tests may likely want to create their own PassengerFlightInfo, Airport, or AirportEvent, which would lead to very similar code showing up between tests.

To help improve the readability of our arrange method, we can introduce fields for the two airports and set them up in the constructor:

```
public class FlightSchedulerTests {
  private readonly Airport _airport1;
  private readonly Airport _airport2;
  public FlightSchedulerTests() {
    _airport1 = new() {
        Code = "DNA",
        Country = "United States",
        Name = "Dotnet Airport"
    };
    _airport2 = new() {
        Code = "CSI",
        Country = "United Kingdom",
        Name = "C# International Airport"
    };
  }
```

When xUnit runs your test code, it will instantiate the FlightSchedulerTests class once for every unit test in that class. This means that any logic in the constructor or field initializers will run whenever any test in that class is run.

This lets us simplify the *arrange* section of our test considerably:

```
// Arrange
FlightScheduler scheduler = new();
PassengerFlightInfo flight = new() {
    Id = "CS2024",
    Status = FlightStatus.OnTime,
    Departure = new AirportEvent() {
        Location = _airport1,
        Time = DateTime.Now
    },
    Arrival = new AirportEvent() {
        Location = _airport2,
        Time = DateTime.Now.AddHours(2)
    }
};
```

This process can be repeated as needed. For example, if you wanted to reuse the same `PassengerFlightInfo` between tests, you could add a `_flight` field and initialize it in the constructor as well.

The refactoring process isn't about minimizing the size of the *arrange* section; it's about keeping code duplication low while keeping the important aspects of your test visible to other developers reading your code.

Sharing test code with methods

Another technique you can use to keep your code focused is to extract reusable methods from your test code to help accomplish common *arrange* tasks.

For example, if you wanted to test that removing a flight correctly removes the flight from the scheduler, you'd need a test that looks a lot like the test we just covered.

When you think about it, both tests don't care much about the specifics of the flight being added – they care that when a flight is scheduled, it appears in the list of flights and that when a flight is removed, it should no longer be included.

To accomplish this, we can extract a method to create our `Flight` object. This method could take in a flight identifier and return the created flight, as shown here:

```
private PassengerFlightInfo CreateFlight(string id)
    => new() {
        Status = FlightStatus.OnTime,
        Id = id,
        Departure = new AirportEvent() {
```

```
    Location = _airport1,
    Time = DateTime.Now
  },
  Arrival = new AirportEvent() {
    Location = _airport2,
    Time = DateTime.Now.AddHours(2)
  }
};
```

Our prior test can now call this method to create its flight:

```
[Fact]
public void ScheduleFlightShouldAddFlight() {
  // Arrange
  FlightScheduler scheduler = new();
  PassengerFlightInfo flight = CreateFlight("CS2024");
  // Act
  scheduler.ScheduleFlight(flight);
  // Assert
  IEnumerable<IFlightInfo> result =
    scheduler.GetAllFlights();
  Assert.NotNull(result);
  Assert.Contains(flight, result);
}
```

See how much more focused this method is? You can quickly read it and get the intent of the test without having to focus on all the mechanics needed to create the flight.

> **Testing void methods**
>
> One question I often encounter is "How do you test void methods since they don't return anything?" Most of the time, when you write tests, you test the return value of a method, but with void methods, you test the side effects of that method. This ScheduleFlight test is an example of how a void method can be tested. In our case, the side effect of scheduling a flight *should* be that the flight is present later when we're getting all the flights from the scheduler.

Now, let's look at the flight removal test, which uses the same method:

```
[Fact]
public void RemoveShouldRemoveFlight() {
  // Arrange
  FlightScheduler scheduler = new();
  PassengerFlightInfo flight = CreateFlight("CS2024");
  scheduler.ScheduleFlight(flight);
```

```
  // Act
  scheduler.RemoveFlight(flight);
  // Assert
  IEnumerable<IFlightInfo> result =
    scheduler.GetAllFlights();
  Assert.NotNull(result);
  Assert.DoesNotContain(flight, result);
}
```

This method is focused on the task of scheduling a flight and then removing it, and then verifying that the flight is no longer on the list of flights. If adding and removing a flight doesn't remove it from the list of flights, that would be a bug and the test would fail.

> **Sharing methods between test classes**
>
> If you find that many of your test classes would benefit from the same "helper" methods, such as `CreateFlight`, you may want to consider moving these helpers to a static class in your test project. This pattern is sometimes referred to as the **ObjectMother** or Builder pattern and is described further in the *Further reading* section.
>
> Alternatively, you could introduce a base testing class, move your shared methods to that class, and then have your tests inherit from that class. Test classes and test projects are just like normal code and many of the refactoring tricks we used in part 1 of this book will help improve your tests as well.

Before we close out this chapter with a discussion on adopting a testing mindset, let's briefly look at a pair of other popular C# testing frameworks.

Exploring other testing frameworks

Beyond xUnit, the next most popular testing frameworks are **NUnit** and **MSTest**.

These two frameworks operate in very similar ways to xUnit but with slight differences in the syntax you use to declare a unit test.

I've had the opportunity to program professionally and recreationally in all three major testing frameworks and I can tell you that these differences are largely cosmetic. That said, you will find that certain frameworks have specific features that might not be present in the others.

Testing with NUnit

Of the three testing frameworks, NUnit's syntax is my favorite because it uses the `Test` name for both unit tests that require no parameters (equivalent to an xUnit `Fact`) and those that do (equivalent to an xUnit `Theory`).

Here's a parameterized test that verifies the `Load` method on `PassengerFlightInfo`:

```
public class PassengerFlightTests {
    [TestCase(6)]
    public void AddPassengerShouldAdd(int passengers) {
        // Arrange
        PassengerFlightInfo flight = new();
        // Act
        flight.Load(passengers);
        // Assert
        int actual = flight.Passengers;
        Assert.AreEqual(passengers, actual);
        Assert.That(actual, Is.EqualTo(passengers));
    }
}
```

In `NUnit`, Test and `TestCase` replace Theory and `InlineData`. If this test were not parameterized, `TestCase` would become `Test`.

The assert section of this test is a little different. The first thing to note is that NUnit's assertion method is `Assert.AreEqual` instead of `Assert.Equal`. While this is a minor difference, I find that the code reads a bit better.

Below the `Assert.AreEqual` line is the `Assert.That` line. This is NUnit's newer constraint model of unit tests; it reads a bit more fluently and reduces your chances of confusing parameters like the expected and actual values on an assertion. Both ways of writing NUnit tests are valid and work fine.

One final note: in NUnit, all tests in a test class share the same class instance. This means that values stored in fields or properties on your tests will be shared by all tests in that test class. This is different from xUnit which creates a new test class instance for each test that runs.

With NUnit explored, let's look at MSTest.

Testing with MSTest

MSTest's official name was **Visual Studio Unit Testing Framework**, but the framework has come to be known as **MSTest** throughout the community and even throughout Microsoft's internal documentation.

> MSTest V2
>
> While MSTest had a poor reputation for nearly a decade due to a lack of feature parity between it and NUnit and xUnit, Microsoft revised MSTest in 2016, calling it **MSTest V2** and bringing many improvements to the framework to the point where it is now on par with its competitors.

Like NUnit, MSTest uses a single `TestMethod` attribute to mark both parameterized and unparameterized unit tests. However, unlike both NUnit and xUnit, MSTest also requires a `TestClass` attribute on the class itself to make the individual tests discoverable. This is something to watch out for when writing tests in MSTest as it's another thing you can miss to make your tests not show up in the test runner.

Let's look at a sample parameterized test in MSTest that verifies the `FullName` property of the `Passenger` class from our `BoardingProcessor` class from *Chapter 3*:

```
[TestClass]
public class PassengerTests {
  [TestMethod]
  [DataRow("Calvin", "Allen", "Calvin Allen")]
  [DataRow("Matthew", "Groves", "Matthew Groves")]
  [DataRow("Sam", "Gomez", "Sam Gomez")]
  [DataRow("Brad", "Knowles", "Brad Knowles")]
  public void PassengerNameShouldBeCorrect(string first,
    string last, string expected) {
    // Arrange
    Passenger passenger = new() {
      FirstName = first,
      LastName = last,
    };
    // Act
    string fullName = passenger.FullName;
    // Assert
    Assert.AreEqual(expected, fullName);
  }
}
```

Here, this parameterized test evaluates the name of each of this book's technical reviewers from `DataRow`, just like `InlineData` does in xUnit or `TestCase` does in NUnit.

While the MSTest syntax is different, there are many similarities between it and the other test frameworks.

The major differences between MSTest and NUnit are the inclusion of the `TestClass` attribute and the names `TestMethod` and `DataRow` instead of `Test` and `TestCase`, respectively. Even the naming of the `Assert.AreEqual` methods are identical between the two frameworks.

Ultimately, these three testing frameworks are all very similar and serve a powerful role in your goal of high-quality software. I've found that I can work effectively in any of the three frameworks. While I tend to prefer NUnit's syntax, I use xUnit in new projects because xUnit has largely become the community standard.

My recommendation is to pick the library whose syntax you like the most and use that for your projects and focus your efforts on writing good tests and adopting a testing mindset.

Adopting a testing mindset

Let's take a step back and talk about why a book on refactoring features an entire series of chapters around testing. The reason is that code that needs to be refactored is often a bit more volatile and tends to break more easily when changed. Since the art of refactoring is about changing the form of the software without changing its behavior, introducing bugs when refactoring is undesirable and unacceptable.

This is where tests come in. Tests give you the confidence you and your team need to be able to improve your code. Your legacy code may or may not have tests around it already, so the responsibility and necessity of ensuring good tests are present falls to you before you perform any testing work.

This requires you to adopt a testing mindset. This phrase refers to thinking about tests at the *beginning* of the development process as a vital component of software development and refactoring, not as an afterthought.

While we'll explore this concept at length in the next chapter as we discuss **test-driven development**, let's touch on a few considerations that will help you be successful with tests in your organization and adopt a testing mindset.

Incorporating testing into your workflow

Testing should be a standard part of your everyday life as a software engineer.

This means that you should think about testing whenever you make any change to a system, whether the change is a new feature, fixing a bug, or paying down technical debt through refactoring.

This requires a shift of mentality from seeing tests as tedious or something you ought to do to thinking of tests as things that have intrinsic value to the codebase and even to the larger organization. This is because tests provide value through their role as a sort of "living documentation" of your codebase, their ability to provide a safety net against certain types of bugs in the future, and their ability to give you and the business confidence in the code you're writing.

You will, of course, bump into pieces of software that are significantly harder to test. These might be pieces of code working with the user interface or they might be pieces of code with very strong dependencies to other systems.

We'll touch more on dependencies later in this section and again in *Chapters 8* and *9*, but testing the user interface is typically done with specialized tools and libraries and varies based on whether you are testing a web, desktop, or mobile application. As a result, user interface testing is outside the scope of this book. However, isolating dependencies is usually a strong part of that process.

Isolating dependencies

When we talk about isolating dependencies, this means that when we test a piece of code, testing it shouldn't alter anything else.

For example, when we're trying to verify that scheduling a flight adds the flight to the list of flights in the system, we don't want the system to send an email with a flight confirmation every time we run our unit test!

Such an example might look like this:

```
public class FlightScheduler {
  private readonly EmailClient _email = new();
  public void ScheduleFlight(Flight flight) {
      // other logic omitted...
      _email.SendMessage($"Flight {flight.Id} confirmed");
  }
}
```

Here, `FlightScheduler` has an `EmailClient` class and calls `SendMessage` on the client every time a flight is scheduled. This is a strong dependency from `FlightScheduler` to the `EmailClient` class and will result in an undesirable side effect of sending emails when this code is tested.

Side effects such as sending emails or interacting with the filesystem or a database are often undesirable in unit tests, as we'll discuss shortly.

While it's good for systems to be able to do these things, we want to test our units of code in isolation without them having side effects we don't like. We can work around this via a process called **dependency injection**, where a class is no longer responsible for creating the dependencies it needs but gets them from others.

A more testable version of `FlightScheduler` would look like this:

```
public class FlightScheduler {
  private readonly IEmailClient _email;
  public FlightScheduler(IEmailClient email) {
    _email = email;
  }
  public void ScheduleFlight(Flight flight) {
      // other logic omitted...
      _email.SendMessage($"Flight {flight.Id} confirmed");
  }
}
```

Here, the dependency on the `EmailClient` class is injected into this class in its constructor and a new `IEmailClient` interface is used so that we can use a different implementation of this interface for testing. This test-specific version wouldn't have the negative side effect of sending emails, making it more acceptable.

Dependency injection and its related terms, **inversion of control** and **dependency inversion**, are complex topics that take some time to grasp. So, we'll revisit them in *Chapter 8*, *Avoiding Code Anti-Patterns with SOLID*. Additionally, experienced testers may be crying out that a mocking framework such as Moq or NSubstitute can help with some of these concerns. We'll cover these libraries in *Chapter 7*.

For now, let's move on to talking about other factors that constitute good and bad tests.

Evaluating good and bad tests

Good unit tests should be as follows:

- **Fast to run**: If tests take minutes to run, developers won't run them.

- **Reliable and repeatable**: Tests shouldn't randomly fail or pass or fail based on the day of the week, time of day, or which other tests were run earlier.

- **Independent from one another**: One test should never impact another test passing or failing and tests shouldn't need to be run in a certain order.

- **Isolated**: They should be kept independent of dependencies such as databases, files on disk, cloud resources, or external APIs. Not only do these things slow down your tests but if we're testing these interactions, that's an *integration test*, not a unit test.

- **Readable**: Tests serve as examples of how to interact with your classes. Additionally, when a test fails, its failure should be easy to understand.

- **Portable**: Tests shouldn't require significant machine setup and should be runnable on any developer's machine or another machine as part of a **continuous integration/continuous delivery (CI/CD)** pipeline.

In contrast, bad tests take time to run, are "flaky" and randomly fail, cannot be run in parallel or out of order, are difficult to understand regarding what they're testing or why, and require a lot of manual configuration to run reliably.

In general, you want to favor many small unit tests that are fast to run, easy to understand, and reliable over more ambitious tests that test too many things at once, leading to slow tests that lead to unclear and unreliable test failures.

Thoughts on code coverage

I can't talk about unit testing without introducing **code coverage**. Code coverage is the lines of code that run as part of any unit test. If a test causes the line of code to run, it is considered covered; otherwise, it is considered not covered.

Several tools calculate code coverage, including Visual Studio Enterprise and JetBrains ReSharper, which we talked about briefly in *Chapter 2*. If you have Visual Studio Enterprise, you can calculate code coverage by selecting the **Test** menu and then **Analyze Code Coverage for All Tests**. This will show the lines of code that are covered and not covered by unit tests, as shown in *Figure 6.9*:

Hierarchy	Covered (Blocks)	Not Covered (Blocks)	Covered (Lines)	Partially Covered (Lines)	Not Covered (Lines) ▼
Admin_DEEP-THOUGHT 2023-07-23 16_15_36.coverage	185	510	151	0	260
chapter6.dll	117	510	70	0	260
{ } Packt.CloudySkiesAir.Chapter6.Flight.Boarding	8	108	5	0	59
{ } Packt.CloudySkiesAir.Chapter6.Flight	0	81	0	0	58
{ } Packt.CloudySkiesAir.Chapter6.Flight.Scheduling	24	137	19	0	51
{ } Packt.CloudySkiesAir.Chapter6.Flight.Scheduling.Search	0	103	0	0	49
{ } Packt.CloudySkiesAir.Chapter6.Flight.Scheduling.Flights	37	71	15	0	33
{ } Packt.CloudySkiesAir.Chapter6.Flight.Baggage	48	5	31	0	4
{ } Packt.CloudySkiesAir.Chapter6	0	2	0	0	3
{ } Packt.CloudySkiesAir.Chapter6.Helpers	0	3	0	0	3

Figure 6.9 – Overview of Code Coverage Results in Visual Studio Enterprise

These coverage results will highlight any lines that are not covered by unit tests, such as the code of the `Unload` method in `PassengerFlightInfo`, as shown in *Figure 6.10*:

```
     6 references | Matt Eland. 5 days ago | 1 author. 1 change
 3   public class PassengerFlightInfo : FlightInfoBase {
 4       private int _passengers;
         4 references | ● 1/1 passing | Matt Eland. 5 days ago | 1 author. 1 change
 5       public int Passengers {
 6           get => _passengers;
 7           private set => _passengers = value;
 8       }
 9
         1 reference | ● 1/1 passing | Matt Eland. 5 days ago | 1 author. 1 change
10       public void Load(int passengers) =>
11           Passengers = passengers;
12
         0 references | Matt Eland. 5 days ago | 1 author. 1 change
13       public void Unload() =>
14           Passengers = 0;
15
         5 references | Matt Eland. 5 days ago | 1 author. 1 change
16       public override string BuildFlightIdentifier() =>
17           base.BuildFlightIdentifier() +
18           $" carrying {Passengers} people";
19   }
```

Figure 6.10 – Covered lines are highlighted in blue, while lines without tests are highlighted in red (line 14)

Code coverage is one of those topics that can be divisive. On the one hand, code coverage gives you a metric that shows how much of your code is executed by any test. This gives you a meaningful way of measuring the extent of your unit testing safety net.

However, code coverage can be deceptive. Just running a line of code does not mean that the effects of that line are verified by a unit test. This can lead to a false sense of security around your unit tests.

Additionally, when organizations prioritize work that increases the code coverage percentage or requires a certain minimum percentage of code coverage for new work, this can lead to tests that focus on the less risky aspects of your software system. For example, do you need to write a unit test to verify code that throws an `ArgumentNullException` error when a null value is passed to a method, or is your time better spent elsewhere?

Often, the most critical areas of your application may already appear to be covered by your code coverage metrics, but no tests verify that these lines work correctly.

My personal feeling is that code coverage is one of many useful metrics to monitor but should not be used to significantly drive the behavior of your development teams.

See the *Further reading* section for more information on code coverage and how to get started calculating it.

We'll explore other metrics in *Chapter 12, Code Analysis in Visual Studio*, but for now, let's conclude this chapter with some closing thoughts on unit testing.

Summary

Unit testing is a powerful way to verify that refactoring code does not introduce bugs, document your classes, and prevent bugs from occurring in the future.

Unit tests are code that tests other code. In .NET, project unit tests are usually performed with xUnit, NUnit, or MSTest. Each testing framework provides assertions that verify that code behaves correctly or fails a test if the actual value doesn't match the expected value.

When we write unit tests, we typically structure our tests in the *arrange*/*act*/*assert* pattern, which sets up the thing being tested in the *arrange* step, does a single action in the *act* step, and verifies the correctness of the action's result in the *assert* step.

In the next chapter, we'll explore testing more with test-driven development.

Questions

Answer the following questions to test your knowledge of this chapter:

1. Which unit testing framework syntax do you like the most?
2. What are the most complex parts of your application? Are they tested?
3. How would you test a method that calculates the credit score of an applicant?
4. How do you test a `void` method?
5. What things can you do to help test code stay clean and readable?

Further reading

You can find more information about the materials discussed in this chapter by checking out the following resources:

- *Types of Tests*: https://learn.microsoft.com/en-us/dotnet/core/testing/

- *Visual Studio Test Explorer*: https://learn.microsoft.com/en-us/visualstudio/test/run-unit-tests-with-test-explorer

- *xUnit*: https://xunit.net/

- *NUnit*: https://nunit.org/

- *MSTest*: https://learn.microsoft.com/en-us/dotnet/core/testing/unit-testing-with-mstest

- *The ObjectMother Pattern*: https://www.martinfowler.com/bliki/ObjectMother.html

- *Code Coverage*: https://learn.microsoft.com/en-us/visualstudio/test/using-code-coverage-to-determine-how-much-code-is-being-tested

7

Test-Driven Development

Let's continue our discussion of testing and ensuring the quality of our software processes by going in-depth with Test-Driven Development.

While this is a book about refactoring and Test-Driven Development is primarily intended for future development and bug fixing, it has some key lessons to teach us in software quality and the same tools Visual Studio provides to support Test-Driven Development can help immensely in the refactoring process.

In this chapter, we'll cover the following main topics:

- What is Test-Driven Development?
- Test-Driven Development with Visual Studio
- When to use Test-Driven Development

Technical requirements

The starting code for this chapter is available from GitHub at `https://github.com/PacktPublishing/Refactoring-with-CSharp` in the `Chapter07/Ch7BeginningCode` folder.

What is Test-Driven Development?

Test-driven Development (TDD) is the process of writing your tests *before* you write your code for a new feature or to implement a new fix.

Under TDD, you first write a test for the feature you're trying to implement or a test to reproduce the bug you're about to fix. You do this in the most ideal way possible, which may even involve classes or methods that don't exist at the start of your test.

Next, you do the minimum amount of work needed to make your code successfully compile. This isn't to say that it runs perfectly or does the thing it is trying to do, in fact, you're trying to start out with a red failing test that indicates your feature or fix doesn't work.

This makes sense when you consider that at this point you haven't implemented the new feature or made the fix to the code. So, the test *should* be a failing test.

Next, you write the minimum amount of code required to make your test pass. In this step, you are doing what you need to do to meet the specific requirement you are trying to address. Once you are finished, your test should turn into a green passing test.

After that, you refactor the code you added to implement your feature or fix and you refactor your test code as well; taking care to continue to run your unit tests to ensure you haven't broken anything.

Once you're satisfied with the state of your new code and your test, you look at the next requirement on the current work item you're working on, write a test for that, and repeat the process until you have met all requirements. This process is illustrated in *Figure 7.1*:

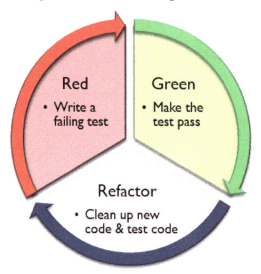

Figure 7.1 – The Test-Driven Development Cycle

Because you start with a failing red test, move on to a green passing test, and then refactor your code before starting again with a new requirement, TDD is sometimes referred to as **Red / Green / Refactor**.

This process has a few key benefits:

- You can be confident your code addresses the problem by starting with a test.
- Code written in this way is guaranteed to be covered by your tests.
- When you start with how your code should be called by others, it tends to lead to more intuitive class designs for others to use later.

This process, and its results, make a lot more sense with a practical example. So, let's jump into some code and implement a new feature for Cloudy Skies Airlines.

Test-Driven Development with Visual Studio

We're starting this chapter with a nearly empty console project and a supporting xUnit test project that has already been linked to the main project as shown in *Chapter 6*. The structure of this project can be seen in *Figure 7.2*:

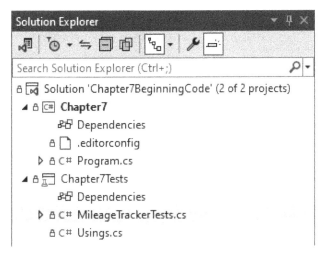

Figure 7.2 – Solution Explorer showing only a few files

Over the course of the rest of this section, we're going to add a new class to track frequent flier miles for Cloudy Skies Airlines.

The requirements we'll be addressing (in order) are:

- When a new Frequent Flier Account is created it should start with a starting balance of 100 miles.
- You should be able to add miles to the frequent flier account.
- You should be able to mark miles as redeemed as long as this wouldn't result in a negative balance.

These are not complex requirements, but they should serve as a starting point for briefly exploring TDD.

We'll start with the starting balance requirement.

Setting the starting balance

Our first requirement involves the account starting with 100 miles already registered.

Under the guidance of TDD, we should start with a failing test. Thankfully, we already have a `MilesTrackerTests.cs` file, so that gives us a good place to start.

However, we have no classes in the `Chapter7` project to represent the mileage tracker, which poses a problem for us in writing the arrange section of our first test.

While there's a temptation to "cheat" a bit by creating the class now, let's follow a strictly TDD approach and write the test code in the way we'd prefer to interact with the class, knowing that the class doesn't exist yet and this will cause some compiler errors for us in a moment.

Such a test might look like this:

```
[Fact]
public void NewAccountShouldHaveStartingBalance() {
  // Arrange
  int expectedMiles = 100;
  // Act
  MileageTracker tracker = new();
  // Assert
  Assert.Equal(expectedMiles, tracker.Balance);
}
```

This test sets an expected starting mileage variable, tries to instantiate a `MileageTracker`, and then asserts that the `Balance` property on this new tracker should be the expected amount.

This is a simple, concise, and readable test with a couple of tiny problems: `MileageTracker` and its `Balance` property don't exist in our code yet, meaning our code won't compile.

Generating classes

These compiler issues when creating new classes and new properties are normal and to be expected when coding under TDD. Thankfully Visual Studio has a Quick Actions refactoring available for us.

Select the `MileageTracker` in your act section and open the Quick Actions menu. From there note the various options to generate this Type as shown in *Figure 7.2*:

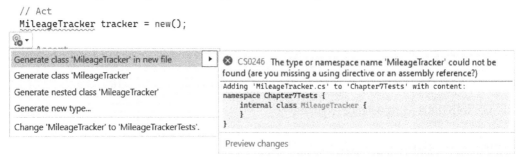

Figure 7.3 – Quick Actions to generate a new Type

These options, as shown here, are great, but most of them would create the new class inside the test project which is not what we want. Since we want to customize the new type being created, select **Generate new type…**

This will open the **Generate Type** dialog allowing you to select the type, name, and location of the new type being generated. Change the **Project** to *Chapter7* and choose to create a new file as shown in *Figure 7.4*:

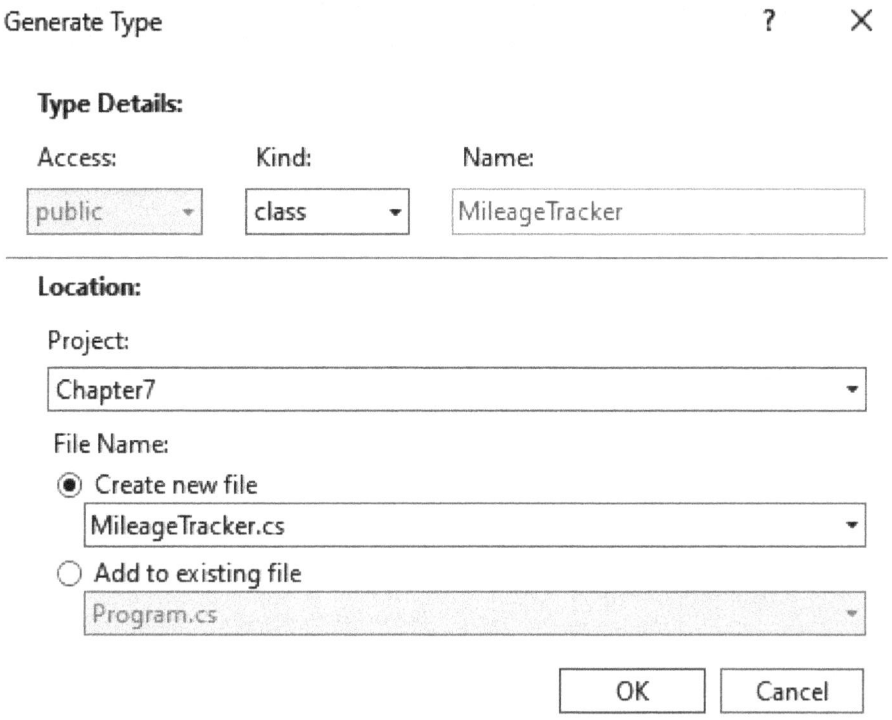

Figure 7.4 – Generating a new class in the Chapter7 project

Next, click **OK** and Visual Studio will generate this class and add a `MileageTracker.cs` file to the main project.

This class is boring at present with nothing in it, but we'll add to it in a moment as we work on the next compiler error.

Generating members

Going back to our test, the *act* section now has no issues, but we still have a compiler error on the reference to `Balance` in the *Assert* section as shown in *Figure 7.5*:

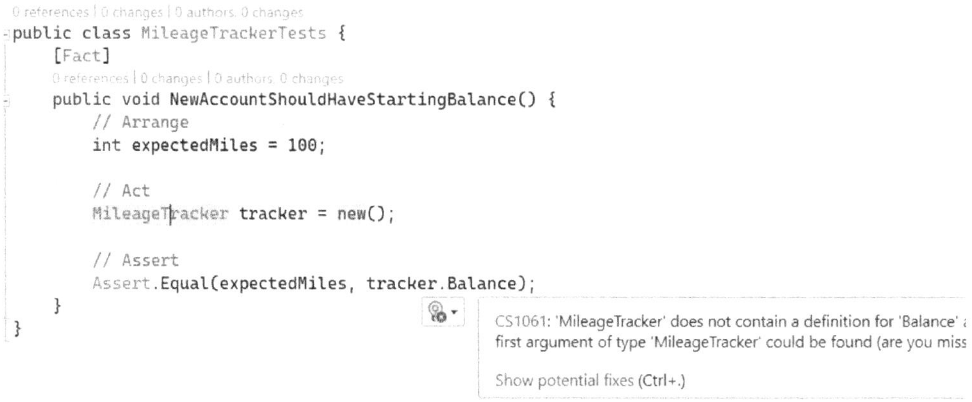

```
0 references | 0 changes | 0 authors, 0 changes
public class MileageTrackerTests {
    [Fact]
    0 references | 0 changes | 0 authors, 0 changes
    public void NewAccountShouldHaveStartingBalance() {
        // Arrange
        int expectedMiles = 100;

        // Act
        MileageTracker tracker = new();

        // Assert
        Assert.Equal(expectedMiles, tracker.Balance);
    }
}
```

CS1061: 'MileageTracker' does not contain a definition for 'Balance' ;
first argument of type 'MileageTracker' could be found (are you miss

Show potential fixes (Ctrl+.)

Figure 7.5 – The C# Compiler pointing out that MileageTracker has Balance property

Thankfully, Visual Studio gives us tools to generate properties. Let's do that now so our code will at least compile.

Select **Balance** and then open the **Quick Actions** menu and choose **Generate property 'Balance'** as shown in *Figure 7.6*:

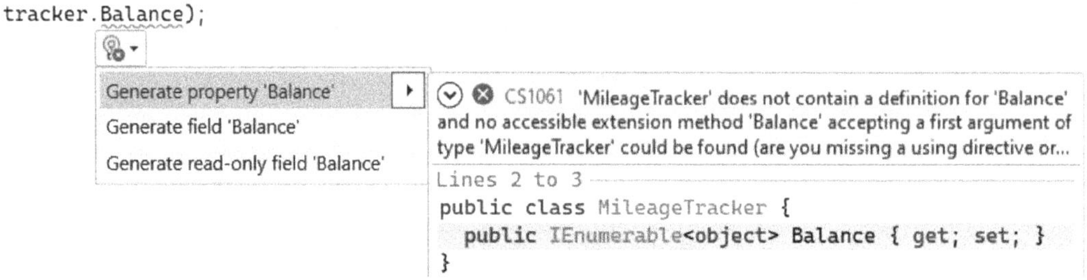

```
tracker.Balance);
```

Generate property 'Balance'
Generate field 'Balance'
Generate read-only field 'Balance'

CS1061 'MileageTracker' does not contain a definition for 'Balance'
and no accessible extension method 'Balance' accepting a first argument of
type 'MileageTracker' could be found (are you missing a using directive or...

```
Lines 2 to 3
public class MileageTracker {
    public IEnumerable<object> Balance { get; set; }
}
```

Figure 7.6 – Generating a new property

Doing so causes Balance to be defined. If you hold down *Ctrl* and click on `Balance`, it will navigate you to `MileageTracker.cs` and we'll see how the class is defined:

```
public class MileageTracker {
  public IEnumerable<object> Balance { get; set; }
}
```

Here, Visual Studio had to guess what property type `Balance` was and it guessed horribly wrong. Since this will otherwise cause compiler errors, change `Balance` to an `int`:

```
public class MileageTracker {
  public int Balance { get; set; }
}
```

With that change, the code should now compile, but let's make one more change before we run our tests.

Remember that TDD requires us to write the minimum amount of code to do what we're trying to do? Technically, Visual Studio has violated this principle by generating both a getter and a setter for our Balance property. In this test, we only need to get the `Balance` and not set it via this property. So, let's protect that `Balance` by removing the setter:

```
public class MileageTracker {
    public int Balance { get; }
}
```

With this bit of added encapsulation in hand and our code compiling, let's run our test. When you do so, you should see the test fail stating that it expected `Balance` to be 100 but it actually was 0 as shown in *Figure 7.7*:

Figure 7.7 – Our first failing test

Under TDD, this is exactly what we'd want. We did the minimum amount of work to get an ideal test to compile, and that test failed because we hadn't fully implemented the feature.

Moving from red to green and onto refactoring

Let's implement the feature now.

While we know that our `MileageTracker` will need some additional things later, let's implement this feature by writing the minimum amount of code possible:

```
public class MileageTracker {
    public int Balance { get; } = 100;
}
```

This now defaults new `MileageTracker` instances to have a starting balance of 100, which meets our needs and causes our test to turn green and pass when re-run.

With a green test, we now look for opportunities to refactor. While our test code is minimal, the `MileageTracker` does have a **magic number** in it. Magic numbers are **code smells** that represent some sort of undocumented business or technical requirement.

Let's fix it by introducing a constant:

```
public class MileageTracker {
    private const int SignUpBonus = 100;
    public int Balance { get; } = SignUpBonus;
}
```

This code is now easier for others to understand, removing the code smell.

> **Naming**
>
> Naming things in software engineering is hard. It's possible the name that occurred to you for this class or the `SignUpBonus` const I introduced was different than the names I picked. That's fine. What's most important about a name is that it *communicates intent* to other developers and is not confused with something else in the system. While the name `StartingBalance` would have been fine for my const, I chose `SignUpBonus` because I thought it more clearly documented the business case for the starting balance.

Running the tests again results in a green passing test once more and there are no other obvious targets for refactoring, so we move on to the next requirement.

Adding miles and generating methods

Our next requirement is *You should be able to add miles to the frequent flier account.*

Let's go back to our tests and add a new test for this requirement. Here we'll again choose the most intuitive syntax and then make the code compile and test pass later:

```
[Fact]
public void AddMileageShouldIncreaseBalance() {
  // Arrange
  MileageTracker tracker = new();
  // Act
  tracker.AddMiles(50);
  // Assert
  Assert.Equal(150, tracker.Balance);
}
```

This test instantiates a `MileageTracker`, then tries to add 50 miles using a not-yet-created `AddMiles` method before verifying that the balance is 150 (100 starting miles plus the 50 we just added).

Of course, there is no `AddMiles` method in `MileageTracker`. Let's add one by selecting `AddMiles` and then choosing **Generate method 'AddMiles'** from the **Quick Actions** menu as shown in *Figure 7.8*:

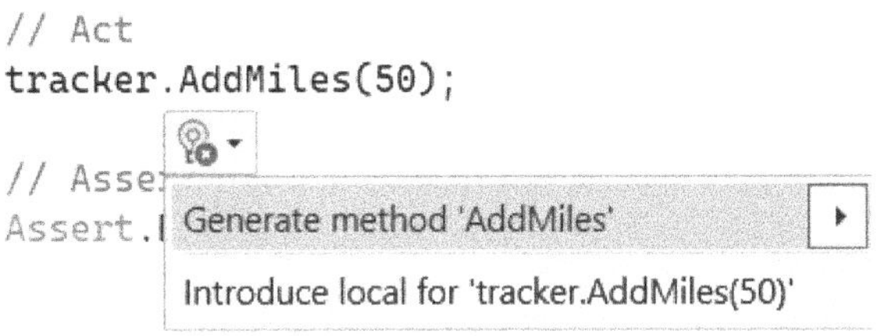

```
// Act
tracker.AddMiles(50);
```

Figure 7.8 – Adding a new method

Adding this method causes it to be created with the following implementation:

```
public void AddMiles(int v) {
    throw new NotImplementedException();
}
```

Obviously, this is not what the method should do. However, let's follow strict TDD and move through the motions one step at a time.

Since our code now compiles, we can run the test and verify that it fails as expected.

Once we're confident we have a test that can detect failing code we write only the minimum amount of code required to get the test to pass. This ensures that our tests are sufficient for finding actual problems with the code later.

A passing implementation of AddMiles might look like this:

```
public class MileageTracker {
    private const int SignUpBonus = 100;
    public int Balance { get; set; } = SignUpBonus;
    public void AddMiles(int miles) {
      Balance += miles;
    }
  }
}
```

As you can see, the code now compiles and results in green tests. This means we should move on to refactoring our code as needed.

The test code is still clean and the only refactoring I can see to apply here might be to use the expression-bodied members that we covered in *Chapter 4*. However, I'm going to leave the code in its current form as the class is still very minimal.

With that requirement complete, let's move on to our final requirement around redeeming miles.

Redeeming miles and refactoring tests

Our final requirement is *You should be able to mark miles as redeemed if this wouldn't cause a negative balance*. This is a bit more complex than the last requirement as it has a condition attached to it.

As we did before, let's start by writing a test:

```
[Fact]
public void RedeemMileageShouldDecreaseBalance() {
    // Arrange
    MileageTracker tracker = new();
    tracker.AddMiles(900);
    // Act
    tracker.RedeemMiles(250);
    // Assert
    Assert.Equal(750, tracker.Balance);
}
```

This test should look very similar to our `AddMiles` test earlier, except it calls out to a new `RedeemMiles` method.

Let's use the *generate method* refactoring shown earlier to generate that empty `RedeemMiles` method and allow the code to compile.

This should result in a red failing test as shown in *Figure 7.9* due to the default `throw new NotImplementedException` line in that method:

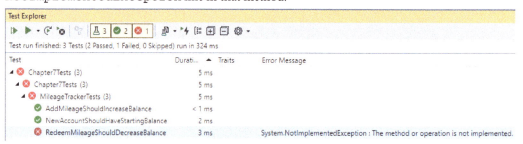

Figure 7.9 – The remove mileage test failing due to an Exception being thrown

However, moving from red to green is again trivial here by mirroring what we did for `AddMiles`:

```
public class MileageTracker {
    private const int SignUpBonus = 100;
    public int Balance { get; set; } = SignUpBonus;
    public void AddMiles(int miles) {
      Balance += miles;
    }
    public void RedeemMiles(int miles) {
```

```
      Balance -= miles;
    }
  }
}
```

This gets our test to pass and so we move on to looking for refactoring options. This code isn't bad, so we continue to look for the next requirement.

In this case, we haven't fully met the requirement we were trying to solve because we don't cover trying to redeem more miles than are in an account. Let's write a new test for that scenario:

```
[Fact]
public void RedeemMileageShouldPreventNegativeBalance() {
    // Arrange
    MileageTracker tracker = new();
    int startingBalance = tracker.Balance;
    // Act
    tracker.RedeemMiles(2500);
    // Assert
    Assert.Equal(startingBalance, tracker.Balance);
}
```

This test creates an account and takes note of its starting balance. The test then attempts to withdraw more miles than accounts start with and verifies that the ending balance is equal to the starting balance.

This doesn't rely on any new methods in the tracker. As a result, our code compiles without changes. However, running this test results in a failure stating that balance was expected to be 100 but was -2400 instead.

With a red test in hand, let's modify the RedeemMiles method to make the test green:

```
public void RedeemMiles(int miles) {
  if (Balance >= miles) {
    Balance -= miles;
  }
}
```

Now, we check to make sure we have enough miles to fulfill the request and only reduce the mileage if that condition is met.

Running the tests again results in a full set of passing tests as shown in *Figure 7.10*:

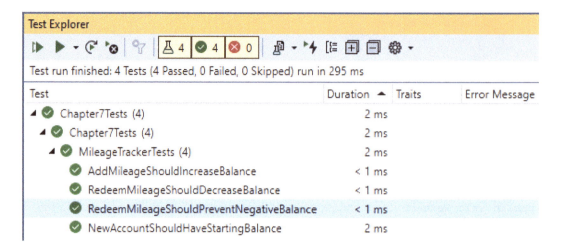

Figure 7.10 – Four passing tests around mileage

With a passing test in hand, we now look at refactoring. Since the `MileageTracker` is succinct and clear, we'll move on to looking at our tests.

> **What about exceptions?**
>
> Right now `RedeemMiles` will silently fail if you request more miles than desired, which might raise some alarm bells for you as a developer. In a real-world application, you'd probably want this method to either return a bool indicating if the redemption was successful or to throw an exception if the redemption was not possible. Both of these scenarios could be handled in TDD as additional requirements to implement, such as "If we try to redeem more miles than possible, an `InvalidOperationException` should be thrown".

Looking at our tests, we do see that our `RemoveMileageShouldDecreaseBalance` and `RemoveMileageShouldPreventNegativeBalance` do similar things.

Due to the duplication between tests, we should combine these into a `Theory` with `InlineData` lines representing individual test cases. This would look something like the following:

```
[Theory]
[InlineData(900, 250, 750)]
[InlineData(0, 2500, 100)]
public void RedeemMileageShouldResultInCorrectBalance(
    int addAmount, int redeemAmount, int expectedBalance) {
      // Arrange
      MileageTracker tracker = new();
      tracker.AddMiles(addAmount);
      // Act
```

```
        tracker.RedeemMiles(redeemAmount);
        // Assert
        Assert.Equal(expectedBalance, tracker.Balance);
    }
```

This form allows many tests to add an initial amount to the balance, redeem some number of miles, and then verify the result matches the expected balance. This also lets us easily add new scenarios as we identify them.

However, the name of the method is less meaningful than the more specific names we could use with individual Fact tests.

With passing tests and refactoring complete, we now move on to either the next requirement in this feature or the next work item in our queue. Let's close the chapter by talking about TDD at a high level and when it's right to use in your projects.

When to use Test-Driven Development

TDD is not always a good match for every task. Some tasks, such as highly visual user interface design may not fit into the TDD workflow very well, while others such as fixing an error observed in production or adding a new special case to a calculation are almost ideal for TDD.

Using TDD results in code that is generally easier to understand, has perfect or near-perfect code coverage on tests, and encourages refactoring along the way.

Many developers follow TDD but don't follow it as strictly as outlined in this chapter. For example, instead of just generating a method, they may go ahead and implement the method and write additional argument validation code not required by their specific test.

Such deviations from TDD are common and often acceptable, though they usually result in a few pieces of code being added that don't have supporting tests.

Ultimately, it's up to you and your team to determine what works best for you and the work that you do, but I can tell you that projects I work on where TDD is possible tend to rapidly reach better quality levels, encourage more refactoring, and have better long-term success.

Summary

In this chapter, we covered Test-Driven Development (TDD) and showed how its process involves writing only the minimum possible amount of code to get to a failing test – make that test pass with the minimum amount of code needed – then, refactor all code as needed before moving on to the next requirement or work item.

We also saw how Visual Studio has Quick Actions that allow you to generate types, properties, and methods and support your efforts in following TDD.

In the next chapter, we'll talk about anti-patterns that can lead to unmaintainable code and SOLID principles that help your code be robust and maintainable.

Questions

1. What areas of your code would be a good fit for using TDD?

2. What areas might be harder to apply TDD to?

Further reading

You can find more information about materials discussed in this chapter at this URL:

*   *Test-Driven Development Walkthrough:* `https://learn.microsoft.com/en-us/visualstudio/test/quick-start-test-driven-development-with-test-explorer`

*   *Is TDD Dead?:* `https://martinfowler.com/articles/is-tdd-dead/`

8
Avoiding Code Anti-Patterns with SOLID

The right design principles can keep your code from quickly going stale. While there are many right ways of writing code, there are anti-patterns and code smells that constitute the wrong way of writing code.

Additionally, the community has identified several principles to keep in mind when building software that can help your code resist accumulating technical debt for as long as possible. In this chapter, we'll cover a number of these principles, including the famous SOLID acronym, and see how they can help you build software that actively resists the gradual decline toward legacy code.

In this chapter, we'll cover the following topics:

- Identifying anti-patterns in C# code
- Writing SOLID code
- Considering other architectural principles

Identifying anti-patterns in C# code

I've often found myself telling new programmers that to build good software, you have to first build a lot of really bad software and learn from it.

While this statement is somewhat in jest, there is some truth to it: almost every developer can recognize code that's written the wrong way and discover things that make it difficult to work with, and doing so helps you write better code the next time.

When your code is bad, there's usually a part of you that knows it. You see little things that you don't love: duplicated pieces of code, inconsistencies in naming or parameter ordering, passing too many parameters around, methods, or even classes that are just too big to manage effectively.

These symptoms are what we commonly refer to as **code smells**, and we'll revisit them later in this section.

Beyond code smells are something called **anti-patterns**, which is code that significantly deviates from community recommendations. Unfortunately, not all anti-patterns are easy to notice or discover on your own, and some even seem like good ideas to individuals or teams until they're fully explored.

A few common C# anti-patterns I see include throwing and catching an `Exception` error instead of a specific type of `Exception` error, not disposing of resources that implement `IDisposable`, and inefficient **Language-Integrated Query (LINQ)** statements. See the *Further reading* section of this chapter for more details on these anti-patterns.

There are far too many anti-patterns to cover in this book, and the established practices of .NET development evolve over time. Because of this constant change, Visual Studio offers code analysis tools to help spot and fix violations of community standards. These tools include code analysis rulesets and built-in **Roslyn Analyzers**, which we'll cover at more length in *Chapter 12, Code Analysis in Visual Studio*.

Not all issues in code are specific to C# code. Many issues in code stem from how classes interact, pass data around to one another, manage variables, and are generally structured. These issues emerge even in code that you intended to be "well structured" as you start to see your systems scale up in size as new capabilities are added.

Thankfully, even new developers have an innate ability to spot code that is difficult to follow, requires more work to maintain and expand than it should, or involves excessive duplication. These types of issues in code are commonly referred to as **code smells**.

What are code smells?

Code smells are prime indicators that your current architecture has some drawbacks and refactoring might be in order. Pay attention to these symptoms when you encounter them in systems, including the code you write yourself. Learning what makes code difficult to work with will help you write better code and refactor existing code into better forms.

For now, let's move on to talk about writing **SOLID code**, which can help you avoid some common code smells and build robust, maintainable, and testable code.

Writing SOLID code

SOLID is an acronym introduced by Michael Feathers summarizing the words of Robert C. Martin. The intent of SOLID is to provide developers with a set of principles that will guide them toward more maintainable code that resists becoming technical debt.

The five principles of SOLID code are:

- **Single Responsibility Principle (SRP)**
- **Open-Closed Principle (OCP)**
- **Liskov Substitution Principle (LSP)**
- **Interface Segregation Principle (ISP)**
- **Dependency Inversion Principle (DIP)**

In this section, we'll cover all five of these principles.

Single Responsibility Principle

The **Single Responsibility Principle (SRP)** says that a class should be responsible for one thing and one thing only. Here are a few examples of classes that follow the SRP:

- A class responsible for saving application data to a specific file format
- A database access class dedicated to executing queries against a database table or set of tables
- An API controller providing REST methods to interact with flight data
- A class representing the user interface in a specific part of your application

Classes violate the SRP by trying to do more than one type of thing in the same class. More formally, if there's ever more than one reason to modify a class, the class violates the SRP.

For example, if a class is responsible for tracking a set of items in a user interface, responding to button presses, parsing user input, and asynchronously fetching data, that class very likely violates the SRP.

Classes that violate the SRP tend to be frequently modified, grow in complexity over time, and be very large classes compared to other classes in the system. These classes can be hard to fully understand or adequately test and can become brittle and buggy as they grow in complexity.

One of the things that I do to help detect violations of the SRP is to have a class-level comment talking about what the class is responsible for. For example, the following XML comment describes the FlightScheduler class from *Part 1* of this book:

```
/// <summary>
/// This class is responsible for tracking information
/// about current and pending flights
/// </summary>
public class FlightScheduler {
  // Details omitted
}
```

Here, the responsibility of `FlightScheduler` is clear: it exists to track active and pending flights within the system. Reasons for modifying this class should be related to the tracking of these flights and not related to other topics.

For this reason, I tend to put class-level comments in all classes whenever I define a new class to help that class stay focused on its mission over the course of its life.

But what if you have a class that already exists and violates the SRP?

When you have a class that's responsible for multiple things, I like to look at everything the class is currently responsible for and group them into related groups of members. For example, if a class has 10 fields, 25 methods, and 6 properties, I might go through them and try to find common topics that those things address.

For example, if the `FlightScheduler` class violated the SRP, it might have members for the following:

- Scheduling and canceling flights
- Assigning crew to flights
- Booking flights for passengers
- Changing seat assignments for passengers
- Moving passengers to different flights
- Generating flight-scheduling documentation for management

This class, clearly, is responsible for more than one type of thing. In a production system, this class might be 2,000 lines long or more and be difficult to fully understand and adequately test. Additionally, changes to one area of the class might impact other areas in unexpected ways.

By looking at the groups of things a class addresses, you can usually identify a few key groups. I like to do this and then focus on the largest group of related responsibilities that are not clearly related to the core goal of the class. Once you identify these groupings, you can extract a new class to manage these aspects. Your original class can reference this class or store it as a field if needed, or the new class could operate completely independently of the old class.

In the case of `FlightScheduler`, I would say that scheduling and canceling flights is the core part of the class, and other aspects currently in the class might belong more elsewhere. Looking at those other areas, there are several things related to managing flight reservations for passengers, so in this case, a `FlightBookingManager` class might be introduced to contain these related pieces of logic.

By iteratively introducing new classes from functionality not related to the core responsibility of a class, you can shrink large classes down to manageable sizes and resist the complexity, quality, and testability issues found in classes that ignore the SRP.

The SRP doesn't apply just to classes but can apply to methods as well. A method should have a single core task it is responsible for, and that purpose should be communicated by the name of the method.

When a method is responsible for multiple things or starts getting too large, it's a good sign that you might need to extract a method and pull some logic out of the original method to keep the size of the method maintainable.

Personally, if there were one programming principle I could impart to my younger self –or most early/intermediate developers out there, it would be the importance of the SRP in keeping your code easy to understand, test, expand, and maintain.

My personal guideline is to strive for classes under 200 lines of code long and methods under 20 lines of code long, but both can be challenging, and there are certainly exceptions to be made to these guidelines depending on the nature of the code you're maintaining – remember that these are principles and guidelines, not firm rules or commandments.

If you only remember one part of SOLID, remember the SRP; it's that important to the health of your application. However, there are four more principles to explore.

Open-Closed Principle

Classes are said to follow the **Open-Closed Principle (OCP)** when they are *open to extension* but *closed to modification.*

This principle was originally written for C++ modules, and it doesn't translate as cleanly to C# as some of the other SOLID principles, but this is essentially a principle about following **object-oriented programming (OOP)** principles when designing your classes.

If you build something to follow the OCP, you are designing a class to have its behavior extended through other classes inheriting it, through customizable properties or parameters, or through composition where you compose your class of other objects that change how it behaves.

An example of using composition was covered in *Chapter 5: Object-oriented Refactoring* and involved providing different cargo items for a flight.

The rest of this section will focus on using inheritance to fulfill the OCP.

In C#, methods do not allow overriding by default. This means you'll need to explicitly opt-in to allow others to override your methods by declaring them as `virtual`.

> Counterpoint
>
> I've heard some developers argue that declaring methods as `virtual` without any classes overriding them is confusing, adds unnecessary keywords to your code, and even slightly harms the performance of your code at runtime. All these things can be true, but if you are in a scenario where you cannot predict how others will use your code and you know they won't be able to modify your source code, marking key methods as `virtual` is usually a good idea. In these scenarios, `virtual` adds extra flexibility.
>
> Remember that SOLID principles *are guidelines to keep in mind* while building software, not firm rules you need to always follow.

As a specific example of the OCP, let's look at a sample `ItineraryManager` class representing information about a passenger's flight itinerary as they travel via Cloudy Skies Airlines:

```
public class ItineraryManager {
  public int MilesAccumulated {get; private set;}
  public FlightInfo? Flight {get; private set;}
  public virtual void FlightCompleted(FlightInfo? next) {
    if (Flight != null) {
      AccumulateMiles(Flight.Miles);
    }
    Flight = next;
  }
  public virtual void ChangeFlight(FlightInfo newFlight,
    bool isInvoluntary) =>
    Flight = newFlight;
  public void AccumulateMiles(int miles) =>
    MilesAccumulated += miles;
}
```

Here, we have a class that tracks the total miles a passenger has accrued, as well as the next flight the passenger is scheduled to fly (which may be `null` when their trip is completed). The class has two `virtual` methods related to handling completed flights as well as canceled flights. Additionally, the class has a non-`virtual` method called `AccumulateMiles` that updates the miles the passenger has accumulated on this trip.

While this class meets the needs of the airline, let's say that the airline wants to introduce a new logic for reward customers that gives them 100 extra miles for every flight they complete and rewards the scheduled mileage for a flight when the passenger is involuntarily moved to a new flight.

Under the OCP, we should be able to do this without having to modify our base class, assuming that the class is open to modification. It turns out we can do this with the following `RewardsItineraryManager` class:

```
public class RewardsItineraryManager : ItineraryManager {
  private const int BonusMilesPerFlight = 100;
  public override void FlightCompleted(FlightInfo? next) {
    base.FlightCompleted(next);
    AccumulateMiles(BonusMilesPerFlight);
  }
  public override void ChangeFlight(FlightInfo newFlight,
      bool isInvoluntary) {
    if (isInvoluntary && Flight != null) {
      AccumulateMiles(Flight.Miles);
```

```
    }
    base.ChangeFlight(newFlight, isInvoluntary);
  }
}
```

Without modifying our base class, we can extend the implementation of ItineraryManager with our new class that follows a slightly different logic. Thanks to the magic of polymorphism, we can use a RewardsItineraryManager class anywhere an ItineraryManager class is accepted, further supporting the closed-to-modification aspect of the OCP.

Liskov Substitution Principle

The **Liskov Substitution Principle (LSP)** says that polymorphic code should not need to be aware of what specific types of objects it is working with.

That's still a somewhat vague description, so let's take another look at the FlightCompleted method from earlier:

```
public virtual void FlightCompleted(FlightInfo? next) {
  if (Flight != null) {
    AccumulateMiles(Flight.Miles);
  }
  Flight = next;
}
```

This method takes in a flight that it stores in the Flight property. If a prior flight was stored in that Flight property, the code will call the AccumulateMiles method with that flight's Miles property.

The application has several classes that inherit from FlightInfo: PassengerFlightInfo and CargoFlightInfo. That means our next parameter may be any one of these three classes – or some other class that inherits from them.

The LSP says that *any* valid instance of FlightInfo should not error when you call its Miles property (or any other method). For example, this version of CargoFlightInfo would be a violation of the LSP because its Miles property errors when called:

```
public class CargoFlightInfo : FlightInfo {
  public decimal TonsOfCargo { get; set; }
  public override int RewardMiles =>
    throw new NotSupportedException();
}
```

Essentially, when following the LSP, the method should not have any reason to need to know which subclass of FlightInfo it's dealing with.

Because the LSP is focused on polymorphism, it applies to both class inheritance and interface implementations in .NET code.

Speaking of interfaces, let's move on to the ISP.

Interface Segregation Principle

The **Interface Segregation Principle** (ISP) is a fancy way of saying that you should prefer many smaller specialized interfaces focused on related capabilities over one large interface that encompasses everything your class does.

For example, imagine we had a `FlightRepository` class that managed database access to individual flights. In many systems, this class might implement an `IFlightRepository` interface that could be defined as follows with all public members of the class as part of the interface:

```
public interface IFlightRepository {
  FlightInfo AddFlight(FlightInfo flight);
  FlightInfo UpdateFlight(FlightInfo flight);
  void CancelFlight(FlightInfo flight);
  FlightInfo? FindFlight(string id);
  IEnumerable<FlightInfo> GetActiveFlights();
  IEnumerable<FlightInfo> GetPendingFlights();
  IEnumerable<FlightInfo> GetCompletedFlights();
}
```

As you can see, this manages common operations related to flights and provides some means of finding information about many flights. In a more real-world example, there would likely be many additional methods that would need to be added over the years to support new features.

In my experience with .NET code, it is very common to have a large interface per major class that includes all public methods in this class. This interface is usually named after the class it was based on and exists mostly to support testability through **dependency injection** (**DI**), as we'll touch on in the next chapter.

However, this approach is usually a violation of the ISP. Because our interfaces are designed around classes instead of discrete sets of capabilities, it becomes harder to introduce a new class that meets some of those capabilities but not all.

For example, let's say that Cloudy Skies Airlines wants to integrate with another subsidiary airline's systems. It doesn't need to add, update, or delete flights, but it does want a way of searching for flights. Under the `IFlightRepository` interface, the `AddFlight`, `UpdateFlight`, and `CancelFlight` methods would either need to do nothing or throw a `NotSupportedException` error when called. By the way, throwing the exception on a not-supported method call as part of a larger interface would be a violation of the LSP mentioned earlier.

Instead of having one large interface per major type, the ISP advocates for small interfaces for tightly related capabilities. In the case of `FlightRepository`, it's essentially doing two things:

- Adding, editing, and deleting flights
- Searching for existing flights

If we wanted to introduce interfaces, we could introduce interfaces for these separate sets of related capabilities, as shown here:

```
public interface IFlightUpdater {
  FlightInfo AddFlight(FlightInfo flight);
  FlightInfo UpdateFlight(FlightInfo flight);
  void CancelFlight(FlightInfo flight);
}
public interface IFlightProvider {
  FlightInfo? FindFlight(string id);
  IEnumerable<FlightInfo> GetActiveFlights();
  IEnumerable<FlightInfo> GetPendingFlights();
  IEnumerable<FlightInfo> GetCompletedFlights();
}
```

In this example, our `FlightRepository` class would implement both the `IFlightUpdater` interface and the `IFlightProvider` interface. If we wanted to integrate with another airline's systems but didn't have the ability to modify their flights, the `IFlightProvider` interface could be implemented without the `IFlightUpdater` interface.

By segmenting our interfaces into small interfaces that denote distinct sets of capabilities, we make it easier to provide alternative implementations of those capabilities as well as test our code later.

We've touched on DI a few times now; let's explore that topic in more detail by covering the DIP and rounding out our SOLID principles.

Dependency Inversion Principle

The **Dependency Inversion Principle** (**DIP**) states that your code should generally depend on abstractions instead of on specific implementations.

To illustrate this, let's look at a `FlightBookingManager` class that helps passengers book flights. This class needs to register booking requests and send confirmation messages for the booking. Here's its current code:

```
public class FlightBookingManager {
  private readonly SpecificMailClient _email;
  public FlightBookingManager(string connectionString) {
    _email = new SpecificMailClient(connectionString);
```

```
  }

  public bool BookFlight(Passenger passenger,
    PassengerFlightInfo flight, string seat) {
    if (!flight.IsSeatAvailable(seat)) {
      return false;
    }
    flight.AssignSeat(passenger, seat);
    string message = "Your seat is confirmed";
    _email.SendMessage(passenger.Email, message);
    return true;
  }
}
```

This code allows passengers to book a flight by checking if a seat is available, then reserving that seat and sending a message using the _email field. This field is set in the constructor to a new instance of SpecificMailClient, which is a made-up class representing some very specific implementation of an email client. The constructor needs to get a connection string to instantiate this class.

This code violates the DIP because our FlightBookingManager class is tightly coupled with a specific email client. If we ever wanted to write unit tests against this class, the class would always try to send messages to that email client, which usually isn't what you want when testing.

Additionally, if the organization wanted to change email providers and you needed to switch to a different email client, the FlightBookingManager class would need to change along with anywhere else in the system where we were tightly coupled to use the SpecificMailClient class.

Dependency inversion flips this on its head by having our classes instead depend on abstractions of the specific things they depend on. This is usually done by depending on a base class such as EmailClientBase that is then inherited or through taking in an interface such as IEmailClient that specific clients can implement.

We typically take in these dependencies in the constructor as a constructor parameter. This version of our FlightBookingManager class would look like this:

```
public class FlightBookingManager {
  private readonly IEmailClient _email;
  public FlightBookingManager(IEmailClient email) {
    _email = email;
  }

  public bool BookFlight(Passenger passenger,
    PassengerFlightInfo flight, string seat) {
    if (!flight.IsSeatAvailable(seat)) {
      return false;
```

```
    }
    flight.AssignSeat(passenger, seat);
    string message = "Your seat is confirmed";
    _email.SendMessage(passenger.Email, message);
    return true;
  }
}
```

Here, instead of taking in a connection string, we now take in an `IEmailClient` class. This means our class doesn't need to know which implementation it is dealing with or how to instantiate an instance of that class, doesn't need a connection string, doesn't need to change if the specific email provider ever changes, and can be tested easier by passing in a fake email client instead of a real one (we'll talk more about this in the next chapter when discussing Moq).

This process of taking in a dependency from something else is called **Dependency Inversion** and is often an intimidating topic for new and intermediate developers, but at its core, Dependency Inversion is all about classes getting their dependencies passed into them instead of having to create specific instances themselves.

Following the DIP leads to more maintainable, flexible, and testable code.

This concludes the five principles in SOLID, but we still have a few more design principles to cover before closing out the chapter.

Considering other architectural principles

Before we close out the chapter, let me share three brief principles that have helped me in my own journey toward good software.

Learning the DRY principle

Don't Repeat Yourself (**DRY**) is an important tenant in software development. The DRY principle is oriented around making sure you don't repeat the same patterns in code throughout your application. Code takes a while to write, read, and maintain, and bugs inevitably do occur at a certain rate per line of code. As a result, you want to strive to solve problems once in a centralized place and then reuse that solution.

Let's look at some sample code that violates the DRY principle. This code takes in a **comma-separated value** (**CSV**) string such as `"CSA1234,CMH,ORD"` and translates it into a `FlightInfo` object:

```
public FlightInfo ReadFlightFromCsv(string csvLine) {
  string[] parts = csvLine.Split(',');
  const string fallback = "Unknown";
  FlightInfo flight = new();
  if (parts.Length > 0) {
```

```
      flight.Id = parts[0]?.Trim() ?? fallback;
    } else {
      flight.Id = fallback;
    }
    if (parts.Length > 1) {
      flight.DepartureAirport = parts[1]?.Trim() ?? fallback;
    } else {
      flight.DepartureAirport = fallback;
    }
    if (parts.Length > 2) {
      flight.ArrivalAirport = parts[2]?.Trim() ?? fallback;
    } else {
      flight.ArrivalAirport = fallback;
    }
    // Other parsing logic omitted
    return flight;
  }
```

Notice how the logic for parsing in each part of the CSV string is wrapped in checks against `null` values and the array of parts is empty. This code is very repetitive, and it's easy to imagine that if a new field got added to the CSV data, the developer making the change would just copy and paste those five lines of code.

There are a few problems with repeating code patterns such as this:

- It encourages copying and pasting, which tends to produce poor code or results in bugs due to things that should have been changed on paste not being changed

- If the logic for parsing an individual field needs to change (for example, to protect against empty strings), it now needs to be changed in many places

We can fix this by extracting a method containing the logic for parsing fields:

```
private string ReadFromCsv(string[] parts, int index,
  string fallback = "Unknown") {
  if (parts.Length > index) {
    return parts[index]?.Trim() ?? fallback;
  } else {
    return fallback;
  }
}
public FlightInfo ReadFlightFromCsv(string csvLine) {
  string[] parts = csvLine.Split(',');
  FlightInfo flight = new();
  flight.Id = ReadFromCsv(parts, 0);
```

```
    flight.DepartureAirport = ReadFromCsv(parts, 1);
    flight.ArrivalAirport = ReadFromCsv(parts, 2);
    // Other parsing logic omitted
    return flight;
}
```

Not only is this new version easier to maintain, but it also results in less code overall and helps focus your attention on parts of the logic that are different from section to section. This improves the readability of your code while also reducing your likelihood of making mistakes.

KISS principle

"**Keep it simple, stupid**" (abbreviated as **KISS** and sometimes called "**Keep it simple, silly**") is a principle focused on the complexity of software systems. As software engineers, we sometimes overthink things and make things incredibly complex when they don't need to be. KISS encourages you to keep your code and classes as simple as possible and expand the complexity only when truly necessary.

Typically, the more complexity you have in your systems, the longer it takes you to add new features, diagnose problems, onboard new team members, and resolve customer-facing issues. With more moving parts to your application, there are also more things that can break, meaning that complexity has a real chance of creating customer-facing issues—all for potential solutions to problems your organization won't have for a few years.

Complexity tends to grow over time and rarely ever decreases (particularly in database schemas). Keep it simple until you see a pressing and compelling reason to add more complexity.

Understanding high cohesion and low coupling

Finally, let's close the chapter out by reviewing two terms you'll hear occasionally in software engineering: **cohesion** and **coupling**.

Cohesion has to do with how related different parts of the class are to the same thing. In a high-cohesion class, almost all parts of the class are oriented on the same types of capabilities. Let's look again at the `IFlightUpdater` interface from earlier for an example:

```
public interface IFlightUpdater {
    FlightInfo AddFlight(FlightInfo flight);
    FlightInfo UpdateFlight(FlightInfo flight);
    void CancelFlight(FlightInfo flight);
}
```

A class that implemented everything in this interface and added no other members would be a good example of *high cohesion* because all members in this interface are related to working with the same type of item. A *low-cohesion* class would start with these methods but also add many methods related to booking flights, generating reports, searching data, or other capabilities.

Classes that have low cohesion usually also violate the SRP.

Coupling refers to how tightly paired together with other classes a single class is. The more classes an individual class needs to know about to do its job, the more tightly coupled it is. Classes with higher coupling are harder to test due to a larger number of dependencies and need to be modified more frequently as their related classes evolve over time.

The DIP provides a great way for classes to reduce their coupling.

So, when you hear people talk about wanting high cohesion and low coupling, they're advocating for classes that are very tightly focused on a specific area and rely on as few other classes as possible to achieve that objective. When this combination is met, classes tend to be very focused and easy to maintain.

Summary

In this chapter, we discussed code smells and anti-patterns. The right design principles can help keep your code focused and minimal and slow the rate at which it naturally accumulates complexity. This helps keep your code in good form and resist accumulating technical debt.

The most common maxim for quality programming is SOLID, following the Single Responsibility Principle (SRP), making code open for extension while being closed to modification, the Liskov Substitution Principle (LSP) advocating for low coupling with polymorphic code, the interface segregation principle focused on several smaller interfaces over one larger interface, and the Dependency Inversion Principle (DIP) which talks about reducing coupling by having classes take in the things they need from outside of the class.

Now that we've established how to write SOLID code, we'll explore some advanced testing techniques that can help test code built using these principles.

Questions

1. How does the SRP affect cohesion?

2. Which areas of your code violate the SRP or DRY?

3. What are the advantages of DI? How does it affect coupling?

Further reading

You can find more information about materials discussed in this chapter at these URLs:

*   *SOLID Principles in C# with Examples*: `https://www.c-sharpcorner.com/UploadFile/damubetha/solid-principles-in-C-Sharp/`

- *15 of the Worst C# Anti-Patterns Developers Keep Using (And How to Avoid Them)*: `https://methodpoet.com/worst-anti-patterns/`

- *Top 10 Dotnet Exception Anti-Patterns in C#*: `https://newdevsguide.com/2022/11/06/exception-anti-patterns-in-csharp/`

- *Using objects that implement IDisposable*: `https://learn.microsoft.com/en-us/dotnet/standard/garbage-collection/using-objects`

- *LINQ: Caveats and pitfalls*: `https://dev.to/samfieldscc/linq-37k3`

9

Advanced Unit Testing

As we've seen, testing is incredible and can give you the freedom to effectively refactor your code in relative safety. Sometimes, code is written in a way that makes testing difficult and you need a few more tools. In this chapter, we'll explore a handful of popular .NET libraries that can improve the readability of your tests and give you more options for testing code – including those tricky classes with complex data or dependencies.

We'll cover the following topics in this chapter:

- Creating readable tests with Shouldly
- Generating test data with Bogus
- Mocking dependencies with Moq and NSubstitute
- Pinning tests with Snapper
- Experimenting with Scientist .NET

Technical requirements

The code for this chapter is available from GitHub at `https://github.com/PacktPublishing/Refactoring-with-CSharp` in the `Chapter09` folder.

Libraries change with new releases and some of these changes may cause issues with code in this chapter. Because of this, here are the exact names and versions of the libraries that are used in this chapter at the time of writing:

- **Bogus 34.0.2**
- **FluentAssertions 6.11.0**
- **Moq 4.20.2**
- **NSubstitute 5.0.0**
- **Scientist 2.0.0**

- **Shouldly 4.2.1**

- **Snapper 2.4.0**

Creating readable tests with Shouldly

In *Chapter 6*, we saw how the `Assert` class is used to verify the behavior of existing classes through code such as the following:

```
Assert.Equal(35, passengerCount);
```

This code verifies that `passengerCount` is equal to `35` and fails the test if it is a different number.

Unfortunately, this code has two problems:

- Assert methods take in the expected value first and the actual value second. This is different than how most people think about things and can lead to confusing test failure messages, as we saw in *Chapter 6*.

- The code doesn't read incredibly well in English, which can slow you down as you are reading tests.

Several open-source libraries address this issue by providing an alternative syntax for writing assertions in unit tests through sets of extension methods they introduce.

The most popular of these libraries are FluentAssertions and Shouldly. While FluentAssertions is by far the more popular library, I find Shouldly to read more naturally, so we'll start with that.

Let's look at installing Shouldly and getting started with its syntax before looking at a similar example with FluentAssertions.

Installing the Shouldly NuGet package

Shouldly is not a library that is included by default in any project template built into Visual Studio. Because of this, we need to add it to our project.

In Visual Studio, we use a **package manager** called **NuGet Package Manager** to install external dependencies from package sources such as the one at `nuget.org`.

If you've programmed in JavaScript, this concept is very similar to JavaScript package managers such as Yarn or NPM. While other package managers download the code and have you compile it, NuGet downloads *compiled* versions of external code and allows your code to reference things defined in those projects without slowing your build process.

To install a package, right-click on the `Chapter9Tests` project in **Solution Explorer** and choose **Manage NuGet Packages**.

Next, click on the **Browse** navigation link in the top-left corner and type `Shouldly` in the search bar. Your search results should look something like those in *Figure 9.1*:

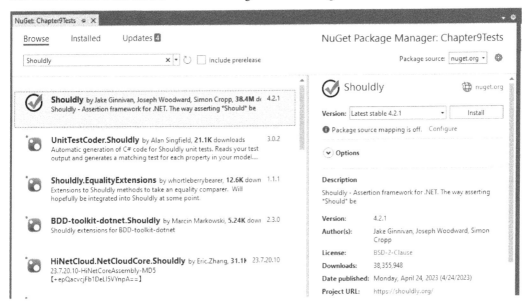

Figure 9.1 – NuGet Package Manager showing results for Shouldly

You should see an entry named Shouldly by Jake Ginnivan et al. in the list on the left. Select it by clicking on it. The details on the right will then list information about this package, including its license terms and dependencies.

> **Tip**
> Always check the author and the exact name of the package you are looking for as many have similar names.

Using the **Version** dropdown in the details area on the right, you can choose the specific version of the library to install. Usually, it's fine to leave this as the latest stable version, but occasionally, you may need to select a prior version for compatibility purposes.

When you click **Install**, Shouldly and anything it depends on will automatically be downloaded and installed into your project. When installing packages, a window may open showing you various license terms or dependencies, such as those shown in *Figure 9.2*. Read these carefully, especially if you are using a library in your workplace:

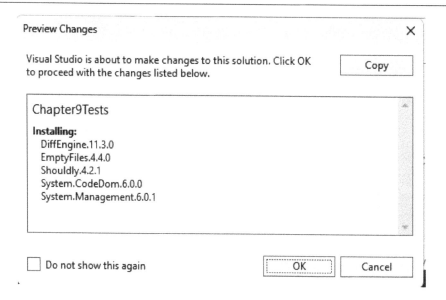

Figure 9.2 – Dependencies needed to install Shouldly

Now that we have Shouldly installed, let's learn how to work with it.

Writing readable assertions with Shouldly

In `PassengerTests.cs`, there's an existing `PassengerFullNameShouldBeAccurate` test that instantiates a `Passenger` object, grabs the value out of the object's `FullName` field, and makes sure the resulting name matches the expected value, as shown in the following code:

```
[Fact]
public void PassengerFullNameShouldBeAccurate() {
    // Arrange
    Passenger passenger = new() {
        FirstName = "Dot",
        LastName = "Nette",
    };
    // Act
    string name = passenger.FullName;
    // Assert
    Assert.Equal("Dot Nette", name);
}
```

Using Shouldly, we can make this assertion a lot more readable.

First, let's add a **global using** to the `Usings.cs` file by adding a `using` for Shouldly at the end of that file:

```
global using Xunit;
global using Shouldly;
```

This `global using` directive allows you to work with things in the Shouldly namespace anywhere in the `Chapter9Tests` project. Put another way, it is the equivalent of if every file in the project had a `using Shouldly;` statement at the top of the file.

Now that we have Shouldly installed and its namespace imported, we can rewrite the assertion from earlier by using one of the many extension methods provided by Shouldly, as shown here:

```
[Fact]
public void PassengerFullNameShouldBeAccurate() {
    // Arrange
    Passenger passenger = new() {
        FirstName = "Dot",
        LastName = "Nette",
    };
    // Act
    string name = passenger.FullName;
    // Assert
    name.ShouldBe("Dot Nette");
}
```

Here, Shouldly adds a `ShouldBe` extension method to the `string`, allowing us to call this method in a very readable way. This code is functionally equivalent to `Assert.Equal`, but it is significantly more readable. Additionally, you are far less likely to confuse which parameter is the expected value versus the actual value under this way of working with things.

Shouldly has a wide variety of extension methods, including `ShouldBe`, `ShouldNotBe`, `ShouldBeGreaterThan`/`ShouldBeLessThan`, `ShouldContain`, `ShouldNotBeNull`/`ShouldBeNull`, `ShouldStartWith`/`ShouldEndWith`, and more.

To illustrate this, let's look at a more complex test written without Shouldly:

```
[Fact]
public void ScheduleFlightShouldAddFlight() {
    // Arrange
    FlightScheduler scheduler = new();
    PassengerFlightInfo flight = _flightFaker.Generate();
    // Act
    scheduler.ScheduleFlight(flight);
    // Assert
```

```
    var result = scheduler.GetAllFlights();
    Assert.NotNull(result);
    Assert.Equal(1, result.Count());
    Assert.Contains(flight, result);
}
```

This code uses `FlightScheduler` to schedule a flight using the Bogus library, which we'll discuss later in this chapter. Once a flight has been scheduled, the code gets all the flights and asserts that the resulting collection is not null, has only one item, and the flight we scheduled is in that collection.

This code isn't too bad, but I still prefer the Shouldly version:

```
[Fact]
public void ScheduleFlightShouldAddFlight() {
    // Arrange
    FlightScheduler scheduler = new();
    PassengerFlightInfo flight = _flightFaker.Generate();
    // Act
    scheduler.ScheduleFlight(flight);
    // Assert
    var result = scheduler.GetAllFlights();
    result.ShouldNotBeNull();
    result.Count().ShouldBe(1);
    result.ShouldContain(flight);
}
```

In general, I find the Shouldly library to have more consistent parameter ordering and result in more readable tests. Because of this, I find myself more productive and use Shouldly wherever I can.

> **Practice exercise**
>
> As an exercise, I'd encourage you to take the starting code for this chapter and convert the various tests so that they use Shouldly instead of standard assertions. Feel free to experiment with other assertions as you go. This chapter's final code uses Shouldly if you want to check your answers.

Before we see what else Shouldly can do, let's look at FluentAssertions, a popular library fulfilling a similar role as Shouldly.

Writing readable assertions with FluentAssertions

FluentAssertions does the same thing that Shouldly does, but the approach of its syntax is less oriented on calling single methods like Shouldly's `ShouldContain`. Instead, FluentAssertions prefers chaining together several method calls to produce a similar result.

Let's look at a test of the baggage pricing system as an illustration:

```
[Fact]
public void CarryOnBaggageIsPricedCorrectly() {
    // Arrange
    BaggageCalculator calculator = new();
    int carryOnBags = 2;
    int checkedBags = 0;
    int passengers = 1;
    bool isHoliday = false;
    // Act
    decimal result = calculator.CalculatePrice(checkedBags,
        carryOnBags, passengers, isHoliday);
    // Assert
    result.Should().Be(60m);
}
```

This code creates `BaggageCalculator` and then sends a series of factors to that calculator's `CalculatePrice` method before performing its assertions via the `Should().Be(60m)` syntax.

Before we explore this in more depth, I should point out that, like Shouldly, FluentAssertions does not come pre-installed. You'll need to install FluentAssertions with NuGet Package Manager, the same way you did earlier for Shouldly. You'll also need to add a `using FluentAssertions;` statement to your code file to see the FluentAssertions extension methods.

Now that we've established how to get started with FluentAssertions, let's take a closer look at that `result.Should().Be(60m)` syntax.

Most actions in FluentAssertions flow out of the `Should` methods. Notice that there are multiple `Should` methods in FluentAssertions, with each one related to a specific type of data you might work with.

These `Should` methods return a strongly-typed object such as `NumericAssertions<decimal>` in the case of the calculator assertions. These assertion objects contain various constraint methods, allowing you to do targeted assertions such as `Be`, `NotBe`, `BeLessThan`, `BePositive`, `BeOneOf`, and others.

There are a few advantages to the FluentAssertions approach:

- It's easier to find assertion methods since they all go through `Should()`

- The constraint methods allow you to combine assertions such as `result.Should().BePositive().And.BeInRange(50, 70)`

Unfortunately, FluentAssertions has a slightly higher learning curve and is a little more verbose than Shouldly, which might result in slightly less readable tests.

Ultimately, it's up to you and your team as to what style you prefer, but both Shouldly and FluentAssertions can significantly improve the readability of your tests and your enjoyment of the test writing experience.

Before we introduce our next new library, let's talk about one more thing Shouldly can do that might be helpful.

Testing performance with Shouldly

One of the reasons people find themselves refactoring code is to look for ways of improving the performance of code that is known to be slow.

Imagine you are following **Test-Driven Development (TDD)** and are investigating code that takes an unacceptably long time to iterate through a list of items.

The first step in TDD is to write a failing test, so you now need to write a test that fails if the performance of a method is too slow.

We'll talk about reasons why you might not want to write a test around performance in a bit, but let's explore how you would go about testing performance first.

In order to fail tests involving code that performs too slowly, you'd need to be able to measure how long that code took to run. To do that, you could create a `Stopwatch` object, start it, stop it, and then verify the duration of that watch, as shown here:

```
[Fact]
public void ScheduleFlightShouldNotBeSlow() {
    // Arrange
    FlightScheduler scheduler = new();
    PassengerFlightInfo flight = _flightFaker.Generate();
    int maxTime = 100;
    Stopwatch stopwatch = new();
    // Act
    stopwatch.Start();
    scheduler.ScheduleFlight(flight);
    stopwatch.Stop();
    long milliSeconds = stopwatch.ElapsedMilliseconds;
    // Assert
    milliSeconds.ShouldBeLessThanOrEqualTo(maxTime);
}
```

This code will fail if it takes more than 100 milliseconds (0.1 seconds) to run `ScheduleFlight`, but this approach has a couple of disadvantages:

- There's a lot of setup code required for this approach. In this case, over half of the test method is devoted to `Stopwatch`.

- The test waits for the method to complete before the test is failed. If it takes 10 seconds to complete the method, the test waits the full time. This is inefficient because once the 100-millisecond threshold is crossed, the test will never pass.

Shouldly gives us a more compact `Should.CompleteIn` method that solves both problems:

```
[Fact]
public void ScheduleFlightShouldNotBeSlow() {
  // Arrange
  FlightScheduler scheduler = new();
  PassengerFlightInfo flight = _flightFaker.Generate();
  TimeSpan maxTime = TimeSpan.FromMilliseconds(100);
  // Act
  Action testAction = () => scheduler.ScheduleFlight(flight);
  // Assert
  Should.CompleteIn(testAction, maxTime);
}
```

This code creates an action to schedule the flight that Shouldly will invoke as part of the test. This action isn't invoked until it is passed into the `Should.CompleteIn` method, which also requires a maximum amount of time to allow the method to run.

When Shouldly runs your action, it tracks the elapsed time internally and will cancel your action and fail the test once that threshold is reached. This results in more compact test code that won't take longer than the maximum allowable amount of time.

So, now that we know how to write simple performance tests using Shouldly or plain old .NET with `Stopwatch`, let's talk about why you might not want to do this.

Good tests should be fast and result in a repeatable result. Tests will be run by a variety of machines in a variety of different circumstances, such as when the processor has relatively little work to do or when the processor is completely overloaded. Tests may also be run in isolation or parallel, alongside, other tests. Additionally, with .NET, it is normal to see variations in performance from run to run.

All these things mean that performance testing is going to be more chaotic than you like and the maximum allowable duration is something you should consider carefully. If your tests are run in a **continuous integration/continuous delivery (CI/CD)** pipeline (which they should be, as we'll talk about in *Part 4* of this book), it's likely that the build machine's CPU and memory characteristics look nothing like a developer workstation. To combat this, you may need to pick a significantly higher number than you normally would to avoid random failures due to a slow test environment. On the other hand, if you make your timeout too long, you won't detect legitimate performance issues.

My general stance is that performance testing is something that should rarely ever be codified into unit tests due to the chaotic nature of performance metrics and the wide variety of machines that might run tests. Instead, I tend to prefer periodic profiling using a dedicated tool such as **Visual Studio Enterprise** or **JetBrains dotTrace** for those areas that are truly critical to performance.

That said, there is value in performance tests, but you may spend more time than you'd expect finding a good maximum test duration number.

Let's move on to another library that makes your life easier when testing: **Bogus**.

Generating test data with Bogus

In *Chapter 6*, I mentioned that tests are a form of documentation that explains how your system should work.

Keeping that in mind, look at the following test, which tests the interaction of the `Passenger` and `BoardingProcessor` classes:

```
[Fact]
public void BoardingMessageShouldBeAccurate() {
  // Arrange
  Passenger passenger = new() {
    BoardingGroup = 7,
    FirstName = "Dot",
    LastName = "Nette",
    MailingCity = "Columbus",
    MailingStateOrProvince = "Ohio",
    MailingCountry = "United States",
    MailingPostalCode = "43081",
    Email = "noreply@packt.com",
    RewardsId = "CSA88121",
    RewardMiles = 360,
    IsMilitary = false,
    NeedsHelp = false,
  };
  BoardingProcessor boarding =
    new(BoardingStatus.Boarding, group:3);
  // Act
  string message = boarding.BuildMessage(passenger);
  // Assert
  message.ShouldBe("Please Wait");
}
```

A lot of setup is needed in the *Arrange* phase before `BuildMessage` can be called. But what aspects of that setup are important? Which parts of the `Passenger` object contribute to that person being allowed to board versus being told to wait?

While it's important to create test objects that look accurate, mixing irrelevant properties with vital properties can lead to difficulties interpreting what's important about test data or why a test should pass instead of fail.

Bogus is a library that generates realistic random data of different types. Bogus helps solve this problem by giving you a good way of generating random data for those less critical parts of your objects.

This has the simultaneous benefit of focusing your attention on the more critical portions of your tests while also generating random data to test your assertion that the values in the other properties truly don't matter.

Like the other libraries in this chapter, Bogus must be installed via NuGet and then referenced in a `using Bogus;` statement.

Let's look at the *Arrange* section of the earlier test using Bogus:

```
// Arrange
Faker<Passenger> faker = new();
faker.RuleFor(p => p.FirstName, f => f.Person.FirstName)
  .RuleFor(p => p.LastName, f => f.Person.LastName)
  .RuleFor(p => p.Email, f => f.Person.Email)
  .RuleFor(p => p.MailingCity, f => f.Address.City())
  .RuleFor(p => p.MailingCountry, f => f.Address.Country())
  .RuleFor(p => p.MailingState, f =>f.Address.State())
  .RuleFor(p => p.MailingPostalCode, f=>f.Address.ZipCode())
  .RuleFor(p => p.RewardsId, f => f.Random.String2(8))
  .RuleFor(p => p.RewardMiles,
          f => f.Random.Number(int.MaxValue));
Passenger passenger = faker.Generate();
passenger.BoardingGroup = 7;
passenger.NeedsHelp = false;
passenger.IsMilitary = false;
```

As you've likely noticed, this code is significantly different than the earlier code. It uses a `Faker<Passenger>` object from Bogus that will generate a different random `Passenger` object every time the `Generate()` method is called.

These `Passenger` objects will use Bogus' library of random data to generate reasonable test data, as shown in *Figure 9.3*:

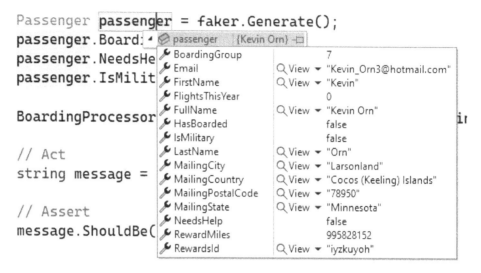

Figure 9.3 – A randomized passenger with somewhat realistic values

The way this works is that you can set rules that `Faker` will follow when it sees a given property using the `RuleFor` method.

Using `RuleFor`, you can specify the property you want to program a response to in the first argument and then specify a function to get a value in the second parameter.

As an example, the `RuleFor(p => p.Email, f => f.Person.Email)` line has two function parameters. The first one uses `p` to represent the `Passenger` object and focuses on that object's `Email` property. The second parameter takes in a `Faker` instance as `f` and the function may choose to use it to generate a value that `Faker` will use when generating a person.

`Faker` contains many different types of data, from fake company names to ZIP codes to product names, IP addresses, and even absurd things such as hacker speak and "rants" such as reviews.

Now, if you look closely at the data `Faker` generates, it doesn't always make sense. For example, *Figure 9.3* listed the person as living in Larsonland, Minnesota with a postal code of 78950 and a country of "Cocos (Keeling) Islands." Individually, these things are fine, but these different properties conflict wildly with one another.

If you need your data to make sense, you'll need to write more nuanced rules for how these properties interact. Despite these limitations, Bogus gives you a great way of adding randomness to your code for the inconsequential data.

Often, when using Bogus, you'll create your `Faker` instance in a separate method or the test constructor, which simplifies your code significantly:

```
[Fact]
public void BoardingMessageShouldBeAccurate() {
  Faker<Passenger> faker = BuildPersonFaker();
  Passenger passenger = faker.Generate();
  passenger.BoardingGroup = 7;
  passenger.NeedsHelp = false;
  passenger.IsMilitary = false;
  BoardingProcessor boarding =
    new(BoardingStatus.Boarding, group: 3);
  // Act
  string message = boarding.BuildMessage(passenger);
  // Assert
  message.ShouldBe("Please Wait");
}
```

Notice how this approach minimizes Bogus' role in things and focuses your attention on how the randomly generated person is further configured. This helps you see that the important factors for someone not boarding the plane yet are as follows:

- They are in a higher boarding group than the current group
- They are not military
- They do not need help boarding the plane

Bogus isn't just for tests. For example, I've used Bogus successfully for prototyping user interfaces and generating data for small game projects. However, Bogus is a valuable addition to your testing toolbox.

Let's move on to look at ways of isolating dependencies with a pair of mocking libraries.

Mocking dependencies with Moq and NSubstitute

So far, we've looked at a few libraries that improve the readability of your tests. In this section, we'll look at **mocking frameworks** and see how libraries can help you more effectively test your code.

Understanding the need for mocking libraries

Let's discuss why mocking frameworks are necessary by revisiting the `FlightBookingManager` example we introduced in the previous chapter while discussing dependency injection:

```
public class FlightBookingManager {
  private readonly IEmailClient _email;
```

```
public FlightBookingManager(IEmailClient email) {
  _email = email;
}
public bool BookFlight(Passenger passenger,
  FlightInfo flight, string seat) {
  if (!flight.IsSeatAvailable(seat)) {
    return false;
  }
  flight.AssignSeat(passenger, seat);
  string message = "Your seat is confirmed";
  return _email.SendMessage(passenger.Email, message);
}
}
```

Here, this class requires IEmailClient when FlightBookingManager is created. The client is then stored in the _email field and this is later used to send a message when a flight is booked. Passing in IEmailClient as a parameter to the constructor is an example of dependency injection and allows our class to work with anything that implements the IEmailClient interface.

Unfortunately, it also means that to test the class, we must provide an implementation of IEmailClient, even if we're not explicitly testing something email-related.

Since we generally don't want to send emails when unit testing our code, that means we'd need a separate implementation of IEmailClient. We could make one by declaring a class and implementing the IEmailClient interface with a minimal implementation.

Let's say that IEmailClient was defined as follows:

```
public interface IEmailClient {
  bool SendMessage(string email, string message);
}
```

You could create a TestEmailClient that meets this requirement:

```
public class TestEmailClient : IEmailClient {
  public bool SendMessage(string email, string message)
    => true;
}
```

Here, the implementation of the test client is very simple and does the minimum possible needed to compile the code, which in this case is returning true, indicating a message was successfully sent. This type of class is sometimes called a **test double**, a **test stub**, or simply a **mock object**. These names are due to these classes looking like real implementations for testing purposes without having all their functionality. In this chapter, I will refer to these as mock objects since that will help mocking frameworks make more sense later.

This lets us write a test using the `TestEmailClient` mock object we created:

```
[Fact]
public void BookingFlightShouldSucceedForEmptyFlight() {
  // Arrange
  TestEmailClient emailClient = new();
  FlightBookingManager manager = new(emailClient);
  Passenger passenger = GenerateTestPassenger();
  FlightInfo flight = GenerateEmptyFlight("Paris",
    "Toronto");
  // Act
  bool booked = manager.BookFlight(passenger, flight,"2B");
  // Assert
  booked.ShouldBeTrue();
}
```

Here, we can safely test a flight without sending an email by providing `TestEmailClient` instead of a real email client.

Unfortunately, mock objects have their drawbacks. Let's say we wanted to write another test that verifies that trying to book a seat that's already occupied doesn't send an email. In that case, we'd need to create another mock object with a different implementation.

In this case, we'd want to fail the test if the `SendMessage` method was called, so that method should throw an exception or use the `Assert.Fail` method to cause the test to fail, as shown here:

```
public class SendingNotAllowedEmailClient : IEmailClient {
  public bool SendMessage(string email, string message) {
    Assert.Fail("You should not have sent an email");
    return false;
  }
}
```

Let's consider a more nuanced example. Let's say you want to verify that the `BookFlight` method calls the `SendMessage` method on its `IEmailClient` one time and one time only.

We could test this by building a specialized mock object that had a counter of all the times it was called, but that's yet more complexity in our test code that we don't necessarily need. If the definition of what's in `IEmailClient` ever changes, all our mock objects that implement that interface will also need to be updated.

Because so many tests need mock objects and each test tests something slightly different, writing and maintaining mock objects manually can be a lot of work. This is the core problem that mocking libraries exist to solve.

While there are several popular mocking libraries in .NET, the most popular for many years has been Moq. We'll explore Moq next before looking at an alternative.

Creating mock objects with Moq

Moq, pronounced either "Mock" or "Mock-you" in the words of its creator, *is a mocking library built around using LINQ to create, configure, and verify the behavior of mock objects.*

Just like the other libraries in this chapter, you'll need to install Moq from NuGet Package Manager and import it into your file via a `using Moq;` statement.

With Moq, you don't create mock objects on your own; instead, you tell Moq the interface you want to implement or the class you want to inherit and Moq automatically creates an object that meets these requirements.

Let's revisit our flight booking test from earlier in this chapter using Moq:

```
[Fact]
public void BookingFlightShouldSucceedForEmptyFlight() {
  // Arrange
  Mock<IEmailClient> clientMock = new();
  IEmailClient emailClient = clientMock.Object;
  FlightBookingManager manager = new(emailClient);
  Passenger passenger = GenerateTestPassenger();
  FlightInfo flight = GenerateEmptyFlight("Hamburg",
    "Cairo");
  // Act
  bool booked = manager.BookFlight(passenger, flight,"2B");
  // Assert
  booked.ShouldBeTrue();
}
```

Here, we instantiate a `Mock` instance named `clientMock` that will create a new mock object in the form of `IEmailClient`. We then call the `Object` property on `clientMock` and the Moq library automatically generates an object that implements `IEmailClient` in the simplest way possible.

Since we don't care how the email client works in this example, this is all we need to do to generate a simple mock object that we can pass to `FlightBookingManager`. Not only is this less code, but we can stay in the test method while defining our mock object, and if the definition for `IEmailClient` ever changes, we don't need to update the mock object since Moq takes care of that for us.

Of course, there's a lot more that Moq can do, so let's see how you can use it to configure how your mock objects behave.

Programming Moq return values

By default, methods on Moq's mock objects will return the default value for that type. For example, a method returning a `bool` object would return `false`, and a method returning an `int` object would return `0`.

Sometimes, you need Moq to return something different. In these cases, you can set up your mock object by calling Moq's `Setup` method. For example, if you needed the `SendMessage` method to return `true` instead of `false` for any value that was passed in, you could write the following code:

```
Mock<IEmailClient> mockClient = new();
mockClient.Setup(c => c.SendMessage(It.IsAny<string>(),
                                    It.IsAny<string>())
                ).Returns(true);
IEmailClient emailClient = mockClient.Object;
```

Here, the `Setup` method requires you to tell it what method or property you are configuring. Since we're configuring the `SendMessage` method, we specify it in the arrow function.

Next, Moq needs to know when it should apply this rule. You can program your mock objects to reply differently based on different parameters, so you could have a `Setup` call for different parameter values to the same method.

In our case, we want the method to always return `true`, regardless of what is passed in, so we specify that with Moq's `It.IsAny` syntax.

Before we finish our discussion of Moq, we'll look at a final example and teach you how to verify how many times a given method was called on your mock objects.

Verifying Moq calls

Sometimes, you want to test the behavior of a method and verify that calling one method causes it to call something on another object. Moq lets you do this by verifying that a method has been called a specific number of times.

This can include verifying that a method wasn't called, which can be helpful for cases like the example we discussed earlier involving making sure emails aren't sent out in cases where a seat couldn't be reserved.

To accomplish this, we can call Moq's `Verify` methods, as shown in the following case, which verifies that an email was sent once and only once when booking a flight:

```
[Fact]
public void BookingFlightShouldSendEmails() {
    // Arrange
    Mock<IEmailClient> mockClient = new();
    mockClient.Setup(c => c.SendMessage(It.IsAny<string>(),
```

```
        It.IsAny<string>())).Returns(true);
    IEmailClient emailClient = mockClient.Object;
    FlightBookingManager manager = new(emailClient);
    Passenger passenger = GenerateTestPassenger();
    FlightInfo flight = GenerateEmptyFlight("Sydney","LA");
    // Act
    bool result= manager.BookFlight(passenger,flight,"2C");
    // Assert
    result.ShouldBeTrue();
    mockClient.Verify(c => c.SendMessage(passenger.Email,
        It.IsAny<string>()), Times.Once);
    mockClient.VerifyNoOtherCalls();
}
```

Here, we call `Verify` on our `Mock` instance to verify that the `SendMessage` method was called exactly one time with the passenger's email address and any email body. If the method wasn't called or was called multiple times, this will fail our test.

In other words, this one `Verify` line protects us from cases where the system didn't email the user when it should have, as well as cases where it might have sent too many emails.

Next, the code calls `VerifyNoOtherCalls`. This method will cause the test to fail if some other method on our `IEmailClient` was called that was not verified by a previous `Verify` statement. This can be handy for ensuring that the code is not doing unexpected things with the objects you provide it.

> **A note on verifying behavior**
>
> The developer community has historically been divided on whether it is good practice to verify that calling code calls some other piece of code in your unit tests. The argument against verifying the behavior of your tests is that it shouldn't matter how a method implements something if it produces the right results. The counter-argument is that sometimes, the desired result of your method is the callout to the external code, such as our code here, which calls the `SendMessage` call. You and your team will need to decide when it is appropriate to use `Verify` in your tests.

Moq can seem complex to work with initially, but you don't need to use all its features to benefit from it. As we saw earlier, just using Moq to generate simple mock objects can save you significant work in maintaining a growing number of manually created mock objects over time.

You won't always need to use Moq's `Setup` or `Verify` methods, but they're very helpful when you want them.

For years, Moq has been the dominant mocking library in .NET, but recently, NSubstitute has been gaining popularity. This results in a higher likelihood that you may encounter it in the workplace as a substitute for Moq. Let's explore NSubstitute briefly and see how it accomplishes similar things to Moq using a different syntax.

Mocking with NSubstitute

NSubstitute is a similar mocking library to Moq, but its approach is to avoid arrow functions where possible and prefer code that looks more like standard method calls.

Like other libraries in this chapter, you'll need to install NSubstitute via NuGet Package Manager and then import it via a `using NSubstitute;` statement.

Once you have NSubstitute installed and imported, you can use it in code, as follows:

```
[Fact]
public void BookingFlightShouldSendEmailsNSubstitute() {
  // Arrange
  IEmailClient emailClient= Substitute.For<IEmailClient>();
  emailClient.SendMessage(Arg.Any<string>(),
                          Arg.Any<string>()
                         ).Returns(true);
  FlightBookingManager manager = new(emailClient);
  Passenger passenger = GenerateTestPassenger();
  FlightInfo flight = GenerateEmptyFlight("Sydney","LA");
  // Act
  bool result = manager.BookFlight(passenger, flight,"2C");
  // Assert
  result.ShouldBeTrue();
  emailClient.Received()
             .SendMessage(passenger.Email,
                          Arg.Any<string>());
}
```

Note how NSubstitute's `Substitute.For` returns the object you're creating instead of creating an object like `Mock<IEmailClient>` did with Moq. This change makes your code a little simpler to work with but also means you now need to call methods like `Received()` and `DidNotReceive()` to get access to the method to verify.

In general, NSubsitute is very similar to Moq but with a simpler syntax. This simplicity has its advantages, particularly in code readability and a lowered learning curve for new developers. Unfortunately, this sometimes comes at the price of NSubstitute not having the full range of features you're used to with Moq.

Now that we've explored mocking libraries, let's move on to completely different types of unit tests.

Pinning tests with Snapper

Let's say you've inherited some complex legacy code that returns an object with a lot of properties. Some of these properties may, in turn, contain other complex objects with their own nest of properties. You're just starting to work with this code and need to make a change, but there aren't any tests in place and you're not even sure what properties are important to verify.

I've seen this scenario a few times now and can attest that a special testing library called Snapper is a fantastic solution to this problem.

What Snapper does is it creates a snapshot of an object and stores it to disk in a JSON file. When Snapper next runs, it generates another snapshot and then compares it to the snapshot it stored previously. If the snapshots differ at all, Snapper will fail the test and alert you to that problem.

> **Snapper and Jest**
>
> For those of you with a JavaScript background, Snapper was inspired by the snapshot testing capabilities found in JavaScript's Jest testing library.

Let's see what a sample test looks like with Snapper.

As usual, first, we install Snapper via NuGet and add a `using Snapper;` statement.

After that, we'll write a test against a complex object, `FlightManifest`:

```
[Fact]
public void FlightManifestShouldMatchExpectations() {
  // Arrange
  FlightInfo flight = GenerateEmptyFlight("Alta", "Laos");
  Passenger p1 = new("Dot", "Netta");
  Passenger p2 = new("See", "Sharp");
  flight.AssignSeat(p1, "1A");
  flight.AssignSeat(p2, "1B");
  LegacyManifestGenerator generator = new();
  // Act
  FlightManifest manifest = generator.Build(flight);
  // Assert
  manifest.ShouldMatchSnapshot();
}
```

Here, we call `ShouldMatchSnapshot` to verify that the object matches the current snapshot.

This will generate the snapshot the first time, but subsequent runs will compare the object's snapshot to the stored snapshot. If the resulting snapshot is different, you'll see a test failure with details about the difference, such as the one that occurs when a passenger's name is changed, as shown in *Figure 9.4*:

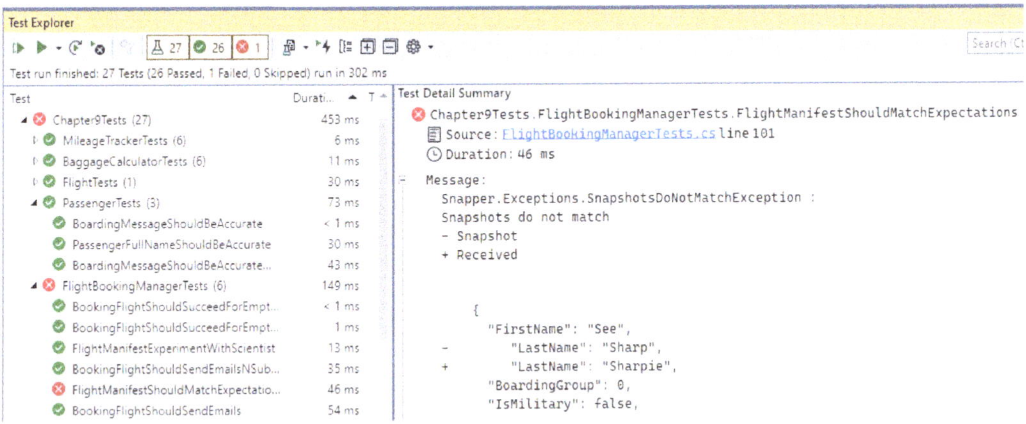

Figure 9.4 – A failing snapshot test showing the difference between two properties

Sometimes, you'll add new properties or realize that the stored snapshot was based on buggy data and you'll want to update your snapshots. You can do this by temporarily adding an `UpdateSnapshots` attribute to your test method, as shown here:

```
[Fact]
[UpdateSnapshots]
public void FlightManifestShouldMatchExpectations() {
```

After this, re-run your test to update the stored snapshot, then remove the `UpdateSnapshots` attribute. This final step is important because the test with `UpdateSnapshots` included will never fail a snapshot test but rather replace the snapshot every time.

Snapshot testing is not for every project and not for every team. It is a very useful broad safety net that you can include as the first test for complex return values, but it is far less useful as a test that documents the behavior of a system. Additionally, snapshot tests can be very brittle and cause tests to fail for trivial things such as modified dates being different between two otherwise identical sets of data.

Still, I find that Snapper and snapshot testing can be an appropriate opening move while trying to bring tests to particularly complex areas of legacy systems.

Now, let's close this chapter out with a similar library that helps you compare several different implementations with each other.

Experimenting with Scientist .NET

Scientist .NET is a library built by GitHub for scientifically refactoring the critical parts of your application.

Let's say you have a portion of your application that is vital to what the business does but has a significant amount of technical debt. You want to refactor it, but you're afraid of breaking anything and your existing tests are not sufficient to address those fears, but you're not sure what tests you need to add. In your estimation, the only thing that will let you feel good about your new code is to see how it does in production.

This is what Scientist .NET helps with. Scientist .NET lets you deploy your new code alongside the legacy code it hopes to replace and compares the results of the two pieces of code. Alternatively, Scientist .NET can be used in unit tests to verify that the old version of a component and the new version of the component achieves the same results.

This concept will hopefully be a bit clearer in a moment. Let's jump into a specific example that looks at replacing LegacyManifestGenerator with RewrittenManifestGenerator.

Like before, we'll need to install the Scientist package from NuGet and then add a using GitHub; statement to the top of our file.

Next, let's look at the science experiment comparing the two manifest generators:

```
[Fact]
public void FlightManifestExperimentWithScientist() {
    FlightInfo flight = GenerateEmptyFlight("Alta", "Laos");
    Passenger p1 = new("Dot", "Netta");
    Passenger p2 = new("See", "Sharp");
    Scientist.Science<FlightManifest>("Manifest", exp => {
        exp.Use(() => {
            LegacyManifestGenerator generator = new();
            return generator.Build(flight);
        });
        exp.Try(() => {
            RewrittenManifestGenerator generator = new();
            return generator.Build(flight);
        });
        exp.Compare((a, b)=> a.Arrival == b.Arrival &&
                            a.Departure == b.Departure &&
                            a.PassengerCount==b.PassengerCount
                  );
        exp.ThrowOnMismatches = true;
    });
}
```

That's a lot of code, so let's unpack everything here bit by bit.

First, the `Scientist.Science<FlightManifest>` line tells Scientist you're starting a new experiment that will return `FlightManifest`. In this example, we're ignoring this result value, but in a production scenario, you might assign the result to a variable and work with it after the call to the Scientist.

Scientist requires you to name every experiment in the first parameter to the `Science` call because you may be performing multiple experiments. This experiment is simply named "Manifest."

Next, the Scientist requires an action to configure the experiment you're about to perform. You might configure a few things, but here, we're specifying four different things that we'll talk about in sequence.

First, we call the `Use` method to tell the experiment what to use as the result of the call to the `Scientist.Science`. This should be the legacy implementation of the system you're looking at replacing.

Next, we need to give Scientist one or more alternative implementations to consider and compare against the "control" version in the legacy system. We do this via a `Try` method that looks very similar to the `Use` method, but it represents the experimental version.

What Scientist does with these two versions is it makes the call to both implementations, compares the two results, and sends metrics on to something called a result publisher. This process is illustrated in *Figure 9.5*:

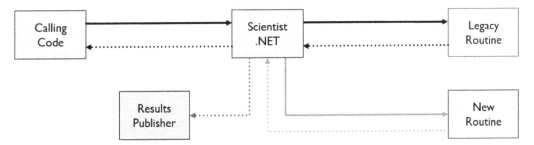

Figure 9.5 – Scientist .NET performing an experiment

Scientist always returns the result of the legacy version defined during `Use`, so your new implementation will not impact the existing logic and you'll be able to identify cases where the new and old implementations do not match. This allows you to verify your new logic's behavior without risking any logic bugs impacting end users.

Once you are satisfied that your new implementation is without issues, you can remove Scientist and the legacy implementation from your code and use the new implementation in their place.

For Scientist to tell if two results are equivalent, it needs to know how to compare them. You can configure this with the `Compare` method, which takes in a function that will return a `bool` object indicating if the two objects should be considered equivalent.

Finally, our code sets `ThrowOnMismatches` to `true`. You can set this property in Scientist to have it throw an exception when the experiment and the control do not match for a given input. This is only intended for use in unit tests like our code here and is not intended for use if you're using Scientist in a production application.

Instead, you would implement Scientist's `IResultPublisher` interface and set `Scientist.ResultPublisher` equal to your custom result publisher. This would allow you to report mismatches to a database, App Insights on Azure, or some other mechanism you might consider using to capture these mismatches. Getting into result publishers is outside the scope of this book, but see the *Further reading* section in this chapter for more resources.

Scientist .NET is a complex solution you won't use frequently, but it allows you to compare how two different implementations of an algorithm perform against a variety of inputs, either in a unit testing scenario or in a production application. I've personally seen Scientist .NET enable teams to collect the data they needed to successfully refactor highly complex code without impacting end users.

> **Warning**
>
> It's important to note that when you run an experiment in Scientist, both the original version in your `Use` statement and any experiments you defined in the `Try` calls will be called. This means that if your code has any side effects such as inserting into a database or sending an email, these things will occur twice. This might result in duplicate rows being inserted into a database or duplicate emails being sent.

You can potentially avoid this downside by providing the experimental versions of mock objects as their dependencies instead of real versions of a database client or an email provider.

Summary

In this chapter, we saw several different open-source libraries that can improve the readability and capabilities of your tests.

- Shouldly and FluentAssertions give you the readable syntax for writing assertions.
- Bogus allows you to generate randomized test data for values that don't matter.
- Moq and NSubstitute help you isolate dependencies and provide alternative implementations for testing.
- Snapper and Scientist .NET help catch issues where complex objects change in subtle ways.

Not every project will benefit from each of these libraries. However, knowing the tools at your disposal will help you as you refactor and maintain your code and expand your tests.

While it's possible to do all the things in this chapter without using these libraries, all of these libraries represent established community projects dedicated to solving specific technical concerns.

In the next chapter, we'll close out this section of this book with a discussion of defensive coding practices using modern C#.

Questions

1. What areas of your test code could be more readable? Are there any libraries in this chapter that might help?

2. How do mocking libraries such as Moq and NSubstitute help in testing?

3. Do you see any areas of your code where the complexity is high enough that Snapper or Scientist .NET might be able to help?

Further reading

You can find more information about the libraries discussed in this chapter at these URLs:

- *Shouldly*: https://github.com/shouldly/shouldly

- *FluentAssertions*: https://fluentassertions.com/

- *Bogus*: https://github.com/bchavez/Bogus

- *Moq*: https://github.com/moq/moq

- *NSubstitute*: https://nsubstitute.github.io/

- *Snapper*: https://github.com/theramis/Snapper

- *Scientist .NET*: https://github.com/scientistproject/Scientist.net

10

Defensive Coding Techniques

Code is almost organic and evolves over its lifetime as new features are added, fixes are implemented, and refactorings occur at regular intervals. As code changes and developers enter and leave the project, there's a chance that some of these changes may introduce bugs.

In *Part 2* of this book, we discussed testing strategies for detecting these bugs before they reach production. In this chapter, we'll talk about a few additional techniques that help developers catch and resolve bugs during development. Along the way, we'll also explore a few newer features in C# and their roles in keeping your code stable and healthy.

We'll cover the following topics in this chapter:

- Validating inputs
- Protecting against null
- Moving beyond classes
- Advanced type usage

Technical requirements

The starting code for this chapter is available from GitHub at `https://github.com/PacktPublishing/Refactoring-with-CSharp` in the `Chapter10/Ch10BeginningCode` folder.

The code in this chapter talks to a REST API, which will require an active internet connection.

Introducing the Cloudy Skies API

Our fictitious sample organization, Cloudy Skies, has a pre-existing set of web services in the form of a public **REST API**. This API intends to allow interested organizations to pull information about Cloudy Skies flights through the API. However, a steady amount of support tickets has proven that organizations are having a hard time adopting the API and using it in approved ways.

In response, Cloudy Skies has built a .NET library to help others more easily use the API.

Early testing of this library is promising, but some developers are still encountering confusing errors that ultimately appear to be related to the data they're passing the library.

The development team decided that validating parameters to public methods would help improve the adoption of their library by finding issues sooner. We'll explore this change in the next section.

Validating inputs

Input validation is the act of verifying that any inputs to your code, such as parameters or current property values, are correct before performing the requested work. We validate inputs to public methods to detect potential issues early on.

To illustrate the importance of this, let's look at a method that doesn't validate its inputs:

```
public FlightInfo? GetFlight(string id, string apiKey) {
  RestRequest request = new($"/flights/{id.ToLower()}");
  request.AddHeader("x-api-key", apiKey);
  LogApiCall(request.Resource);
  return _client.Get<FlightInfo?>(request);
}
```

The GetFlight method takes in an id parameter indicating a flight number, such as "CSA1234," whereas the apiKey parameter represents a token that must be supplied to interact with the API and get a response. Think of the token as something like a digital keycard that Cloudy Skies issues to interested organizations that want to interact with its APIs. Every request that goes to the Cloudy Skies API must include a token to authenticate and get a result.

The id parameter is important because it is used to identify the flight that we're interested in. This parameter gets added to the URL that the code makes an HTTP GET request to using the RestSharp library, which is one of many ways of interacting with web services in modern .NET.

> **Don't panic!**
> If any of the web services code or handling of authentication tokens is beyond your comfort zone, don't worry. While these are concepts you should learn as you grow, the actual mechanics of the web API are not important for this chapter. Instead, we're focusing on parameter validation.

Now that we've established what this method is doing, let's talk about how it could be better.

First of all, any value for a string is valid here for both id and apiKey. This includes values such as null and empty or whitespace strings. While you might not think that a developer might try those values for those parameters, I can think of compelling reasons someone might try either one:

- Someone might try to pass null for the `id` parameter, thinking that it would get the next flight, all flights, or possibly even a random flight
- A developer without an API key may think that API keys are only required for requests that modify data on the server or that you can interact with the API in low volumes without an API key

While both assumptions are incorrect for this API, I could see someone without knowledge of the system trying either one. In the case of Cloudy Skies, not providing a valid API key will result in a 401 unauthorized error coming back from the server.

On the other hand, not providing an `id` parameter results in a `NullReferenceException` error when the code tries to convert `id` into lowercase, as shown in *Figure 10.1*:

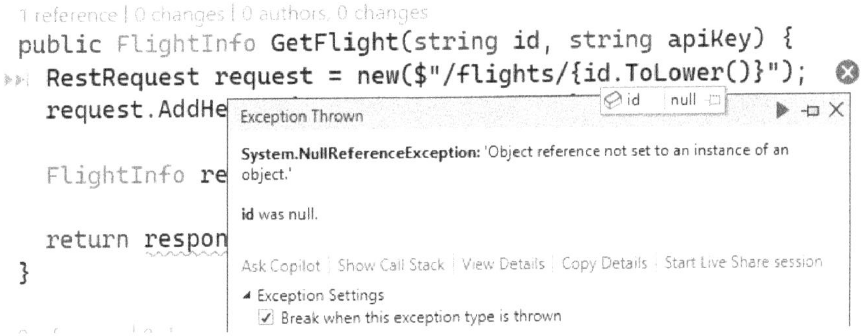

Figure 10.1 – A NullReferenceException error due to id being null when ToLower was called

Both of these errors are things that a developer trying to interact with this code could encounter, and neither one of these errors adequately tells the developer that they made a mistake in the parameters they passed in. Let's fix this with validation.

Performing basic validation

The goal of validation is to detect bad inputs early on and explicitly point out these issues before bad data gets deeper into our system. In building a library, this means that we want to validate parameters sent to our code as early as possible, preferably in the public methods other developers will interact with.

Here's a version of `GetFlight` that performs some additional validation steps:

```
public FlightInfo? GetFlight(string id, string apiKey) {
    if (string.IsNullOrEmpty(apiKey)) {
        throw new ArgumentNullException("apiKey");
    }
    if (string.IsNullOrEmpty(id)) {
        throw new ArgumentNullException("id");
    }
```

```
if (!id.StartsWith("CSA",
                    StringComparison.OrdinalIgnoreCase)) {
  throw new ArgumentOutOfRangeException("id", "Cannot
      lookup non-CSA flights");
}
RestRequest request = new($"/flights/{id.ToLower()}");
request.AddHeader("x-api-key", apiKey);
LogApiCall(request.Resource);
return _client.Get<FlightInfo?>(request);
}
```

Here, we check if `apiKey` or `id` are either null or empty strings. If that's true, we throw an `ArgumentNullException` error to tell whoever called this method that they are not providing a valid value for a specific parameter.

We also perform a check on `id` to determine whether it refers to a flight with a Cloudy Skies Airline prefix. If it doesn't, this flight will never be found since it isn't tracked by the system. In this case, it makes sense to alert the caller with an `ArgumentOutOfRangeException` error. This exception type is also commonly used with numbers or dates that are outside of acceptable ranges for a method.

> **Should we really throw exceptions here?**
>
> Many new developers think that exceptions are bad. Most developers hate encountering exceptions, and throwing exceptions can indeed be relatively slow. Keeping these things in mind, when you get invalid values, sometimes, the best option is to throw a specific exception that highlights the issue. This helps catch mistakes quickly and prevents errors that can occur from letting invalid values deeper into a system.

You may have noticed that the revised code has a lot of validation relative to the other logic in the method. There are a few ways of improving this, as we'll see in the upcoming sections, but let's work toward that goal incrementally. We'll start by looking at a better way of referring to bad parameter values.

Using the nameof keyword

Right now, the code validates parameters and throws exceptions with code like this:

```
throw new ArgumentNullException("apiKey");
```

In this example, `"apiKey"` refers to the name of the parameter, which helps developers identify which parameter the exception is complaining about.

Now, what happens if someone renames that parameter later to apiToken? This change wouldn't cause any compiler errors and the exception could still be thrown. Unfortunately, the exception would reference the old apiKey parameter name that was no longer present, which would confuse the developer encountering the error.

To help with this, C# gives us the nameof keyword, which looks like this:

```
public FlightInfo? GetFlight(string id, string apiKey) {
  if (string.IsNullOrEmpty(apiKey)) {
    throw new ArgumentNullException(nameof(apiKey));
  }
```

When your code is compiled, the nameof keyword evaluates the name of the parameter, method, or class it is used on. A string with the result of that nameof evaluation is then included in the compiled code. In other words, it's identical to the code we had before – except that if the parameter is ever renamed, our code no longer compiles until the nameof keyword is updated to refer to the renamed parameter.

This allows us to rely on the compiler to help ensure our parameter validation uses the correct parameter names, even if those parameters are renamed in the future.

Let's introduce a more concise way of throwing exceptions.

Validation with guard clauses

Right now, our validation logic consists of an if statement followed by a conditional throw statement. This validation is so common and can take up many lines of code when validation is complex that .NET now gives us a more concise way of interacting with it in the form of **guard clauses**.

We can take our validation down to a single line of code by calling ArgumentException. ThrowIfNullOrEmpty, as shown here:

```
public FlightInfo? GetFlight(string id, string apiKey) {
  ArgumentException.ThrowIfNullOrEmpty(id, nameof(id));
```

This method will check the value of the parameter it is passed in and will throw either an ArgumentNullException error if the value is null or an ArgumentException error if the value is an empty string.

There aren't a lot of these validations built into .NET right now, but if you like the idea and want validations for things such as negative values or numeric or date ranges, you'll love Steve Smith's excellent **GuardClauses library**.

Guard clauses with the GuardClauses library

To help augment the built-in guard clauses, Steve Smith created the **Ardalis.GuardClauses** library.

To use the GuardClauses library, install the latest version of Ardallis.GuardClauses via NuGet Package Manager, as we've done in prior chapters.

Next, add `using Ardalis.GuardClauses;` to the top of your `.cs` file.

Once that's been installed and referenced, you'll be able to use guard syntax, as shown in the following code:

```
public Flights GetFlightsByMiles(int maxMiles,
  string apiKey) {
  Guard.Against.NegativeOrZero(maxMiles);
  Guard.Against.NullOrWhiteSpace(apiKey);

  // Other logic omitted…
}
```

Here, the GuardClauses library provides various static methods inside `Guard.Against` syntax that allow you to validate a great many things.

If a validation condition is met – for example, if `maxMiles` is 4 when `NegativeOrZero` is called – the program continues as normal. However, if the condition is not met, an `ArgumentException` error will be thrown containing the name of the parameter that violated the condition.

I've found this library to be intuitive to write and read, and it also leads to efficient and effective guard clauses that require a minimal amount of effort.

The full extent of the GuardClauses library is well beyond the scope of this book, but you can install it and see the methods available or check out the documentation referenced in the *Further reading* section at the end of this chapter.

> **But wait – there's more!**
>
> This book's wonderful technical reviewers rightly pointed out the popular **FluentValidation library**, which offers a rich set of validation rules that can be applied to your classes. You can learn more about this library in the *Further reading* section.

Before we move on, I want to point out one aspect of the `Ardalis.GuardClauses` library that you might not have noticed.

Let's say you call a guard clause with `Guard.Against.Null(apiKey);`.

If this validation rule fails it will throw an `ArgumentException` error. This exception will have a `ParamName` property with a value of `apiKey`. Additionally, the resulting message will mention the `apiKey` parameter by name, *even though you didn't provide the name when you called the guard clause.*

This works due to the library's use of the `CallerArgumentExpression` attribute, which we'll explore next.

Using CallerMemberInformation attributes

The `nameof` keyword proved so successful in eliminating strings referring to things that were later renamed that C# grew to accompany four separate attributes that can tell you things about any given method.

Each of these attributes is applied to a method parameter. Like the `nameof` keyword, these attributes are evaluated at compile time and result in a `string` or `int` type being used in the final compiled code in their place.

The four available caller member attributes are as follows:

- **CallerFilePath** contains a string with the name and path of the file of the code calling to the method on the machine compiling the code

- **CallerLineNumber** contains an `int` type with the line number for the method call

- **CallerMemberName** contains the name of the method or property where the method call occurred

- **CallerArgumentExpression** converts the expression passed into the method into a string, before evaluating the expression

Let's look at `LogApiCall` for an example of this:

```
public static void LogApiCall(string url,
    [CallerFilePath] string file = "",
    [CallerLineNumber] int line = 0,
    [CallerMemberName] string name = "",
    [CallerArgumentExpression(nameof(url))] string expr = "")
{
    Console.WriteLine($"Making API Call to {url}");
    Console.WriteLine("Called in:");
    Console.WriteLine($"{file}:{line} at {name}");
    Console.WriteLine($"Url expression: {expr}");
}
```

This method takes in five parameters, where the first is a standard string parameter and the other four use the various caller member information attributes. Notice how these attributes all have a default value specified. When values are not specified for these parameters, the compiler will replace each parameter with values it detected during compilation.

Let's look at an example call:

```
public IEnumerable<FlightInfo> GetFlightsByMiles(
  int maxMiles, string apiKey) {
  // Validation omitted...
  string url = $"/flights/uptodistance/{maxMiles}";
  RestRequest request = new(url);
  request.AddHeader("x-api-key", apiKey);
  LogApiCall(request.Resource);
  IEnumerable<FlightInfo>? response =
    _client.Get<IEnumerable<FlightInfo>>(request);
  return response ?? Enumerable.Empty<FlightInfo>();
}
```

Notice how when `LogApiCall` is invoked, only the string parameter is specified. The remaining parameters are provided values during compilation due to the attributes on each parameter.

Also, note that the expression that was used to get that string is `request.Resource`. This expression is what `CallerArgumentExpression` uses to generate its string because the `CallerArgumentExpression` attribute requires the name of another parameter. In this case, we specified `[CallerArgumentExpression(nameof(url))]` to have it look at the expression that was passed into the `url` parameter – the first parameter the method takes in.

When this code runs, we will see the following message logged in the console:

```
Making API Call to /flights/uptodistance/500
Called in:
C:\RefactorBook\Chapter10\CloudySkiesFlightProvider.cs:51
  at GetFlightsByMiles
Url expression: request.Resource
```

As you can see, it logged the full path to the file on my hard drive, as well as the line number of the `LogApiCall` method call.

The expression of `request.Resource` is the exact string of code that's used to call that method, as shown here:

```
LogApiCall(request.Resource);
```

Caller member information attributes are very handy for certain types of things, such as logging and validation, or certain specialized scenarios such as raising `INotifyProperty` changed in **Windows Presentation Foundation** (**WPF**) applications.

Now that we've sufficiently explored working with parameters for our methods, let's look at how modern C# lets us work safely with null values.

Protecting against null

British computer scientist, Tony Hoare, is generally credited as the inventor of the null reference in programming. In 2008, he famously apologized for it, calling it his "billion-dollar mistake." This was due to the countless bugs and crashes that have occurred in various programming languages when code attempted to interact with variables currently holding null values. While I can't fault Tony Hoare, nulls can certainly be dangerous.

In .NET, this comes in the form of a `NullReferenceException` error, as we saw earlier in this chapter. You get a `NullReferenceException` error any time you attempt to invoke a method or evaluate a property on a variable that currently holds a null value.

Before C# 8, developers needed to be explicitly aware that any reference type could hold a null value and write conditional logic, such as the following code:

```
if (flight != null) {
  Console.WriteLine($"Flight {flight.Id}: {flight.Status}");
}
```

This pattern of checking for nullability and then conditionally acting became prevalent in C# because when it didn't, developers encountered `NullReferenceException` errors. Unfortunately, this led to null checks occurring throughout the code, including in many places where nulls would never be encountered.

In C# 8, nullable reference types were introduced, which helped developers understand when and where they were likely to encounter null values so that they would have active reminders to guard against null values in those places. Additionally, these improvements made it easier to remove unnecessary null checks in places where nulls were not expected.

In C# 8 and beyond, when nullability analysis is enabled, you can indicate that any reference type may be null by adding ? after the type indicator, as shown here for `FlightInfo`:

```
public FlightInfo? GetFlight(string id, string apiKey) {
  ArgumentException.ThrowIfNullOrEmpty(id);
  ArgumentException.ThrowIfNullOrEmpty(apiKey);
  RestRequest request = new($"/flights/{id.ToLower()}");
  request.AddHeader("x-Api-key", apiKey);
  LogApiCall(request.Resource);
  return client.Get<FlightInfo?>(request);
}
```

In this case, this indicates that the `GetFlight` method will return either a `FlightInfo` instance or a null value. Additionally, this indicates that the `id` and `apiKey` parameters will always have a string that is not null. If these accepted null values, they would be declared as `string? Id, string? apiKey` instead.

> **Important note**
>
> Nullability analysis in C# does not prevent you from passing null to things that say they do not accept null values, nor does it prevent you from returning null values from methods that claim to return a non-null return type. Instead, nullability analysis flags these cases as warnings, which will help you address these issues. We'll talk more about code analysis warnings in *Chapter 12*.

If we wanted to say that GetFlight could never return null, we would remove ? from the FlightInfo return type and validate that the result from the API was not null:

```
public FlightInfo GetFlight(string id, string apiKey) {
  ArgumentException.ThrowIfNullOrEmpty(id);
  ArgumentException.ThrowIfNullOrEmpty(apiKey);
  RestRequest request = new($"/flights/{id.ToLower()}");
  request.AddHeader("x-api-key", apiKey);
  LogApiCall(request.Resource);
  FlightInfo? flightInfo=_client.Get<FlightInfo?>(request);
  if (flightInfo == null) {
    string message = $"Could not find flight {id}";
    throw new InvalidOperationException(message);
  }
  return flightInfo;
}
```

The request to the API via `_client.Get` still might return a nullable value, so the code must now check for null and conditionally throw an exception if a null value is encountered. However, this guarantees that the code returns only a non-null value, which is what the return type of FlightInfo indicates with nullability analysis active.

Let's look at how to enable and disable nullability analysis in Visual Studio.

Enabling nullability analysis in C#

Since .NET 6, nullable reference types are enabled by default in new projects going forward.

However, you can enable nullable reference types in any project using C# 8 or above by adding a <Nullable>enable</Nullable> node to your project's .csproj file:

```
<Project Sdk="Microsoft.NET.Sdk">
  <PropertyGroup>
    <OutputType>Library</OutputType>
    <TargetFramework>net8.0</TargetFramework>
    <ImplicitUsings>enable</ImplicitUsings>
    <Nullable>enable</Nullable>
    <RootNamespace>Packt.CloudySkiesAir</RootNamespace>
```

```
    </PropertyGroup>
  </Project>
```

You can edit this file either in a text editor such as Notepad, or you can double-click on the project node in **Solution Explorer** to edit the file inside Visual Studio.

If you don't want nullability analysis enabled for your entire project, you can enable and disable nullability analysis with preprocessor statements such as #nullable enable and #nullable disable. For example, the following code temporarily disables nullability analysis for a class definition:

```
#nullable disable
public class FlightInfo {
    public string Id { get; set; }
    public FlightStatus Status { get; set; }
    public string Origin { get; set; }
    public string Destination { get; set; }
    public DateTime DepartureTime { get; set; }
    public DateTime ArrivalTime { get; set; }
    public int Miles { get; set; }
    public override string ToString() =>
      $"{Id} from {Origin} to {Destination} " +
      $"on {DepartureTime}. Status: {Status}";
}
#nullable restore
```

I'd encourage you to use project-level nullability analysis and avoid using #nullable when possible. I've known many developers who get nauseated every time they see a preprocessor statement. My opinion is that #nullable should be reserved for when you are moving a larger project to use nullability analysis but are not yet ready to enable it for the entire project.

Using nullability operators

Earlier, we talked about how ? indicates that a type may contain a null value, but there are several other operators related to nullability you should be aware of in C#.

First of all, the non-null assertion operator of ! tells C# that something is not going to be null and to ignore nullability warnings on that value.

One common place I use this is when working with Console.ReadLine(). This method indicates it may return a null value, but in practice, it never does in normal operation. This can be suppressed using !, as shown here:

```
Console.WriteLine("Enter a flight #: ");
string id = Console.ReadLine()!;
```

Here, we are taking `ReadLine`, which is defined as having a `string?` result and storing it in `string`. The `!` operator says that the `string?` result should be treated as if it was `string`.

Other nullability operators include the following:

- The **null-conditional operator** (`?`), which conditionally calls methods only if the object they're being invoked on is not null. For example, `_conn?.Dispose()` calls the `Dispose` method only if `_conn` is not null.

- The **null coalescing operator** (`??`), which uses a backup value in case something is null. For example, `int miles = flight?.Miles ?? 0;` uses null-conditional and null coalescing operators to safely get `Miles` out of a flight or use `0` when no flight is present.

- The **null coalescing assignment operator** (`??=`) assigns a value to a variable only if the variable is null already. For example, `message ??= "An unexpected error has occurred";` will only set the new error message in `message` if `message` is null. This allows us to effectively replace null values with backup values.

The combination of nullability analysis and nullability operators helps us make intelligent decisions around null values in concise ways. This keeps our code efficient and focused while guiding us toward having a cohesive strategy around handling null values in code.

Let's take a broader look at changes we can make at the class level to help design more robust applications.

Moving beyond classes

In C# 9 and beyond, Microsoft has made concerted efforts to give developers new options for working with classes through things such as record types, init-only properties, primary constructors, and more.

In this section, we'll explore how these newer C# constructs can improve the design of your classes.

Preferring immutable classes

In recent years, immutable classes have become more and more popular. This immutability refers to the inability to change an object after it has been created.

What this means is that once an object exists, you cannot modify its state and instead are limited to creating new objects that are like the original. If you're familiar with working with string and DateTime objects in .NET, you've seen this concept with methods such as `ToLower` on string and `AddDays` on DateTime returning a new object instead of modifying the original object.

Let's look at a small class representing a boarding pass that is currently mutable (changeable) and then convert it into an immutable class:

```
public class BoardingPass {
  public FlightInfo Flight { get; set; }
```

```
    public string Passenger { get; set; }
    public int Group { get; set; }
    public string Seat { get; set; }
}
```

This is a "plain old C# object" with properties with getters and setters. Thinking about the class logically, there are several problems:

- There's nothing preventing `Flight`, `Passenger`, or `Seat` from having a null value.

- Once a pass is created, properties such as `passenger`, `boarding group`, `seat`, and even `flight` can be changed. This doesn't make sense in the context of an airline business where a new boarding pass would need to be issued to change these.

We can change this object so that it's immutable and requires valid values for these parameters by removing their setters and adding a constructor with validation:

```
public BoardingPass(FlightInfo flight, string passenger,
    string seat, int group) {
    ArgumentNullException.ThrowIfNull(flight);
    ArgumentException.ThrowIfNullOrEmpty(passenger);
    ArgumentException.ThrowIfNullOrEmpty(seat);
    if (group < 1 || group > 8) {
        throw new ArgumentOutOfRangeException(nameof(group));
    }
    Flight = flight;
    Passenger = passenger;
    Seat = seat;
    Group = group;
}
```

This constructor now requires that valid values are present for all properties on the object in object creation. Meanwhile, the removal of setters for the properties ensures that the class stays valid and cannot be changed.

If we needed to, we could add new methods to the `BoardingPass` class that create and return a new `BoardingPass` object with similar characteristics to the original in a similar manner to how various string and DateTime methods work. However, `with expressions` give us a more interesting way of doing this, as we'll see later in this chapter.

While using immutability may seem more inconvenient than beneficial at first, there are a few key advantages of using immutable classes:

- Immutable classes can be validated during creation and ensured that they are in a valid state. Once created, this valid state cannot change.

- When objects can be modified anywhere in your code, this makes it harder to track down what changed an object when multiple other classes may have a reference to it. Immutable objects prevent this from occurring.

- Some concepts just make more sense as immutable objects, such as a prior version of a document or a boarding pass for a passenger at an airport.

- Since immutable objects don't change, they can be reliably worked with in multi-threaded applications. Without immutability, you'd need to rely on using `Interlocked`, the `lock` keyword, or thread-safe collections to avoid bugs.

Of course, having to specify all the properties of an object in its constructor can be cumbersome for classes with many properties. Additionally, not every class in your project needs to be immutable. For those classes that would benefit from immutability, C#'s required keyword and init-only properties help alleviate this burden.

Using required and init-only properties

The downside of adding every property as a parameter to class constructors is that your constructors can start to become larger than you'd like. Additionally, creating objects that require many constructor parameters is tedious and error-prone and the creation of individual objects can be tedious and confusing, particularly when many constructor parameters are needed.

On the other hand, object initializers can be more readable, but until recently, they lacked a way of ensuring properties are present.

Look at the two ways of creating a `BoardingPass` object and see which appears more readable to you:

```
BoardingPass p1 = new(myFlight, "Amleth Hamlet", "2B", 1);
BoardingPass p2 = {
  Flight = myFlight,
  Passenger = "Amleth Hamlet",
  Seat = "2B",
  Group = 1
};
```

The object initializer version used in p2 is more readable and maintainable, particularly as the number of properties you might want to set in the class grows over time.

The traditional downside of this approach was that a developer using the object initializer might forget to set important required properties. C# 11 introduced the `required` keyword, which will fail to compile if a required property is not explicitly initialized during object initialization or in the constructor when the `Passenger` property is omitted, as shown in *Figure 10.2*:

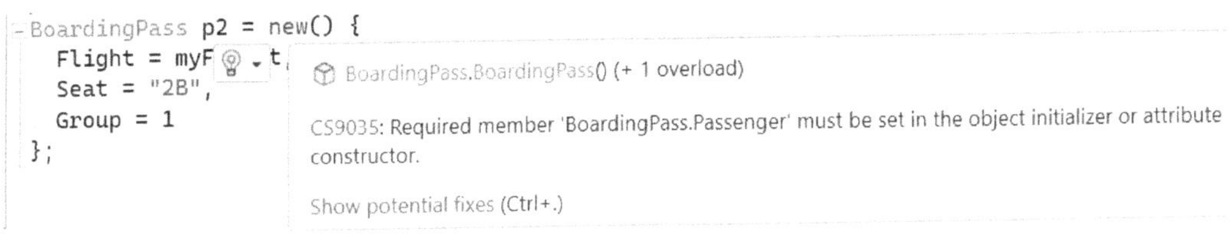

```
- BoardingPass p2 = new() {
    Flight = myF  ⊕ . t
    Seat = "2B",
    Group = 1
  };
```

⊕ BoardingPass.BoardingPass() (+ 1 overload)

CS9035: Required member 'BoardingPass.Passenger' must be set in the object initializer or attribute constructor.

Show potential fixes (Ctrl+.)

Figure 10.2 – A compiler error due to Passenger not being set

To achieve this, we can add `required` to any property definitions on the class that we want to make sure they are explicitly set by the time the object-initializer completes. The following version of `BoardingPass` features required properties:

```
public class BoardingPass {
    public required FlightInfo Flight { get; init; }
    public required string Passenger { get; init; }
    public required int Group { get; init; }
    public required string Seat { get; init; }
}
```

You may have also noticed that this class definition defines these properties as `{ get; init; }` instead of `{ get; }` or `{ get; set; }`. While the traditional `get; set;` combination allows a property to be changed at any time, this violates immutability. The `get;` version removes the ability to set the property anywhere but the constructor, which means properties defined as `get;` cannot be set in object initializers.

The newer `get; init;` combination that was added in C# 9 allows the property to be set in the constructor or initializer, but no longer allows setting after the object is initialized. This helps us support our immutable class design while not restricting the user to using constructors.

I believe that object initializers are the future of .NET and nowadays tend to favor required properties with `get; init;` when designing classes for immutability.

Speaking of the future, let's look at a brand-new feature in C# 12: primary constructors for reference types.

Primary constructors

Primary constructors are constructors that must be called to initialize the class and provide a way of automatically creating fields in your class. We'll talk more about what that "must be called" phrase entails in a moment, but let's start by looking at a simple example:

```
public class BoardingPass(string Passenger) {
    public required FlightInfo Flight { get; init; }
    public required int Group { get; init; }
    public required string Seat { get; init; }
```

```
    public override string ToString() =>
      $"{Passenger} in group {Group} " +
      $"for seat {Seat} of {Flight.Id}";
}
```

This version of `BoardingPass` has parentheses and a parameter list immediately following the class declaration. This is the primary constructor for the class.

Any parameters declared in the primary constructor are available as if they were init-only properties. This makes a primary constructor roughly equivalent to the following C# code:

```
public class BoardingPass {
  public BoardingPass(string passenger) {
    this.Passenger = passenger;
  }
  public string Passenger {get; init; }
  // Other members omitted for brevity...
}
```

The advantage of primary constructors is that they are very concise and do not require you to define a constructor or field definitions.

Primary constructors can work with other constructors, though any other constructor you declare must call the primary constructor using the `this` keyword, as shown here:

```
public class BoardingPass(string Passenger) {
  public BoardingPass(FlightInfo flight, string passenger)
   : this(passenger) {
    Flight = flight;
  }
  // other members omitted for brevity...
}
```

Essentially, your primary constructor must always be called – either on its own or from another constructor via the `this` keyword.

Primary constructors are not unique to classes and exist for records starting in C# 9.

Converting classes into record classes

Throughout this book, I've alluded to **record classes** several times without defining them or going into detail on why you'd want to use one.

To understand record classes, let's talk briefly about equality in classes. By default, two objects are considered equal if they both live in the same memory address in the heap.

This means that, by default, two separate objects with identical properties are not equal. For example, the following code would evaluate these two boarding passes as different from each other:

```
BoardingPass pass1 = new("Amleth Hamlet") {
    Flight = nextFlight,
    Seat = "2B",
    Group = 2
};
BoardingPass pass2 = new("Amleth Hamlet") {
    Flight = nextFlight,
    Seat = "2B",
    Group = 2
};
Console.WriteLine(pass1 == pass2); // false
```

You can change this behavior by overriding Equals and GetHashCode on the BoardingPass class, as we did in *Chapter 5*. However, record types give us an easier way of managing this.

Record classes are like normal C# classes except equality works by comparing all properties to each other. In other words, record classes are like normal C# classes that have overridden Equals and GetHashCode.

Let's redeclare our boarding pass as a record class:

```
public record class BoardingPass(string Passenger) {
  public required FlightInfo Flight { get; init; }
  public required int Group { get; init; }
  public required string Seat { get; init; }
  public override string ToString() =>
    $"{Passenger} in group {Group} " +
    $"for seat {Seat} of {Flight.Id}";
}
```

Now, we can successfully compare two boarding passes using just their values:

```
BoardingPass pass1 = new("Amleth Hamlet") {
    Flight = nextFlight,
    Seat = "2B",
    Group = 2
};
BoardingPass pass2 = new("Amleth Hamlet") {
    Flight = nextFlight,
    Seat = "2B",
    Group = 2
};
Console.WriteLine(pass1 == pass2); // true
```

These two classes are considered equal because they carry the same values. Note that the `Flight` property refers to a `FlightInfo` object, which is still a standard C# class and uses traditional reference equality. This means that boarding passes must point to the same `FlightInfo` object in memory; otherwise, they will not be considered equal. This can be changed by making `FlightInfo` a record class as well.

I recommend using record classes for small objects that you might want to compare to each other. They also might be helpful for classes that might be frequently instantiated, such as objects coming from the database or an external API call.

Let's move on to talk about my favorite new way of creating objects: `with` expressions.

Cloning objects using with expressions

with expressions are a shorthand way of creating an object that's like another object but with a few differences. `with` expressions work very well with immutable records by allowing you to clone and slightly tweak the source record without making any modifications to the original record.

Let's say that Hamlet's boarding pass for seat 2B on the flight needed to be changed. The system could instantiate a new boarding pass that was just like the original one except for seat 2C using the following code:

```
BoardingPass pass = new("Amleth Hamlet") {
    Flight = nextFlight,
    Seat = "2B",
    Group = 2
};
BoardingPass newPass = pass with { Seat = "3B" };
```

This creates a new boarding pass based on the original one but with one property slightly different.

If we wanted to move Hamlet to have a new seat but an earlier boarding group, we could do that as well by listing an additional property, as shown here:

```
BoardingPass newPass2 = pass with {Seat = "3B", Group = 1};
```

I find `with` expressions to be one of the most exciting things about working with record classes in C# and I love the direction the language is going in to streamline the creation of objects.

This style of referring to property values is not unique to the `with` expression, as we'll see in the next section with pattern matching.

Advanced type usage

In this final section of this chapter, we'll see how new and old language features help you build better types.

Exploring pattern matching

It turns out that we can use the same style of syntax we used with expressions earlier to conditionally match different objects through **pattern matching**.

To explain what I mean, let's start with an example that loops over different boarding passes:

```
List<BoardingPass> passes = PassGenerator.Generate();
foreach (BoardingPass pass in passes) {
  if (pass is { Group: 1 or 2 or 3,
                Flight.Status: FlightStatus.Pending
              }) {
    Console.WriteLine($"{pass.Passenger} board now");
  } else if (pass is { Flight.Status: FlightStatus.Active
                       or FlightStatus.Completed
                     }) {
    Console.WriteLine($"{pass.Passenger} flight missed");
  } else {
    Console.WriteLine($"{pass.Passenger} please wait");
  }
}
```

This code loops over a collection of boarding passes and does one of three things:

- If the flight is `Pending` and the passenger is in group 1, 2, or 3, we tell them to board

If the flight is `Active` or `Completed`, we tell the passenger they missed their flight

If neither of these cases is true, the flight must be `Pending`, but the passenger's group is not boarding, so we tell them to wait

The code is a little arbitrary, particularly in how it deals with the boarding group, but it illustrates some of the capabilities of pattern matching.

Using pattern matching, you can evaluate one or more properties on an object in an `if` statement to concisely check multiple things at once.

While you can use pattern matching in `if` statements, they are also commonly used in switch expressions, as we saw in *Chapter 3*. We could rewrite our code from earlier into a switch expression, as follows:

```
List<BoardingPass> passes = PassGenerator.Generate();
foreach (BoardingPass pass in passes) {
  string message = pass switch {
    { Flight.Status: FlightStatus.Pending,
      Group: 1 or 2 or 3 }
      => $"{pass.passenger} board now",
```

```
    { Flight.Status: not FlightStatus.Pending }
      => $"{pass.passenger} flight missed",
      _ => $"{pass.passenger} please wait",
  };
  Console.WriteLine(message);
}
```

Here, we can see the switch expressions concept combined with the power of pattern matching to set a string in the `message` variable. Note that the code uses `not FlightStatus.Pending` instead of `FlightStatus.Active` or `FlightStatus.Completed` for brevity and to illustrate the usage of the `not` keyword in negating or inverting pattern matching expressions.

While this code takes some adjustment to learn to read, there's also very little "waste" in this syntax. Almost the entirety of every line of code is centered around either the conditions that must be true or the value to use when they are true. Additionally, this syntax can handle more complex scenarios such as or and not statements more easily than normal C# logic can.

Of course, as with any new C# language feature, if the readability cost is too high for you and your team, you are free to avoid switch expressions and pattern matching entirely.

Now that we've seen how pattern matching and switch expressions work together in the latest versions of C#, let's look at one of C#'s earliest enhancements: generics.

Using generics to reduce duplication

Generics are a concept that every .NET developer encounters and works with daily.

When you work with `List<string>` (pronounced "list of strings"), you are working with a generic `List` object that can hold something of a specific type – in this case, strings.

Generics work by specifying at least one type parameter that goes into either a class or a method and allows the class or method to be structured around that type.

To illustrate the advantage of generics, let's look at a very simple `FlightDictionary` class that stores `FlightInfo` objects by their identifiers using a dictionary and incorporates some light console logging:

```
public class FlightDictionary {
  private readonly Dictionary<string, FlightInfo> _items =
    new();
  public bool Contains(string identifier)
    => _items.ContainsKey(identifier);
  public void AddItem(string id, FlightInfo item) {
    Console.WriteLine($"Adding {id}");
    _items[id] = item;
  }
```

```
  public FlightInfo? GetItem(string id) {
    if (Contains(id)) {
      Console.WriteLine($"Found {id}");
      return _items[id];
    }
    Console.WriteLine($"Could not find {id}");
    return null;
  }
}
```

This class is the beginning of a new collection class, like the `Dictionary` class provided by .NET. It allows external callers to add, retrieve, and check for `FlightInfo` by a string identifier.

While this code is very simple and missing several features I'd expect from a real collection class, it should serve to illustrate the need for generics by asking the following question: What happens if we like this class so much for `FlightInfo` objects that we want to use something like it for `BoardingPass` objects?

Often, this would result in someone copying and pasting the `FlightDictionary` class to create a new `BoardingPassDictionary`, as shown here:

```
public class BoardingPassDictionary {
  private readonly Dictionary<string, BoardingPass> _items
    = new();
  public bool Contains(string identifier)
    => _items.ContainsKey(identifier);
  public void AddItem(string id, BoardingPass item) {
    Console.WriteLine($"Adding {id}");
    _items[id] = item;
  }
  public BoardingPass? GetItem(string id) {
    if (Contains(id)) {
      Console.WriteLine($"Found {id}");
      return _items[id];
    }
    Console.WriteLine($"Could not find {id}");
    return null;
  }
}
```

The only difference between these two classes is the type of item being stored.

What generics let us do is declare a class that takes in parameters of the types it should use for different operations.

Now, let's look at a more reusable version of this class that accepts generic type parameters for the type used as a key for each item, as well as the type used as a value:

```
public class LoggingDictionary<TKey, TValue> {
  private readonly Dictionary<TKey, TValue> _items
    = new();
  public bool Contains(TKey identifier)
    => _items.ContainsKey(identifier);
  public void AddItem(TKey id, TValue item) {
    Console.WriteLine($"Adding {id}");
    _items[id] = item;
  }
  public TValue? GetItem(TKey id) {
    if (Contains(id)) {
      Console.WriteLine($"Found {id}");
      return _items[id];
    }
    Console.WriteLine($"Could not find {id}");
    return default(TValue);
  }
}
```

This implementation of the class depends on two generic type arguments: TKey and TValue. These parameters can be whatever names you want them to be, but the convention is to use **PascalCasing** and start each type parameter with the letter T.

With this class, a new LoggingDictionary can be created for any types you might want to support using the following syntax:

```
LoggingDictionary<string, BoardingPass> passDict = new();
LoggingDictionary<string, FlightInfo> flightDict = new();
```

Generics are something that has been around since .NET Framework 2.0 but still offers value today in adding reusability to classes.

Let's close this chapter out with a brief look into a new C# 12 feature: **type aliases**.

Introducing type aliases with the using directive

Let's say you're developing a system and you need to work with a set of data types you're not certain about and may need to change in the future. Alternatively, you might have a routine need for some hideous-looking types, such as needing to deal with List<string, Dictionary<Passenger, List<FlightInfo>>> throughout a class.

While one approach for the latter problem might be to introduce your class to hide away some of this complexity, a new option in C# 12 is to use **type aliases** via the `using` statement.

Let's look at simplifying some of the code in `CloudySkiesFlightProvider.cs` to reduce the places where `IEnumerable<FlightInfo>` appears. We'll use the `GetFlightsByMiles` method as an example:

```
public IEnumerable<FlightInfo> GetFlightsByMiles(
  int maxMiles, string apiKey) {
  RestRequest request =
    new($"/flights/uptodistance/{maxMiles}");
  request.AddHeader("x-api-key", apiKey);
  LogApiCall(request.Resource);
  IEnumerable<FlightInfo>? response =
    _client.Get<IEnumerable<FlightInfo>>(request);
  return response ?? Enumerable.Empty<FlightInfo>();
}
```

This code isn't bad, but imagine that you felt very strongly that you didn't like looking at `IEnumerable<FlightInfo>` everywhere and you'd rather have a custom type defined for this.

Using C# 12, you could add the following line to the `using` statements in the file:

```
using Flights = System.Collections.Generic.IEnumerable<
Packt.CloudySkiesAir.Chapter10.FlightInfo>;
```

With this one change, you can now change your method to use your new type alias:

```
public Flights GetFlightsByMiles(int maxMiles,
  string apiKey) {
  RestRequest request =
    new($"/flights/uptodistance/{maxMiles}");
  request.AddHeader("x-api-key", apiKey);
  LogApiCall(request.Resource);
  Flights? response = _client.Get<Flights>(request);
  return response ?? Enumerable.Empty<FlightInfo>();
}
```

This code doesn't change that you're dealing with `IEnumerable<FlightInfo>` in this method, but it does reduce the amount of code you have to type and simplifies the code for reading.

Additionally, if you ever wanted to change to a different type in these places, you now just need to modify the `using` statement to use a different type instead.

I'm not sure if obscuring the underlying type offers more benefit than potential confusion, but I could see some places where it might be helpful, particularly in dealing with complex generic types or working with tuples (collections of multiple values).

Time will tell on the effectiveness of type aliases and the best places to use them, but I'm glad we now have the option.

Summary

In this chapter, we looked at a variety of ways of ensuring your classes are safe and reusable through means such as argument validation, caller member information, nullability analysis, and using modern C# features such as record classes, primary constructors, pattern matching, and enhanced properties with the `required` and `init` keywords.

These language features help you detect issues earlier in development, work with objects more effectively, and write fewer lines of code overall.

This concludes *Part 2* of this book. In *Part 3*, we'll look at how AI and code analysis tools can help you and your team sustainably build better software.

Questions

Answers the following questions to test your knowledge of this chapter:

1. How can throwing exceptions be beneficial to your code?
2. What are the various ways you can declare a property in C#?
3. What are the various ways you can instantiate an object in C#?
4. What are the differences between classes and record classes?

Further reading

You can find more information about features discussed in this chapter at these URLs:

- *Guard Clauses library*: `https://github.com/ardalis/GuardClauses`
- *Fluent Validation library*: `https://github.com/FluentValidation/FluentValidation`
- *Caller Member Information*: `https://learn.microsoft.com/en-us/dotnet/csharp/language-reference/attributes/caller-information`
- *Primary constructors and using aliases*: `https://devblogs.microsoft.com/dotnet/check-out-csharp-12-preview/`

- *Safer Nullability in Modern C#*: `https://newdevsguide.com/2023/02/25/csharp-nullability/`

- *Classes, structs, and records in C#*: `https://learn.microsoft.com/en-us/dotnet/csharp/fundamentals/object-oriented/`

- *Choosing Between Exceptions or Validation:* `https://ardalis.com/guard-clauses-and-exceptions-or-validation/`

Part 3: Advanced Refactoring with AI and Code Analysis

The third part of this book focuses on advanced refactoring techniques using artificial intelligence and modern code analysis capabilities built into Visual Studio.

This chapter introduces GitHub Copilot Chat as a way to refactor, generate, inspect, document, and test code.

We then extensively cover the code analysis capabilities of Visual Studio by introducing the code analysis tooling and rulesets as well as some third-party tools that can help catch additional issues. Finally, we explore how Visual Studio's code analysis is based on Roslyn Analyzers by building and deploying our own Roslyn Analyzer as both a Visual Studio extension and as a NuGet package.

This chapter will give you a deep understanding of code analysis issues as well as new productivity tools to help detect and resolve issues in their code.

This part contains the following chapters:

- *Chapter 11, AI-Assisted Refactoring with GitHub Copilot*
- *Chapter 12, Code Analysis in Visual Studio*
- *Chapter 13, Creating a Roslyn Analyzer*
- *Chapter 14, Refactoring Code with Roslyn Analyzers*

11

AI-Assisted Refactoring with GitHub Copilot

Change is a constant in technology, and that's certainly true in the .NET ecosystem. Every year, Microsoft releases a new version of .NET and C# packed with new features to keep the language exciting, useful, and relevant as technology changes. But perhaps the most significant changes to .NET development in the last two years have come not from the major language releases, but in the field of artificial intelligence through AI agents such as GitHub Copilot and ChatGPT.

In this chapter, we'll explore how GitHub Copilot integrates into Visual Studio and brings ChatGPT-like conversational AI into your editor. We'll also explore some of the interesting possibilities this opens and some of the things we must keep in mind when considering whether this new technology has a place in our toolset.

We'll cover the following topics in this chapter:

- Introducing GitHub Copilot
- Getting started with GitHub Copilot in Visual Studio
- Refactoring with GitHub Copilot Chat
- Drafting documentation with GitHub Copilot Chat
- Generating test ideas with GitHub Copilot Chat
- Understanding the limits of GitHub Copilot

Technical requirements

The starting code for this chapter is available from GitHub at `https://github.com/PacktPublishing/Refactoring-with-CSharp` in the `Chapter11/Ch11BeginningCode` folder.

Introducing GitHub Copilot

In 2021, GitHub announced a new artificial intelligence tool called **GitHub Copilot**. GitHub Copilot is an editor extension that integrates into different editors including JetBrains Rider, VS Code, and all editions of Visual Studio 2022.

What GitHub Copilot does is it looks at the code you just typed and generates predictions for the code it thinks you're about to type. If it has a prediction and you are not currently typing, GitHub Copilot displays the prediction in grey text in front of your cursor for you to evaluate and possibly add to your code, as shown in *Figure 11.1*:

```
public static void Main(string[] args) {
    int x = 2;
    int y = 2;

    // Add and display the two numbers
    Console.WriteLine(x + y);
}
    ▲ 8 of 18 ▼  void Console.WriteLine(int value)
```

Figure 11.1 – GitHub Copilot suggesting code to add as the developer types

Copilot does this by using a predictive machine learning model that has been trained on various pieces of code in many different programming languages, including C#, F#, JavaScript, and SQL.

Understanding GitHub's predictive model

If this sounds familiar, it's because GitHub Copilot's model is a specialized machine learning model built around a promising new model training technique called **transformers**.

Transformers, introduced in 2017 in a paper called *Attention is All You Need* (https://research.google/pubs/pub46201/), allow machine learning models to be trained on larger bodies of text while still retaining the context of how different pieces of text related to each other.

This innovation has led to technologies such as Google BERT (which powered Google search predictions), MidJourney, and DALL-E (which can generate art from textual prompts), and the extremely popular ChatGPT by OpenAI that can mimic conversations with humans.

Transformer-based models are now commonly referred to as **large language models** (**LLMs**). Their superpower is their ability to memorize patterns in text and generate new text that mimics patterns it has internalized in its model.

> **Ever wondered what GPT stood for?**
>
> The GPT acronym (found in ChatGPT, GPT-4, and similar) stands for **generative pre-trained transformer**. In other words, this is a transformer-based model used to generate new content, and the model has been trained on a large volume of data.

These LLMs take in a textual prompt and generate some form of output. With chat LLMs, the prompt might be a question such as "What is .NET?" and the output might be a short description of .NET, as pictured in this interaction with Bing Chat (`https://www.bing.com/`) in *Figure 11.2*:

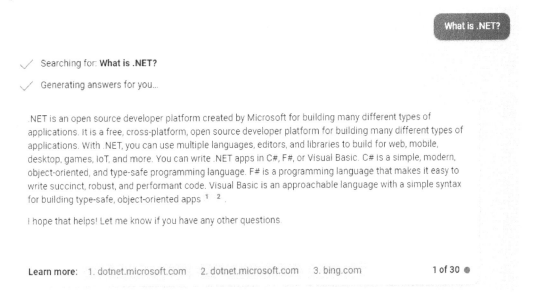

Figure 11.2 – Bing Chat describing .NET in response to a short prompt

There is no intelligent understanding built into an LLM. These models do not think or have thoughts of their own, but rather use mathematics to identify similarities between the text they receive and the large volumes of text the model was trained on.

While LLM systems may seem eerily intelligent at times, this is because they are emulating the intelligence of the authors of the various books, blog posts, tweets, and other materials they've been trained on.

GitHub Copilot uses an LLM called **Codex**. The Codex model is produced by OpenAI and was trained not on blog posts or tweets but on open-source software repositories.

This means that when you type something into your editor, the text you type can be used as a prompt to predict the next line of code you might type. This is very similar to how Google search predicts the next few words in a search term or how ChatGPT generates textual replies.

We'll talk more about the use of open-source code in GitHub Copilot and whether it is appropriate to use GitHub Copilot in a workplace project near the end of this chapter. For now, let's move on to some of the newer aspects of GitHub Copilot.

Starting the conversation with GitHub Copilot Chat

GitHub extended Copilot's code generation capabilities by introducing **GitHub Copilot Chat**. GitHub Copilot Chat gives you the ability to interact with a conversational AI agent like ChatGPT directly in your editor.

This means that you can chat with an LLM in Visual Studio and do things such as the following:

- Ask it to explain a block of code

- Generate new code using textual prompts

- Ask Copilot for ways to improve the quality of your code

- Have Copilot draft unit tests or documentation for methods

I've even used Copilot to generate intentionally messy code just to practice refactoring.

A typical interaction with GitHub Copilot Chat involves the user selecting some code and then pressing *Alt + /* to start a conversation. For example, *Figure 11.3* shows the user typing a text prompt to GitHub Copilot Chat with a small block of code selected:

```
 6    public static List<BoardingPass> Generate() {
 7        Faker faker = new();
 8        List<BoardingPass> passes = new();
 9
10        for (int i = 0; i < 15; i++) {
11            BoardingPass pass = new(faker.Name.FullName()) {
```

> Explain the current selected lines
>
> AI suggestions might be inaccurate.
>
> I'm confused by this code. What does this do?

```
12            Flight = GenerateFlight(faker),
13            Seat = faker.Random.Int(1, 60) + faker.Random.String2(2, "ABCDEF"),
14            Group = faker.Random.Number(1, 8)
15        };
16
17        passes.Add(pass);
18        }
19
20        return passes;
21    }
```

Figure 11.3 – Asking GitHub Copilot Chat a question

From there, GitHub Copilot Chat generates a textual response that is shown to the user, as seen in *Figure 11.4*:

This code is a static class that generates 15 **BoardingPass** instances. **BoardingPass** is a class that represents a boarding pass, which is an authorization pass that lets passengers board a particular flight. For each **BoardingPass** created, the passenger's full name is set as the constructor parameter. The **Flight**, **Seat**, and **Group** details of each **BoardingPass** are then obtained from a call to the private **GenerateFlight** method. The **Flight** property of the **BoardingPass** is set to the **FlightInfo** value that the **GenerateFlight** method returns. **GenerateFlight** method is responsible for creating a new instance of the **FlightInfo** class and populating it with random values. The values generated include the **Miles**, **Status**, **Id**, **ArrivalTime**, **DepartureTime**, **Origin** and **Destination**.

✧ What is the `Faker` class used for?

Figure 11.4 – GitHub Copilot generating an explanation of the block of code

If you feel you're too experienced with C# to fully benefit from this feature, I want to assure you that it has value beyond basic programming. Sometimes when maintaining code, you'll encounter strange method calls that don't make sense and you don't have any documentation to tell you what the developer was trying to do. When this happens, having Chat's opinion can be very valuable in understanding the intent of the developer who wrote the code.

Of course, Chat can be used to generate code, as we'll see in the next section.

The bottom line for me is that programming with GitHub Copilot Chat is something that not only amplifies my capabilities as a developer but also helps keep me focused since I have fewer reasons to go check the documentation or leave my editor. Between the automation capabilities built into the Chat LLM and this added extra focus, GitHub Copilot Chat is a significant boost to my productivity and capabilities.

I suspect you'll like GitHub Copilot Chat too, so let's see how to get started.

Getting started with GitHub Copilot in Visual Studio

In order to work with GitHub Copilot, you'll need to have a GitHub account. If you don't have one, you can sign up for a free GitHub account at `https://github.com/signup`.

GitHub Copilot also requires that you work with Visual Studio 2022 version 17.4.4 or later. If you haven't installed Visual Studio, you can download a copy at `https://visualstudio.microsoft.com/downloads/`.

If you need to update or check your Visual Studio version, a quick way of doing either task is to launch the **Visual Studio Installer** from the Windows menu. This will let you see your current version and optionally update your edition of Visual Studio, as shown in *Figure 11.5*:

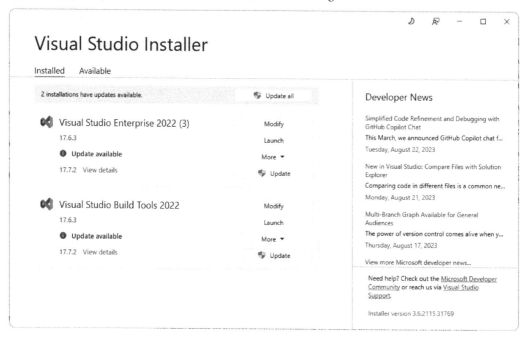

Figure 11.5 – Updating Visual Studio from the Visual Studio Installer

Once you have a GitHub account and an up-to-date edition of Visual Studio, you can install the GitHub Copilot extension.

Installing and activating GitHub Copilot

To install GitHub Copilot, launch Visual Studio, choose the **Extensions** menu, and then select **Manage Extensions**. Next, search for **GitHub Copilot** and download and install the extension, as shown in *Figure 11.6*:

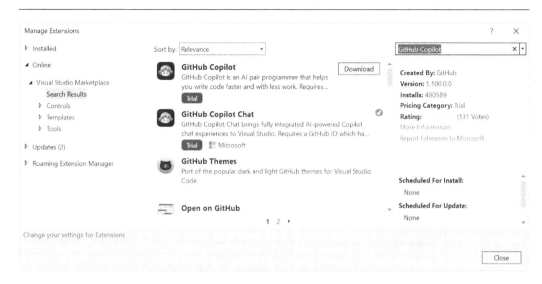

Figure 11.6 – Installing GitHub Copilot in Visual Studio

Next, you will need to log in to GitHub within Visual Studio to link the extension to your GitHub account. Follow the instructions at `https://docs.github.com/en/copilot/getting-started-with-github-copilot?tool=visualstudio` for the most up-to-date instructions on how to do this.

GitHub Copilot Chat is currently a separate extension from GitHub Copilot. If you want to try Chat, I recommend you install Copilot on its own and ensure it works first. Once you've done this, repeat the installation process for the Chat extension.

Some GitHub Copilot features, such as Chat, may need to be enabled or require additional configuration. You can do so by going to the **Tools** menu and then selecting **Options…** and finding the **GitHub** node in the list.

Getting access to GitHub Copilot

While GitHub itself is free, GitHub Copilot is a premium feature that requires you to have a GitHub Premium license or be part of GitHub Copilot for Business account. We'll talk more about the benefits of Copilot for Business near the end of this chapter.

At the time of this writing, GitHub charges $10 USD/month for individuals or $19/month per user for a Copilot for Business account. As with any emerging technology, pricing and availability may change over time.

Now that we've covered how to install and get access to Copilot, let's see it in action.

Generating suggestions with GitHub Copilot

In your `Program.cs` file for this chapter's code, type a comment such as `// Populate a list of random numbers`, then move down to the next line.

Next, type the letters Ra and wait a moment before continuing. If everything is configured right, you should hopefully see a suggestion similar to the one I encountered in *Figure 11.7*:

```
// Populate a list of random numbers
Random rand = new Random();
}    Random
     RandomAccess
     Range
```

Figure 11.7 – GitHub Copilot helping at Random

Here, GitHub Copilot has suggested some code based on the context it has observed in the area. In my case, its suggestion was `Random rand = new Random();`, which is a valid C# code.

In your case, it may suggest something different, including something that potentially doesn't even make sense or compile.

Keep in mind that LLMs such as GitHub Copilot are not intelligent, but they memorize patterns and trends in their training data. Sometimes those trends work, while other times they look plausible but reference properties or capabilities that simply don't exist.

Because GitHub Copilot and systems like it are trained on older code, you'll sometimes notice Copilot generating out-of-date code or code using obsolete APIs. It's also entirely possible that Copilot generates code with bugs, security vulnerabilities, performance issues, or other bad things. It's your responsibility as a programmer to identify good and bad code.

Now that we've covered the basics of working with Copilot, let's see what this has to do with refactoring by working with GitHub Copilot Chat.

Interacting with GitHub Copilot Chat

With GitHub Copilot Chat installed and configured, let's try our experiment again with a list of random numbers.

Remove any code you added after the comment on populating a list of random numbers. Next, move your typing cursor to the line below the comment as if you were about to start typing a line of code there.

From here, let's show the GitHub Copilot Chat window by selecting **View** and then choosing **GitHub Copilot Chat**. You should see the **GitHub Copilot Chat** pane, shown in *Figure 11.8*:

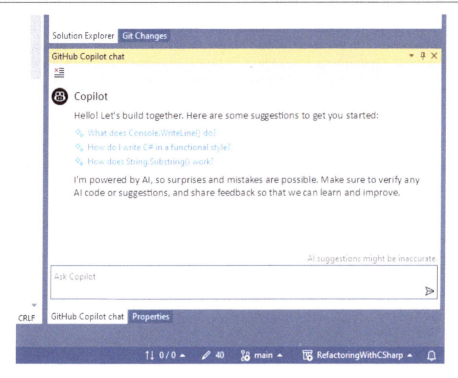

Figure 11.8 – The GitHub Copilot Chat pane

In the text box, type in `Generate a list of 10 random numbers` and press *Enter*. With any luck, you should see something like *Figure 11.9*:

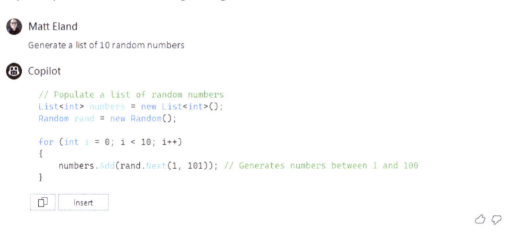

Figure 11.9 – A code suggestion from GitHub Copilot Chat

If you've ever interacted with ChatGPT or similar conversational AI agents, this should look very similar to that experience. In this case, Copilot Chat generated some code that we can accept either by clicking on the first button to copy the code or the **Insert** button to add it to the editor directly.

After clicking **Insert**, you should see a preview of code appear in your Main method. Click **Accept** and the code will be inserted.

> **Tip**
>
> If you don't like working with the GitHub Copilot Chat pane, you can bring up GitHub Copilot Chat suggestions at any time with the *Alt + /* keyboard shortcut.

If GitHub Copilot Chat doesn't seem like it's working, open the **Output** view and choose **Show output from: GitHub Copilot Chat**, as shown in *Figure 11.10*:

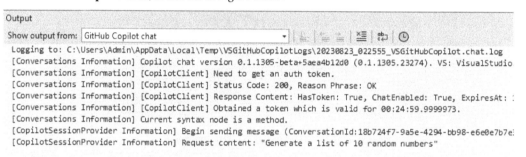

Figure 11.10 – Diagnostic information from GitHub Copilot Chat

This diagnostic information has helped me track down a few issues, but equally often the solution is simply to re-open Visual Studio. Thankfully, this diagnostic information is rarely ever needed, but it's nice to know where to find it if you need it.

Now that we've seen Copilot at work, let's use it to refactor some code.

Refactoring with GitHub Copilot Chat

Because GitHub Copilot Chat was trained on open-source repositories, it has had a lot of exposure to people writing about code. Because of this, its likelihood of being able to provide helpful insight is high.

To see this, we'll refactor the aptly-named RefactorMe.cs file, which looks like this:

```
namespace Packt.CloudySkiesAir.Chapter11;
public class RefactorMe {
  public void DisplayRandomNumbers() {
    List<int> numbers = new List<int>();
```

```
    for (int i = 1; i <= 10; i++) {
      Random rand = new Random();
      int n = rand.Next(1, 101);
      numbers.Add(n);
    }
    String output = string.Join(", ", numbers.ToArray());
    Console.WriteLine(output);
  }
}
```

This code has some deliberate inefficiencies, and there's even a potentially dangerous bug I sometimes see with Random. I'll give you a few paragraphs to see if you can spot the issue, but let's see if GitHub Copilot Chat can spot it.

Select the `DisplayRandomNumbers` method and then press *Alt + /* to open the chat prompt. Next, ask Copilot `How would you improve this code?`

When I asked Copilot, I got several suggestions, as shown in *Figure 11.11*:

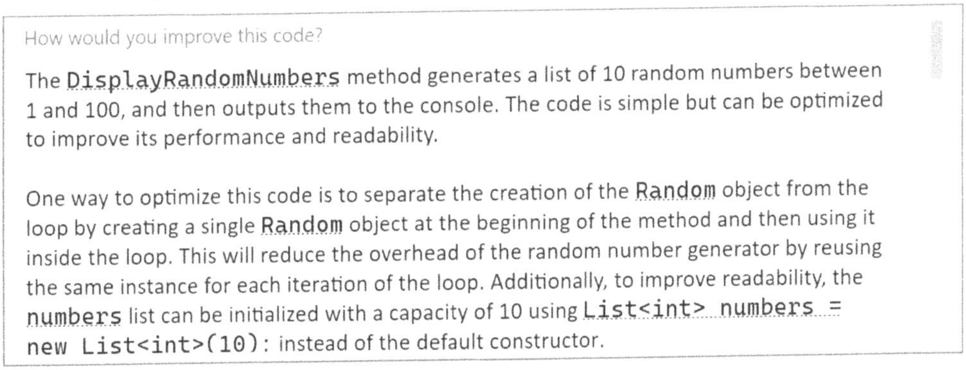

How would you improve this code?

The `DisplayRandomNumbers` method generates a list of 10 random numbers between 1 and 100, and then outputs them to the console. The code is simple but can be optimized to improve its performance and readability.

One way to optimize this code is to separate the creation of the `Random` object from the loop by creating a single `Random` object at the beginning of the method and then using it inside the loop. This will reduce the overhead of the random number generator by reusing the same instance for each iteration of the loop. Additionally, to improve readability, the `numbers` list can be initialized with a capacity of 10 using `List<int> numbers = new List<int>(10);` instead of the default constructor.

Figure 11.11 – GitHub Copilot Chat acting as a code reviewer

Looking over the suggestions I encountered (which might be different from the ones you see following this same experiment), I can summarize them into a few bullet points:

- Declare the `Random` outside of the loop for performance reasons

- Since you know the size of the list, declare it as `new List<int>(10)`

- Use a `foreach` and an `Enumerable.Range` instead of a `for` loop

Not only did GitHub Copilot Chat generate ideas for improvement, but it even suggested the following code to fulfill its suggestions:

```csharp
public void DisplayRandomNumbers() {
  List<int> numbers = new List<int>(10);
  Random rand = new Random();
  foreach (int i in Enumerable.Range(0, 10)) {
    int n = rand.Next(1, 101);
    numbers.Add(n);
  }
  string output = string.Join(", ", numbers);
  Console.WriteLine(output);
}
```

Here, Copilot suggested some improvements I was considering, such as moving Random outside of the loop, and a few I wasn't, such as using `Enumerable.Range`.

What was the bug?

If you're curious about the potential bug I mentioned, it had to do with `Random` being instantiated in the loop. Every time you run `new Random()`, it uses the current system time as a random seed to generate new numbers. If you do this in a fast loop, the clock stays the same, resulting in the same sequence of "random" numbers every iteration.

Looking at the recommended code, I notice a few opportunities for improvement, such as renaming the n variable to something more meaningful, using target-typed `new` to instantiate the objects, and discarding the unused i variable with the _ operator.

Between GitHub and myself, our final code for this method is as follows:

```csharp
public void DisplayRandomNumbers() {
  List<int> numbers = new(10);
  Random rand = new();
  foreach (int _ in Enumerable.Range(0, 10)) {
    int number = rand.Next(1, 101);
    numbers.Add(number);
  }
  string output = string.Join(", ", numbers);
  Console.WriteLine(output);
}
```

The resulting code is more concise, slightly more performant in its list allocation, and ultimately represents a slightly better result for a small piece of code.

The purpose of this section wasn't to show you how to generate random numbers, but instead for you to see the potential value chat offers as a "brainless" programming buddy who can review your code and generate suggestions. These suggestions won't always make sense or even compile, but they can give you a quick external perspective when your coworkers are unavailable.

GitHub Copilot Chat as a code reviewer

GitHub Copilot Chat's value for refactoring isn't just limited to code generation. You can also ask GitHub Copilot Chat questions such as the following:

- Can you review this code as if you were a senior engineer in a code review?

- What performance optimizations can be made to this method?

- How can I make this method more readable?

- Where would this method encounter errors?

- Are there any ways of reducing or combining lines that don't hurt the overall readability?

Of course, it's important to remember that you're effectively getting advice from an LLM that is essentially a glorified autocompletion/sentence prediction engine and not a being with intelligent or original thought.

Amusingly, I've noticed that asking GitHub Copilot Chat for its opinion on methods several times can yield different results. These results can even reverse the opinion of the original recommendations that Copilot provided! Still, this can be valuable in getting a variety of perspectives.

Before we move on, let's look at another example of refactoring code.

Targeted refactoring with GitHub Copilot Chat

This refactoring example focuses on the `BaggageCalculator.cs` file. This file holds the final version of the `BaggageCalculator` class from the end of *Chapter 2*.

As a quick reminder, this class has a `CalculatePrice` method that calculates and displays the baggage fee for a customer based on the number of checked-in and carry-on bags and whether they're traveling on a holiday.

Supporting the public `CalculatePrice` method is a private static `ApplyCheckedBagFee` method that calculates the fee of a checked bag.

We'll focus largely on the `CalculatePrice` method, which looks a little repetitive:

```
public decimal CalculatePrice(int bags, int carryOn,
   int passengers, bool isHoliday) {
   decimal total = 0;
   if (carryOn > 0) {
```

```
      decimal fee = carryOn * CarryOnFee;
      Console.WriteLine($"Carry-on: {fee}");
      total += fee;
    }
    if (bags > 0) {
      decimal bagFee = ApplyCheckedBagFee(bags, passengers);
      Console.WriteLine($"Checked: {bagFee}");
      total += bagFee;
    }
    if (isHoliday) {
      decimal holidayFee = total * HolidayFeePercent;
      Console.WriteLine("Holiday Fee: " + holidayFee);
      total += holidayFee;
    }
    return total;
  }
```

Looking at this code, we see three similar blocks that check a condition, calculate a fee, display that fee, and then add it to total.

This repetitive nature of the code strikes me as a code smell that could potentially be improved. One solution would be to extract a method for each of these three blocks, but these methods would still be very similar to each other.

Instead, I naturally wonder if there's a solution that might involve an Action or a Func, but I'm not immediately certain of what such a solution might look like.

Thankfully, we can ask Copilot about this by selecting the entire method and telling GitHub Copilot Chat Refactor this method to use an Action that writes the fee out and adds it to total so the three blocks are less repetitive.

For me, this resulted in the following method:

```
public decimal CalculatePrice(int bags, int carryOn,
  int passengers, bool isHoliday) {
  decimal total = 0;
  Action<decimal> addFeeToTotal = fee => {
    Console.WriteLine($"Fee: {fee}");
    total += fee;
  };
  if (carryOn > 0) {
    decimal fee = carryOn * CarryOnFee;
    addFeeToTotal(fee);
  }
  if (bags > 0) {
```

```
    decimal bagFee = ApplyCheckedBagFee(bags, passengers);
    addFeeToTotal(bagFee);
  }
  if (isHoliday) {
    decimal holidayFee = total * HolidayFeePercent;
    Console.WriteLine("Holiday Fee: " + holidayFee);
    addFeeToTotal(holidayFee);
  }
  return total;
}
```

Here, Copilot introduced a local `addFeeToTotal` variable storing an `Action` that writes the `fee` to the console and increments `total`. It then calls this `Action` from each of the three branches.

However, this refactoring was incorrect in a few regards. First, the messages being displayed now start with Fee instead of the appropriate fee name. Second, the refactoring didn't remove the `WriteLine` for the holiday fee, so that `fee` would be displayed twice.

Still, the refactoring does give us an idea of how the code could be improved. With a little clean-up, you end up with a more correct method:

```
public decimal CalculatePrice(int bags, int carryOn,
  int passengers, bool isHoliday) {
  decimal total = 0;
  Action<string, decimal> addFeeToTotal = (name, fee) => {
    Console.WriteLine($"{name}: {fee}");
    total += fee;
  };
  if (carryOn > 0) {
    decimal fee = carryOn * CarryOnFee;
    addFeeToTotal("Carry-on", fee);
  }
  if (bags > 0) {
    decimal bagFee = ApplyCheckedBagFee(bags, passengers);
    addFeeToTotal("Checked", bagFee);
  }
  if (isHoliday) {
    decimal holidayFee = total * HolidayFeePercent;
    addFeeToTotal("Holiday Fee", holidayFee);
  }
  return total;
}
```

This code now works properly and reduces duplication. In this particular case, Copilot was able to suggest a path forward, but accurately implementing it without introducing bugs was beyond its current abilities.

This limit underscores both the need for tests and the role of Copilot as the *partner* of the human programmer and not a *replacement* for the human.

> **Reminder**
>
> Remember that GitHub Copilot Chat, ChatGPT, and other generative AI systems based on large language models are just prediction machines that generate text that follows patterns from their training data. There is nothing guaranteeing that these generated values are correct, optimal, or free of bugs.

Now that we've covered a few refactoring scenarios, let's see what else we can do with GitHub Copilot Chat.

Drafting documentation with GitHub Copilot Chat

Over the years, I've learned that developers don't always like to document their code. While some code truly is self-documenting as developers claim, other areas require proper documentation.

In C#, we document public methods with XML documentation, such as the sample comment for the `DisplayRandomNumbers` method:

```
/// <summary>
/// Displays a sequence of 10 random numbers.
/// </summary>
public void DisplayRandomNumbers() {
```

This specially formatted comment is interpreted by Visual Studio to display additional help in the editor. This extra information appears in the editor when you are trying to invoke your method, as shown in *Figure 11.12*:

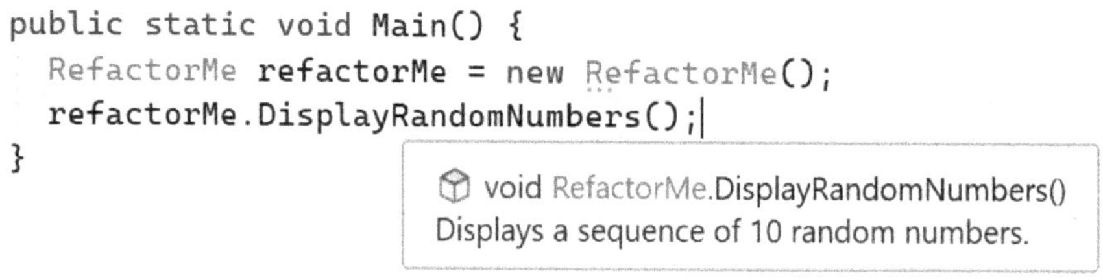

```
public static void Main() {
    RefactorMe refactorMe = new RefactorMe();
    refactorMe.DisplayRandomNumbers();
}
```

> void RefactorMe.DisplayRandomNumbers()
> Displays a sequence of 10 random numbers.

Figure 11.12 – Visual Studio showing a tooltip containing the method comment

Although the sample documentation we saw a moment ago was relatively straightforward, documentation gets a bit more complex when you have return values and parameters.

Let's use GitHub Copilot Chat to document a method. We'll start with the `AddEvenNumbers` method in `DocumentMe.cs`:

```
public int AddEvenNumbers(int[]? numbers, int total = 0) {
  if (numbers == null || numbers.Length == 0) {
    string message = "There must be at least 1 element";
    throw new ArgumentException(message, nameof(numbers));
  }
  return total + numbers.Where(n => n % 2 == 0).Sum();
}
```

This method takes in an array of numbers and, optionally, a number to add to the resulting sum. If at least one number was provided, the method returns the sum of all even numbers in that array added to the optional `total` parameter. If no elements were provided, an `ArgumentException` will be thrown instead.

Now that you've read *my* description of this, let's see how GitHub Copilot describes it. Press *Alt + /* to open the chat interface and then tell Copilot to `Document AddEvenNumbers`. Copilot should suggest documentation changes such as the ones shown in the preview in *Figure 11.12*:

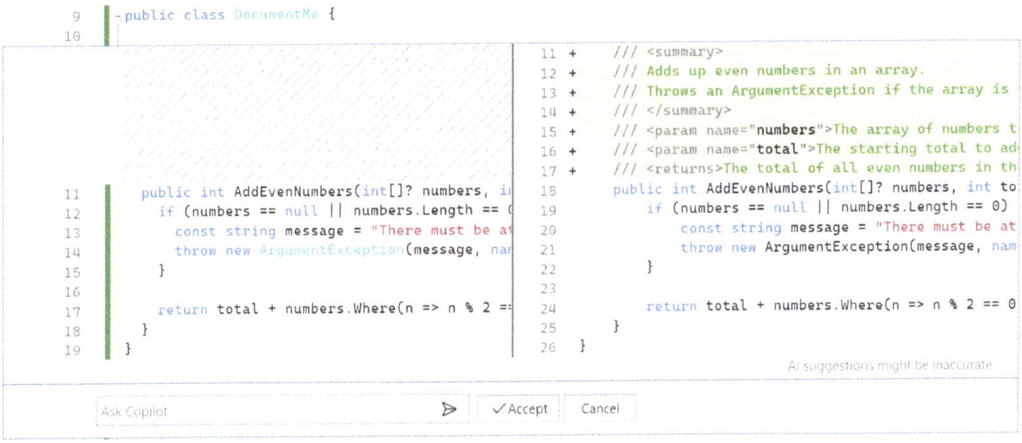

Figure 11.13 – GitHub Copilot suggesting documentation

Click **Accept** and the comments will be added to your method.

For me, the documentation generated was reasonably good:

```
/// <summary>
/// Adds up even numbers in an array. Throws an
/// ArgumentException if the array is null or empty.
/// </summary>
/// <param name="numbers">
/// The array of numbers to add.
/// </param>
/// <param name="total">
/// The starting total to add to. Defaults to 0.
/// </param>
/// <returns>
/// The total of all even numbers in the array.
/// </returns>
```

This is a very accurate piece of documentation. The one change I would make is to add the following line of XML documenting the potential exception:

```
/// <exception cref="ArgumentException">Thrown when the array is null
or empty.</exception>
```

This adds the exception to the list shown in the method tooltip, as seen in *Figure 11.13*:

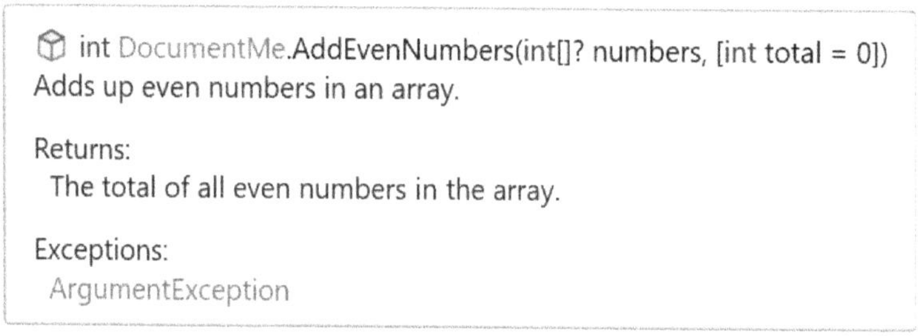

Figure 11.14 – Exception documentation in Visual Studio

Communicating exceptions allows other code to catch them in an appropriate manner.

Human-generated documentation will usually be better than AI documentation, but when humans and AI can work together, it can be a huge productivity boost.

In the next section, we'll see how these productivity boosts apply to testing as well.

Generating test stubs with GitHub Copilot Chat

For our final technical section of this chapter, let's look at a method that finds the largest number in a sequence of numbers, provided that the number doesn't have a "7" in it somewhere, such as a 71 or 17. This method is located inside of `TestMe.cs`:

```
public static class TestMe {
  public static int CalculateLargestNumberWithoutASeven(
    INumberProvider provider) {
    IEnumerable<int> numbers = provider.GenerateNumbers();
    return numbers.Where(x => !x.ToString().Contains("7"))
              .Max();
  }
}
```

This `CalculateLargestNumberWithoutASeven` method takes in an `INumberProvider` that allows us to call `GenerateNumbers` and get a sequence of integers.

Next, the method looks at the resulting sequence, finds the numbers that don't have a seven somewhere in their string representation, and then returns the largest number.

> **Dependency injection**
>
> As a brief refresher, our method is effectively getting its dependency on an `INumberProvider` injected into it as an external parameter. This means the code works with anything that implements that interface without having to know the details.

While this method seems utterly useless as something you might write in the real world, think for a moment about how you would test this method. Specifically, how would you call this method? What would you give it as an `INumberProvider`? What value would you expect it to return?

While you're thinking that over, let's see how GitHub Copilot would handle this by opening the GitHub Copilot Chat pane and typing in `Generate tests for CalculateLargestNumberWithoutASeven`.

> **Note**
>
> While I usually prefer to use the *Alt + /* method of interacting with Copilot, if you want Copilot to generate a new file you should use the GitHub Copilot Chat pane for best results.

For me, Copilot generated a C# code for a new test class. I'll share that code shortly, but what's most interesting to me about the code generation are the three buttons at the bottom of the recommendation, shown in *Figure 11.14*:

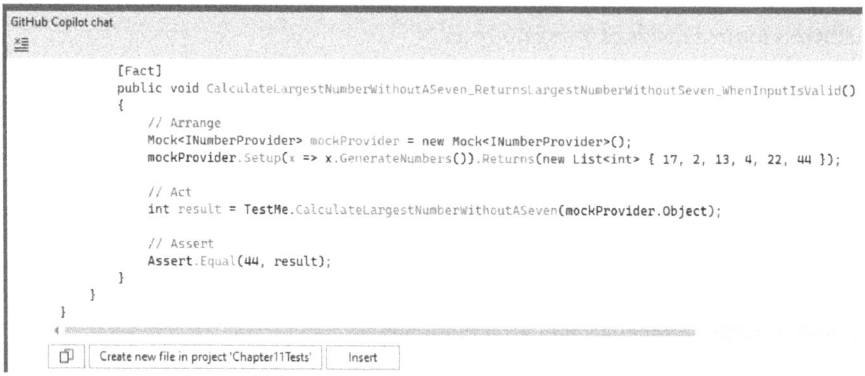

Figure 11.15 – GitHub Copilot offering to create a new file

These three buttons allow you to copy the new code to your clipboard, create a new file, and insert the code in the current editor, respectively.

Since we want the tests to live in the test project, click **Create new file**.

This will create a new file in your test project with any test(s) generated by Copilot. For me, it generated two tests, as shown at a high level in *Figure 11.16*:

Figure 11.16 – A pair of XUnit tests generated by GitHub Copilot Chat

The tests aren't the most important thing here, so I don't want to focus on the code other than to make a few observations on Copilot's strategy when I asked it for tests:

- Copilot generated a pair of tests using xUnit and Moq, which were both installed in the test project already. These tests compile and pass.

- The first test ensured the method threw an exception when given a null input.

- The second test provided a series of numbers at random and asserted that the method returned the largest number without a seven.

- Both tests used Moq to create a fake `INumberProvider` that is programmed to generate the desired sequence of numbers.

So, have we discovered the silver bullet that allows us to forget about writing tests going forward? Probably not.

While both tests verify something legitimate, their readability could be better. Additionally, the tests don't consider all the paths that should be tested. For example, it didn't test with an empty sequence of elements, with only a single number, with a single number with a seven in it, with only negative numbers, or with the largest number having a seven in it. These are all legitimate cases that a human tester would likely consider.

So, GitHub Copilot won't absolve you of your responsibility to test your code (and think about your tests), but it's not completely worthless either.

GitHub Copilot has a lot of value for identifying test cases and considering new ways of testing particularly hard-to-test classes. I've come to view it as a catalyst – or copilot –that helps get your momentum going when writing tests of your own.

Now that we've seen the value GitHub Copilot provides, let's talk about its limits.

Understanding the limits of GitHub Copilot

By this point in the chapter, many readers are probably thinking "This is great, but can I actually use this in my job?" That's a valid question, so let's talk about the two common objections: privacy of source code and license concerns with public code.

Data privacy and GitHub Copilot

Many organizations considering GitHub Copilot are concerned that integrating an AI tool into their code editor means exposing their code to GitHub. Some also raise the potential that GitHub might even use the organization's private code to generate new large language models in the future where these new models might generate code based on the organization's proprietary logic.

These are valid concerns, and depending on which edition of GitHub Copilot you are using, there may be some basis for them.

With **GitHub Copilot for Individuals**, the prompts you send to GitHub Copilot, including surrounding code and Copilot's suggested code, may be retained for analysis unless you have disabled the code snippet collection in your settings.

This setting can be disabled at `https://github.com/settings/copilot` by unchecking the **Allow GitHub to use my code snippets for product improvements** checkbox, as shown in *Figure 11.17*:

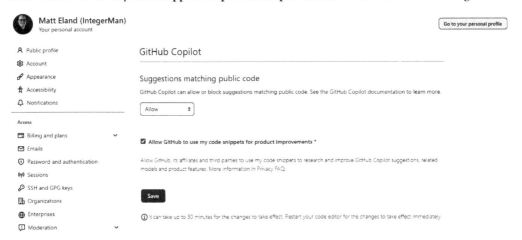

Figure 11.17 – GitHub Copilot settings

While GitHub Copilot for Individuals has some data privacy concerns by default, these can be easily opted out if you are working with sensitive code.

It should also be noted that GitHub Copilot for Individuals also collects telemetry on GitHub Copilot usage to detect how frequently the service is used and detect and resolve errors.

On the other hand, **GitHub Copilot for Business** is private by default and also offers additional organization-wide policy settings that businesses can configure to globally enable or disable Copilot. These features can also be used to prevent Copilot from generating code matching known public code for everyone in your organization.

According to the **GitHub Copilot Trust Center**, *"GitHub Copilot [for business] does not use Prompts or Suggestions to train AI models. These inputs are not retained or utilized in the training process of AI models for GitHub Copilot"*. This means that the code you send to GitHub Copilot and the suggestions it generates for you are private from human consumption and will not be used to give others insight into your codebase.

> **Disclaimer**
>
> This book is intended to help you understand the basics of GitHub Copilot and was written with the best understanding available of an early technology. As with any technology, GitHub Copilot continues to evolve and grow. As it does so, the privacy policy, data retention policy, and pricing model will likely change over time. Readers are encouraged to verify the information in this chapter against current information provided by GitHub before making any usage decisions.

Glory Francke, head of privacy at GitHub, states "We only process your code to provide the service. It is not retained, human eyes don't see it, and it is not being used for any AI model improvements" (GitHub Copilot Trust Center – `https://resources.github.com/copilot-trust-center/`).

In general, I find the GitHub Copilot Trust Center to be a very useful tool in addressing enterprise concerns around the security, privacy, and accessibility of the tool. You can read more about the trust center in the *Further reading* section of this chapter, but for now, let's talk more about GitHub Copilot and public code.

Concerns around GitHub Copilot and public code

Most open-source code is accompanied by a license dictating the terms developers must follow when using the source code. There are several common licenses that developers choose, such as the MIT License, Apache License, GNU General Public License, and so on.

While many of these licenses are very permissive, some include clauses requiring additional actions such as attributing the source code, making your organization's code open source, or not being able to use the code in commercial software projects.

Because of restrictions like this, and because GitHub Copilot was trained on open-source software code, there's a small chance that GitHub Copilot might accidentally generate code identical to code from a public repository.

Because of this concern, GitHub Copilot now allows individuals and businesses to block the generation of code that is identical to known public code. Additionally, GitHub is currently rolling out a new feature called GitHub Copilot code referencing, which allows you to detect whether Copilot has suggested public code. This feature lets you unleash Copilot's full creativity while allowing you to see what repositories the code was found and the licenses for those repositories.

At the time of writing this chapter, this feature was not yet available for GitHub Copilot for Visual Studio, but it's likely that this capability will make it to Visual Studio sometime after the publication of this book.

Let's close the chapter with a case study on GitHub Copilot Chat at our fictitious airline.

Case study: Cloudy Skies Airline

The use of AI at Cloudy Skies Airlines started first with individual developers, as often happens with productivity tools and new technologies. James, an eager young developer on the team, shared with his coworkers how he's been trying GitHub Copilot, feeling more capable and empowered, and even learning new things. His coworkers were excited, but his manager, Mya, had a few concerns.

Looping in the chief technology officer (CTO), Mya and James demonstrated the capabilities of the tool and talked about how it worked. The CTO was worried about legal compliance and the safety of the company's intellectual property. As a result, the use of Copilot and other AI tools was temporarily suspended while the team investigated the implications of the technology.

After some research, and with the help of the GitHub Copilot Trust Center, the Cloudy Skies Airlines team agreed to a multi-stage plan:

1. **Pilot the program**: A small group of developers, including James, will try GitHub Copilot with code snippet collection disabled for two weeks

2. **Review**: The team will evaluate any impacts on productivity, code quality, and general developer feedback from the pilot program and decide whether the tool should be adopted

3. **Rollout**: If GitHub Copilot is found to be beneficial, it will either be allowed for individuals organizational-wide with guidelines or be managed through a GitHub Copilot for Business account, depending on the results of the technology review

The developers in the pilot program reported having an easier time focusing on code, employing helpful practices for speeding up "boring" aspects of coding, and learning some new practices and concepts from the code that Copilot generated.

As a result, Cloudy Skies Airlines embraced GitHub Copilot and adopted a GitHub Copilot for Business account to ensure snippet collection was disabled and that appropriate policies on things such as public code sources were set at an organizational level.

Summary

In this chapter, we saw how GitHub Copilot and GitHub Copilot Chat can help developers understand, refactor, document, and even test their code.

We talked about how GitHub Copilot is not an intelligent AI overlord, but instead a predictive model built around patterns in text found in open-source repositories. As a result, the code it generates may not even compile and may contain security vulnerabilities, bugs, performance issues, or other undesirable effects.

We closed this chapter with a discussion of privacy and open-source licensing that organizations must care about for security and compliance purposes and how GitHub Copilot helps organizations meet those needs.

In the next chapter, we'll explore code analysis in Visual Studio and see how code analysis can help you detect potential issues and targets for refactoring in your code.

Questions

1. How do GitHub Copilot and GitHub Copilot Chat work?
2. How can you address data privacy and compliance concerns with Copilot?

Further reading

You can find more information about GitHub Copilot at these URLs:

*   About the GitHub Copilot extension for Visual Studio: `https://learn.microsoft.com/en-us/visualstudio/ide/visual-studio-github-copilot-extension`
*   GitHub Copilot Trust Center: `https://resources.github.com/copilot-trust-center/`
*   *GitHub Copilot Chat*: `https://docs.github.com/en/copilot/github-copilot-chat/about-github-copilot-chat`

12

Code Analysis in Visual Studio

Thus far, we've covered how to refactor our code in a safe, effective, reliable, and productive manner.

In this chapter, we'll determine areas of code that might need refactoring using code metrics and code analysis tools. Along the way, we'll cover the following topics:

- Calculating code metrics in Visual Studio
- Performing code analysis in Visual Studio
- Exploring advanced code analysis tools

Technical requirements

The starting code for this chapter is available from GitHub at `https://github.com/PacktPublishing/Refactoring-with-CSharp` in the `Chapter12/Ch12BeginningCode` folder.

Calculating code metrics in Visual Studio

Every codebase I've ever worked with has had a few maintainability hot spots. These are areas that are frequently changed, have a higher degree of complexity than other areas of code, and represent serious quality risks to the software project.

These areas are usually some of the most critical to refactor and they tend to be easily discoverable using **code metrics**.

Code metrics calculate a handful of useful statistics about every file, class, method, and property in your C# code. This lets you spot hot spots in your code that have significantly higher complexity or lower maintainability. Code metrics can even help you find classes that are too large and likely violate the Single Responsibility Principle (SRP) as we discussed in *Chapter 8*.

To calculate code metrics, open your solution in Visual Studio and then click the **Analyze** menu, followed by **Calculate Code Metrics**, and then **For Solution**, as shown in *Figure 12.1*:

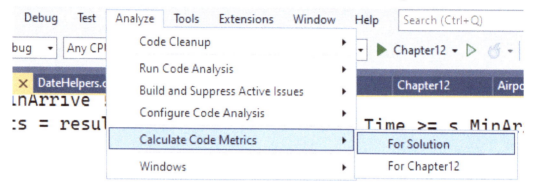

Figure 12.1 – Calculating code metrics

This will open the **Code Metrics Results** pane, as shown in *Figure 12.2*:

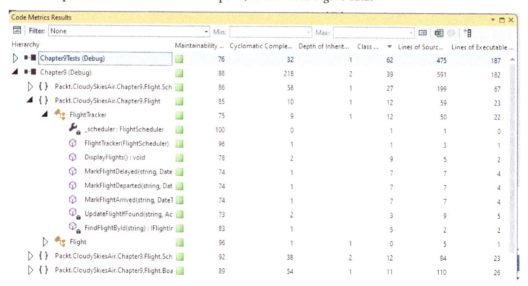

Figure 12.2 – Code Metrics Results

This pane displays a hierarchical view of your solution, along with the following six metrics:

- **Lines of Source Code**: The number of lines of code for the class or method.

- **Lines of Executable Code**: The lines of source code that ignore blank lines and comments.

- **Cyclomatic Complexity**: A metric that specifies the unique number of paths that exist through your code. Each `if` statement, loop, switch case, and similar type of branching instruction increases this by 1.

- **Maintainability Index**: A calculated value based on cyclomatic complexity, lines of code, and the number of operations performed in a method. This value ranges from 0 to 100, indicating how maintainable your code is. Values from 0 to 9 are bad, 10 to 20 are warning areas, and 21 and above are areas to watch.

- **Depth of Inheritance**: The number of classes this class inherits from before it reaches `System.Object`, which all classes ultimately inherit from.

- **Class Coupling**: The number of other classes your code depends on.

Each of these metrics is useful individually, but together, they tell a broader picture.

The maintainability index gives you a quick metric for an area of code. Unlike other columns, which sum up values for all code in a class, namespace, or project, the maintainability index acts as an average, which can help you quickly drill into problem areas.

Cyclomatic complexity can identify areas that are hard to test or hard to understand since it identifies the number of distinct paths through a method. *Figure 12.3* illustrates a cyclomatic complexity of the `CalculatePrice` method:

```
 10    public decimal CalculatePrice(int bags, int carryOn,
 11      int passengers, bool isHoliday) {
 12
 13      decimal total = 0;
 14
 15      if (carryOn > 0) {
 16        decimal fee = carryOn * CarryOnFee;
 17        Console.WriteLine($"Carry-on: {fee}");
 18        total += fee;
 19      }
 20
 21      if (bags > 0) {
 22        decimal bagFee = ApplyCheckedBagFee(bags, passengers);
 23        Console.WriteLine($"Checked: {bagFee}");
 24        total += bagFee;
 25      }
 26
 27      if (isHoliday) {
 28        decimal holidayFee = total * HolidayFeePercent;
 29        Console.WriteLine("Holiday Fee: " + holidayFee);
 30
 31        total += holidayFee;
 32      }
 33
 34      return total;
 35    }
```

Figure 12.3 – Calculating cyclomatic complexity

Here, the `CalculatePrice` method has a cyclomatic complexity of 4. All methods start with a cyclomatic complexity of 1, representing a single path through the method. Each branching statement, such as the `if` statements here, increments the cyclomatic complexity by 1, resulting in a total of 4.

I find cyclomatic complexity to be generally useful and try to keep this as low as possible. Keep in mind that cyclomatic complexity is biased against methods that use `switch` statements since each `case` statement adds to the complexity. Simple `switch` statements with only a line or two of code are generally not hard to maintain, so treat cyclomatic complexity as only one indicator of code quality. Microsoft recommends a maximum cyclomatic complexity of 10 for each method, but in my experience, I tend to be happiest with a cyclomatic complexity of 7 or less.

Depth of inheritance and class coupling can help you identify places where you may be over-using inheritance or have too high of coupling to other classes, as we covered in *Chapter 8*. Microsoft encourages a maximum depth of inheritance of 6 and a maximum class coupling of 9.

The lines of code metrics are quite useful. I find that having many lines of code in a class is frequently one of the greatest signs that a class violates the SRP and needs to be refactored. Similarly, if a method is too large, it's usually hard to understand, maintain, and test.

I try to keep classes under 200 lines of code and methods to 20 lines or less. In both cases, I look for things I can pull out of the method or class and am hesitant to expand an already large class or method with new logic unless I can pull logic out of the code first.

Keep in mind that these are general guidelines I've found generally effective. These are not concrete rules that you must always follow.

I encourage you to spend some time looking over code metrics for the sample code for this chapter or some code you maintain. In the case of the code for this chapter, I'm most concerned about the following methods:

- `BaggageCalculator.CalculatePrice` in the `Flight.Baggage` namespace has a maintainability index of 58, cyclomatic complexity of 4, and 26 lines of source code

- `FlightScheduler.Search`, which takes in a `FlightSearch` object in the `Flight.Scheduling` namespace, has a maintainability index of 48, a cyclomatic complexity of 9, a class coupling of 11, and 37 lines of source code

Both methods are flagged by the metrics because they have several `if` statements that they need to run. Neither method is very complex, but at the same time, if either needs to grow significantly more, I'd like to see refactorings like the ones we applied in *Chapter 5* to move complexity out of these methods and into other objects.

Now that we've covered code metrics, let's see how code analysis can give us another way of looking at our code.

Performing code analysis in Visual Studio

Microsoft knows that as C# and .NET changes, it can be very difficult to keep up with evolving standards in a broad and changing language.

To address this, Microsoft gave us tools beyond code metrics in the form of analyzers that inspect our C# code for issues. These analyzers look at our code and flag potential issues and optimizations. This helps ensure our code complies with standards and is secure, reliable, and maintainable.

Analyzing your solution using the default ruleset

To see an analyzer in action, build this chapter's solution in Visual Studio and notice the three warnings that appear in the **Output** pane, as shown in *Figure 12.4*:

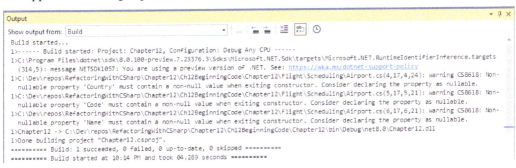

Figure 12.4 – An overview of the build results showing warnings

These three lines represent separate compiler warnings for the CS8618 code analysis rule, which we'll look at shortly.

Before we do that, click on the **View** menu and then select **Error List**. You should see the same warnings formatted in an easier-to-read manner, as shown in *Figure 12.5*:

Figure 12.5 – An overview of the compiler warnings in Error List

If these warnings don't show up, make sure the **Errors**, **Warnings**, and **Messages** buttons are checked, as shown in *Figure 12.5*.

Since these warnings are all associated with `Airport.cs`, let's review its code:

```
public class Airport {
    public string Country { get; set; }
    public string Code { get; set; }
    public string Name { get; set; }
    // Non-relevant code omitted...
}
```

When looking at this code in Visual Studio, you'll see a "green squiggly" underneath each of these three properties. As shown in *Figure 12.6*, hovering the mouse cursor over any of these "squigglies" shows details about the warning or suggestion:

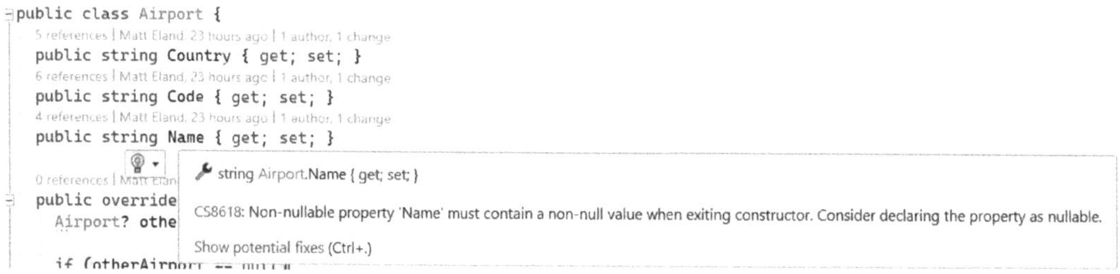

Figure 12.6 – The CS8618 compiler warning associated with the Name property

In this case, the warning tells us that these three properties are non-nullable, meaning that they are declared as `string` instead of `string?`, as we discussed in *Chapter 10* when discussing nullability analysis.

Since the default value for any `string` property in .NET is null and the `Airport` class doesn't have any logic to initialize these three properties, the compiler warning is telling us that when `Airport` instances are created, they'll have null values in properties we told it couldn't be null!

> **Nullability analysis in .NET**
>
> Remember that although strings are reference types and can be null, nullability analysis in C# indicates if a property is expected to have a null value at any point in time. Here, the `string` type indicator means that we never expect these properties to have a null value. On the other hand, a `string?` type indicator would indicate that we might expect null values. See *Chapter 10* for more information on nullability analysis in C#.

There are a few ways to address this compiler warning:

- Default these properties to an empty string
- Change these properties to `string?` instead of `string`

- Add a constructor that sets these properties to non-null values

- Mark these properties as `required` so that they must be set on creation

As shown here, the simplest fix is to mark these properties as `required`:

```
public class Airport {
  public required string Country { get; set; }
  public required string Code { get; set; }
  public required string Name { get; set; }
  // Non-relevant code omitted...
}
```

This resolves the three code analysis warnings, leaving two less severe suggestions for us to investigate, both dealing with the `Equals` method of `Airport`:

```
public override bool Equals(object? obj) {
  Airport? otherAirport = obj as Airport;
  if (otherAirport == null)
    return false;
  string otherName = otherAirport.Name;
  string otherCountry = otherAirport.Country;
  string otherCode = otherAirport.Code;
  return Country == otherCountry &&
          Code == otherCode;
}
```

The first warning is IDE0019, which suggests using pattern matching when declaring `otherAirport`. Thankfully, this analyzer provides a **Quick Action** to resolve the suggestion. Hovering over the three dots underneath the `Airport?` type reveals the **Use pattern matching Quick Action**, as shown in *Figure 12.7*:

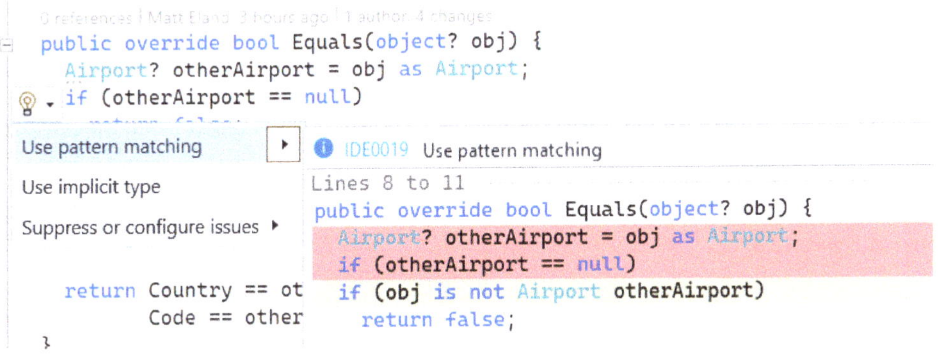

Figure 12.7 – Applying the Use pattern matching refactoring

Applying this refactoring resolves the suggestion and makes our code more concise:

```
if (obj is not Airport otherAirport)
        return false;
```

The last remaining warning is *IDE0059: Unnecessary assignment of a value to 'otherName'*. This highlights that we've declared a variable and assigned a value to that variable but never used the variable after that point, as shown here with `otherName`:

```
string otherName = otherAirport.Name;
string otherCountry = otherAirport.Country;
string otherCode = otherAirport.Code;
return Country == otherCountry &&
        Code == otherCode;
```

Looking at this code, it's a toss-up as to whether `otherName` should be included in the equality check or if the variable is simply not needed. In this case, you might ask a business stakeholder if an airport could ever have multiple names but be the same airport. If you get a "yes," then the fix would be to remove the `otherName` variable, while a "no" would indicate that a `Name` check should be added to the `return` statement.

The correct fix for code issues is not always obvious without gathering more information about the business domain you're modeling.

Configuring code analysis rulesets

There are a large and growing number of analyzers in .NET and not every analyzer shares the same levels of importance. Because of this, Microsoft provides different sets of analyzers so that you can start with a small subset of the most useful ones and gradually expand into additional sets of analyzers as your maturity grows.

Let's look at our code analysis settings for the `Chapter12` project by right-clicking on the `Chapter12` project in **Solution Explorer** and then selecting **Properties**.

This will open the properties view of the project. This view lists all configurable properties associated with the project and can be scrolled through from top to bottom or navigated using the navigation pane on the left-hand side.

Click on **Code Analysis** in the navigation pane; you should see the project's code analysis settings, as shown in *Figure 12.8*:

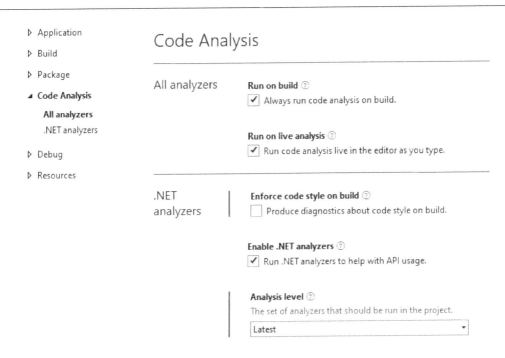

Figure 12.8 – Code Analysis settings for the project

As you can see from the **Run on build** setting, the compiler will analyze code every time the project is built.

The exact set of analyzers used is controlled by the **Analysis level** setting, which defaults to **Latest** for new projects.

There is a wide variety of analysis rulesets supported by Visual Studio, but let's focus on the four rulesets that start with "Latest" as these are the most recent rulesets available, and the patterns in these rules will help you understand the other rules options. These options are as follows:

- **Latest**: The default set of rules. This is a set of rules that is intended to be broadly applicable to any type of project.

- **Latest Minimum**: Everything in **Latest** plus additional rules. This represents the minimum set of rules that Microsoft recommends using in a project.

- **Latest Recommended**: Everything in **Latest Minimum** plus some additional rules. This contains a robust set of rules designed to help you maintain a business application that can run in any locale securely and reliably.

- **Latest All**: All available rules are enabled. Not every rule may be relevant for the application you're trying to build, but it maximizes your chances of building a robust and reliable application.

Let's see what happens when we change our project from **Latest** to **Latest Recommended** and then build.

Responding to code analysis rules

After changing the project to use the **Latest Recommended** ruleset, three new warnings will appear, as shown in *Figure 12.9*:

Code	Description
⚠ CA1822	Member 'BuildMessage' does not access instance data and can be marked as static
⚠ CA1305	The behavior of 'StringBuilder.Append(ref StringBuilder.AppendInterpolatedStringHandler)' could vary based on the current user's locale settings. Replace this call in 'CharterFlightInfo.BuildFlightIdentifier()' with a call to 'StringBuilder.Append(IFormatProvider, ref StringBuilder.AppendInterpolatedStringHandler)'.
⚠ CA1305	The behavior of 'DateTime.ToString(string)' could vary based on the current user's locale settings. Replace this call in 'DateTime.Format()' with a call to 'DateTime.ToString(string, IFormatProvider)'.

Figure 12.9 – New compiler warnings after moving to a stricter ruleset

Let's start with the first warning. This corresponds to the `Flight` class, which is currently defined in only a few lines of code:

```
public class Flight {
  public string BuildMessage(string id, string status) {
    return $"Flight {id} is {status}";
  }
}
```

The CA1822 warning tells us *Member 'BuildMessage' does not access instance data and can be marked as static.*

This analyzer is suggesting we make the `BuildMessage` method `static` because it doesn't deal with any specific information from the overall `Flight` class.

In this case, making the method `static` could make it easier to test and allow the compiler to make a few performance optimizations as well.

We could resolve this warning by performing the *Make method static* refactoring we covered in *Chapter 4*, but instead, let's explore suppressing specific warnings.

In this case, let's say that we intend `BuildMessage` to deal with instance-specific properties at some point in the future, but haven't gotten there yet. Because of this, we want the warning to go away without making the method static.

Use the **Quick Action** menu on the `BuildMessage` method and then select the **Suppress or configure issues** submenu. From there, choose **Suppress CA1822**. This will reveal three different options for suppressing the issue, as shown in *Figure 12.10*:

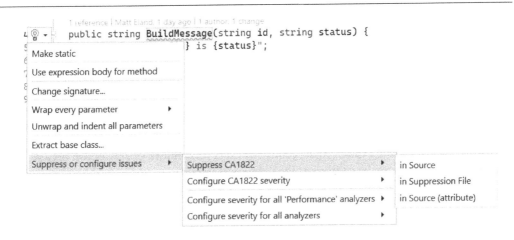

Figure 12.10 – Options for suppressing the code analysis warnings

These options are as follows:

- **in Source**: This adds several `#pragma` statements above and below your code to disable the code analysis warning temporarily

- **in Suppression File**: This creates a separate file with code telling code analysis not to care about this specific issue for this specific method

- **in Source (attribute)**: This adds `SuppressMessageAttribute` above the method, suppressing the code analysis issue

All three of these approaches will suppress the issue, but all do so in different styles. I generally prefer to avoid preprocessor directives such as `#pragma` to have cleaner and more maintainable code. This leaves the suppression file and attribute approaches.

The advantage of a suppression file is that code analysis suppressions do not clutter your source code and instead live in a separate file. However, that's also their disadvantage. By hiding away suppressions in another file, you reduce the odds of resolving them in the future since they're "out of sight, out of mind."

Using the **in Source (attribute)** approach and then adding a `using` statement for `System.Diagnostic.CodeAnalysis` results in the following file:

```
using System.Diagnostics.CodeAnalysis;
namespace Packt.CloudySkiesAir.Chapter12.Flight;
public class Flight {
  [SuppressMessage("Performance",
    "CA1822:Mark members as static",
    Justification = "Intend to work with instance data in future
      release")]
  public string BuildMessage(string id, string status) {
```

```
      return $"Flight {id} is {status}";
    }
  }
```

The SuppressMessage attribute above the method marks the category of the code analysis issue as "Performance." Next, it names the individual analysis rule being suppressed before providing a justification.

This justification is a string explaining to your coworkers (and future you) why you believe the code analysis rule should not be addressed at this time and should be excluded from the list of code analysis results.

I will never suppress a code analysis warning without providing a valid justification for the suppression. If a rule was important enough for someone to provide an analyzer for, it should either be resolved or I should have a valid justification for why I am choosing to ignore it. In case you were wondering, "I don't feel like addressing it" is not a valid justification.

With the first warning out of the way, let's look at the other two warnings together as they're related.

The first warning is CA1305, which is associated with the DateHelpers class, as shown here:

```
public static class DateHelpers {
  public static string Format(this DateTime time) {
    return time.ToString("ddd MMM dd HH:mm tt");
  }
}
```

This warning states that the ToString call might result in a different result, depending on the user's locale and language settings. My settings, as someone speaking English in the United States, may be different than someone running the same code with French as their primary locale.

The next warning is on BuildFlightIdentifier in CharterFlightInfo:

```
public class CharterFlightInfo : FlightInfoBase {
  public List<ICargoItem> Cargo { get; } = new();
  public override string BuildFlightIdentifier() {
    StringBuilder sb = new(base.BuildFlightIdentifier());
    if (Cargo.Count != 0) {
      sb.Append(" carrying ");
      foreach (var cargo in Cargo) {
        sb.Append($"{cargo}, ");
      }
    }
    return sb.ToString();
  }
}
```

This warning is complaining about a similar localization issue stating that the behavior of `StringBuilder.Append` could differ based on the user's locale.

> **Recommended rules versus minimum and default rules**
>
> These formatting rules are examples of rules that are not relevant to all projects. These rules are not enabled in the default or minimum rulesets for a reason: not all applications you create will need to behave consistently, regardless of where they're running. If you're building a hobby application or an application that runs only on a single server or in your office, this rule probably isn't important for you. However, if you're building something that is distributed throughout the globe to customers of all cultures, this is going to be a rule you care about.

The fix for these two warnings is to provide an explicit culture that you want to be used when formatting strings. This changes our append code to the following line:

```
sb.Append(CultureInfo.InvariantCulture, $"{cargo}, ");
```

Our date formatting code changes in a similar manner:

```
CultureInfo culture = CultureInfo.InvariantCulture;
return time.ToString("ddd MMM dd HH:mm tt", culture);
```

With these changes made, we are now free of code analysis warnings. Let's finish this section by looking at a way of making sure we stay free of warnings.

Treating warnings as errors

I've met many developers who treat warnings like they treat speed limits while driving: they ignore them and cruise by at unsafe speeds.

There are a few ways of making sure developers ensure their code is free of warnings. Perhaps the easiest way of doing so is to tell the C# compiler to treat any warning as if it were a compiler error.

You can have the C# compiler treat all warnings as errors by right-clicking on the project and then selecting **Properties**, as we did before. From there, expand **Build** in the navigation pane and then click **Errors and warnings**. Once you do so, you should see something like *Figure 12.11*:

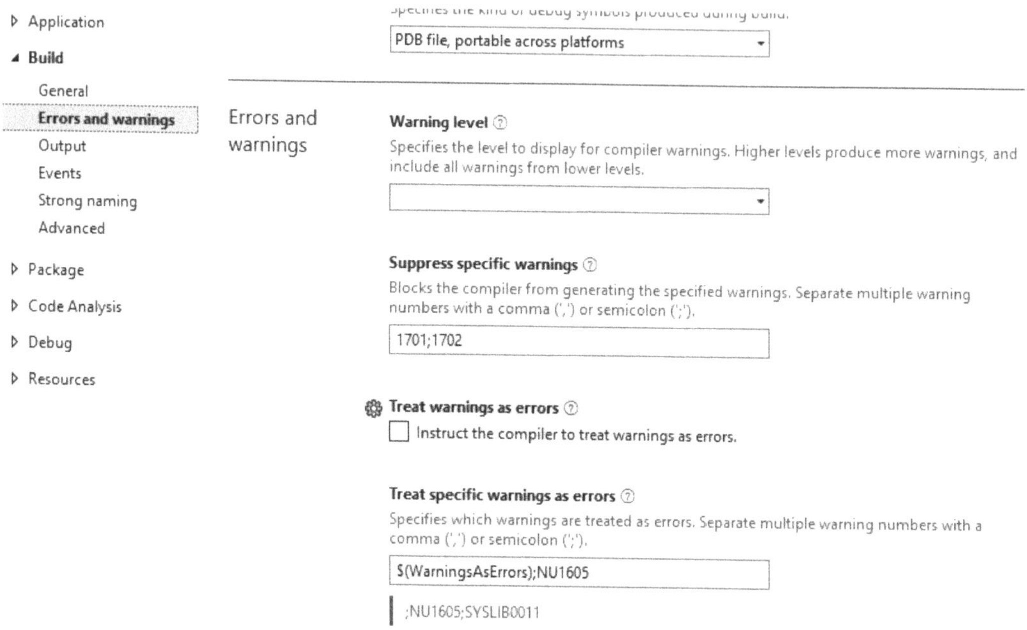

Figure 12.11 – Configuring errors and warnings for a project

You can check **Treat warnings as errors** to have all warnings result in errors.

Since developers pay attention to things that stop their code from running at all, causing any warning to stop them from building their code will certainly get their attention! Be careful when using this as they may not be very happy about the severity of the interruption.

A less extreme option is to configure the **Treat specific warnings as errors** setting and include the identifiers of specific warnings you believe should always be addressed.

For example, if we wanted to force developers to respond to suggestions of making methods `static` (CA1822), you could set the **Suppress specific warnings** value to `$(WarningsAsErrors);NU1605;CA1822;` by doing so, any place where the warning occurred and was not suppressed would result in a compiler error.

Now that we've covered the code analysis features of Visual Studio, let's take a look at a pair of additional options in the form of third-party tools that work well with C# code.

Exploring advanced code analysis tools

The built-in code analysis and code metrics tools are very good for engineers wanting to pinpoint bad code and ensure code follows best practices for .NET projects, but they lack some enterprise-level features.

In this section, we'll look at two different commercial analysis tools that I've found to provide additional value for .NET projects: **SonarCloud** and **NDepend**.

I won't be covering how to set up these tools as both tools have comprehensive documentation that I've provided links to in the *Further reading* section at the end of this chapter. Instead, we'll focus on the types of insights that dedicated code analysis tools can give you beyond what's available in Visual Studio.

Tracking code metrics with SonarCloud and SonarQube

SonarCloud and SonarQube are a pair of commercial code analysis tools offered by SonarSource. Both products look at Git repositories containing code in a variety of popular programming languages and generate a series of recommendations.

The primary difference between SonarCloud and SonarQube is that SonarCloud is hosted on and analyzed by servers maintained by SonarSource while SonarQube is software you can install on your servers.

Both pieces of software can analyze code in Git repositories and provide heat maps of problem areas in your code in the areas of reliability, maintainability, security, and code duplication. These views give you a simple graphical representation of your code that helps easily flag problem areas, as shown in *Figure 12.12*:

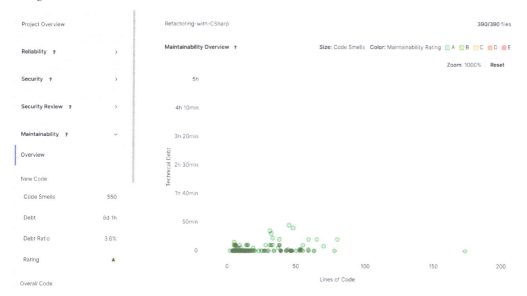

Figure 12.12 – SonarCloud analysis highlighting technical debt areas

These tools have built-in analyzers that analyze your code and flag reliability, security, and performance issues for remediation.

Once an issue has been flagged, you can use the web user interface shown in *Figure 12.13* to assign it to a team member, add comments to it, or mark it as resolved or ignored:

Figure 12.13 – Code analysis recommendations per line of code

For me, SonarCloud and SonarQube have a few major selling points:

- They help expose technical debt to non-developers in a very user-friendly way. An engineering manager or chief technology officer can look at the project in their web browser and get an understanding of the weak areas without ever having to install Visual Studio. This helps make technical debt transparent.

- Items flagged by SonarCloud and SonarQube tend to be worth investigating, perhaps even more so than items flagged by Visual Studio code analyzers.

- You tend to get a good result with these tools out of the box without needing additional configuration, though the configuration is available for customization should you wish to do so.

SonarCloud and SonarQube are commercial products that are priced based on the lines of code in your projects. SonarCloud is also freely available for any public GitHub repository.

Since the code in this book is public on GitHub, you can see its code analysis results at `https://sonarcloud.io/summary/overall?id=IntegerMan_Refactoring-with-CSharp`. I'd also strongly recommend that you create an account and have SonarCloud analyze some open-source code you've written or are familiar with, just to walk through the setup and analysis process and see the recommendations it gives you.

While SonarCloud and SonarQube are not .NET-specific tools, I do find they work well with .NET projects, which is why they're highlighted in this book.

Next, let's look at a tool explicitly built for .NET and C# projects in particular: NDepend.

In-depth .NET analysis with NDepend

NDepend is a power tool designed to help architects and software engineers get the most out of their C# projects.

NDepend can operate as a Visual Studio extension such as GitHub Copilot Chat, as a standalone application, or as a build agent integrated into an Azure DevOps build pipeline.

When NDepend runs its analysis, it produces an HTML report (pictured in *Figure 12.14*) and populates a dashboard view with the same information in Visual Studio:

Figure 12.14 – NDepend report showing code analysis results

This report highlights the number of code analysis rules violated by the project, the current unit test code coverage percentages, and how metrics have changed over time.

> **Try it out**
>
> You can view a sample NDepend report for this chapter in the `Chapter12/Ch12FinalCode/NDependOut/NDependReport.html` file in this book's GitHub repository.

If you and your engineering team are trying to answer questions such as "Are we getting better or worse?", "What are our major problems?", or "What areas need to be fixed the most?", NDepend will help you with that.

Like SonarCloud, NDepend operates on a series of analyzers called "rules." These rules are written using LINQ against a model representing your source code. The default rules ship with their source code included and can be customized to your team's needs. You can also write your own rules – much as we'll write our own Roslyn Analyzers in the next two chapters.

These rules also allow you to compare how your code has changed since it was last baselined and estimate the amount of time it will take to resolve the technical debt they represent.

NDepend's strengths go past its primary report, rules list, and list of rules violations. The real strength of NDepend is in its data visualizations.

The dependency matrix is what NDepend was originally known for and allows you to see a two-dimensional matrix of different namespaces and types, as shown in *Figure 12.15*:

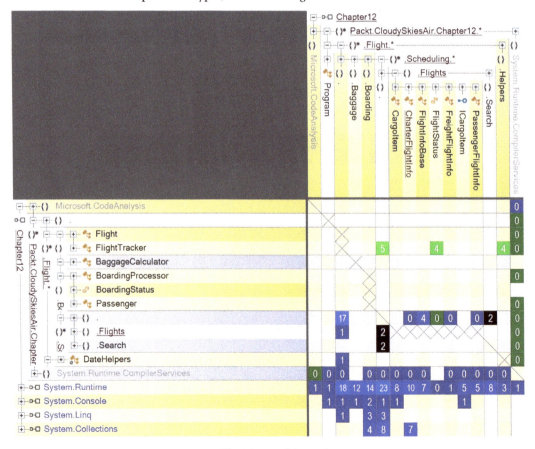

Figure 12.15 – The NDepend dependency matrix

This matrix helps you detect namespaces or types that are dependent on each other. When different types or namespaces are mutually dependent on each other, this typically represents incorrectly segmented software architecture, and NDepend makes this highly visible when violations are present.

NDepend's visualizations don't stop there, however. My favorite visualization built into NDepend is its heat view, which allows you to view types or methods inside your project in a hierarchical tree with different rectangles representing different types or methods.

This view is similar to a tree map in data visualization tools, but each rectangle is colorized and sized based on various metrics calculated by NDepend. These metrics go well beyond the metrics Visual Studio calculates on its own and include things such as the lines of code, cyclomatic complexity, percentage of unit test coverage, or even the amount of comments in the file.

This heat map, pictured in *Figure 12.16*, is the most intuitive way I've found of helping me zero in on potentially problematic code – and communicate problem areas visually to key stakeholders:

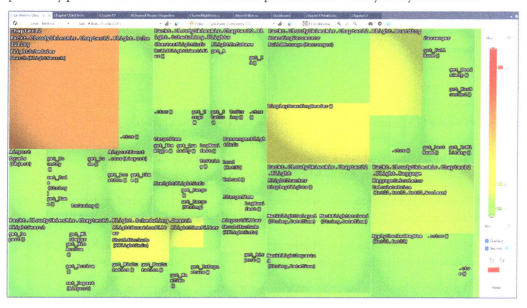

Figure 12.16 – An NDepend heat map showing lines of code and cyclomatic complexity

NDepend also offers a dependency graph view. This graph allows you to see how assemblies, namespaces, types, methods, properties, events, and even fields interact with each other richly and interactively, as shown in *Figure 12.17*:

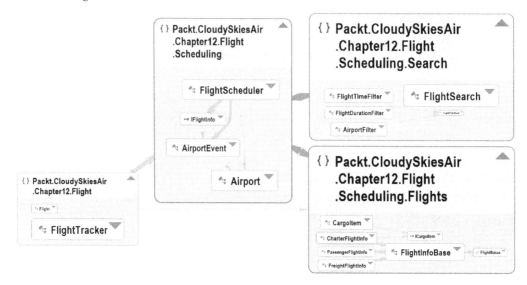

Figure 12.17 – Namespace and type interactions within the Chapter12 project

This allows you to visualize your software architecture and communicate that architecture to others on your team. This is particularly handy when onboarding new developers.

The graph view also allows you to spot problem areas such as types that depend on too many other types, different namespaces dependent on each other, and classes that likely violate the SRP.

In my experience, NDepend takes some additional time to configure and investigate, but it represents a very effective way of visualizing, communicating, and navigating problem areas in your code.

Let's finish this chapter by exploring code analysis at our fictional organization.

Case study – Cloudy Skies Airline

Cloudy Skies Airlines knew they had a lot of technical debt and code issues, but they weren't sure which areas they should prioritize. Each engineer had different opinions on what was most important. As you would expect, these opinions were usually influenced by what each engineer had worked on most recently.

To resolve this issue, engineering leadership turned to the data. They started analyzing the available code metrics in Visual Studio and cataloging where most code analysis warnings seemed to be located.

Engineering management then compared the problem areas with the areas that had changed within the past 3 months and the areas the organization expects will need to change to support the team's upcoming initiatives. This approach helped engineering management prioritize technical debt resolution in strategic areas that supported business objectives.

To help resolve the backlog of warnings, developers were given a new mandate: each commit you make should not increase the number of active code analysis warnings. Decreasing the warning count or having it stay the same is fine, but increasing it will not be acceptable in code review.

This policy built additional awareness of code analysis warnings and the warnings were gradually reduced over time. Once the team got acclimated to paying attention to warnings, they moved to a larger code analysis ruleset. This caused a new series of warnings to come in, but those warnings helped identify potential or actual problems, as well as optimizations for the application.

To help provide insight into the health of its code, the organization is currently evaluating SonarCloud and NDepend to provide the team with a quality dashboard that will help them focus on key areas and ensure quality remains high going forward.

Summary

In this chapter, we saw how code metrics and code analysis tools can help you spot problem areas in your code, follow best practices, and prioritize areas of technical debt. This will help you understand the issues you and your team struggle with. Once you know the areas you struggle with, you can focus on remediating them going forward. This also helps you prioritize areas of technical debt and communicate those areas to others.

These built-in analyzers are incredibly handy and it turns out you can build some on your own. Over the next two chapters, we'll do just that as we build our own code analyzer that can detect and automatically fix issues.

Questions

Answer the following questions to test your knowledge of this chapter:

1. What are the areas you consider to be most problematic about your code?
2. What do the code metrics say about these problem areas?
3. What is cyclomatic complexity and how is it calculated?
4. What are the things you should consider when picking a code analysis ruleset?

Further reading

You can find more information about code analysis at these URLs:

- *Code Metrics Values*: https://learn.microsoft.com/en-us/visualstudio/code-quality/code-metrics-values

- *Overview of .NET source code analysis*: https://learn.microsoft.com/en-us/dotnet/fundamentals/code-analysis/overview

- *SonarCloud*: https://www.sonarsource.com/products/sonarcloud/

- *NDepend*: https://www.ndepend.com/

13

Creating a Roslyn Analyzer

In the previous chapter, we covered the use of code analyzers to detect issues in code. But what happens when your team has common issues that aren't detected by any existing analysis rules?

It turns out that modern C# provides a means for building custom analyzers through something called **Roslyn Analyzers**. In this chapter, we'll see how Roslyn Analyzers work in action by building an analyzer of our own.

This chapter covers the following topics:

- Understanding Roslyn Analyzers
- Creating a Roslyn Analyzer
- Testing Roslyn Analyzers with `RoslynTestKit`
- Sharing analyzers as Visual Studio extensions

Technical requirements

Unlike other chapters, we won't be starting with sample code. Instead, we'll be starting with a blank solution and gradually adding new projects to that solution.

The starting empty solution and final code for this chapter are available from GitHub at `https://github.com/PacktPublishing/Refactoring-with-CSharp` in the `Chapter13` folder.

Understanding Roslyn Analyzers

Before we can go into what a Roslyn Analyzer is, let's talk about Roslyn.

Roslyn is the codename for the reimagined **.NET Compiler Platform** that was released alongside Visual Studio 2015. Since ".NET Compiler Platform" is a lot to say, most people refer to this as the Roslyn compiler or simply Roslyn for short.

Before Roslyn, if a tool wanted to understand C#, VB, or F# source code, developers needed to write their own language parser for these code files. This involved a significant amount of time and complexity, and this effort needed to be repeated every time these programming languages changed. This led to tools being slower to support new language features, lost productivity, and bugs.

One of the explicit goals of the Rosyln compiler was to provide visibility into the structure of code in a standardized way. This way, plugins could work with the Roslyn APIs to get live information about code without having to write their own parser.

To do this, projects can create **Roslyn Analyzers**, which integrate into the code analysis and compilation process. This lets you do the following:

- Provide warnings and errors when anti-patterns in code are present
- Integrate into the **Quick Actions** menu, allowing developers to automatically fix known issues using established solutions
- Provide refactoring capabilities, thereby improving developer productivity

You've been working with Roslyn Analyzers this whole time with the various code warnings, suggestions, and **Quick Action** refactorings you've seen in Visual Studio.

You can explore the built-in analyzers in your projects by going to **Solution Explorer** and then expanding a project's **Dependencies** node, followed by its **Analyzers** node and specific analyzer assemblies, as shown in *Figure 13.1*:

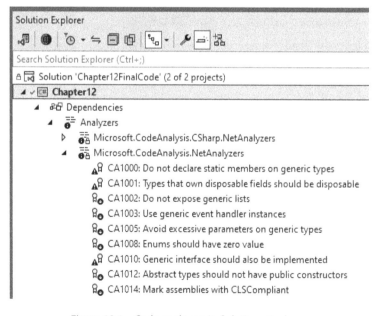

Figure 13.1 – Code analyzers in Solutions Explorer

Through the rest of this chapter, we'll create a Roslyn Analyzer of our own, but before we do, let's talk about how Roslyn sees C# code.

Installing the extension development workload and DGML editor

When you're developing with Roslyn Analyzers, two additions to Visual Studio will help you create and debug your own analyzers. Let's install these by launching **Visual Studio Installer** from the Windows start menu. Next, select your installation of Visual Studio and click **Modify**.

This will bring up a list of workloads and features that are available. These change over time, but you'll want to make sure that the **Visual Studio extension development** workload is checked in the **Workloads** tab, as shown in *Figure 13.2*:

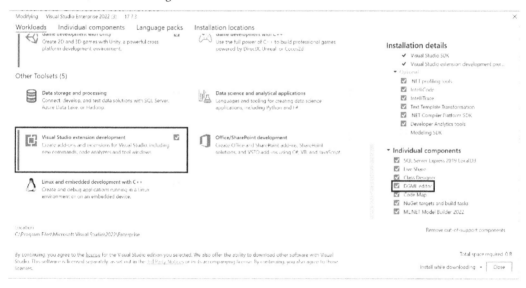

Figure 13.2 – Installing Visual Studio extension development and DGML editor

Next, find **DGML editor** in the **Individual components** tab and check it as well before clicking **Modify** to install the additional components.

The Visual Studio extension development workload is useful when you are trying to create a VSIX extension project for Visual Studio. This type of project allows you to add custom user interface elements, analyzers, and new features to Visual Studio. We'll talk more about VSIX extensions periodically throughout the rest of this chapter and the next.

The DGML editor works with **Directed Graph Markup Language** (**DGML**) to show interactive visualizations in Visual Studio. It also happens to install a very useful view that will help us understand Roslyn more: **Syntax Visualizer**.

Introducing Syntax Visualizer

Syntax Visualizer is a view in Visual Studio that allows you to see the structure of source code from the Roslyn API's point of view.

To see this in action, open a C# file in your editor and then open **Syntax Visualizer** by clicking the **View** menu, followed by **Other Windows** and then **Syntax Visualizer**.

This should show you a hierarchy of various nodes corresponding to the code in your editor, as shown in *Figure 13.3*:

Figure 13.3 – Syntax Visualizer synchronizing with the current code selection

Click on various keywords, variables, methods, and values in your code and watch **Syntax Visualizer** change to reflect what you've selected.

This is a very good way of understanding how code is structured in Roslyn's APIs, but the tool can also be helpful when you're not sure what class inside of the Roslyn API refers to the type of code element you want to work with.

Now that we have a slightly greater understanding of what the Roslyn API is, let's create our first Roslyn Analyzer.

Creating a Roslyn Analyzer

People create custom Roslyn Analyzers when they experience common issues in their code that no existing analyzer addresses. These custom analyzers help enforce rules that specific organizations or teams find to be useful. However, these organization-specific rules tend to be less relevant to the larger .NET community.

Here are a few examples of when you might want to build a custom analyzer:

- Your team has been having issues with too many `FormatException` errors from things such as `int.Parse` and wants to make `int.TryParse` their standard

- Due to large files and limited memory, your team wants to avoid the `File.ReadAllText` method and use stream-based approaches instead

- Your team mandates that all classes must override the `ToString` method to improve the debugging and logging experience

Note that none of these approaches relate to styling or syntax. Instead, these analyzers deal with team-specific decisions about how to best use .NET. We'll explore ways of enforcing styling and syntax choices in *Chapter 16, Adopting Code Standards*.

Let's say that Cloudy Skies Airlines is spending a lot of time debugging and troubleshooting code and suspects that overriding `ToString` in more places would lead to a better developer experience for their team.

> **Note**
>
> It's not an established best practice to override `ToString` in all classes. There are likely some performance drawbacks to doing so, but for this chapter, we'll assume this rule makes sense for the Cloudy Skies team.

Throughout the rest of this chapter, we'll create this analyzer, starting from a blank solution.

Adding the analyzer project to our solution

While there are templates for creating Roslyn Analyzers built into Visual Studio, these are older templates and they hide some of the implementation details. Instead, we're going to walk through the steps of creating and deploying a Roslyn Analyzer from an empty solution.

We'll start by adding a class library that will contain our analyzer. Class libraries are a special type of project that provides code to other projects but cannot run on their own.

Starting with the `Chapter13BeginningCode` solution, we'll right-click on the solution in **Solution Explorer** and then choose **Add** and then **New Project…**.

From there, we'll select the type of project we want to create, select a **Class Library** project using the C# language, as shown in *Figure 13.4*, and click **Next**:

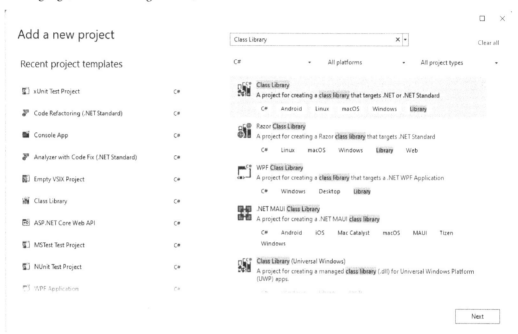

Figure 13.4 – Adding a C# Class Library project to our solution

> **Warning**
> There are multiple projects with the name Class Library in different languages. Look for the green C# icon and the C# label in the list.

Next, we'll need to provide a name for our class library. This is the library that will hold the code analyzer we're creating this chapter, so let's call it `Packt.Analyzers` since the name of the project will become the default namespace of the project.

After this, you'll be asked to select the framework the project should use. Select **.NET Standard 2.0** and click **Create**. The new project will be added to your solution.

> **Why .NET Standard?**
>
> Unlike other projects in this book, we're using .NET Standard here. This is a special version of .NET that was designed to run on a variety of different .NET runtimes. This makes .NET Standard a great choice for when you don't know which version of .NET your code will be running in. See the *Further reading* section for more information.

To create a Roslyn Analyzer, we'll need to add a few NuGet packages to our class library. To do this, right-click on the class library in **Solution Explorer** and then choose **Manage NuGet Packages…**.

Once you're in **NuGet Package Manager**, go to the **Browse** tab and then search for and install version 4.0.1 of the `Microsoft.CodeAnalysis` package, as shown in *Figure 13.5*:

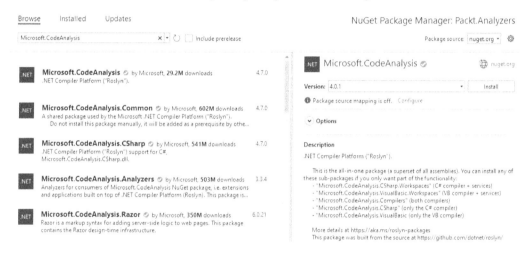

Figure 13.5 – Installing version 4.0.1 of Microsoft.CodeAnalysis

Note that version 4.0.1 is not the most recent version of this package. This specific version was chosen to avoid a conflict with the testing library we'll use later.

Now that the package has been installed, we're ready to start creating our Roslyn Analyzer.

Defining a code analysis rule

Let's start by renaming the `Class1.cs` file to `ToStringAnalyzer.cs` and replacing its contents with the following:

```
using System;
using System.Linq;
using System.Collections.Immutable;
using Microsoft.CodeAnalysis;
using Microsoft.CodeAnalysis.Diagnostics;
```

```
namespace Packt.Analyzers {
  [DiagnosticAnalyzer(LanguageNames.CSharp)]
  public class ToStringAnalyzer : DiagnosticAnalyzer {
  }
}
```

This is the minimum we need to have a compiling analyzer. Let's explore what's here.

First of all, the ToStringAnalyzer class inherits from DiagnosticAnalyzer, which is a base class for all Roslyn Analyzers that provide warnings to the user.

The class has a DiagnosticAnalyzer attribute that says the analyzer applies to code written in C#.

> **Note**
>
> It's possible to write analyzers that apply to C#, F#, Visual Basic, or some combination of these languages.

Inheriting from the abstract DiagnosticAnalyzers class forces us to override the SupportedDiagnostics property and the Initialize method. Let's do that now in the simplest way possible:

```
public override ImmutableArray<DiagnosticDescriptor>
  SupportedDiagnostics => null;
public override void Initialize(AnalysisContext con) {
}
```

The SupportedDiagnostics property returns ImmutableArray, which contains all diagnostic rules the analyzer provides to the editor. In our case, we'll want it to return the warning the user might see if the rule is violated.

Let's add a new property and update our SupportedDiagnostics property, as shown here:

```
public static readonly DiagnosticDescriptor Rule =
  new DiagnosticDescriptor(
    id: "CSA1001",
    title: "Override ToString()",
    messageFormat: "Override ToString on {0}",
    category: "Maintainability",
    defaultSeverity: DiagnosticSeverity.Info,
    isEnabledByDefault: true,
    description: "Override ToString to help debugging.");
public override ImmutableArray<DiagnosticDescriptor>
  SupportedDiagnostics => ImmutableArray.Create(Rule);
```

Here, we've added a static `Rule` property that defines the `DiagnosticDescriptor` object that's defining our rule. This rule is then included in the `SupportedDiagnostics` property.

> **Localization note**
>
> `DiagnosticDescriptor` objects can be created with either raw strings, as we're using here, or by using `LocalizableString` parameters. `LocalizableString` works better in different languages, so you'll want to use it if you are trying to create a Roslyn Analyzer intended to be used throughout the globe.

The `DiagnosticDescriptor` object that this code defines will show up in the **Error List** pane and build output if the rule is ever violated. The rule needs the following parts:

- **ID**: A piece of code starting with letters identifying a provider and then a numeric code. We chose the code CSA for Cloudy Skies Airlines.

- **Title**: The short name of the code analysis warning. This is what will appear in tooltips when the rule is violated.

- **Message format**: A formattable string that will appear in the Visual Studio tooltip.

- **Category**: The broad rule category. Common categories include `Naming`, `Performance`, `Maintainability`, `Security`, `Reliability`, `Design`, and `Usage`.

- **Default severity**: The severity of the code analysis rule without the user adjusting it. This will be `Hidden`, `Info`, `Warning`, or `Error`.

- **Enabled by default**: Whether the rule starts as enabled.

- **Description**: A detailed description of the rule and why it's important. This shows up in the **Error List** pane when a rule violation is expanded.

Defining your rule as a separate property is helpful when other code needs to refer to your exact rule definition.

Now that our rule has been defined, let's write the code that detects when the rule is violated.

Analyzing symbols with our Roslyn Analyzer

Let's start by building out our `Initialize` method:

```
public override void Initialize(AnalysisContext con) {
  con.ConfigureGeneratedCodeAnalysis(
    GeneratedCodeAnalysisFlags.None);
  con.EnableConcurrentExecution();
  con.RegisterSymbolAction(Analyze, SymbolKind.NamedType);
}
```

This method now does a few additional things:

- First, we configure the analyzer to ignore any auto-generated code for analysis purposes. These are files that the user didn't write but various tools generate and so it doesn't make sense to analyze them.

- Secondly, we tell Roslyn that it's fine to evaluate multiple pieces of code with this rule at the same time. This is always the preferred option from a performance standpoint.

Finally, we tell the analyzer that whenever it encounters a named Type during code analysis, we want to know about it. Specifically, the code should call a new Analyze method for each Type that is detected.

We haven't written that Analyze method yet, so let's do so now:

```
private static void Analyze(
  SymbolAnalysisContext con) {
  INamedTypeSymbol sym = (INamedTypeSymbol)con.Symbol;
  IMethodSymbol toString =
    sym.GetMembers()
      .OfType<IMethodSymbol>()
      .FirstOrDefault(m => m.Name == "ToString"
                        && m.IsOverride
                        && m.Parameters.Length == 0);
  if (toString == null) {
    Diagnostic diagnostic = Diagnostic.Create(
      Rule, sym.Locations[0], sym.Name);
    con.ReportDiagnostic(diagnostic);
  }
}
```

This code is not easy to write or read, so let's go over it before discussing *how* to write analyzer code.

First, since we know this method is called on named types, we can cast the symbol Roslyn gives us to INamedTypeSymbol, which lets us query further.

Using this symbol, we can ask for all members such as properties and methods using GetMembers. Next, we can use LINQ to filter these down to just ones that are methods. Once we have these, we can use FirstOrDefault to see if we have a method named ToString that takes in zero parameters and is an override.

> **Why not check the return type?**
> We could check if the return type was a string, but the C# compiler doesn't allow multiple methods with the same parameters and different return types. We also know all objects have string ToString(), so the return type will be string.

If we didn't find a `ToString` override, our analyzer should flag this as a violation of the rule. It does so by creating a `Diagnostic` object referencing the `Rule` property we defined earlier, as well as the name and location of the symbol that violated the rule. Here, the symbol will be a `Type` definition that does not override `ToString`.

Before we go into verifying our analyzer works, let's talk about writing analyzer code.

Tips for writing Roslyn Analyzers

In my experience, Roslyn Analyzers are one of the tougher pieces of code to write. With Roslyn, you're looking at your C# code in a completely different light.

Each analyzer you write will likely be analyzing something completely different than the last one, making discussing the breadth of options available in Roslyn difficult.

I've found two key things helpful for writing Roslyn Analyzers:

- **Looking at other Roslyn Analyzers**: There are a lot of other Roslyn Analyzers out there (including the ones built into .NET) and most are open source. This means you can find an existing analyzer similar to what you're interested in and then look at its source code and do something similar.

  See the *Further reading* section of this chapter for a few popular collections of Roslyn Analyzers.

- **GitHub Copilot Chat**: Starting with an empty `Analyze` method, you can give Copilot a prompt such as "I want to find all methods contained in this type" or "How would I check if this type is marked as public?"

  You still need to provide high-level guidance, but in my experience, Copilot can be extremely effective at helping you write complex and unfamiliar analyzer code.

Now that we've built our Roslyn Analyzer, let's look at how we can make sure it works.

Testing Roslyn Analyzers with RoslynTestKit

We'll show how to use your Roslyn Analyzers in projects of your own at the end of this chapter, but we'll start by writing unit tests around our existing analyzer.

At a high level, we want to test two things with our analyzer:

- The analyzer doesn't trigger for code that doesn't violate its rule.
- The analyzer correctly flags code that it should.

We'll do this with two unit tests in a new unit test project.

Adding a Roslyn Analyzer test project

Our tests can be written in **MSTest**, **xUnit**, or **NUnit**. We'll use xUnit for consistency.

We'll start by adding a new xUnit project to the solution by right-clicking on the solution and then choosing **Add** and then **New Project…**, as we've done before.

After this, select the C# version of **xUnit Test Project** and click **Next**. Name your project `Packt.Analyzers.Tests` and click **Next**. When prompted with the framework, select **.NET 8.0** and click **Create**.

Once the project has been created, add a project reference to `Packt.Analyzers` by right-clicking on the **Dependencies** node in the `Packt.Analyzers.Tests` project and then selecting **Add Project Reference…**, as shown in *Figure 13.6*:

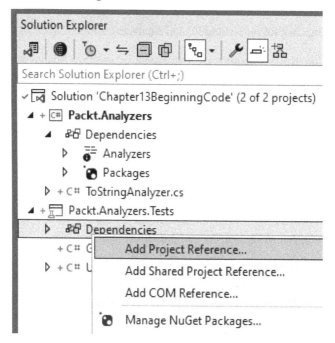

Figure 13.6 – Add Project Reference…

Check the box next to `Packt.Analyzers` and click **OK**. This will allow you to reference your analyzers from the test project.

Next, we'll need to add a reference to the **RoslynTestKit** NuGet package. This is a testing framework-agnostic library that lets us unit-test Roslyn Analyzers by extending from certain test fixture classes, as we'll see in a moment.

Right-click `Packt.Analyzers.Tests` and click **Manage NuGet Packages…**. Next, go to the **Browse** tab and install `SmartAnalyzers.RoslynTestKit`.

> Troubleshooting installation issues
>
> You may encounter a conflict between the latest versions of `Microsoft.CodeAnalysis` and `SmartAnalyzers.RoslynTestKit`. See this chapter's final code on GitHub for recommended versions of NuGet packages to resolve this issue.

With the project setup out of the way, let's create our test fixture.

Creating AnalyzerTestFixture

We'll start by renaming `UnitTest1.cs` to `ToStringAnalyzerTests.cs` and replacing its contents with the following code:

```
using Microsoft.CodeAnalysis;
using Microsoft.CodeAnalysis.Diagnostics;
using RoslynTestKit;
namespace Packt.Analyzers.Tests;
public class ToStringAnalyzerTests : AnalyzerTestFixture {
  protected override string LanguageName
    => LanguageNames.CSharp;
  protected override DiagnosticAnalyzer CreateAnalyzer()
    => new ToStringAnalyzer();
}
```

This class inherits from `AnalyzerTestFixture` in `RoslynTestKit`. This forces the class to provide the language it works with and a method to create the analyzer we want to test. Since we're working with C#, we return `LanguageNames.CSharp` for the language. In `CreateAnalyzer`, we instantiate and return an instance of our `ToStringAnalyzer` from the `Packt.Analyzers` project.

This lets `RoslynTestKit` know how to create our analyzer and what languages we're working with, but we haven't defined a test yet. Let's write our first test now.

Verifying that our Roslyn Analyzer doesn't flag good code

Our first test will be to ensure that code that doesn't violate our analyzer won't get flagged as a rule violation. We'll test this by defining a string containing valid code and then verifying that the analyzer didn't find any issues with it.

We declare the "good" code as follows:

```
public const string GoodCode = @"
using System;
public class Flight
{
  public string Id {get; set;}
  public string DepartAirport {get; set;}
  public string ArriveAirport {get; set;}
  public override string ToString() => Id;
}";
```

This multi-line string defines C# for a simple class declaration of a `Flight` class, which includes an override of the `ToString` method. Because `ToString` is overridden, our rule should not find issues with this class definition.

We can verify this with the following code:

```
[Fact]
public void AnalyzerShouldNotFlagGoodCode() {
    NoDiagnostic(GoodCode, ToStringAnalyzer.Rule.Id);
}
```

Here, we use the `NoDiagnostic` method from the `RoslynTestKit's AnalyzerTestFixture` class to check that the code doesn't violate our rule.

`RoslynTestKit` needs to know the ID of the rule we're checking for, so we use the `Rule` property we defined on `ToStringAnalyzer` earlier to provide its `id` value.

Now that our test passes without issues, let's move on to the second test.

Verifying that our Roslyn Analyzer flags bad code

To verify that bad code triggers the analyzer rule, we'll use a similar approach: we'll pass in known bad code and ensure that the rule is triggered.

This is slightly more complicated because we want to make sure the rule is triggered for the right symbol in the code. So, when we define our bad code, we need to add `[|` and `|]` markers to denote which symbol should be flagged, as shown here:

```
public const string BadCode = @"
using System;
public class [|Flight|]
{
  public string Id {get; set;}
  public string DepartAirport {get; set;}
```

```
  public string ArriveAirport {get; set;}
}";
```

This code doesn't have a `ToString` override, so the `Flight` class should be flagged as a rule violation. We can verify this with the `HasDiagnostic` method:

```
[Fact]
public void AnalyzerShouldFlagViolations() {
  HasDiagnostic(BadCode, ToStringAnalyzer.Rule.Id);
}
```

This code is very similar to our approach to validating good code and will fail if the rule was not triggered or was not triggered explicitly for the `Flight` symbol.

We could continue to expand our tests with additional examples and counter-examples, but let's move on to talking briefly about debugging our Roslyn Analyzers.

Debugging Roslyn Analyzers

When you write a Roslyn Analyzer, it's unlikely that you'll get it right the first time.

Unit tests help detect failures in your analyzer, but let's talk about how you would debug a Roslyn Analyzer.

My recommended approach with Roslyn Analyzers is to follow the approach of this chapter: *create a class library containing your analyzer and a test project that tests it.*

If your analyzer isn't properly triggering for certain code, you can put breakpoints in your analyzer code and step through the code for a specific instance by right-clicking on a specific test and selecting **Debug**, as shown in *Figure 13.7*:

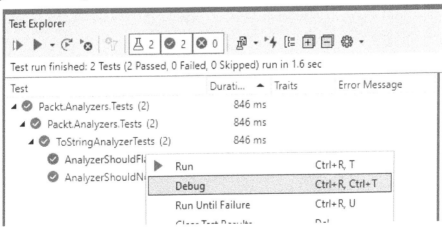

Figure 13.7 – Debugging a specific test case

I've found this approach to be generally very helpful when analyzing specific test cases. In these scenarios, I can see the exact objects the analyzer encounters from the test scenario. From there, I wrote enough code to get the analyzer to handle that scenario. Once the analyzer has handled that test case, I'm usually at a point where I'm ready to try the analyzer on a wider range of code, which we'll discuss next.

Sharing analyzers as Visual Studio extensions

Once you're ready to try an analyzer on more code or share it with your peers, there are a few options available:

- Deploy the analyzer as a NuGet package, as we'll discuss in the next chapter

- Create a **Visual Studio Installer** (**VSIX**) to install the analyzers locally

- Create a new project and add an explicit reference to the analyzers by editing the `.csproj` file and adding an `Analyzer` node, as shown here:

```
<ItemGroup>
  <Analyzer Include="..\some\path\Your.Analyzer.dll" />
</ItemGroup>
```

This last approach is one you might consider if you had a large solution and wanted your analyzer to only apply to other projects in that solution. However, I've found this approach to be buggy and require frequent reloads of Visual Studio for changes in the analyzers to take hold, so we'll use the VSIX approach as we close out this chapter.

Creating a Visual Studio extension (VSIX) for your Roslyn Analyzer

Visual Studio extension projects (VSIX projects) allow you to bundle a diverse set of capabilities into an extension that can then be installed into Visual Studio.

Let's create a new VSIX project, add our analyzer to it, and then use it in a new instance of Visual Studio.

We'll start as we usually do: by right-clicking on the solution in **Solution Explorer**, choosing **Add**, and then **New Project…**.

Next, select the **Empty VSIX Project** template with C# as the language. Name this project `Packt.Analyzers.Installer` and click **Create**.

This empty project consists of a single `source.extension.vsixmanifest` file, which we'll refer to as the manifest. This manifest is the only file we'll need. Double-click on it to open the designer, as shown in *Figure 13.8*:

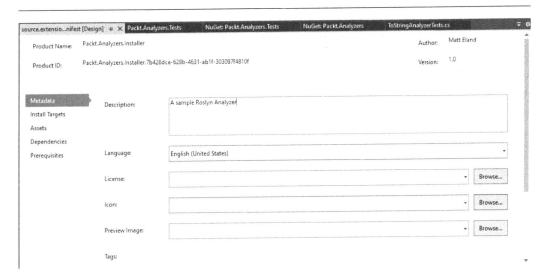

Figure 13.8 – The manifest in the design view

This opens the metadata view, which contains different settings you can configure. We'll ignore those and click on the **Assets** blade on the left sidebar.

The **Assets** blade specifies the different components that are included in the extension. We want to include our analyzer, so click **New** to open the **Add New Asset** dialogue.

Next, specify the **Analyzer** type, use **A project in current solution** as your source, and then select the Packt.Analyzers project, as shown in *Figure 13.9*:

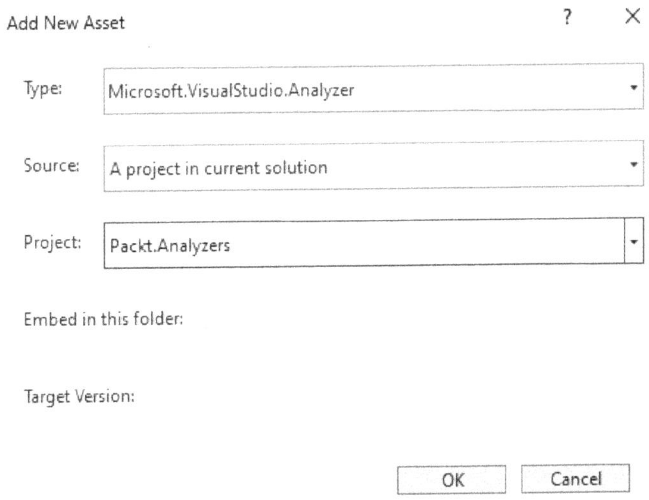

Figure 13.9 – Adding the Roslyn Analyzer to your VSIX project as an asset

Click **OK**; your analyzer should now appear in the list of assets.

With that change, our VSIX project is now ready for us to use. To test this project, right-click on the `Packt.Analyzers.Installer` project and choose **Set as Startup Project**. Next, run your project – a new experimental instance of Visual Studio will open.

> **Note**
>
> It can take a few minutes for Visual Studio to open after you run the project. The version of Visual Studio that opens is built specifically for developing extensions and needs additional time to launch. It is not recommended to use this version of Visual Studio for actual development. Instead, use it to test your extensions and then close it.

After a few minutes, a new instance of Visual Studio will open with your VSIX project installed. Using this instance of Visual Studio, you can open any other project and the Roslyn Analyzer you built in this chapter will be active.

Specifically, our analyzer will show up as a suggestion on classes that don't override `ToString`, such as the `SkillController` class in *Figure 13.10*:

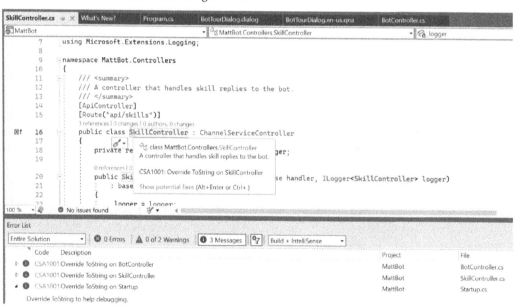

Figure 13.10 – Our Roslyn Analyzer suggests overriding ToString

Warnings for your analyzer will also show up in the error list, though if you marked them as having a severity, as we did in the chapter, you'll need to make sure that messages are displayed in those results. See the highlighted button in *Figure 13.10* for the message filter.

> **DebuggerDisplay attributes versus ToString overrides**
>
> This chapter uses `ToString` as an example, and overriding `ToString` can help with the debugger experience. An alternative to this would be to add a `[DebuggerDisplay]` attribute above your class definition to describe how it appears in the debugger without needing to override `ToString`.

Once you are satisfied with your test, close the new instance of Visual Studio.

Building and testing your installer will have created a `Packt.Analyzers.Installer.vsix` file in the `bin/Debug` folder within your extension project. This `.vsix` file will let other people install your custom extension and use your analyzers in their projects.

> **Note**
>
> You could also distribute your installer on the Visual Studio marketplace. This would make the extension publicly available and easier for others to locate and download.

Any time you update your analyzer, you'll need to share a new version of the extension and your team will need to upgrade. This makes managing Roslyn Analyzers via `.vsix` files challenging.

Fortunately, NuGet packages offer a better way of sharing Roslyn Analyzers, as we'll see in the next chapter.

Summary

In this chapter, we created our first Roslyn Analyzer, tested it with `RoslynTestKit`, and built a VSIX extension to integrate it into Visual Studio.

We saw how Roslyn Analyzers power all the warnings we interact with in Visual Studio and how you and your team can create new Roslyn Analyzers to detect and flag issues that are unique to your team and its codebase.

In the next chapter, we'll see how Roslyn Analyzers can be used to fix the issues they find and help safely refactor your code.

Questions

1. How do Roslyn Analyzers work?
2. When would you want to create your own Roslyn Analyzer?
3. How can you verify that Roslyn Analyzers work correctly?

Further reading

You can find more information about the topics that were covered in this chapter at these URLs:

- *Roslyn Analyzers*: `https://learn.microsoft.com/en-us/visualstudio/code-quality/roslyn-analyzers-overview`

- *Install third-party analyzers*: `https://learn.microsoft.com/en-us/visualstudio/code-quality/install-roslyn-analyzers`

- *Awesome Roslyn*: `https://github.com/ironcev/awesome-roslyn`

- *.NET Standard*: `https://learn.microsoft.com/en-us/dotnet/standard/net-standard`

Here are some popular open-source Roslyn Analyzers on GitHub:

- *Roslyn Analyzers*: *https://github.com/dotnet/roslyn-analyzers*

- *StyleCop*: `https://github.com/DotNetAnalyzers/StyleCopAnalyzers`

14

Refactoring Code with Roslyn Analyzers

In the last chapter, we saw how you can build Roslyn analyzers to flag issues in your code. In this chapter, we'll improve our analyzers by giving them the ability to fix code issues by providing **Quick Actions** the user can invoke to modify their source code. We'll also discuss some additional ways of deploying Roslyn analyzers that improve your ability to provide a consistent experience to your team members.

This chapter covers the following:

- Building a Roslyn Analyzer code fix
- Testing code fixes with RoslynTestKit
- Publishing Roslyn analyzers as NuGet packages

Technical requirements

In this chapter, we're starting right where we left off in *Chapter 13*.

The starting code for this chapter is available from GitHub at `https://github.com/PacktPublishing/Refactoring-with-CSharp` in the `Chapter14/Ch14BeginningCode` folder.

Case study – Cloudy Skies Airlines

In *Chapter 13*, we built a `ToStringAnalyzer` that detects classes that do not override the `ToString` method. This results in suggestions in the Visual Studio editor and a message in the error list.

Cloudy Skies Airlines has deployed this internally and found it to be generally helpful, but there are a few things that need improvement:

- Although violations of the `ToString` override rule are flagged by the analyzer, not every developer is addressing this issue. When discussed internally, some developers stated they didn't want to take the time to address it. Additionally, some of the newer developers didn't fully understand the rule or what fixing it would look like.

- Whenever a new analyzer is created or a bug in an existing analyzer is addressed, a new VSIX file must be created. Developers then need to download and install it to get the updated version. Because of this, it's hard for the team to know which developers have the analyzer installed or which version each developer is using.

In this chapter, we'll address these concerns. We'll look at creating and testing a code fix provider that can automatically resolve detected issues. After that, we'll explore publishing analyzers via **NuGet packages** and show how they can help your team have a consistent analyzer experience.

Building a Roslyn Analyzer code fix

Roslyn Analyzers allow you to provide options for users to automatically fix issues your analyzers detect in your code. They do this through something called a **code fix provider**, which can modify your document in an automated manner to resolve the diagnostic warning.

Think of it this way: diagnostic analyzers, like our `OverrideToStringAnalyzer`, help *detect* issues in your team's code. On the other hand, code fix providers give you a way of *fixing* these issues.

Not all diagnostic analyzers will have code-fix providers, but in my experience, those that also provide code-fix providers tend to get addressed earlier and more consistently.

Let's see how one works.

Creating a CodeFixProvider

First, we'll add a new class to the `Packt.Analyzers` class library. We'll call this class `ToStringCodeFix`. Replace its contents with the following code for a basic code fix:

```
using Microsoft.CodeAnalysis;
using Microsoft.CodeAnalysis.CodeActions;
using Microsoft.CodeAnalysis.CodeFixes;
using Microsoft.CodeAnalysis.CSharp;
using Microsoft.CodeAnalysis.CSharp.Syntax;
using Microsoft.CodeAnalysis.Text;
using System.Collections.Immutable;
using System.Composition;
using System.Linq;
```

```
using System.Threading.Tasks;
namespace Packt.Analyzers {

  [Shared]
  [ExportCodeFixProvider(LanguageNames.CSharp,
    Name = nameof(ToStringCodeFix))]
  public class ToStringCodeFix : CodeFixProvider {
    public override ImmutableArray<string>
      FixableDiagnosticIds =>
        ImmutableArray.Create(ToStringAnalyzer.Rule.Id);
    public override FixAllProvider GetFixAllProvider()
      => WellKnownFixAllProviders.BatchFixer;
    public async override Task RegisterCodeFixesAsync(
      CodeFixContext context) {
      throw new NotImplementedException();
    }
  }
}
```

This is the minimum amount of code we need in order to have a compiling code fix provider. Before we build out the rest of this class, let's examine what's here already.

First, we're declaring a `ToStringCodeFix` class that inherits from `CodeFixProvider`. `CodeFixProvider` is the abstract class used for providing a fix for one or more diagnostics.

Note that we named our code fix `ToStringCodeFix` to pair with the `ToStringAnalyzer` class it provides a code fix for. This is a convention I like to follow to help clearly associate analyzers and their code fixes.

The class has two attributes assigned to it:

- The `ExportCodeFixProviderAttribute` tells Roslyn that the class represents a code fix, what the name of the code fix is, and the languages the code fix applies to
- The `SharedAttribute` doesn't do anything on its own, but it is needed for Roslyn to be comfortable registering your code fix in Visual Studio

These two attributes should be on every code fix you create. Failing to use them will result in your code fix provider not appearing for some users (don't ask me how I know).

The `ToStringCodeFix` class has three members at the moment:

- **FixableDiagnosticIds**: This lists the unique identifier of all analyzer rules this code fix can provide solutions to. In our case, this uses the ID of the `ToStringAnalyzer` rule, meaning it says it can fix that issue.

- **GetFixAllProvider**: By default, code fixes don't support the "fix-all" functionality in Visual Studio. By overriding this method and returning `WellKnownFixAllProviders.BatchFixer`, we tell Visual Studio to allow the user to try to fix all issues of that type in the file, project, or even solution.

- **RegisterCodeFixesAsync**: This is where we can register our code fix and tell Visual Studio what to do if the user chooses to apply it.

The bulk of our logic will be in `RegisterCodeFixesAsync`, so let's implement that method now.

Registering a code fix

The job of `RegisterCodeFixesAsync` is to interpret code that violates the diagnostic rule we've set up and register an action that will let the user fix it.

The code to do this is fairly involved, so let's look at parts of it at a time. The first part has to do with interpreting where in the document the diagnostic violation occurred:

```
public async override Task RegisterCodeFixesAsync(
   CodeFixContext context) {
   Diagnostic diagnostic = context.Diagnostics.First();
   TextSpan span = diagnostic.Location.SourceSpan;
   Document doc = context.Document;
```

Here, we get a `CodeFixContext` object that contains information about the code analysis diagnostic violations.

These `Diagnostic` objects contain information about the exact span of text within the document that triggered the rule. In our case, this should be the text for the name of the class that doesn't override `ToString`.

Next, we get a reference to the `Document` containing the violation. Think of a `Document` as a file of source code somewhere in your solution. It's possible to have analyzers and code fixes that look over your entire solution, so this `Document` helps narrow down the scope to the file containing the offending code.

With this `Document`, we can gain access to the syntax tree and its `type` declarations:

```
SyntaxNode root = await doc
   .GetSyntaxRootAsync(context.CancellationToken)
   .ConfigureAwait(false);
TypeDeclarationSyntax typeDec =
   root.FindToken(span.Start)
       .Parent
       .AncestorsAndSelf()
       .OfType<TypeDeclarationSyntax>()
```

```
      .First();
```

Here, we're getting the `SyntaxRoot` element representing the base of our document and then finding the declaration of the class by the location of that span of text within the document.

This lets us jump from the raw text we had in the span to an object representing the `Type` declaration. Having this object allows us to make changes and provide a fix.

The final portion of the method registers the code action to fix the issue:

```
  CodeAction fix = CodeAction.Create(
    title: "Override ToString",
    createChangedDocument: c => FixAsync(doc, typeDec)
  );
  context.RegisterCodeFix(fix, diagnostic);
}
```

This code creates a `CodeAction` and registers it as a fix for the diagnostic rule. This fix has a title representing the text the user will see in the **Quick Actions** menu when making the fix and an action to invoke when the user is attempting to invoke the code fix. In this case, the code fix invokes the `FixAsync` method we've yet to see.

Additional options

There are several overloads and optional parameters to `CodeAction.Create` that let you change the entire solution instead of a single document or resolve conflicts when multiple code fixes have the same title.

Now that we've registered our code fix, let's see how the fix action works.

Modifying the document with a code fix

The final step in implementing our code fix is the `FixAsync` method. This method's job is to modify the `Document` so that it no longer violates the diagnostic rule.

In our case, the fix will be to generate code such as this:

```
public override string ToString()
{
  throw new NotImplementedException();
}
```

Sadly, it's a lot easier to write the raw C# here than it is to build it with the Roslyn API.

To add this with Roslyn, we'll follow these steps:

1. Create a method body that throws a `NotImplementedException`.

2. Create a list of modifiers that go with the method (`public` and `override`).

3. Create a method declaration with the appropriate name and return type and make sure this method has the list of modifiers and the method body.

4. Create a version of the `Type` declaration that has the new method.

5. Find the `Type` declaration in the `Document` and replace it with our new one.

Let's see how this works, starting with the code that declares the new method body:

```
private Task<Document> FixAsync(Document doc,
  TypeDeclarationSyntax typeDec) {
  const string exType = "NotImplementedException";
  IdentifierNameSyntax exId =
    SyntaxFactory.IdentifierName(exType);
  BlockSyntax methodBody = SyntaxFactory.Block(
    SyntaxFactory.ThrowStatement(
      SyntaxFactory.ObjectCreationExpression(exId)
        .WithArgumentList(SyntaxFactory.ArgumentList())
    )
  );
```

As you can see, the code to declare anything in Roslyn can get a bit dense. When you take a step back, though, this code is just declaring a method block that instantiates and throws a `NotImplementedException`.

Next, we'll define the method definition that uses this method body:

```
SyntaxToken[] modifiers = new SyntaxToken[] {
  SyntaxFactory.Token(SyntaxKind.PublicKeyword),
  SyntaxFactory.Token(SyntaxKind.OverrideKeyword)
};
SyntaxToken returnType =
  SyntaxFactory.Token(SyntaxKind.StringKeyword);
MethodDeclarationSyntax newMethod =
  SyntaxFactory.MethodDeclaration(
    SyntaxFactory.PredefinedType(returnType),
    SyntaxFactory.Identifier("ToString")
  )
  .WithModifiers(SyntaxFactory.TokenList(modifiers))
  .WithBody(methodBody);
```

This code is almost as dense as the last block, but all it really does is declare the method. This method brings together a return type of `string`, a name of `ToString`, the `public` and `override` modifiers, and the body we declared in the previous block.

The final step in the fix is to modify the editor's code with our code fix. We do this with the following code:

```
TypeDeclarationSyntax newType =
  typeDec.AddMembers(newMethod);
SyntaxNode root = typeDec.SyntaxTree.GetRoot();
SyntaxNode newRoot = root.ReplaceNode(typeDec, newType);
Document newDoc = doc.WithSyntaxRoot(newRoot);
return Task.FromResult(newDoc);
}
```

This code creates a new version of the `Type` declaration that has our new method. We then find the old `Type` declaration in the `Document` and replace it with the new one. This creates a new `Document` that we then return from our code fix, and Visual Studio updates our code accordingly.

With that, we now have a working code fix. How do we know it's working? We test it!

Testing Code Fixes with RoslynTestKit

In *Chapter 13*, we saw how the `RoslynTestKit` library helps your diagnostic analyzers flag code issues appropriately. In this chapter, we'll revisit the library to verify our new code fix.

We will start by creating a new class in our test project named `ToStringCodeFixTests` due to our common naming conventions.

This class will start by declaring a test fixture like it did with the analyzer:

```
using Microsoft.CodeAnalysis;
using Microsoft.CodeAnalysis.CodeFixes;
using Microsoft.CodeAnalysis.Diagnostics;
using RoslynTestKit;
namespace Packt.Analyzers.Tests;
public class ToStringCodeFixTests : CodeFixTestFixture {
 protected override string LanguageName
   => LanguageNames.CSharp;
 protected override CodeFixProvider CreateProvider()
   => new ToStringCodeFix();
 protected override IReadOnlyCollection<DiagnosticAnalyzer>
   CreateAdditionalAnalyzers()
   => new[] { new ToStringAnalyzer() };
```

Like before, our test class inherits from a test fixture, but this time it's a `CodeFixTestFixture` since we're testing a code fix.

Also like before, we need to specify that our code fix affects the C# programming language and provide a reference to our class through the `CreateProvider` method.

Unlike before, we also need to provide the code analyzer we're testing through the `CreateAdditionalAnalyzers` method. The compiler will allow you to not override this method, but if you forget to do so, your analyzer will never trigger in the steps ahead, so be sure to include your analyzer here.

Next, we test our code fix by providing a block of bad code and a block of good code and verifying that the code fix successfully moves from the bad code to the good code:

```csharp
  public const string BadCode = @"
using System;
public class [|Flight|]
{
    public string Id {get; set;}
    public string DepartAirport {get; set;}
    public string ArriveAirport {get; set;}
}";

  public const string GoodCode = @"
using System;
public class Flight
{
    public string Id {get; set;}
    public string DepartAirport {get; set;}
    public string ArriveAirport {get; set;}

    public override string ToString()
    {
        throw new NotImplementedException();
    }
}";
  [Fact]
  public void CodeFixShouldMoveBadCodeToGood() {
    string ruleId = ToStringAnalyzer.Rule.Id;
    TestCodeFix(BadCode, GoodCode, ruleId);
  }
}
```

This code should be somewhat familiar from the last chapter. Just like with analyzers, we need to denote the location the fix is triggered from using the [| and |] markers as we see on [|Flight|].

The actual verification step occurs through the TestCodeFix method call. This method call will convert your bad code to a new form using the code fix and then compare that result to the expected good code.

This comparison is very sensitive, and any extra space, line breaks, or differences at all will result in a failing test with the observed differences between the two strings highlighted, as shown in *Figure 14.1*:

```
Test Detail Summary
  ⊗ Packt.Analyzers.Tests.ToStringCodeFixTests.CodeFixShouldMoveBadCodeToGood
    ▤ Source: ToStringCodeFixTests.cs line 41
    ⊕ Duration: 837 ms

  Message:
    RoslynTestKit.TransformedCodeDifferentThanExpectedException : Transformed code is different than expected:
    ============================
    From line 9:
    -  ····public·override·string·ToString()·{¶↵
    +  ····public·override·string·ToString()¶↵
    +  ····{¶↵
```

Figure 14.1 – A test failure showing a string difference due to styling choices

Assuming your formatting is consistent, your test should now pass, proving you have a good code fix.

If you want, you can now launch your VSIX extension project and verify the code fix in Visual Studio. After that, you could share the VSIX file with colleagues or people in the .NET community and they'd have access to your analyzer and its fix.

However, VSIX deployment has some downsides as we'll soon see. Let's close the chapter by looking at using NuGet packages to share your code fixes in a more controlled manner.

Publishing Roslyn Analyzers as NuGet packages

Using VSIX files to share code analyzers works, but isn't an ideal solution.

Since VSIX files must be manually installed and updated, this means that with a team of software engineers, you're never sure who has the extension installed at all or who is on which version of the extension.

Because each developer must install the VSIX themselves and keep it updated, this makes it harder to onboard new team members, release new analyzers or code fixes, or issue patches for issues found in your existing analyzers.

Thankfully, there's a better option: *NuGet package deployment*.

Understanding NuGet package deployment

Analyzers and code fixes can be packed into NuGet packages and deployed to a NuGet feed so others can find them. Once in a NuGet feed, any developer on the team can install the package into one or more projects.

Once a NuGet package is installed, any developer who opens the project will automatically have the package downloaded through the largely invisible NuGet package restore step. If you install a NuGet package and then add, commit, and push the change, other developers will see it automatically installed when they pull your changes and open the project in Visual Studio.

This means that only one developer on your team needs to install any NuGet package, including a package containing Roslyn Analyzers. Additionally, if you ever need to update the package to include new analyzers, any developer on the team can update the version of the package that is installed.

By using NuGet package deployment for Roslyn Analyzers, your analyzers become:

- Easy to install
- Easy to update
- Consistently available across all developers on the team
- Intentionally associated with the project

That last point is an interesting one. With VSIX deployment, analyzers apply to any code that a developer opens on their machine. There is no formal link between the analyzer and your team's source code, but if a developer has a VSIX analyzer installed, they'll see its recommendations.

With NuGet packages, you're explicit about which analyzers should analyze which projects because you explicitly associate them via the NuGet install process. This means that you can look at any project in your solution and get a sense of what analyzer rules should apply for all developers on your project, which is very hard to accomplish through VSIX deployment.

Because of these things, I strongly recommend deploying your analyzers and code fixes as NuGet packages.

Let's see how that's done.

Building a NuGet package

Visual Studio gives you an easy way of packaging most .NET projects: just right-click on a project in **Solution Explorer**, select **Properties**, and then find the **General** blade under **Package** in the navigator. From there, you can check the **Produce a package file during build operations** checkbox, as shown in *Figure 14.2*:

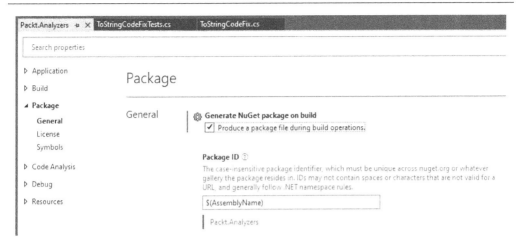

Figure 14.2 – Enabling NuGet package creation in Visual Studio

When this box is checked, you should see something like the following in your build output after building:

```
1>Successfully created package 'C:\PacktBook\Chapter14\
Ch14BeginningCode\Packt.Analyzers\bin\Debug\Packt.
Analyzers.1.0.0.nupkg'.
1>Done building project "Packt.Analyzers.csproj".
```

The general blade also lets you configure many of the pieces of metadata associated with the package. This lets you specify a readme file or a logo, enter any legal information you need, and more. These pieces of information will later be visible to users considering installing your package.

The many things to consider when configuring a NuGet package for publishing to the public are beyond the scope of this book, but additional resources are listed in the *Further reading* section at the end of this chapter.

Unfortunately, when building packages for Roslyn Analyzers, you need to customize more than Visual Studio makes available in the properties user interface.

Double-click on `Packt.Analyzers` in **Solution Explorer** to open its `.csproj` file and replace it with this:

```
<Project Sdk="Microsoft.NET.Sdk">
 <PropertyGroup>
   <TargetFramework>netstandard2.0</TargetFramework>
   <GeneratePackageOnBuild>True</GeneratePackageOnBuild>
   <IncludeBuildOutput>false</IncludeBuildOutput>
   <Authors>YourName</Authors>
   <Company>YourCompany</Company>
   <PackageId>YourCompany.Analyzers</PackageId>
   <PackageVersion>1.0.0</PackageVersion>
```

```
    <PackageLicenseExpression>MIT</PackageLicenseExpression>
    <Description>
        Sample analyzer with fix from "Refactoring with C#"
        by Matt Eland via Packt Publishing.
    </Description>
    <PackageProjectUrl>
https://github.com/PacktPublishing/Refactoring-with-CSharp
    </PackageProjectUrl>
    <RepositoryUrl>https://github.com/PacktPublishing/
Refactoring-with-CSharp</RepositoryUrl>
  </PropertyGroup>
  <ItemGroup>
    <PackageReference Include="Microsoft.CodeAnalysis"
                      Version="4.0.1" />
    <None Include="$(OutputPath)\Packt.Analyzers.dll"
          Pack="true"
          PackagePath="analyzers/dotnet/cs"
          Visible="false" />
  </ItemGroup>
</Project>
```

These additional pieces of metadata customize how your package will be installed. Let's talk about each one of the relevant changes separately:

- **GeneratePackageOnBuild** is the same thing as checking the box on the properties page to build the package on build.

- **IncludeBuildOutput** tells the packaging process not to include the results of compilation in the generated package. Instead, we'll do something different to include these files using the `ItemGroup` section.

- **PackageId** is a unique identifier for your NuGet package. While the code in this book uses `Packt.Analyzers`, I recommend using your name without spaces or punctuation in place of `Packt` to avoid conflicts publishing this.

- **PackageVersion** is the release version number of your package. The latest version of a package is typically what people install using NuGet.

- **PackageLicenseExpression** is optional, but it allows you to tell others what open-source license, if any, applies to the usage of your package. The various license types and their legal implications are beyond the scope of this book.

- **Description** is a short user-friendly description of what the package does and why someone might want to install it.

- **RepositoryUrl** is optional and tells others where the package code is available.

The really critical part of this file is the `None` element in the `ItemGroup`. This step tells the packaging process to take the compiled DLL of the analyzer project and put it in the `analyzers/dotnet/cs` directory of the NuGet package.

This directory is a special directory that .NET looks at when loading Roslyn Analyzers from various sources. If it doesn't see your analyzers there, those analyzers will not be loaded.

With these steps configured and the file saved, rebuild the project and you should see your NuGet package created inside the `bin\Debug` or `bin\Release` directory of your `Packt.Analyzers` project.

> **Debug vs Release builds**
>
> When publishing software, you'll want to use the `Release` configuration instead of `Debug`. The `Debug` configuration suppresses certain compiler optimizations and adds extra build byproducts that help you debug your applications. `Release` builds tend to be smaller and faster and are generally recommended. You can change which configuration is active using the main toolbar in Visual Studio.

Once your `.nupkg` file is created, you're ready to publish it for others to use.

Deploying the NuGet package

Now that we have a `.nupkg` file, we can deploy it to any NuGet feed. This can be a feed you set up yourself at your organization, a private NuGet registry on GitHub, or a public NuGet feed such as the one at `NuGet.org`.

Because `NuGet.org` is the standard place for sharing open-source code packages, we'll explore this path in this chapter. If your code is proprietary and you only want to share it within your organization, it should not go on `NuGet.org`.

> **NuGet hosting options**
>
> If you'd like to host your NuGet packages outside of `NuGet.org`, you have a few options including setting up a private NuGet server or using a team-shared NuGet repository service such as those offered on GitHub. See the *Further reading* section for more information.

To get started, navigate to `NuGet.org`, create a user, and then log in as that user.

Once you are authenticated, click on the **Upload** tab to begin the process of uploading a NuGet package. This will allow you to drag and drop or click **Browse…** to find your NuGet package, as shown in *Figure 14.3*:

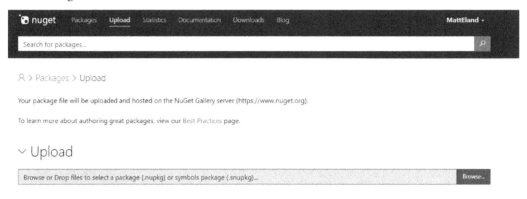

Figure 14.3 – Uploading a NuGet package

If you need help finding your `.nupkg` file, it should be inside of the `Packt.Analyzers` project in the `\bin\Debug` folder or the `\bin\Release` folder depending on if you build your project in `Debug` or `Release` mode.

> **Tip**
> It's always best to publish `Release` builds when sharing code with others.

Once you've selected your NuGet package, the page will update with the information it detects about your package. This includes the version number, license file, readme file, and other information. While it's best to configure these values in Visual Studio, some things, such as the readme file, can be customized here before publishing.

If something doesn't look right, you can create a new `.nupkg` file and upload that file.

Once you're satisfied with the information on the preview screen, click **Submit** and `NuGet.org` will begin checking your file for anything harmful and indexing the package so others can import it.

This process typically takes 5 to 15 minutes but can vary. If you want to check on the status of your package, you can refresh the package details page found in *Figure 14.4* to check on the status.

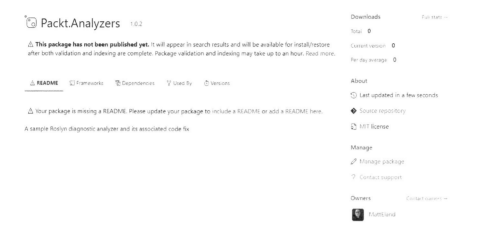

Figure 14.4 – NuGet.org checking and indexing a package

Once this process finishes, you're ready to reference the package in Visual Studio.

Referencing the NuGet package

Once your package is published on NuGet.org, you can reference it in any compatible .NET project.

To prove this, open a solution from a previous chapter or create a new console application. Next, choose **Manage NuGet Packages…** for that project in **Solution Explorer**.

Once **NuGet Package Manager** comes up, go to the **Browse** tab and search for your package by its name. Assuming the name is correct and your package has finished indexing, you should see the package in *Figure 14.5*:

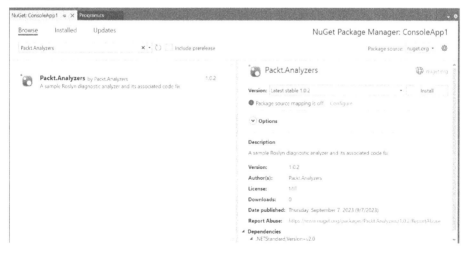

Figure 14.5 – Referencing your package in NuGet Package Manager

Click **Install** to install the latest published version of your package and notice the dependencies and license terms that appear based on your choices when creating the NuGet package.

Once your package is installed, your analyzer will now be active and will appear inside of the **Analyzers** node nested inside of the project's **Dependencies** node in **Solution Explorer**, as shown in *Figure 14.6*:

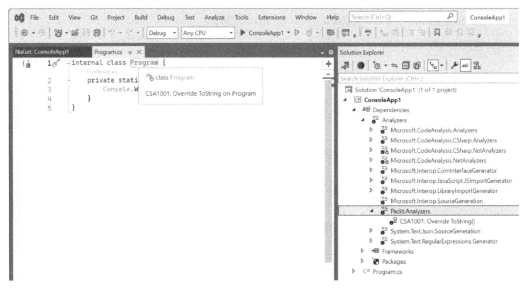

Figure 14.6 – Our analyzers package installed and active in a project

The analyzer will also be active for any class in your project and it will provide suggestions and code fixes.

Once you commit and push your changes to the project, others on your team will pull down the reference to the new NuGet dependency. Visual Studio will then restore your NuGet packages and install the analyzer locally into that project for your coworkers.

If you ever need to update your NuGet package, you can create a new version of the package and upload it to NuGet.org. Once the new version is indexed, you'll be able to update the installed version of the package from NuGet Package Manager.

The NuGet deployment process makes it easy to install and update packages in your project that are then available to every developer on your team. This is why this process is my default recommendation for sharing your Roslyn Analyzers with your team.

Packaging a CodeFixProvider as an extension

If you want to package your code fix in a VSIX extension, you can do that in largely the same way as we did in *Chapter 13* with one additional change.

To get your `CodeFixProvider` to work in the extension, you'll need to add a **Managed Extensibility Framework (MEF)** asset to your installer's manifest.

To do this, go to the **Assets** pane of your Installer project's manifest and click **New**.

Next, select **Microsoft.VisualStudio.MefComponent** as the type, specify the source as **A project in current solution**, and specify your analyzers project as the project (see *Figure 14.7* for an example).

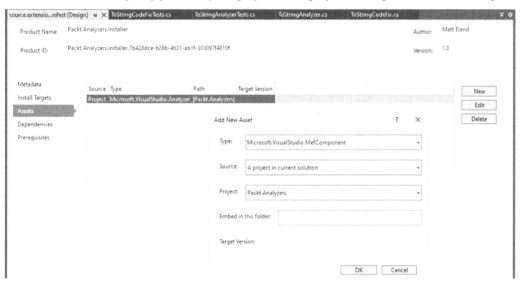

Figure 14.7 – Adding an MEF component asset to the installer manifest

This change will ensure your code fix is properly registered by the installer.

In my experience, it's usually easier to maintain analyzers via a NuGet package than a VSIX installer, but both deployment models have their advantages. Pick the approach that makes the most sense for your installation, updating, and security needs.

Summary

In this chapter, we saw how Roslyn Analyzers can be extended to provide code fixes along with the diagnostic information they already provided.

Code fixes work by interpreting the tree structure of your code and making modifications to that structure, resulting in a new document or solution. Visual Studio then reacts to these changes by updating the source code.

This means that code fixes can automatically make pre-configured modifications to your code to address known issues in a repeatable and safe manner.

We also discussed how NuGet package deployment allows you to wrap up your Roslyn Analyzers into a package and share them with other developers – either other developers on your team or other developers worldwide.

This concludes *Part 3* of this book. In the final part of this book, we'll explore some of the unique challenges and opportunities found in refactoring code in real-world organizations and teams.

Questions

1. What is the relationship between a `DiagnosticAnalyzer` and a `CodeFixProvider`?
2. How can you test a code fix?
3. What are some of the advantages of NuGet deployment versus VSIX deployment?

Further reading

You can find more information about materials from this chapter at the following URLs:

- *Get started with syntax transformation*: https://learn.microsoft.com/en-us/dotnet/csharp/roslyn-sdk/get-started/syntax-transformation
- *Configuring and Publishing NuGet Packages*: https://learn.microsoft.com/en-us/nuget/quickstart/create-and-publish-a-package-using-visual-studio?tabs=netcore-cli
- *Hosting your own NuGet feeds*: https://learn.microsoft.com/en-us/nuget/hosting-packages/overview
- *Working with NuGet on GitHub*: https://docs.github.com/en/packages/working-with-a-github-packages-registry/working-with-the-nuget-registry

Part 4: Refactoring in the Enterprise

In the fourth and final part of the book, we focus on the social aspects of refactoring: communicating technical debt to others, adopting code standards as an engineering organization, and refactoring in agile environments.

Convincing a large team or organization of the importance of refactoring can be a critical battle, and so this part looks at how software engineers can partner with business leaders. These chapters contain key tips and tricks to ensure that refactoring actually happens and that the right areas of technical debt get refactored first.

We specifically focus on refactoring in an agile environment and how to handle refactoring scenarios that are so large that it feels like a complete rewrite is necessary.

This part contains the following chapters:

- *Chapter 15, Communicating Technical Debt*
- *Chapter 16, Adopting Code Standards*
- *Chapter 17, Agile Refactoring*

15

Communicating Technical Debt

Most developers have worked in environments where they are unable to pay down technical debt, not due to the technical difficulty of the task, but because of organizational priorities, fears, urgent deadlines, and a lack of clear understanding of the full impact of technical debt on their software.

In this chapter, we'll explore some of these factors that can prevent you and your team from resolving technical debt and introduce some ways of helping the organization understand and value the refactoring process.

We're going to cover the following main topics:

- Overcoming barriers to refactoring
- Communicating technical debt
- Prioritizing technical debt
- Getting organizational buy-in

Overcoming barriers to refactoring

When I speak with developers in the technical community, almost everyone has stories of being told that they were not allowed to spend time refactoring their code.

Sometimes this mandate came from upper management and sometimes from product management or someone involved in the agile process. However, just as often, the directive would come from engineering leadership such as a team lead or engineering manager.

The reasons for this can vary by the organization and project you're working on, but some common reasons include the following:

- There's an urgent deadline and the team must focus on meeting it
- Refactoring the code isn't perceived to provide any business value

- The change would be to a risky area of the application with a lot of technical debt and there's a risk of introducing bugs

- Developers are told "Don't worry about the quality of the code; this is just a prototype and won't go into production" (it usually will)

- The team is assured "Don't worry about the quality of the code; we're going to completely rewrite this application" (you usually won't)

Let's talk about some of these objections.

Urgent deadlines

The "we're on a deadline" objection is a very common one for many teams. Sometimes, teams are truly on a critical deadline that can't be missed. During these times, it can often be "all hands on deck," with people working in high-stress environments and typically working late hours as well. When this is the case, spending time to address technical debt can be disruptive to the team and its chances of meeting the deadline.

In other words, *sometimes, this objection is a legitimate one that makes sense for the business during a specific and limited period of time.*

However, these high-urgency time periods cause technical debt to accumulate at a very high rate since developers aren't given the time to do things the right way. While a team may be able to achieve amazing things in a short period of time, these things are rarely accomplished in a way that results in maintainable code that will stand the test of time.

Additionally, many organizations flow from urgent deadline to urgent deadline, causing long stretches of time where the team accumulates technical debt at a staggering rate while not being able to pay it down.

Sometimes deadlines cannot be altered or avoided, such as deadlines for the end of a fiscal year or a trade show or other conference. It can also be strategically beneficial to accumulate technical debt in the short term in return for meeting key business objectives that need to happen before a specific date.

However, it is your responsibility as a software engineer or engineering leader to clearly, succinctly, and regularly communicate technical debt and its impact to management. Once management adequately understands the obstacle, you must then work with them on long-term remediation steps and scheduling of the work needed for that effort.

We'll talk more about this remediation process later in this chapter.

"Don't touch high-risk code"

The objection that certain portions of code are too brittle to touch more than needed, so we shouldn't improve them, is a laughable one when you think about it. After all, if code has decayed to the point where you're afraid to even try to improve it, the need for refactoring is likely one that has been postponed for some time.

While this code is dangerous to touch, not refactoring it could lead to disastrous results when the team is finally forced to make a change to it. Let's examine the argument against refactoring this code.

The core concern in this case is often a combination of the following fears:

- Touching this code is likely to introduce bugs
- We don't understand how this code *should* work
- There are no tests that would catch defects that might be introduced

I find that this objection often occurs after key people leave a team and nobody else has any knowledge of a complex area that those individuals maintained. The code in question usually has little to no documentation and very few unit tests, if any are present at all.

These concerns don't mean you can't successfully improve or replace the code in question. In fact, some of the strategies we talked about in *Part 2* of this book around testing code can significantly help with the fears behind this objection.

First, you can write unit tests around the code you're changing before you make any changes. Some of the advanced testing tools we explored in *Chapter 9* such as Snapper and Scientist .NET can help with this.

Deploying software in phased rollouts or with the option of rolling back can also help alleviate some fears, as we'll see in *Chapter 17, Agile Refactoring* when we talk about things such as feature flags and blue/green deployments.

"This code is going away, don't spend time on it"

The objection that specific code is temporary and you shouldn't worry about its quality typically occurs either at the *beginning* of software projects, during prototyping phases, or at the *end* of software projects, when you've determined whether you must replace or retire the entire application.

This often occurs when a team wants to test out a concept by building a quick "throwaway" prototype that can explore a concept or prove that a course of action is viable.

Unfortunately, many "throwaway" prototypes survive to become the foundation of a future application, despite being built for speed in proving a concept and having been designed intentionally to not worry about performance, security, or reliability.

A good prototype can get people so excited about the project that the following may occur:

- They forget they're not dealing with "real" software and that the prototype was intended to be a temporary "throwaway"

- They view the functionality provided in the prototype as already complete

- The project gets an urgent deadline

While there are certainly valid arguments that promoting a throwaway prototype to a real application is a symptom of mismanagement, let's talk about productive things that members of the development team can do about this.

First, understand that your "throwaway" prototypes have a good chance of being viewed as working pieces of software. Some teams use rough styling or sketch-style user interfaces, such as the one in *Figure 15.1*, to help others remember the application is just a prototype:

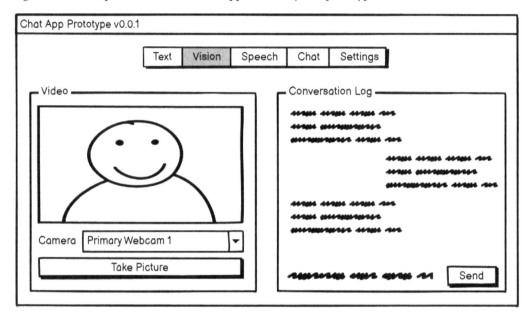

Figure 15.1 – A sample user interface wireframe

Second, you can treat all code as production code deserving of refactoring, tests, and documentation, reducing your prototyping speed accordingly and somewhat defeating the idea of putting together a quick prototype.

Third, in the event that a throwaway prototype is promoted to an operational piece of software, the first pieces of work should be around reworking the prototype as needed to serve as the basis for the application's future.

End-of-life applications

The other time that code is viewed as non-permanent is when the application you're developing is either at the end of its lifespan and about to be retired, or when people decide that the current level of technical debt requires a complete rewrite.

In the case when applications truly are end-of-life and will not be maintained for much longer, the technical debt may not be a critical problem – assuming the application actually does go offline in the near future. In this case, the team should know roughly when the application will go offline and this date should be confirmed regularly.

> **Tip**
>
> It is important to check in regularly with management on the end-of-life status of the application. If the deactivation date is postponed or the decision to retire the application entirely seems less sure, you can change your posture to be more aggressive in your refactoring efforts.

If you have an application that has so much technical debt that you believe it cannot be solved without a rewrite, be very careful. I have seen many teams assume that their application will be retired and replaced by a successor, only to see the rewrite get delayed farther and farther down the road or even canceled entirely.

If you are depending on a rewrite to end your technical debt, I strongly recommend you have an estimated date for when that rewrite will start and when the old project will be retired. While software estimation can be challenging (as numerous books on the topic demonstrate), it is irresponsible to not improve your existing codebase without a believable timeline for the replacement coming online.

I have seen dozens of software projects over the last 20 years as a software engineer. Over that time, I have only seen two projects get completely rewritten. One of these projects was due to a technical necessity since its technology would no longer function past a certain date and the other involved extraordinary efforts by a lead engineer who was frustrated by maintaining the old version of the application.

You and your team will be better off if you assume that a complete rewrite will not happen and instead focus on paying down technical debt piece by piece.

We'll talk more about strategies for gradually renewing and replacing applications in *Chapter 17, Agile Refactoring.*

"Just do the minimum required"

Occasionally, you'll hear something to the effect of "Why are you spending all this time refactoring or testing? Just do the work required to complete the task."

These statements can arise from a few different causes:

- The project being behind schedule

- A lack of trust in the development team due to past delays

- A lack of understanding of the importance of refactoring

Whenever I encounter this objection, I think of a camping analogy I've heard before.

When you go camping, you are expected to leave the campsite as good as you found it or slightly better. At the campsite, you are expected to not leave your trash strewn about, even though it is faster to do so than to spend time cleaning up after yourself. This is sometimes called the **Boy Scout Rule**.

Secondly, if you go camping and you find your campsite to be a mess, it is entirely rational to spend some time cleaning up the campsite instead of setting up your tent on top of a pile of garbage!

Applying this analogy to development, when you go to make a change, you may need to modify some areas of your code that are not up to current standards, not tested, or in need of cleanup in general. It is not unreasonable for changes to a file to include fixes to other unrelated pieces of work.

Let's say you are working on a small set of changes that affect a number of places throughout your application. You discover that one of those places has a significant amount of technical debt and likely needs several days of cleanup work to meet current standards. In this case, the appropriate thing to do would be to implement the small change in that area and talk about the additional refactorings needed during your next stand-up meeting. Often, the team will create a new separate work item for that larger refactoring effort.

> **Agile refactoring**
>
> We'll talk more about tracking technical debt later in this chapter, and about refactoring in agile environments in *Chapter 17, Agile Refactoring*.

While cleaning up code is important, try to keep the amount of cleanup work you're doing proportional to the size of the work item you're working on.

"Refactoring doesn't provide business value"

One of the most dangerous objections to refactoring that I've encountered has been the assumption that refactoring doesn't provide any value beyond the development team.

That is to say that there is often an implicit assumption that developers only provide value to the organization when they add features or fix bugs. Under this mentality, things such as unit testing, refactoring, and documentation are all *waste activities* that developers do but do not provide meaningful value to the organization.

This is a dangerous assumption because managers are usually rewarded for minimizing waste and maximizing the most value possible to the organization. When refactoring and testing are not valued by leadership, organizations trade technical debt accumulation for short-term boosts in things they value, such as new features being delivered. This results in long-term consequences as technical debt grows rampant, development slows to a crawl, and bugs are introduced with nearly every change.

One reason for this devaluation of refactoring work is that new features are visible and often understandable to management, while technical debt is something they only hear about and cannot see.

Anything you as a developer or engineering leader can do to help management understand the scope and effects of technical debt will help resolve this objection.

In the next section, we'll explore ways of helping improve the visibility of technical debt to non-developers.

Communicating technical debt

Explaining **technical debt** to non-developers can be challenging. Even when management trusts the development team, it is difficult for managers to understand what engineers deal with or how technical debt slows the software engineering process and introduces tremendous quality risks whenever the application is changed.

Technical debt as risk

In the course of my career, I've learned that while management has trouble understanding technical debt, there's something they have a much better understanding of: *risk*.

This may sound strange, but I've found the best way to help management understand technical debt is to present it in terms of risk management.

Every aspect of technical debt in your system has both a **probability** and an **impact**.

The **probability** of a piece of technical debt is the likelihood that the piece of technical debt will impact the development team during development or when the application is running in production.

The **impact** is how much the technical debt will hurt things if it *does* impact the developers or deployed applications.

For example, code in a critical area with medium complexity that is lacking tests might have a low or medium probability of producing issues, but would have a critical impact if those issues arose. That is to say that the code isn't currently causing issues, but we think there's a medium probability that it may be changed in the future in such a way that introduces a bug we won't catch due to the complexity of the system. If this does occur, we believe that the impact on end users will be severe.

When you can represent each risk in your codebase with an impact and probability, it allows management to start understanding the level of risk the current slate of technical debt represents.

Creating a risk register

These risk entries should be arranged into a spreadsheet or other series of tracked items (such as work items in the system) called a **risk register**. The risk register becomes a centralized place for management and development leaders to review the current risks present in software engineering projects.

Your risk register might benefit from including the following pieces of information:

- **ID** – A unique identifier for the risk
- **Title** – A name for the risk, such as "High complexity code in the `FlightManager's ScheduleFlight` method"
- **Status** – Whether the risk is open, in the process of being remediated, or closed
- **Probability** – The probability that the risk affects future development or users of the system
- **Impact** – The severity of the impact of the risk if it materializes
- **Priority** – A priority for the risk based on its probability and impact

A sample risk register for Cloudy Skies Airlines would look like the following:

ID	Title	Status	Area	Probability	Impact	Priority
RISK-1	High complexity code in FlightManager	In Progres	Flight	Medium	Medium	Medium
RISK-2	Scalability Concerns in Booking System	Open	Booking	Medium	High	High
RISK-3	Untested complex logic in staff scheduler	Open	Staff Scheduling	Low	Medium	Low
RISK-4	High quantity of regression bugs in luggage router	Closed	Luggage	High	Medium	High

Figure 15.2 – A sample risk register

Your register doesn't have to be limited to these columns. The person the risk is assigned to, the area or component the risk is in, and the estimated effort to resolve it are all fields you might want to consider adding, depending on your needs.

When delays or production issues inevitably occur, you can point to existing risks in the risk register. This should help management understand that the risks have materialized into **issues**.

> **Risks versus issues**
>
> In risk management terminology, a risk is something that may occur while an issue is a risk that has materialized by actually occurring.

This helps resist the temptation to blame the engineers involved in the change and instead helps focus the conversation on the risks present in the existing technical debt.

By forming a shared risk register with management, you can actively involve them in the process of managing and resolving technical debt. This is an ongoing process involving regular risk review meetings, where the team must actively maintain the register as new risks are discovered or opinions on the potential impact or probability of existing risks change.

In these risk review meetings, the group should review the current risk register and discuss any changes that have occurred since the previous month.

Alternatives to a risk register

I understand that not every developer, engineering leader, or even member of upper management feels comfortable working with a formal risk register.

If you'd be more comfortable with a simpler process, you can achieve a similar amount of value by trying one of the following things:

- Having a simple bulleted list in a Word document – perhaps organized by major project or area
- Creating a new *technical risk* type of item in work item tracking software, such as **Jira** or **Azure DevOps**
- Having a regular newsletter that goes out to developers and business stakeholders with the "top 10 most wanted" pieces of technical debt

The format of the risk register isn't the most important part of the process. The important part of the process is that your team is actively itemizing technical debt as it is detected and regularly reviewing it with management to involve them in the process of resolving it.

Prioritizing technical debt

Tracking and communicating technical debt is a critical part of the process of paying it down. However, it's just one step in the process.

While refactoring code as related code is modified can be a viable strategy for paying down technical debt, this approach isn't suitable for tackling large pieces of technical debt or debt that is related to the overall design of the software.

In *Chapter 17, Agile Refactoring*, we'll talk more about managing these larger pieces of work in an agile environment, but for now, let's look at how you determine which pieces of technical debt should be prioritized.

You want to prioritize addressing the items that are most likely to occur and those that will hurt the most if they do occur. In other words, if you have a high probability risk, you should prioritize that. Additionally, you should prioritize your high-impact pieces of technical debt.

Calculating risk priorities with a risk score

I've seen some organizations create a **risk score** out of the impact and probability of each technical risk they track. This risk score is a math equation where the probability of occurrence of a piece of technical debt is written as a number from 0 to 1, with 1 being 100% certain to happen and 0 meaning it will never happen.

This results in a formula where you can calculate the priority of a piece of technical debt by multiplying its probability by its impact. This formula is as follows:

```
risk = impact * probability
```

For example, a high-probability, low-impact piece of technical debt might have a 0.9 probability score and an impact of 3, resulting in a risk score of 2.7.

> **Units and risk scores**
>
> 2.7 what, exactly? Well, we're not really measuring anything tangible unless you choose to represent impact in hours or dollars, so I refer to this number as simply the "risk score" representing the overall expected negative impact the business expects by having the technical debt item present. This is useful for comparing two risks to each other.

Let's look at a different scenario with a high-impact, low-probability tech debt item, scored at 0.15 probability and an impact of 21, resulting in a risk score of 3.15.

Here, the organization typically would focus on the second item because its overall risk score of 3.15 is higher than the 2.7 risk score of the first item, meaning it represents a larger threat to the organization.

Further refinements to this approach might also factor in the estimated hours needed to resolve a piece of technical debt, so items that can be resolved faster can be prioritized over equivalent items that would take longer.

The "gut feeling" approach

It can be hard to numerically quantify things with any precision and estimates can sometimes feel more like wishful thinking than scientifically accurate predictions. I do think there's value in getting some rough numbers on risks, but typically, team members will have a deeper "gut feeling" about the magnitude of some items over others.

My stance is that numerical guides can be helpful, but your brain can point out other things that are important but hard to measure.

> **Tip**
>
> My rule of thumb is that you should focus on fixing the things that scare you the most. If there's an area of your code that keeps you up at night, it's usually a good idea to start there.

This isn't to say that you should stop all new development until technical debt is resolved (though sometimes this is needed in severe scenarios). I'm saying that when you get to pick what should be resolved, you should pick the area your team believes is the largest threat to the organization's success. Once you're done with the biggest problem, move on to the next one and then the next after that, while continuing to support the needs of the business.

Getting organizational buy-in

We've seen how we can track and prioritize technical debt, and we've seen how involving management in the process of tracking technical risk can help build trust and understanding, but let's talk about scenarios where development leadership must "pitch" a major refactoring effort to management.

These conversations can be stressful and represent a critical turning point in software projects. In these high-stakes conversations, your goal is to communicate the following things succinctly and respectfully:

- The problem facing the team and its impact if it is not resolved
- The proposed solution (or a set of proposed solutions to consider)
- The cost of the refactoring effort in terms of developer hours
- The timetable of the refactoring effort
- What you'd like management to do

Note that your goal here *isn't* to get them to agree to what you are proposing. Your goal is to get them to understand the issue and work with you on determining when and how it should be resolved.

When your focus is on getting your way at all costs, this can result in a loss of trust, growing hostilities between development and management, and a feeling that developers cannot think in terms of business needs.

Instead, if you view your partners in management as having legitimate insights and value to add to the organization, the conversation can become something different – a partnership where engineering and management work together for both the long-term and short-term needs of the business.

Setting up the conversation

Before you can even have a conversation about the problem, you need to be able to effectively communicate the problem and the scope of its potential solutions.

This will take some consideration and planning. You don't need to have a detailed project plan in place for this, but you do need to think through the scope of the project, the pieces that will need to change, and the people who will need to be involved.

You'll also need to consider your team's current projects and what the people you're looking to involve are currently working on, or slated to be working on soon.

Remember that for your organization to say "yes" to your refactoring effort, they'll need to say "no" to something else for the duration of your refactoring effort.

Once you have a sufficient understanding of the scope of the problem and its solution, you should bring it to management. This can be done either as part of a regular check-in meeting between engineering leadership and management or as its own meeting.

How you approach the meeting invite will depend on the individual you're approaching.

Some leaders may be receptive to you stopping by their office or sending them a direct message and saying something to the effect of "I have some concerns about the project. Do you have 30 minutes sometime to talk about this in more detail?"

On the other hand, other leaders will want to have the conversation as soon as you broach the topic. For this reason, I recommend you prepare for the conversation and find a time when their calendar appears clear.

Anticipating questions and objections

As you present your concerns and options to management, you should keep in mind the types of questions or objections they might raise. Be prepared to drill into the technical details of the current problem as well as your proposed solutions.

It's also typical for management to want details on project timelines. This can include not only how long you expect the refactoring effort to take, but also *how long the project can wait to be started.*

Remember that most organizations have major projects tentatively scheduled for at least the next quarter. Taking on a refactoring effort typically requires rearranging current and planned work in other areas. As an example, look at *Figure 15.3* for a sample breakdown of major initiatives by quarter for the web, services, and integration teams:

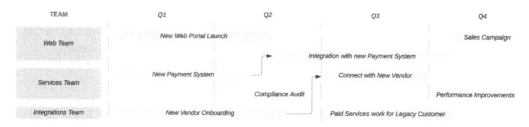

Figure 15.3 – A project roadmap broken down by team and quarter

While the integration team may want to spend time in Q2 working on a piece of technical debt, doing so would risk the services team's planned work on connecting to a new vendor and potentially delay the integration team's own planned paid services work, both slated to begin in Q3.

Be honest about the urgency of the issues your team is facing. Sometimes the answer is that it can wait, but the longer it is delayed the greater the penalty the team faces. At other times, refactoring efforts are needed to resolve urgent and already pressing issues the team is encountering with the current system.

Additionally, keep in mind the background of the person you're talking to and the people they talk to. If you're talking to a very security-oriented person and you haven't thought through the security ramifications of your change, that conversation is likely not going to go well.

You don't need to have an answer for every question you are asked, and it is acceptable to say "I don't know; let me look into that and get back to you."

The bottom line is that changes to project schedules are serious matters and if you appear to have not taken the time to think about the most obvious concerns, it will not inspire confidence among management.

Different approaches for different leaders

I've met a lot of different people in management and it's amazing how different two skilled leaders can be from one another.

Some leaders are extremely analytical and incredibly data-driven, wanting to pore over reports and spreadsheets. Others are people-oriented and driven not as much by raw numbers as they are by *specific stories* of how something affects specific individuals.

For leaders focused on the overall data, I usually present key metrics and highlight interesting findings. I often provide all relevant data to them for further analysis, either preemptively or upon request.

An example metric might be that we spent 15 hours over the last 3 sprints dealing with this problem, or that 15% of the bugs from the last quarter could be traced back to this area.

As far as sharing specific stories goes, I usually come prepared with two or three examples of how a problem impacts developers, end users, or other relevant stakeholders. This might be something such as "Last sprint, Priya tried to work on a new feature we thought would only take a few hours, but because of how this is architected, it actually took her 3 days," or "Garret is a very competent developer, but he tried to modify this area of code and it wound up causing this critical production bug due to the code's lack of maintainability."

An approach that works well with one individual may have very little impact on a different person. As a result, I find it best to have a few interesting metrics and a few relevant scenarios whenever I have these critical conversations on major refactoring efforts.

The importance of communication

One thing I hope you've picked up on in this chapter is that while you want to resolve technical debt, your goal is the short-term and long-term success of the organization.

This means that any conversation about technical debt should be a two-way conversation where both parties listen to each other and can have their voices heard.

Sometimes, the legitimate short-term needs of a business are to ship something as fast as possible or to meet a deadline with an external partner or agency.

As an engineering leader, your goal is to ensure management understands the impact, urgency, and risk that technical debt represents and the importance of both small and large refactoring efforts. However, your focus is typically on the code, while management's focus is centered on strategic initiatives or even simply keeping the business afloat and the lights on. Both roles and their perspectives are critically important to a healthy organization.

At the end of the day, what you're really after is open and honest communication between engineering and management where management can appreciate the risk and impact of technical debt and engineering can understand the pressures facing the organization.

This communication starts with trust and respecting the contributions that management brings to the table in terms of steering the overall organization toward its goals and balancing priorities and needs that often compete with one another.

Case study – Cloudy Skies Airlines

As we close the chapter, let's look at our case study from Cloudy Skies Airlines.

Brian, a lead developer, has been investigating a growing number of problems with the reservation and payment processing part of the application.

These issues, initially thought to be isolated, seem to occur during peak usage times when many customers are trying to book flights or modify their existing flight reservations.

After investigating, Brian and his team discover that the problems are related to the current design and architecture of the system. While the system could handle the old number of users, it is simply not able to adequately scale to handle peak workloads given its current inefficiencies.

Ordinarily, such a system could be scaled out to have multiple servers running in parallel with a load balancer distributing traffic between them (see *Figure 15.4*):

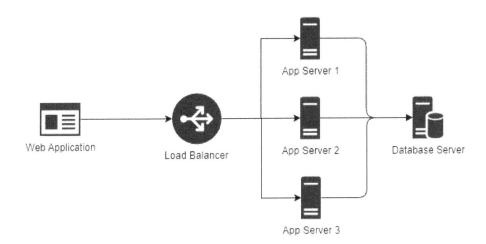

Figure 15.4 – A load balancer distributing requests to different application servers

However, the system was not designed to support multiple copies of the application running at once without significant rework.

While the team is able to make some short-term performance and stability improvements to resolve the current issues, they understand that as the business grows, these problems will just resurface – particularly in peak travel seasons.

After careful consideration, the team comes up with a plan that would allow the system to run multiple copies in parallel but would require a significant amount of rework.

One of the engineers also suggests potentially moving from a model where the server does all the work and returns a successful response to the user to a model where the request is quickly validated and then put in a queue for processing. This approach would handle spikes in incoming requests but would require changes to how request processing currently works.

Armed with these ideas and knowledge of the scope of the current problem and possible fixes, Brian schedules a meeting with Maddie, the Chief Technology Officer.

During the meeting, Brian lays out the performance problem, the recent steps the team has taken to restore service, and the likelihood that it will occur again as the business grows and peak seasons approach.

Once Brian is sure Maddie understands the basics of the problem, he gives an overview of the two possible remediation plans, as well as his personal recommendation to stick with the relatively simpler change of working to allow the application server to support multiple copies in parallel.

Maddie asks several technical questions about scalability, particularly around why the current system is unable to have multiple copies running at once. After Brian explains the problems that would cause, Maddie understands the reasoning and the need for remediation and the conversation shifts toward scheduling.

The next focus for the team was going to be integrating a newly acquired subsidiary airline into Cloudy Skies systems, as shown in *Figure 15.5*:

Figure 15.5 – The planned schedule showing major projects by quarter and the current date

Upon reviewing the problem, Maddie and Brian both agree that having a long-term solution in place for the scalability problems is more important, particularly with some peak travel seasons approaching.

Maddie brings other executives into the conversation on the specifics of the plan and Brian answers their questions, while the team begins planning the architectural changes needed and the technical details of how the application could be scaled out as needed to handle additional traffic loads.

After a short delay, the project is approved and the majority of Brian's team is assigned to the effort, with the understanding that the previously planned work would begin later than originally scheduled to make room for the new scalability project, as shown in *Figure 15.6*:

Figure 15.6 – The adjusted schedule with the scalability project added in the near future

Brian and Maddie continue to check in on the progress of the work, and the scalability concerns are addressed before the peak travel times arrive.

In the meantime, some team members are able to make progress in integrating the new subsidiary into the Cloudy Skies systems. As engineers finish their work on the scalability concerns, they transition over to that project, resulting in only a minor delay to that project's initially planned delivery date.

In the end, the business gets a more stable and scalable system as well as their planned integration of the new subsidiary, in addition to an improved communication channel between management and the software engineering team.

Summary

In this chapter, we explored common objections to refactoring code and paying down technical debt and some reasons and remedies for them.

We also talked about communicating technical debt to management, particularly the idea of technical debt being viewed as a risk to the organization's systems and productivity. We also introduced the idea of using a risk register to track technical debt over time and improve the visibility of technical debt to non-developers.

We closed with a discussion about prioritizing technical debt, getting permission from management for larger refactoring projects, and the importance of trust, communication, and establishing a partnership with management in the remediation effort.

In the next chapter, we'll explore the value of code standards in terms of minimizing technical debt over time and how to choose an existing standard or build your own.

Questions

1. What obstacles are you currently encountering in getting time to prioritize technical debt?

2. If management understood the problems you're dealing with, how could they help you with them in terms of time, resources, or organizational support?

3. What can you and your team do to build a collaborative relationship with management going forward?

4. How well does management understand technical debt and its risks?

5. Does it make sense for you to formally track technical debt as risk?

Further reading

You can find more thoughts on technical debt as risk, communication with engineering leadership, and risk management in general at the following URLs:

*   *Technical Debt as Risk*: `https://killalldefects.com/2019/12/24/technical-debt-as-risks/`

*   *Escaping the black hole of technical debt*: `https://www.atlassian.com/agile/software-development/technical-debt`

*   *How to use a technical debt register*: `https://blog.logrocket.com/product-management/how-to-use-technical-debt-register/`

*   *Communicating with Management About Technical Debt*: `https://devops.com/communicating-with-management-about-technical-debt/`

16
Adopting Code Standards

In this chapter, we'll talk about the importance of establishing clear **code standards** with the right degree of flexibility. We'll also cover some built-in tooling in Visual Studio that will help your team adopt a consistent set of coding standards. This in turn helps you focus on the right things during code review.

This chapter covers the following topics:

- Understanding code standards

- Establishing code standards

- Formatting and code cleanup in Visual Studio

- Applying code standards with `EditorConfig`

Technical requirements

The starting code for this chapter is available from GitHub at `https://github.com/PacktPublishing/Refactoring-with-CSharp` in the `Chapter16/Ch16BeginningCode` folder.

Understanding code standards

In this chapter, we're going to explore the idea of code standards.

Code standards are an agreed-upon set of standards your team decides should be applied to any new code created by the team.

These standards have an important role in resolving disputes, focusing attention on the areas that truly matter, reducing the amount of technical debt teams naturally accumulate, and helping pay down existing technical debt.

The importance of code standards

One of the most frustrating experiences I've ever had as a developer is when I've sent a carefully thought-out change to another developer for review and I've heard back remarks such as the following:

- *I don't like your curly brace formatting*

- *Your indentation doesn't match mine. I use spaces instead of tabs*

- *I'd like it if you'd use* `var` *instead of the Type*

In these scenarios, the developer in question ignores the *substance* of the change and instead focuses on the *style* of the change – specifically where the style differs from their preferences.

The cure for this is to adopt a set of code standards that you and your team agree upon. These standards establish what your team cares about with regard to new code going forward. The standards might also contain the rationale behind the team's style and code preferences.

Some examples of code standard decisions might include the following:

- We use file-scoped namespaces because they result in less nesting

- Unit test classes should be named after the classes they test

- We prefer using target-typed `new` when instantiating objects

- Class definitions should be clearly organized and start with fields, then move on to constructors, properties, and finally methods

These standards don't have to be so rigid that developers don't have any decisions to make or live in constant fear of violating them.

Your code standards should be prescriptive enough that they address the major points of contention and confusion. This helps you focus on creating and maintaining code in a way that maximizes your ability to provide value to the organization.

How code standards influence refactoring

When you have a definitive set of standards that you and your team agree on, it opens the floodgates for refactoring.

Without a set of standards, when you talk about old code, you might say "I don't like this very much," or "This isn't how I would have written this," or "This seems poorly put together."

These things may be true, but they aren't compelling arguments for refactoring.

Instead, when you can say "This class violates our code standards in these areas," the conversation becomes much more productive. This is especially true when you can establish that some of your standards are critical while others are important but less critical.

There are certain aspects of code standards that I believe are critical and worth going in and making changes to just to get the code onto the new standards. For me, these areas often revolve around the handling of `IDisposable` resources and using proper exception management practices.

Whatever you and your team agree upon is critical. These standards will impact your priorities and the decisions you make while maintaining code. Standards violations can be issues that get dedicated work items assigned to people to go in and fix without any other reason for touching the code in question. We'll talk more about this in the final chapter of this book.

Applying code standards to existing code

The non-critical standards are used to guide the work developers do every day. All code changes are expected to comply with these code standards. Often, the standards encourage developers to update nearby pre-existing code that is out of compliance.

For example, your team might have a code standard to not use the `var` keyword when you can help it (or to always prefer `var`, if that's your jam). The team's expectation would be that as developers write new code, the new code will comply with this rule.

When standards are defined, teams sometimes expect that code near the code you're changing will also be updated to comply with the standards. This is particularly true for code in the same method. After all, you've spent effort testing your new code to validate the changes you made. This testing effort can help catch any issues introduced by refactoring the rest of the method.

Over time, these code standards will help reduce the rate at which your team accumulates technical debt. This ongoing improvement of the existing code will also help pay down existing technical debt in frequently changed areas.

Establishing code standards

So, now that I've convinced you how code standards can reduce conflict in your team, focus code reviews, and guide refactoring efforts, let's talk about where these standards come from and how we adopt them in our teams.

Collective code standards

Every software development team already has code standards.

I say this because each software development team already has, by definition, at least one developer. Every developer, whether they're aware of it or not, has their own set of internalized code standards.

They may not have thought about their preferences or be able to list them out, but if you look at each developer on your team and the code they write in isolation, there will be a certain amount of consistency to it.

The problem teams encounter is not that they don't have standards, but rather that they have too many standards. Each developer operates from their own internal set of standards and preferences and the team must now come together and interact with each other's unique styles and preferences.

Usually, teams will gravitate toward certain styles as developers tend to mimic the existing style in code files. As time goes on and teams grow, there are usually conflicts over certain choices. When this happens, your team will need to decide whether the creative freedom of not having defined any collective standards is worth the friction and distractions caused by these differing preferences.

Eventually, most teams formalize a set of standards around the things that really matter to those teams. Let's talk about what should go on that list.

Selecting what is important

Programming is a creative endeavor and so we don't want to place too many restrictions on how developers write code. On the other hand, when there are too few rules, it can result in somewhat eclectic areas of code that are suited to one developer's preferences but not the larger team.

So, how does a development team figure out what should go in its standards?

I like to start with the standards that keep teams safe. These involve following established best practices such as those defined in the .NET's **Framework Design Guidelines** (see *Further reading* for more information). These practices are less oriented around individual opinions. This lets them have a high impact while being relatively free of drama as a result.

Next, look at the major sticking points your team bumps into in code review. If you're sick of discussions around tabs versus spaces – whether or not the { belongs on its own line, or the use of `var` – these are things to consider adding to your team's standards.

If these areas are major sources of disagreements, you have a couple of choices:

- Pick a stance on the area of contention and adopt it as a team
- Make having no official stance on the topic your team's official position

Picking a stance and adopting it as a team may cause temporary arguments and hurt feelings. In the long term, adopting a stance tends to be beneficial since your team can operate with a consistent style. While developers may feel less appreciated or valued by the position, most tend to naturally warm to the new style over time, though this can lead to turnover in some cases when developers feel very strongly about a topic or that their opinions weren't considered.

You may not think that explicitly saying your team has no stance on an aspect of code would be very beneficial. However, I've seen this approach have a massive impact on the conversations teams have. By explicitly having no policy on the topic, the contentious topic now becomes something quickly resolved.

Instead of debating whether `var` belongs in your code, the team can point to its standards that say individual developers can make their own choices on this matter. This moves your team past contentious areas and on to more productive topics. The primary downside is that your overall code will be less consistent.

> **The value of consistency**
>
> Code that follows consistent styling and design decisions feels more professional, makes it easier for developers to work in areas they've not worked in before and keeps developers productive and focused on the function of code instead of its form.

Make sure the engineering team is represented when creating code standards and determining what goes in those standards. This can be done by involving the entire team or by picking a subset that represents the various experience levels and preferences of the engineers in your organization. Additionally, if you have individuals who may react particularly strongly to a new style, make sure their concerns are fully heard and – where possible – involve them in the process.

Sources of code standards

Sometimes, creating a standard of your own can be too difficult or polarizing, or you may find that you don't know where to start when creating code standards.

When this happens, I recommend starting from an established set of code standards and customizing those as needed.

In *Chapter 12*, we covered the built-in code analysis rulesets and how you can progressively move your ruleset from the latest ruleset to the latest minimum, then the latest recommended, and finally all the latest rulesets. These code analysis rules can help enforce best practices.

If you'd like a little more formality to things, Microsoft has documented C# coding conventions and framework design guidelines that give you a good starting point for your team. Both documents are referenced at the end of this chapter in the *Further reading* section and are fantastic, evergreen sources of wisdom around .NET and C#.

Evolving code standards

I mention "evergreen" because C# is not a dormant language. Every November, Microsoft ships new versions of C# with new language features building upon the previous year's improvements. This makes the C# language feel more organic as it evolves over time.

Additionally, the context in which we program changes over time. When .NET was first introduced, it was essentially a productivity improvement for developers primarily performing Windows desktop development. Since then, we've seen .NET become open source and cross-platform. At the same time, many organizations have migrated from on-premises data centers as cloud computing on platforms such as Azure and AWS has become the norm.

Things that were best practices back in the original days of C# have since faded in popularity as new language features have arrived to take their place and as the .NET platform grows new features.

I've been working with .NET since the beginning and have felt this in my own coding style. Throughout this book, I've discussed `var` because it's an easy language feature to talk about, but it is a good example of how C# changes over time.

Prior to `var`, you'd declare a dictionary of `Guid` keys and `int` values as follows:

```
Dictionary<Guid, int> data = new Dictionary<Guid, int>();
```

When `var` was introduced, the standard shifted to using `var` to simplify your declaration since the Type was obvious:

```
var data = new Dictionary<Guid, int>();
```

This resulted in less duplicated syntax and improved developer productivity while still keeping the Type obvious.

With the recent addition of target-typed `new`, my preference changed to use it as follows:

```
Dictionary<Guid, int> data = new();
```

I'm sharing my own personal journey on standards here because it's a microcosm of what engineering teams will go through.

You'll adapt to standards and then C# will change over time, and you'll adjust your standards to keep up. What you may consider a "best" practice right now may later turn out to not work well a few months into implementation. It's also natural for the obstacles facing your team to change. When this happens, this forces you and your team to adopt new strategies to overcome these obstacles.

It's okay to change your standards over time. That's normal and is a sign of an evolving language and the evolving context of our daily programming jobs.

Integrating standards into your processes

Code standards affect a few different places in software development, from how you approach building new features to the way in which you maintain code.

Your code standards should be clearly documented and stored in a central location, such as a team wiki or shared document. These standards should be communicated to new developers who join the team to help them familiarize themselves with the team's expectations on code standards.

Code standards should also be reinforced in the code review process after all other concerns on the substance of code changes are discussed. These issues should be resolved before the code is approved and the work item is completed, but this shouldn't be done in a punitive manner.

It's important to understand that internalizing code standards takes some time for new developers on the team. It's normal for it to take a few months with the team before your new developers think in terms of the team's standards.

One thing that can help is to incorporate tools into the process that make it easy for your team to validate whether its code meets standards before it sends the code on for peer review. Code analysis rules and Roslyn Analyzers can help with this, but Visual Studio places a few more tools at your disposal that can help standardize code before code reaches human review: code formatting and `.editorconfig` files.

Formatting and code cleanup in Visual Studio

It turns out that Visual Studio can automatically arrange and even clean up your code in a consistent manner through built-in features.

Formatting documents

One of the easiest ways to do this is with the **Format Document** feature, either by pressing *Ctrl + K* and then *Ctrl + D* or by opening the **Edit** menu, then going to **Advanced** and selecting **Format Document**, as shown in *Figure 16.1*:

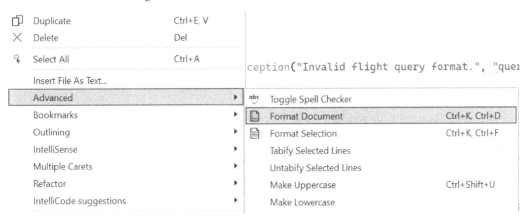

Figure 16.1 – Formatting the active editor document

This will change the code in your current file to match the preferences you've configured in Visual Studio.

These settings can be configured by opening the **Tools** menu and then selecting **Options…**. From there, expand the **Text Editor**, **C#**, **Code Style**, and **Formatting** nodes until you see the various preferences for indentation, new lines, spacing, and wrapping.

These settings blades allow you to configure the formatting preferences of Visual Studio and preview the formatting choices, as shown in *Figure 16.2*:

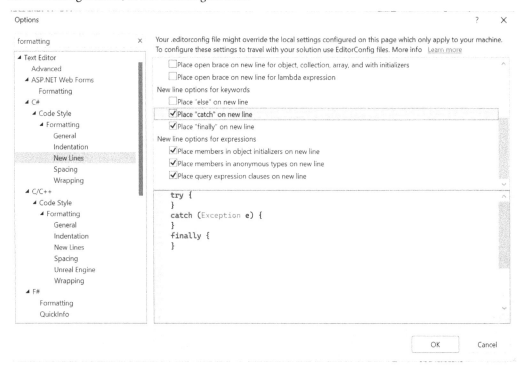

Figure 16.2 – Changing how Visual Studio formats catch statements

Once you've customized your settings, these settings will be used any time you use the **Format Document** feature.

Many developers learn the *Ctrl + K* and *Ctrl + D* shortcuts to format documents early on and use them reflexively, but you can actually get Visual Studio to apply code cleanup automatically.

Automatically formatting documents

Visual Studio has a **Code Cleanup** feature that allows you to format your code either manually or automatically whenever the file is saved.

This is done through **Code Cleanup** profiles. These profiles can do things such as remove unused using statements, sort the members in your classes into a more consistent order, and apply your code formatting preferences to a file.

To configure a code cleanup profile, go to the **Options** dialog again and this time, find **Code Cleanup** in the **Text Editor** node, as shown in *Figure 16.3*:

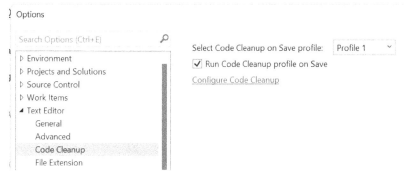

Figure 16.3 – Enabling code cleanup when files are saved

From here, you can check **Run Code Cleanup profile on Save** to have your cleanup profile automatically applied.

I also recommend you click **Configure Code Cleanup** to view your cleanup profiles.

This shows you the fixers that will be applied as part of each profile, as shown in *Figure 16.4*, and allows you to configure what is and isn't included in the code cleanup action:

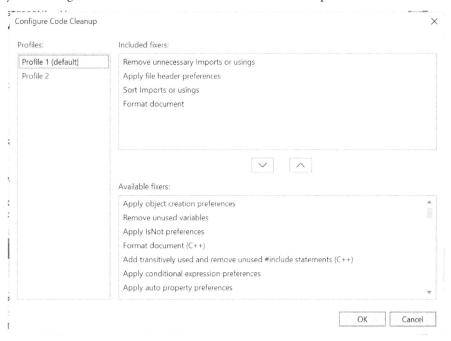

Figure 16.4 – Configuring code cleanup profiles

Automatically cleaning up code on save can be helpful, but it does have some downsides. If your code hasn't been cleaned up in a while, your cleanup action could appear to create many changes in the file. This can be confusing in git when multiple authors are trying to modify the same file or even see what has changed.

Configuring code style settings

Believe it or not, when we covered the C# settings for new lines and indentation earlier, this wasn't the limit of what Visual Studio can do.

Visual Studio provides a **Code Style** settings section that allows you to configure your individual preferences around most language features found in C#.

These settings are found in the **Options** dialog under **Text Editor**, **C#**, **Code Style**, and then **General**, as shown in *Figure 16.5*:

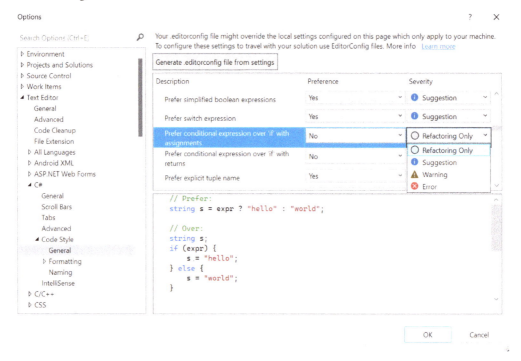

Figure 16.5 – Configuring Code Style rules in Visual Studio

In this user interface, you can configure which rules you care about, what your preferences are on each rule, and how much you care about each rule. Also notice the **Generate .editorconfig file from settings** button, as we'll talk about that more later.

For each rule, you get to select whether the rule only appears as a refactoring option, whether Visual Studio subtly suggests the rule through green underlines on identifiers, or whether Visual Studio should be more aggressive, such as using compiler warnings or compiler errors for violations from standards.

There are a lot of these settings, but they allow you to fine-tune your individual preferences for which C# features you prefer and how you like them formatted.

However, these are your *individual* settings that get applied to the code you work with on your own machine. In the next section, we'll talk about how to make these settings apply to your entire team.

Applying code standards with EditorConfig

Let's take a look at how you can take the same code style settings found in the options dialog and attach them to a project through an `.editorconfig` file.

The **EditorConfig** feature uses `.editorconfig` files that contain style and language usage rules that apply to your project. Any violation of your `EditorConfig` rules will result in compiler warnings and suggestions in the Visual Studio editor.

> **EditorConfig files outside of Visual Studio**
>
> At the time of this writing, `.editorconfig` files work in Visual Studio and JetBrains Rider natively. In VS Code, EditorConfig files are supported as long as you install the C# Dev Kit and the EditorConfig for VS Code extension. See the *Further reading* section for instructions on enabling these features in VS Code and JetBrains Rider.

The key benefit of `EditorConfig` files is that they allow all developers working on a project to work with a consistent set of formatting and styling preferences.

Reviewing our starter code

The code we'll be formatting lives in our *Chapter 16* solution, which has a `FlightQueryDecoder` console app and an associated `xUnit` test project. This code is minimal for this chapter and revolves around the `FlightQueryParser` class.

Let's start with the first half of `FlightQueryParser`, which parses a flight search string such as `AD08FEBDENLHR` into a `FlightQuery` object:

```
namespace Packt.FlightQueryDecoder;
public class FlightQueryParser
{
  public FlightQuery ParseQuery(string query) {
    if (query.StartsWith("AD") && query.Length == 13)
    {
      var flightQuery = new FlightQuery {
```

```
        Date = DateTime.Parse(query.Substring(2, 5)),
        Origin = query.Substring(7, 3),
        Destination = query.Substring(10, 3)
      };
      return flightQuery;
    }
    else {
      throw new ArgumentException("Invalid query format");
    }
  }
```

The actual logic here isn't the focus. What I want to highlight to you is the inconsistency in how the code is formatted within the block.

Let's see the other half of the file, which takes a flight search result string such as DEN LHR 05:50P 09:40A E0/789 8:50 and converts it to a FlightQueryResult:

```
  public FlightQueryResult ParseResult(string result)
  {
    var fqr = new FlightQueryResult();
    var segments = result.Split(' ',
      StringSplitOptions.RemoveEmptyEntries
      | StringSplitOptions.TrimEntries);
    fqr.Origin = segments[0];
    fqr.Destination = segments[1];
    string today = DateTime.Today.ToShortDateString();
    fqr.DepartureTime = DateTime.Parse(
      today + " "+segments[2] + 'M');
    string seg3 = segments[3];
    fqr.ArrivalTime = DateTime.Parse($"{today} {seg3}M");
    fqr.AircraftTypeDesignator = segments[4];
    fqr.FlightDuration = TimeSpan.Parse(segments[5]);
    return fqr;
  }
}
```

While this code is deliberately bad and inconsistently formatted to serve as an example, I'm sure you've seen many larger files in the real world with equally inconsistent styling.

Now that we've introduced this code with its different styling choices, let's add an .editorconfig file to the project and see how that can help enforce styles.

Adding an EditorConfig

To add the .editorconfig file, right-click on the Packt.FlightQueryDecoder project and choose **Add** and then **New EditorConfig** or **New EditorConfig (IntelliCode)**.

> **What is EditorConfig (IntelliCode)?**
>
> There's a difference between the **New EditorConfig** and **New EditorConfig (IntelliCode)** options. The standard option creates an .editorconfig file with the default options, whereas the IntelliCode choice analyzes your project and generates an .editorconfig file from the conventions it observes in your current code. Both are viable options for creating a starting point for your projects.

Depending on which option you selected, you may need to select which folder the .editorconfig file should live in. If you're prompted, select the default choice of the Packt.FlightQueryDecoder folder.

Once this completes, you should see a new .editorconfig file present in your project in **Solution Explorer**.

Before we go on to work with this .editorconfig file, it's worth pointing out that the **Code Style** settings in the **Options** dialog we saw earlier can be used to generate an .editorconfig file based on your current code style choices. This allows you to customize your styles and then create an .editorconfig file out of these choices.

Now that we have an .editorconfig file, let's customize it.

Customizing EditorConfigs

Double-click on the .editorconfig file to open its properties view.

You'll see an editor with tabs allowing you to customize various properties related to white space, code style, naming style, and Roslyn Analyzers.

There are a lot of options here, so we'll focus on just a few very specific ones.

Go to the **Code Style** tab and then scroll down to the bottom for the **var preferences** group.

From here, you can state your team's preferences and the severity of violations of those preferences. For example, if your team wants to avoid `var`, you could set all three `var` rules to **Prefer explicit type** and increase the severity to **Warning** or **Error**, as shown in *Figure 16.6*:

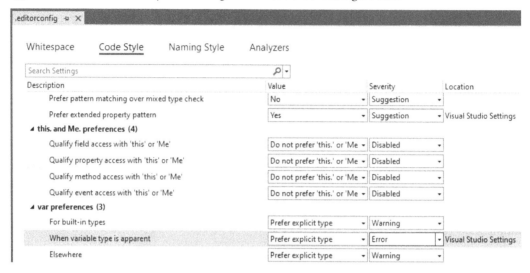

Figure 16.6 – Customizing the var preferences for your project

Save this file and go back into `FlightQueryParser.cs`, and you should now see warnings and errors in your editor for violations of these rules, as seen in *Figure 16.7*:

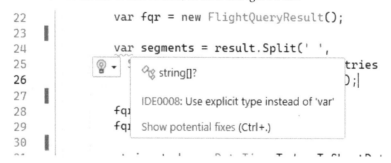

Figure 16.7 – Visual Studio warnings against using var based on code style rules

These rule violations do not cause your code to not compile but they do appear in the **Error List** view, as shown in *Figure 16.8*:

Figure 16.8 – Code violations appearing in Error List

Because `.editorconfig` files are added to source control when you commit your code, other developers on your team will pull down that file and see the exact same styling preferences and warnings you see on your machine.

This makes code standards apparent during the development process and reduces the odds of a peer review of important code changes breaking down into a discussion of the appropriate placement of opening curly braces or the use of `var`.

Summary

Code standards are important for helping your team focus on productive things and ensuring source code can be easily maintained by all developers on your team.

While code standards don't need to include everything, it can be helpful to codify stances on commonly contested items or best practices your team wants to make sure absolutely every change follows.

Visual Studio provides a number of features that help ensure a consistent and high-quality codebase including code formatting, code cleanup profiles, formatting on save, code analysis warning profiles, code styles at the editor level, and EditorConfigs to configure code styles inside of your editor.

In the final chapter of this book, we'll discuss refactoring code as part of a larger organization and as part of an agile software development team.

Questions

1. How do you determine what code standards your team should adopt?
2. What are some ways you can handle disagreements on style rules?
3. What are some options for configuring how Visual Studio formats code?
4. What does the **New EditorConfig (IntelliCode)** option do?

Further reading

You can find more information about materials from this chapter at these URLs:

- *Framework design guidelines*: `https://learn.microsoft.com/en-us/dotnet/standard/design-guidelines/`

- *.NET coding style guidelines*: `https://learn.microsoft.com/en-us/dotnet/csharp/fundamentals/coding-style/coding-conventions`

- *Create portable, custom editor settings with EditorConfig*: `https://learn.microsoft.com/en-us/visualstudio/ide/create-portable-custom-editor-options`

- *Beginner friendly EditorConfig settings*: `https://newdevsguide.com/2022/11/22/beginner-friendly-csharp/`

- *Using EditorConfig in VS Code with C# Dev Kit*: `https://code.visualstudio.com/docs/csharp/formatting-linting#_how-to-support-editorconfig-with-c-dev-kit`

- *Using EditorConfig in JetBrains Rider*: `https://www.jetbrains.com/help/rider/Using_EditorConfig.html`

17

Agile Refactoring

In this final chapter, we'll talk about refactoring as part of an *agile* team, succeeding with larger refactoring efforts, recovering when things go wrong, and incorporating deployment strategies to help make sure they don't go wrong again.

It's possible to win many small refactoring battles with small pieces of offending code but lose the overall "war" when you can't address large-scale design issues. This chapter explores how to continue to fight and win the smaller refactoring battles with your code from sprint to sprint. We will also cover the larger strategic battle of making sure your application has the right design – and correct it to something better when it doesn't.

This chapter covers the following topics:

- Refactoring in an agile environment
- Succeeding with agile refactoring strategies
- Accomplishing large-scale refactorings
- Recovering when refactoring goes wrong
- Deploying large-scale refactorings

Refactoring in an agile environment

Almost all development teams I work with use some form of **agile software development** to manage work over time in the form of short sprints, including any refactoring work.

In this section, we'll cover the basics of agile workflows and how refactoring can fit into this type of environment. This is important because if refactoring work can't fit into an agile workflow, refactoring simply won't happen.

Key elements of agile teams

Agile software development was officially codified in the *Manifesto for Agile Software Development* (commonly called the *Agile Manifesto*) and flows from the following core preferences:

- **Individuals and interactions** over processes and tools

- **Working software** over comprehensive documentation

- **Customer collaboration** over contract negotiation

- **Responding to change** over following a plan

Following these guiding principles, the exact "flavor" of agile differs from team to team, but most teams adopt the following key components:

- **Sprints**: Work is conducted during fixed-duration periods called sprints. These range anywhere from 1 to 4 weeks, but 2 weeks is the norm.

- **User stories**: Work is tracked in the form of work items or user stories. Many teams require that any code change be associated with at least one work item.

- **Backlogs**: The work for each sprint is taken from a prioritized backlog of user stories the team has previously reviewed and refined.

The exact details, roles, and names of things may vary from organization to organization, but these truths generally apply.

This process creates an iterative and cyclical process where the team works on the work items the business considers the most important in one sprint while prioritizing and refining items for the following sprint, as shown in *Figure 17.1*:

Figure 17.1 – The cycle of agile software development

Agile is currently the best methodology we've found for software engineering in a business setting, but it does pose some unique obstacles to refactoring. See the *Further reading* section at the end of this chapter for additional resources on agile.

Understanding obstacles to refactoring

Agile is good for getting teams working on items that are important to the business and working through a prioritized backlog. Unfortunately, agile may not be the best development modality for proactive refactoring work.

Most organizations require all code changes to be associated with at least one user story and developers are expected to be working on user stories when they have spare capacity.

This leaves engineers in a conundrum where they know the areas of code that need to be refactored and have the technical skills and knowledge to refactor them, yet it is not acceptable within the boundaries of their teams for them to proactively improve code outside the bounds of an assigned user story.

This causes technical debt to pile up and eventually decays the team's velocity by slowing down work items. This also results in a greater number of bugs being introduced because the team has not been allowed to proactively manage the risk inherent in their legacy code.

This isn't to say that agile is bad. Agile is the best process we've found so far to manage work in software engineering teams; however, it has some limitations that must be solved to help organizations achieve both short-term and long-term success.

Succeeding with agile refactoring strategies

Ongoing refactoring is important in an agile environment, so let's talk about some ways of making sure code gets refactored regularly.

Dedicated work items for refactoring efforts

Remember that every line of code you and your team write should deliver business value, including your refactoring efforts.

Refactoring focuses on delivering value to the business by addressing known areas of technical risk and improving the speed the team can achieve in the future on related work in the targeted area.

Given these facts, it makes sense that refactoring efforts should be represented inside a sprint as user stories. Just as one developer might get a user story about integrating with a new external system for a partner, another developer might get a user story to refactor and establish additional tests around the data access layer.

In *Chapter 15*, we discussed tracking technical debt in a risk register. I didn't make it explicit in that chapter, but you can use the same system that tracks your user stories to track your known technical risks as a specialized type of user story, such as the one shown in *Figure 17.2*:

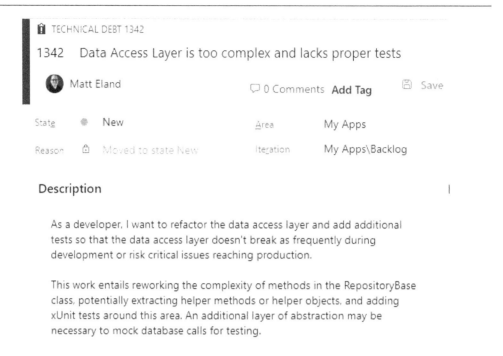

Figure 17.2 – A technical debt item in Azure DevOps

These technical debt user stories should look just like normal user stories and have the same degree of polish and refinement. However, these user stories should have a different type or a property with a different value so that you can identify technical debt items in your backlog and sprints.

Additionally, it should be the responsibility of the developers on the team to write up these technical debt items and not the product owner, though the team will still need to walk the product owner through what the item is, the rough amount of effort needed to remediate it, and the risk the change is looking to resolve.

Healthy agile teams should take a mixture of short-term and long-term items, with technical debt items typically falling in the long-term bucket.

There may be times when you cannot do anything but short-term work and there may be times when you work with a product owner that doesn't understand the risk present in your technical debt. The suggestions from *Chapter 15* may help with this, but sometimes, there won't be an easy answer.

In these times, you may need to shift to a strategy of refactoring any code that changes.

Refactoring code as it changes

Most of the technical debt I've addressed over my career has come from the conscious decision to refactor any code I touch.

This approach of refactoring code that changes has several key benefits:

- It ensures the areas that are changed most frequently get refactored.

- Since I'm working in that area anyway, I know I will be testing the code in question. This means that these testing efforts will help catch any issues that might be addressed as part of refactoring.

- It does not require the overhead of separate user stories for small, trivial refactoring efforts.

In my experience, making it part of your policy to clean up and test the code around the areas you touch results in a much cleaner codebase over time.

This approach has its limitations: when you are making a minor change in one area of code and the code needs serious refactoring efforts, it is typically irresponsible to expand the scope of your work item beyond a certain point.

Additionally, some refactoring efforts cannot be achieved within the context of a single sprint and need more strategic thought and planning behind them.

Refactoring sprints

One concept I've encountered once or twice has been the idea of a **refactoring sprint**. A refactoring sprint follows the mentality of crop rotation in farming.

I'm no farmer, but my understanding of crop rotation is that you can use a field for several seasons, but over time, that field starts to lose the nutrient values from the soil and becomes less productive as years go on.

To combat this, farmers learned to leave these fields fallow and not grow anything in them for a time, as shown in *Figure 17.3*:

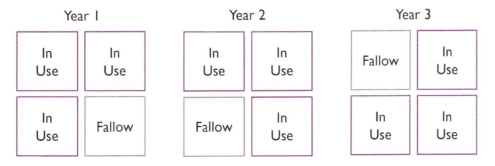

Figure 17.3 – Rotating crops over several years

Applied to agile development, you might spend several sprints working on normal work items, but after a handful of sprints, you introduce a refactoring sprint where the team's effort goes into refactoring the areas of code that concern the team the most.

In refactoring sprints, the development team can take on larger-scale efforts than they might otherwise try as part of a standard sprint.

This also has the side effect of re-energizing your developers and getting them ready for another sequence of sprints around a key long-term business objective.

In practicality, I'm not sure how well these sprints work regularly, but I've seen teams benefit from them tremendously in special scenarios. These refactoring sprints can be used to tackle larger problems or as a way of recharging the team after a major initiative is completed. I've also seen these sprints used as a way of keeping the team engaged during holiday seasons.

Refactoring sabbaticals

Most teams I've worked with simply can't afford to have all their developers work primarily on refactoring efforts, even for a single sprint.

Teams like this may want to take the idea of a refactoring sprint and scale it down so that it applies to just a single team member.

I call this concept a **refactoring sabbatical**, where the developer effectively splits off of the team for a short time to work on a refactoring project, only to rejoin the larger team in the next sprint.

In a future sprint, another developer gets to spend a sprint working on refactoring efforts while others work on traditional work items, as shown in *Figure 17.4*:

Figure 17.4 – A rotating developer sabbatical over several sprints

Under this model, the refactoring efforts the developer wants to take on should be pre-approved, reviewed, and tested by other developers on the team.

The developer on "sabbatical" should still be available for questions and work on emergency items. The only major change is that their work for a sprint is self-directed toward known refactoring goals.

This has some of the same morale-boosting effects as a refactoring sprint but on a smaller scale. This also helps prevent teams from over-relying on any one person on the team, because people rotate into and out of sabbaticals frequently.

While this model may see success in small and medium-sized refactorings, it is less effective in large-scale refactorings. We'll discuss ways of succeeding with larger refactorings next.

Accomplishing large-scale refactorings

In my experience, successfully performing large-scale refactorings is one of the hardest challenges in all of software engineering.

I define large-scale refactoring as something on the scale of replacing an application or a major architectural layer of an application. Moving an application from one database technology to another, replacing a REST API with a gRPC API, upgrading from Web Forms to Blazor, or replacing your entire service layer are all examples of this.

Why large refactorings are difficult

These projects are challenging because they typically take longer than a single sprint to accomplish and must meet feature parity with software that has been developed over the years.

Additionally, software engineering projects are notoriously hard to accurately estimate, which is one of the reasons developers prefer agile software development over more traditional project management methodologies such as **waterfall**. Delays in software development projects can be difficult to predict and manifest in the form of unexpected technical obstacles, such as previously unknown limitations of other components or platforms or subtle bugs slowing development.

Because of these factors, large refactoring efforts are significantly harder to achieve than medium refactoring efforts.

Once completed, the results of these efforts can be daunting to move into production environments as well because they represent such a large change. Later in this chapter, we'll talk about a few ways of reducing this risk, but the decision to replace or upgrade major parts of your application is not one without quality risks.

This problem gets even more pronounced when teams choose to completely rewrite or replace software projects instead of refactoring them.

The rewrite trap

Rewrites take all the problems of large refactoring efforts and multiply them by a factor of at least 10.

In this scenario, you are replacing an application that has been used for some time and typically has a significant number of active users and established features.

It can be a struggle to re-implement years' worth of features while keeping up with production bugs and other short-term work that must happen to keep the business running smoothly.

When a team is actively working on a rewrite, they usually see little value in targeted refactorings of the current system they're working on replacing. This means that if a rewrite is canceled or put on hold, the team gets no value out of their investment and still has a legacy system that needs to be supported.

Since software projects are hard to estimate and manage, rewrites frequently take much longer than you expect them to. During this time, your engineers are working primarily on the rewrite, which takes capacity away from other initiatives.

Remember that a rewrite usually provides no intrinsic value to the business or the users until it is active in a production environment and people are working with it live. This is why so few rewrite projects succeed.

You can remediate this by offering early previews of a partial rewrite, but this is not always possible and may not be the best user experience if important features are not present yet in the rewrite.

Lessons from the ship of Theseus

There's a thought experiment about the Greek hero Theseus that is relevant to refactoring software.

In this thought experiment, **the ship of Theseus**, our hero, Theseus, sets sail on a long journey by sea. Throughout his long voyages, the crew gradually replaced pieces of the ship with spare materials and materials they made or found on their voyages. This continued for some time until there wasn't a single piece of the original ship left in his ship as he returned home.

This thought experiment asks whether the ship that came home is the same, and if it isn't, when did it stop being that ship?

While these are interesting philosophical questions, the concept is relevant to software engineering.

Using refactoring, we can replace the "planks" of our virtual "ship" as technical debt takes hold in various areas. As we gradually refactor the components that need it the most, we continually evolve our software to stay relevant over time.

This is why I view refactoring code as you write code as a critically important practice in software engineering. Technical debt is an inescapable reality of software and you must keep it in mind with every change you make by doing what you can to prevent it from taking hold and paying down existing debt areas through refactoring.

> **Note**
> Gradual refactoring only goes so far. Progressive refactoring may help keep your virtual "boat" afloat, but it won't turn a rowboat into a cruise liner or submarine.

Put more clearly, refactoring won't help you move from an antiquated technology to a more modern one. Let's look at a tool that might help with that.

Upgrading projects with.NET Upgrade Assistant

As new versions of .NET come out and new technologies emerge within the .NET ecosystem, keeping up can be a challenge.

To address this, Microsoft introduced **.NET Upgrade Assistant**, which helps you safely upgrade and modernize your applications. At the time of writing, this tool has been useful with projects written with the following technologies:

- **ASP.NET**
- **Universal Windows Platform (UWP)**
- **Windows Communication Foundation (WCF)**
- **Windows Forms**
- **Windows Presentation Foundation (WPF)**

.NET Upgrade Assistant can be installed either as a global tool or as a Visual Studio extension, as shown in *Figure 17.5*:

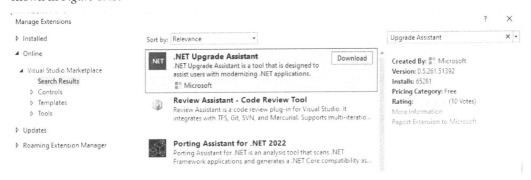

Figure 17.5 – Installing.NET Upgrade Assistant in Visual Studio

Once the extension has been installed, you will be able to right-click on a project in **Solution Explorer** and choose **Upgrade**.

From there, you'll be able to configure a set of options on your project that will vary based on the technologies you use. You'll also be able to configure the scope of the upgrade attempt and include and exclude files of your choosing.

Once the upgrade runs, you'll see a list of projects and files that were updated and see details in the log, as shown in *Figure 17.6*:

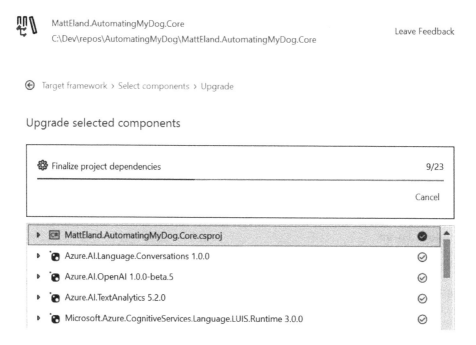

Figure 17.6 – .NET Upgrade Assistant in action

You should make sure your project is properly backed up and in source control before attempting an upgrade and you may need to resolve certain issues yourself, but this tool can be very useful for starting an upgrade in an automated manner.

For applications that can't be easily upgraded with .NET Upgrade Assistant, you may need some more creative strategies, which we'll talk about next.

Refactoring and the strangler fig pattern

In 2004, Martin Folwer introduced the **strangler fig pattern** to the software community in a post he titled *StranglerFigApplication*.

In this post, Martin Fowler describes how certain fig trees, such as the Banyan Tree pictured in *Figure 17.7*, wrap themselves around other trees and gradually replace the structure of the other tree:

Figure 17.7 – Photo of a banyan tree by Ankit Bhattacharjee

Over time, this strangler fig assumes more and more of the structure of the tree and it effectively becomes a whole new tree.

In this metaphor, the tree would be the legacy application you're trying to replace while the various vines from the strangler fig represent your rewrite.

Under this model, you're not trying to rewrite the entire application and replace it with a freshly rewritten application.

Instead, you take a single **vertical slice** of the application encompassing a core set of features and behaviors and you make a new implementation of them in a new technology. This might be a web page or a set of API endpoints, depending on what you're writing.

Once you've rewritten this capability in your new technology, you redirect traffic for that one area from the old application to the new application. This allows you to ship parts of your new application to users incrementally, validate things in production, and then take on another vertical slice of the application.

> **Technical details**
>
> There are a few technologies that can help achieve this goal of replacing vertical slices of an application. Azure API Management can help direct web traffic to an appropriate endpoint in API Management. I've also seen people succeed with **Yet Another Reverse Proxy (YARP)** for these efforts. Links to both can be found in the *Further reading* section.

As you expand your rewrite and validate it works, you can remove portions of the original application so that you no longer need to maintain them.

For areas that your new application doesn't support yet, you can have it link back to existing areas on the old application.

The strangler fig approach has some key advantages compared to a full rewrite:

- It allows you to iteratively deliver your rewrite in stages

- It works better in an agile environment

- It helps validate risk areas early instead of waiting for the full rewrite

- It allows you to remove replaced code from the original if you'd like

- It can be rolled out in parallel with the original as a preview

Perhaps the biggest benefit of this pattern is that its success chance is significantly higher than attempting a total rewrite.

Let's talk about what to do when refactoring isn't as successful.

Recovering when refactoring goes wrong

Sometimes, despite your best efforts, refactoring efforts will fail. It may be due to gaps in your tests or mistaken assumptions about new technologies, but a certain percentage of your refactoring attempts will fail.

The impact of failed refactorings

Failed refactorings can be both frustrating and a serious challenge to future refactoring work. After all, a significant barrier to refactoring is the belief that legacy code is so brittle that touching it will break it. When you change code and it breaks, you make it harder to change code in the future.

When refactoring fails, you sometimes get to make a quick patch to address the issue you introduced. In this case, the code is refactored and service gets restored, but you've lost some of the team's trust.

Other times, failures in refactoring result in code getting rolled back to the previous version before you refactored it. Sometimes, you'll get to make changes, add additional tests, and retry this refactoring, while other times, the team will decide that the refactoring is too dangerous to try again and you'll lose your shot at improving the code for some time.

Ultimately, this conversation boils down to how much the business trusts you to not make mistakes.

Mistakes in software development will happen because people are imperfect and make mistakes, assume things without realizing them, and don't know everything.

Establishing safety in agile environments

What you want to do as a technologist is create an environment where mistakes are infrequent and can easily and safely be caught before they reach production environments.

There are certain things you can do to reduce the odds of breaking software when refactoring:

- **Testing**: Unit tests, manual tests, and having your peers test your code in a different environment can help you catch many mistakes and some assumptions.

- **Code review**: Teams that review changes before they ship to integration and production environments can catch bad assumptions, mistakes, and poor coding practices. Code review is also an opportunity for teams to share knowledge and techniques, as well as share knowledge of the codebase across the dev team.

- **Code analysis**: Using the documented best practices in .NET and adhering to your team's standards, as we talked about in *Part 3* of this book, can prevent issues the team has encountered before from recurring.

- **Automated tests**: Testing is so important I put it on here twice, but this time, I'm stressing that any change getting merged into a release branch needs to have automated tests run against it and pass before it can move on. This ensures that tests are reliably and repeatably run.

- **Active monitoring**: Regular monitoring of error and warning logs can help you detect problems early in production and staging environments.

Be honest and transparent when an issue occurs and follow this sequence of steps:

1. Confirm that the issue exists.
2. Understand the issue enough to resolve it.
3. Resolve the issue and restore service.
4. Determine how you could have prevented the issue from occurring.

When you look at a bug getting past your defensive practices as a way of improving your processes and identifying gaps, it becomes a learning opportunity for your team.

Unfortunately, these learning opportunities do come with a penalty of lost trust from others due to the issue.

I've found that openly and honestly communicating the following things helps encourage understanding and somewhat heal lost trust:

- The steps your team took to verify the item wouldn't cause issues before release

- The nature of the bug and how it got past your team

- What you did to resolve it and restore service

- What you're doing to ensure that things like it won't be issues in the future

This approach treats everyone with respect, shares understanding, provides opportunities for questions and suggestions, and assures them that the quality of the application is important to you and your team.

Before we close this chapter and this book as a whole, let's talk about some helpful practices you may want to consider when deploying software.

Deploying large-scale refactorings

Let's talk about some ways of deploying code that can help you catch any issues that slip through before they become major problems.

Using feature flags

Feature flags are configuration settings that control whether features are active.

When you push out new code that includes a new capability, that code doesn't have to be immediately available. You can deploy as usual with the new feature area disabled in the configuration.

Once you're confident the rest of the software is working as intended, you can enable the new feature. If the feature winds up having issues, you can quickly disable it by flipping the feature flag back to its inactive state.

While feature flags are helpful when you're releasing actual features, you can also use them with major refactoring efforts. For example, a feature flag might govern whether the system uses `LegacyBookingSystem` or `RevisedBookingSystem`.

> **Tip**
> Feature flag libraries pair nicely with A/B testing libraries such as Scientist .NET, which we covered in *Chapter 9*.

Popular feature flag tools include **Azure App Configuration** and **Launchdarkly**, but Microsoft also offers an open-source feature management library called **.NET Feature Management**.

.NET Feature Management is surprisingly capable and integrates directly into your .NET applications, though it lacks some of the web monitoring capabilities a commercial software product might have.

Feature flags add complexity to your application but give you options for when your features go live. This lets you enable a feature, evaluate it for correctness in a production environment, and then either disable it, patch any issues observed, or leave it on.

Phased rollouts and blue/green deployments

Phased rollouts or **blue/green deployments** take the idea of feature flags to a different level. In this model, you have distinct sets of servers, typically referred to as blue and green environments.

In a blue/green deployment, you might start with 100% of your users using one environment. During this time, you patch the other server with your new update and verify that it appears to be running correctly, as shown in *Figure 17.8*:

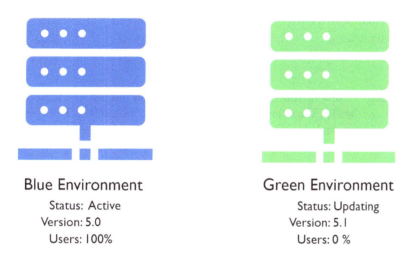

Blue Environment
Status: Active
Version: 5.0
Users: 100%

Green Environment
Status: Updating
Version: 5.1
Users: 0 %

Figure 17.8 – Users using the blue environment while the green one is being updated

Once you're sure the new server is operational and running without issue, you can start diverting a percentage of your users onto the new server.

This subset of users represents real production traffic and can be used to monitor the behavior of your new release with a minimal set of users, as shown in *Figure 17.9*:

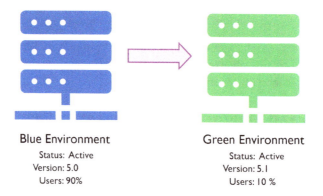

Blue Environment
Status: Active
Version: 5.0
Users: 90%

Green Environment
Status: Active
Version: 5.1
Users: 10 %

Figure 17.9 – The blue environment running most users while a subset of users are on green

If the new environment starts to have issues, you can quickly move users off of that server and onto the old one, then take the new environment offline for maintenance until you've addressed the issues and are ready to try again.

> **Caution**
>
> When migrating to a new revision and then rolling back to the old one, you must take special care to ensure any database migrations still work appropriately. Tools such as Entity Framework's up-and-down scripts can help with this.

If the new environment performs without issues, you can gradually "drain" users from the old environment onto the new environment. Eventually, your old environment will be empty and can be taken offline until the next deployment, as shown in *Figure 17.10*:

Blue Environment
Status: Offline
Version: 5.0
Users: 0%

Green Environment
Status: Active
Version: 5.1
Users: 100 %

Figure 17.10 – The green environment handles all traffic and the blue one goes offline

The next time a deployment occurs, the roles will reverse and users will move from the green environment to the blue environment once the blue environment is updated to the next version.

This sounds complex, and to some extent it is, but a lot of this complexity can be automated and managed by your cloud provider. For example, Azure provides blue/green deployments in many of its services, as detailed in the *Further reading* section.

Once you've migrated over to a blue/green deployment model, the complexity becomes largely irrelevant, and instead, blue/green deployment becomes another tool in your quality toolbox.

The value of continuous integration and continuous delivery

All of this added complexity in the form of deployment and feature management sounds intimidating at first, but this level of maturity helps teams perform at very high levels and reduces the impact of any failures on the end users.

This complexity can be a problem, but thankfully, **continuous integration and continuous delivery (CI/CD)** can help manage it.

CI is about verifying the correctness of your software any time it changes. This means running code analysis, unit tests, and any other checks you need to do any time a change is about to be merged into an integration branch.

CD focuses on automating the deployment of software applications in a repeatable and reliable manner. Instead of deployments being done from one specialized developer's machine, deployments are done using an automated script that is typically run in a cloud environment. Continuous delivery allows you to ship your software in a repeatable and reliable manner to whatever environment you want.

Some interpretations of CI/CD also include **Infrastructure as Code (IaC)** through tools such as **Terraform** or **Bicep**. IaC is used to configure cloud environments that have the same resources, security privileges, and configuration settings based on an IaC script. This means that deployments can be used to create missing cloud resources and secure resources, and generally make it easier for your team to create new environments consistently.

When you put these tools and processes together, you get a well-defined and automated pipeline that checks new code for correctness, runs tests to ensure that the change doesn't break anything, and can deploy changes to whatever environment you'd like – all without the possibility of human error in the process.

Once you have a broad enough library of unit and integration tests, CI/CD allows you to deploy at whatever pace you're comfortable with and is how some teams can deploy hundreds of times a day if they want to.

This degree of process maturity gives teams the freedom to innovate at a rapid pace. These added safety nets of quality checks and automation further support refactoring efforts by taking the fear out of making the changes needed to keep your software clean and healthy.

Case study – Cloudy Skies Airlines

As we close this book, let's take a final look at our case study company: Cloudy Skies Airlines.

Cloudy Skies started with unmaintainable systems they were afraid to touch for fear of introducing critical bugs. They carried out a systematic review of the technical debt in their codebase and the quality issues the team had encountered in the past year.

As a result, the team was able to prioritize a list of key areas of technical debt and identify critical areas lacking unit tests. Cloudy Skies carried out several refactoring sprints to address the most critical areas first, putting a heavy emphasis on expanding their unit tests.

Once the quality hotspots were largely addressed, Cloudy Skies went back to a standard agile development cadence but allocated about 30% of their work each sprint toward paying down technical debt.

Many of the systems Cloudy Skies used were out of date, but Cloudy Skies was able to use .NET Upgrade Assistant to quickly modernize most of them.

For applications that could not be easily upgraded, development teams began following the strangler fig pattern to build a new application to cover vertical slices of the old application and tools such as YARP to route traffic to the new application where possible.

All of this was supported by a culture of trust and transparency and modern application management processes through feature flags and CI/CD.

While it will be some time before the developers are fully proud of their code, Cloudy Skies is heading in the right direction. The team has regained the respect of the larger organization and the added stability and agility is helping the business steer toward sunny horizons.

Summary

In this chapter, we explored the unique challenges of refactoring in an agile environment and strategies for including refactoring work inside agile sprints.

We also looked at ways of accomplishing large-scale refactorings and how to respond when things don't go as planned.

This chapter also touched on some deployment and automation processes that can reduce the impact of issues on end users and minimize the risk of human error through feature flags, blue/green deployments, and CI/CD practices.

Toward more sustainable software

This book took you on a journey from the nature of technical debt to the procedures of refactoring. We talked about how to safely test and structure your software and how to evaluate code for best practices, prioritize, and communicate technical debt.

We also talked about how the C# language and features of Visual Studio support you in this journey toward more sustainable software development.

Every year our world changes a little as Microsoft unveils new C# preview features at the beginning of the year and releases them near the end.

These capabilities give us a wide range of capabilities to tackle the development problems of today and tomorrow, but the reality is that software development continues to change.

Software and software development grows more complex each year. Meanwhile, many teams are stuck maintaining yesterday's code.

It doesn't have to be this way. You can modernize your software, and you can do it in an agile and responsible way while serving the needs of your business and its customers.

I've been writing software in some shape or form for over 35 years now. New developers assume that more experience results in fewer mistakes. While this has some truth to it, I've personally found that the more experience I get, the less I trust my ability to not make mistakes.

Make room for yourself – and others – to make mistakes. Mistakes will happen and bugs will reach production, but when they do, you need to learn from them.

It is my sincere hope that you have learned something new from every chapter. Moreover, I want you to emerge from this book with hope – hope that your code can be a source of joy to you, or at least be less afraid to change.

Through the practices outlined in this book, I believe that you and your team can reach a better place through successfully refactoring with C#.

Questions

1. How can technical debt be paid down inside of an agile setting?
2. Why are large rewrites hard? What processes can help with this?
3. What variances do you see right now in how you deploy and test software?

Further reading

You can find more information about the materials from this chapter at these URLs:

- *Manifesto for Agile Software Development*: *StranglerFigApplication Post*: `https://martinfowler.com/bliki/StranglerFigApplication.html`
- *YARP*: `https://github.com/microsoft/reverse-proxy`
- *Azure API Management*: `https://learn.microsoft.com/en-us/azure/api-management/api-management-key-concepts`

- *Overview of the.NET Upgrade Assistant*: `https://learn.microsoft.com/en-us/dotnet/core/porting/upgrade-assistant-overview`

- *.NET Feature Management*: `https://github.com/microsoft/FeatureManagement-Dotnet`

- *Blue-Green Deployment in Azure Container Apps*: `https://learn.microsoft.com/en-us/azure/container-apps/blue-green-deployment`

- *Vertical Slices:* `https://deviq.com/practices/vertical-slices`

Index

Symbols

Packtpub.com

Subscribe to our online digital library for full access to over 7,000 books and videos, as well as industry leading tools to help you plan your personal development and advance your career. For more information, please visit our website.

Why subscribe?

- Spend less time learning and more time coding with practical eBooks and Videos from over 4,000 industry professionals

- Improve your learning with Skill Plans built especially for you

- Get a free eBook or video every month

- Fully searchable for easy access to vital information

- Copy and paste, print, and bookmark content

Did you know that Packt offers eBook versions of every book published, with PDF and ePub files available? You can upgrade to the eBook version at packtpub.com and as a print book customer, you are entitled to a discount on the eBook copy. Get in touch with us at customercare@packtpub.com for more details.

At www.packtpub.com, you can also read a collection of free technical articles, sign up for a range of free newsletters, and receive exclusive discounts and offers on Packt books and eBooks.

Other Books You May Enjoy

If you enjoyed this book, you may be interested in these other books by Packt:

Clean Code in C#

Jason Alls

ISBN: 978-1-83898-297-3

- Write code that allows software to be modified and adapted over time
- Implement the fail-pass-refactor methodology using a sample C# console application
- Address cross-cutting concerns with the help of software design patterns
- Write custom C# exceptions that provide meaningful information
- Identify poor quality C# code that needs to be refactored
- Secure APIs with API keys and protect data using Azure Key Vault
- Improve your code's performance by using tools for profiling and refactoring

Real-World Implementation of C# Design Patterns

Bruce M. Van Horn II

ISBN: 978-1-80324-273-6

- Get to grips with patterns, and discover how to conceive and document them
- Explore common patterns that may come up in your everyday work
- Recognize common anti-patterns early in the process
- Use creational patterns to create flexible and robust object structures
- Enhance class designs with structural patterns
- Simplify object interaction and behavior with behavioral patterns

Packt is searching for authors like you

If you're interested in becoming an author for Packt, please visit `authors.packtpub.com` and apply today. We have worked with thousands of developers and tech professionals, just like you, to help them share their insight with the global tech community. You can make a general application, apply for a specific hot topic that we are recruiting an author for, or submit your own idea.

Share Your Thoughts

Now you've finished *Refactoring with C#*, we'd love to hear your thoughts! Scan the QR code below to go straight to the Amazon review page for this book and share your feedback or leave a review on the site that you purchased it from.

`https://packt.link/r/1835089984`

Your review is important to us and the tech community and will help us make sure we're delivering excellent quality content.

Download a free PDF copy of this book

Thanks for purchasing this book!

Do you like to read on the go but are unable to carry your print books everywhere?

Is your eBook purchase not compatible with the device of your choice?

Don't worry, now with every Packt book you get a DRM-free PDF version of that book at no cost.

Read anywhere, any place, on any device. Search, copy, and paste code from your favorite technical books directly into your application.

The perks don't stop there, you can get exclusive access to discounts, newsletters, and great free content in your inbox daily

Follow these simple steps to get the benefits:

1. Scan the QR code or visit the link below

https://packt.link/free-ebook/9781835089989

2. Submit your proof of purchase
3. That's it! We'll send your free PDF and other benefits to your email directly

www.ingramcontent.com/pod-product-compliance
Lightning Source LLC
Chambersburg PA
CBHW060648060326
40690CB00020B/4554